The Correspondence of Richard Price

The Correspondence of Richard Price

Joint General Editors: W. Bernard Peach, *Professor of Philosophy, Duke University, and* D.O. Thomas, *formerly Reader in Philosophy, The University College of Wales, Aberystwyth.*

The Correspondence of Richard Price
Vol. II. March 1778–February 1786

Edited by D.O. Thomas

Duke University Press   Durham, N.C.

University of Wales Press   Cardiff

1991

© University of Wales, 1991

British Library Cataloguing in Publication Data

The correspondence of Richard Price.
  Vol. 2: March 1778–February 1786.
  I. Thomas, D. O. (David Oswald)
  192

ISBN 0708310990

Library of Congress Cataloging-in-Publication Data
(Revised for vol. 2)

Price, Richard, 1723–1791.
  The correspondence of Richard Price.

  "A list of the short titles of the published works of Richard Price."; v. 1, p.
  Includes bibliographical references and indexes.
  Contents: v. 1. July 1748–March 1778 – v. 2. March 1778–February 1786.
  1. Price, Richard, 1723–1791—Correspondence. 2. Philosophers—Great Britain—Correspondence.
I. Peach, Bernard, 1918–   . II. Thomas, David Oswald.
III. Title.

B1382 P731   1983   192 [B]   82–14646
ISBN 0–8223–0452–X (v. 1)
ISBN 0–8223–1203–4 (v. 2)

Typeset by BP Integraphics, Bath, England
Printed by Bookcraft, Midsomer Norton, Avon, England

Contents

The Correspondence, March 1778–February 1786

Introduction to Volume II

By the beginning of the period covered by this volume of his correspondence, Richard Price was already well known as a moral philosopher, as a writer on insurance and on demographic and financial matters, and as a political pamphleteer on behalf of the American rebels. His *Two Tracts*, which was published in February 1778, incorporating *Observations on the Nature of Civil Liberty* (1776) and *Additional Observations* (1777), defended the principle of self-government, namely, that the people have the right to govern themselves understood both as an entitlement to representative government and as a defence of national autonomy. It was in the light of the latter that Price defended the American rebels, and throughout the conflict, despite much abuse and scurrilous criticism at home, he remained faithful to them and firm in his conviction that they would eventually succeed in securing the enjoyment of the right to govern themselves. He was able to celebrate the fulfilment of his prophecy with the publication of *Observations on the Importance of the American Revolution* (1784) in which he advised the Americans how to build and strengthen their new state. It is fitting then that this volume should begin with Turgot's famous letter to Price in which he thanked him for his pamphlets on American affairs and in which he offered his own advice to the Americans. This was the letter that Price was to publish together with his *Observations on the Importance of the American Revolution*.

Price had established contact with many Americans long before hostilities broke out; these included Charles Chauncy, Benjamin Franklin, Josiah Quincy, Jr., Henry Marchant, Ezra Stiles, Edward Wigglesworth and John Winthrop. While hostilities continued it proved difficult to sustain a correspondence with these friends, but once the war was over contact was resumed and Price acquired many more American correspondents, notably John Adams (who during the period when he represented the United States in London, attended Gravel Pit Meeting Place at Hackney where Price was minister), James Bowdoin, Thomas Jefferson, Henry Laurens, Nathaniel Gorham, Jonathan Trumbull, the elder, George Washington, Noah Webster, John Wheelock, and Joseph Willard. As these letters testify, Price was warmly regarded by his American friends not only for his publications on their behalf, but also for the attempts he made to relieve the hardships suffered by American prisoners of war in England, as exemplified in his attempts to relieve those incarcerated at Kinsale to whose plight he had been alerted by William Hazlitt, the father of the celebrated essayist. Henry Laurens, who had been held in the Tower during the war, remembered Price's kindnesses with affection, as did Jonathan Trumbull, the elder, whose son John Trumbull, the painter, had been imprisoned at Tothill Fields.

The Americans were not unappreciative of Price's efforts to assist them. In December 1778 he received a very special mark of distinction from Congress in an offer of American citizenship and a request that he should emigrate to America to assist "in regulating their finances" (see Benjamin Franklin, Arthur Lee and John Adams to R.P., 7 Dec. 1778). Further honours followed: on 24 April 1781 the Corporation at Yale voted to confer the degree of LL D. upon him; on 30 January 1782 he was elected to a fellowship of The American Academy of Arts and Sciences at Boston; and on 28 January 1785 he was elected a member of the American Philosophical Society at Philadelphia.

Throughout the period under review Price was a busy man. The first of his duties were those of his ministry; he continued to be the morning preacher at Gravel Pit Meeting Place at Hackney, and until 1783 he was the afternoon preacher at Newington Green. During this period he preached the sermons in which he defined his theological position as an Arian, distinguishing it from orthodox Trinitarianism and the form of Socinianism defended by his friend Joseph Priestley. These addresses were later published in his *Sermons on the Christian Doctrine* (1787). An earlier controversy with Priestley occurred in the exchange of letters published under the title *A Free Discussion of the Doctrines of Materialism, and Philosophical Necessity* in which Price defended a metaphysical dualism and a form of libertarianism against Priestley's materialism and determinism. In the eyes of both participants the manner in which the debate was conducted was as important as the topics discussed. Price and Priestley aimed to give their contemporaries a lesson in literary manners, an exercise in candour in which however great the disagreement on the issues to be debated there was no occasion for lack of courtesy, of consideration or of urbanity.

During this period Price also spent a great deal of time and energy revising his highly successful work on insurance, *Observations on Reversionary Payments*, the fourth edition of which appeared enlarged to two volumes in 1783. In this work he incorporated the Northampton Tables which had been adopted by the Equitable Assurance Society (whose Actuary was Price's nephew, William Morgan), the actuarial tables based upon them, and other mortality tables constructed from materials gathered from a wide range of sources in Britain and in Europe. In this connection the information supplied by the Swedish demographer Per Wilhelm Wargentin was of especial importance (see R.P. to Per Wilhelm Wargentin, 24 Dec. 1781 and 9 June 1783). His interest in demographic matters led him to contribute "An Essay on the Present State of Population in England and Wales" as an appendix to William Morgan's *The Doctrine of Annuities and Assurances on Lives and Survivorships* which appeared in 1779. This essay, published separately in the following year under the title *An Essay on the Population of England*, was an elaboration of the thesis first put forward in a supplement to the second edition of *Observations on Reversionary Payments*, namely, that the population of the kingdom had declined. It provoked a much publicized controversy to which William Eden, John Howlett, and William Wales made notable contributions.

In the early editions of *Observations on Reversionary Payments* (1771–1773) and in *An Appeal to the Public on the Subject of the National Debt* (1772) Price had entered upon what was to remain a major preoccupation for the rest of his career: his concern with what to him seemed to be highly irresponsible methods of government borrowing, and his tireless advocacy that the volume of public debt should be reduced. For many commentators Price's intellectual reputation was tarnished both by his defence of a demographic thesis that turned out to be grievously erroneous and by what was alleged to be an equally misguided insistence upon the need to institute sinking fund operations to reduce the National Debt. Whether Price can be defended on these issues is a matter that cannot be pursued here;[1] for our present purposes it is enough to draw attention to the extent to which his correspondence reveals how extensive were his labours in these fields. Historians have noted the ways in which Price's advocacy of sinking fund operations influenced the formulation of William Pitt's Sinking Fund Bill. What perhaps has not been as fully appreciated, and what the publication of the correspondence between Price and Shelburne and Pitt makes clear, is the extent to which Price was occupied in advising them not only on methods for reducing the National Debt but also on ways in which raising public loans could be beneficially reformed.

The correspondence from the archive at Bowood, now published for the first time, throws considerable light on the relations between Price and Shelburne. As I have already mentioned, Price spent a great deal of energy advising Shelburne on matters of national finance; but this was not the only subject upon which he sought to influence Shelburne's thought. Although in manner Price was deferential, he did not shrink from making clear his disagreements with Shelburne, especially on public matters such as recognizing the independence of the United States, or upon Shelburne's proposal to arrange for the training of the militia on Sundays, and also on more private matters such as the proposal to send Lord Fitzmaurice to Oxford. Their disagreements sometimes led to tension, as when Horne Tooke refused to withdraw the publication of *Facts*, a scathing indictment of North's financial administration in which Horne Tooke and Price had collaborated. The breach between Shelburne and Horne Tooke proved irreparable but Shelburne's friendship with Price survived. When Shelburne came into power there were many, as the correspondence shows, who thought that through Price they could approach him to secure the success of their projects: the gentlemen of Yarmouth, for example, who sought to break the influence of the Townshend connection and promote the interest of the Hurry family in Yarmouth; Solomon Harries, a

1. For a defence of Price's advocacy of Sinking Fund procedures, see my *The Honest Mind*, pp. 234–59, and for an account of his contributions to the demographic problem see my "Richard Price and the Population Controversy", *The Price–Priestley Newsletter*, No. 4 (1980), pp. 43–62.

dissenting minister at Swansea, who sought redress for his son, Houlton Harries, a surgeon in the Army who complained that he had been unjustly passed
over for promotion; William Maltby, a relative of Sarah Price, who sought
some favourable appointment; Adam Jellicoe, First Clerk in the Office of
Paymaster to the Treasury, who became nervous that he might lose his post
when Isaac Barré ceased to be Treasurer to the Navy; and William Russell,
who wished to gain Shelburne's support for a project for constructing canals in
the Midlands, and many more. The closeness of their relationship is evident in
Shelburne's tender concern for Sarah Price who was in failing health throughout this period.

The correspondence shows the wide range of Price's interests: his continuing support for the principle of self-government in politics, whether
through the development of representative government or in the defence of
national autonomy, his interest in moral philosophy, divinity and theology,
his interest in metaphysical questions and in the defence of Newtonian
cosmology, as his lengthy exchanges with Lord Monboddo testify, and his
interest as a Fellow of the Royal Society in recent scientific developments, as
can be seen in the enthusiasm with which he communicated Herschel's discoveries to Joseph Willard and Ezra Stiles. In his letters Price is largely
concerned with public affairs or the exchange of ideas. He does not dwell for
long on private matters and his plain style though eminently perspicuous is
hardly self-revelatory. It is difficult to glimpse the man, especially as he has
little humour and no malice. There is, however, one striking exception to this
almost exclusive concern with public matters: his concern for his wife. She
suffered her first attack of the palsy in 1762 some four or five years after they
were married. Thereafter she suffered a succession of such attacks, each one
more disabling than its precursor. Price looked after her tenderly and affectionately, acknowledging that in their love for each other he had found the
main source of the happiness he had enjoyed in his life, and suffering extreme
anguish at the thought that he might lose her.

Presentation:

In this volume, I have continued to use the conventions that were outlined in
detail in the introduction to the first volume. There is no need to repeat them
here, save to mention one variation. In the first volume a name, event or other
subject was annotated, if sufficient information was to hand, when it was first
mentioned. In this volume that practice is continued except where the item
has already been annotated in the first volume. Where that is the case upon the
first mention a reference is included to the location of the note in the first
volume. Where an item is not annotated the reader may assume that if the
index does not show it to have been annotated earlier, the editor has not been
able to find any illuminating material about it.

Acknowledgments

I wish to thank the staffs of the National Library of Wales, the Library of the University College of Wales, Aberystwyth; the Bodleian Library; the British Library; and Dr Williams's Library for their expert guidance and generous help.

I wish to express my warm appreciation to the following individuals and institutions for their kindness in giving me access to documents in their possession, for allowing me to take copies, for their patience in answering queries, and for permission to publish: The Trustees of the Adams Papers; American Antiquarian Society; American Philosophical Society; Bodleian Library; Library of the Boston Athanaeum; Boston Public Library; The British Library; Cardiff Public Library; Library of Congress; The Connecticut Historical Society; Cornell University Library; Cyfarthfa Castle Museum, Merthyr Tydfil; Viscountess Eccles; Equitable Life Assurance Society; Glasgow University Library; Gloucestershire County Records Office; Archive Department, Library Services, London Borough of Hackney; the late Mr G.V.M. Heap; Houghton Library, Harvard University; Mr Derek Hartley Russell; The Kendall Whaling Museum; Kungl. Svenska Vetenskapsakademiens Bibliothek, Stockholm; the Most Honourable the Marquis of Lansdowne; Library Company of Philadelphia; City of Liverpool: Hornby Library; Col. Arthur B. Lloyd Baker; Massachusetts Historical Society; Historical Society; Ministère des Armées, Vincennes; William L. Clements Library, University of Michigan; The National Library of Scotland; The National Library of Wales; New York Historical Society; New York Public Library; the Historical Society of Pennsylvania; University of Pennsylvania Library; the Pierpont Morgan Library; Princeton University Library; the Public Record Office; Rhode Island Historical Society; Mr R. H. Taylor; the Master and Fellows of Trinity College Cambridge; Mr R.O.M. Williams; Yale University Library.

In addition to those I mentioned in the introduction to the first volume I should like to thank the following for many kindnesses:

Mr Donald Anderle, Miss Lisa Backman; Mr Christopher P. Bickford, Mr M.A.F. Borrie, Mr Neville Carrick, Miss Peggy J. Clark, Viscountess Eccles, Mr P.K. Escreet, Miss Anne E. Fisher, Mr David Francis, Mr Stuart N. Frank, Dr Philip Gaskell, Mr J.A.S. Green, Mr W.R. Hartley Russell, Mr James H. Hutson, Mr Daniel Huws, Mr Marcus A. McCorison, The Revd. A. McLellan, Miss Martha J. McNamara, Mr David Mander, Mr Lionel C. Munn, Dr Brian Nelson, Mr C.A. Ryskamp, Mr Richard Salvato, Miss Margaret H. Sanders, Dr Lars-Erik Sanner, and Dr Arlene P. Shy.

I particularly wish to thank my wife, Beryl, for deciphering Price's shorthand, my daughter, Janet, for help in preparing the final draft, Dr Martin Fitzpatrick, my co-editor of *Enlightenment and Dissent*, and Messrs P.A.L. Jones and John Stephens, my co-editors on Price's bibliography, for many kindnesses in locating manuscripts and providing references, Dr D.A. Rees for his very helpful advice on Greek philosophy, Mr Richard Brinkley for reading and making valuable suggestions on the first draft and Professor Bernard Peach, the co-editor of the series, for his very detailed and very careful examination of the final draft. I also wish to thank Ms Liz Powell of the University of Wales Press for her kindness, patience and skill in preparing the whole document for publication.

Professor Bernard Peach wishes me to express his appreciation to the Program for Editions of the National Endowment for the Humanities for their help in securing the publication of this project.

Abbreviations

Alexander	*The Leibniz–Clarke Correspondence*, ed. H.G. Alexander (Manchester, 1956).
Allibone	S. Austin Allibone, *A Critical Dictionary of English Literature and British and American Authors*, 3 vols. (London, 1859–71).
Autobiography	*Autobiography of Joseph Priestley*, ed. Jack Lindsay (Bath, 1970).
Bailyn	Bernard Bailyn, *Pamphlets of the American Revolution, 1750-1776*, vol.I (Cambridge, Mass., 1965).
Baker	Norman Baker, *Government and Contractors: the British Treasury and War Supplies 1775–1783* (London, 1971).
Binney	J.E.D. Binney, *British Public Finance and Administration, 1774–1792* (Oxford, 1958).
Boatner	Mark M. Boatner, *Cassell's Biographical Dictionary of the American War of Independence, 1763–1783* (London, 1973).
Bodleian	The Bodleian Library, Oxford.
Bonwick	Colin Bonwick, *English Radicals and the American Revolution* (Chapel Hill, North Carolina, 1977).
Bowood	Shelburne Papers in the possession of the Most Honourable the Marquis of Lansdowne at Bowood Park.
Brieven	*Brieven van en aan Joan Derek van der Capellen van de Poll*, ed. W.H. de Beaufort (Utrecht, 1879).
B.L.	The British Library.
Brown	Peter Brown, *The Chathamites* (London, 1967).
Burke's Peerage	*Burke's Genealogical and Heraldic History of the Peerage, Baronetage and Knightage*, 102nd ed. (London, 1969).
Cannon	*The Letters of Sir William Jones*, ed. Garland Cannon, 2 vols. (London, 1969).
"Checklist"	P.A.L. Jones and D.O. Thomas, "A Checklist of the Published Works of Richard Price", *The Price–Priestley Newsletter*, No. 4 (1980), 79–106.
Comm.	Sir William Blackstone, *Commentaries on the Laws of England*, 14th ed. (London, 1803).
Cone	Carl B. Cone, *Torchbearer of Freedom: the Influence of Richard Price on Eighteenth Century Thought* (Lexington, 1952).
Crook	Ronald E. Crook, *A Bibliography of Joseph Priestley* (London, 1966).
D.A.B.	*Dictionary of American Biography.*

D.N.B.	*Dictionary of National Biography.*
D.Sc.B.	*Dictionary of Scientific Biography*, 14 vols., (New York, 1970–76).
D.W.B.	*The Dictionary of Welsh Biography.*
D.W.L.	Dr Williams's Library.
Federal and State	Benjamin Perley Poore, ed. *The Federal and State Constitutions, Colonial Charters, and other Organic Laws of the United States* (Washington, DC, 1875).
Fitzmaurice	Lord Fitzmaurice, *Life of William Earl of Shelburne* 2nd ed., 2 vols. (London, 1912).
Franklin: Bigelow	*The Works of Benjamin Franklin*, ed. J. Bigelow (London, 1904).
Franklin: *Papers*	*The Papers of Benjamin Franklin*, ed. Leonard Labaree et al. (New Haven, 1959–).
A Free Discussion	Richard Price and Joseph Priestley, *A Free Discussion of the Doctrines of Materialism, and Philosophical Necessity* (London, 1778).
Gent. Mag.	*Gentleman's Magazine.*
Gibbs	F.W. Gibbs, *Joseph Priestley: Adventurer in Science and Champion of Truth* (London, 1965).
H.C.J.	*Journals of the House of Commons* (London, 1803–).
Jefferson: Boyd	*The Papers of Thomas Jefferson*, ed Julian F. Boyd (Princeton, 1950–).
"Journal"	"Richard Price's Journal for the period 25 March 1787 to 6 February 1791" deciphered by Beryl Thomas with an Introduction and Notes by D.O.Thomas, *The National Library of Wales Journal*, XXI, No. 4 (Winter), 1980, 366–413.
Knight	W. Knight, *Lord Monboddo and some of his Contemporaries* (London, 1900).
Lecky	W.E.H. Lecky, *A History of England in the Eighteenth Century*, 8 vols. (London, 1879–1904).
M.H.S.P. (1903)	*Proceedings of the Massachusetts Historical Society*, 2nd series, 1903, vol.17 (Boston, 1903).
M.H.S.P. (1909–10)	*Proceedings of the Massachusetts Historical Society*, Oct. 1909–June 1910, vol.43 (Boston, 1910).
Memoirs	William Morgan, *Memoirs of the Life of the Rev. Richard Price, D.D.F.R.S.* (London, 1815).
Mon. Rep.	*The Monthly Repository of Theology and General Literature* (London, 1806–).
Namier and Brooke	Sir Lewis Namier and John Brooke, *The History of Parliament: The House of Commons, 1754-90* (London, 1964).
Nat. Union Cat.	*National Union Catalogue.*

N. Biog. Gén.	*Nouvelle Biographie Générale.*
N.L.W.	The National Library of Wales.
Norris	John Norris, *Shelburne and Reform* (London, 1963),
O.R.P.	Richard Price, *Observations on Reversionary Payments*, 3rd ed. (London, 1773).
Ogborn	M.E. Ogborn, *Equitable Assurances* London, 1962.
Parl. Hist.	*The Parliamentary History of England from the Earliest Period to the Year 1806.* ed. William Cobbett, 36 vols. (London, 1806–20).
Peach	Bernard Peach, *Richard Price and the Ethical Foundations of the American Revolution* (Durham, NC, 1979).
Peerage	*The Complete Peerage*, ed. H.A. Doubleday and Lord Howard de Walden (London, 1932).
Phil. Trans.	*Philosophical Transactions of the Royal Society.*
Principia	Sir Isaac Newton, *The Mathematical Principles of Natural Philosophy*, trans. Andrew Motte (1729), intro. I. Bernard Cohen, 2 vols. (London, 1968).
PRO	Public Record Office.
Review	Richard Price, *A review of the Principal Questions in Morals*, ed. D. D. Raphael (Oxford, 1948, reprinted 1974).
Rush Letters	*Letters of Benjamin Rush*, ed. L. H. Butterfield, 2 vols. (Princeton, 1951).
Rutt	*The Theological and Miscellaneous Works of Joseph Priestley*, ed. J.T. Rutt, 25 vols. (London, 1817–31).
State Trials	*Cobbett's Complete Collection of State Trials and Proceedings for High Treason and other Crimes and Misdemeanours from ... 1163 ... to the Present Time* 33 vols. (London, 1809–28).
D. O. Thomas	D. O. Thomas, *The Honest Mind* (Oxford, 1977).
T.U.H.S.	*Transactions of the Unitarian Historical Society.*
Wallace	D. D. Wallace, *The Life of Henry Laurens* (New York, 1915).

A List of the Short Titles of the Published Works of Richard Price

In chronological order giving the place and date of publication of the first edition.

A Review of the Principal Questions and Difficulties in Morals. London, 1758.

Britain's Happiness and the Proper Improvement of it. London, 1759.

"An Essay towards solving a problem in the Doctrine of Chances." *Phil. Trans.*, LIII, 370–418. London, 1764.

"A Demonstration of the Second Rule in the Essay ... in the Doctrine of Chances." *Phil. Trans.*, LIV, 296–325. London, 1765.

The Nature and Dignity of the Human Soul. London, 1766.

Four Dissertations. London, 1767.

"Observations on the Expectations of Lives." *Phil. Trans.*, LIX, 89–125. London, 1770.

The Vanity, Misery and Infamy of Knowledge without Suitable Practice. London, 1770.

A Letter from Dr. Webster ... and Dr. Price's Answer. Edinburgh, 1771.

An Account of a Scheme for Providing Relief. London, 1771.

"Observations on the Proper Method of Calculating the Values of Reversions." *Phil. Trans.*, LX, 268–76. London, 1771.

Observations on Reversionary Payments. London, 1771.

"On the Effect of the Aberration of Light on the Time of a Transit of Venus." *Phil. Trans.*, LX, 536–40. London, 1771.

An Appeal to the Public on the Subject of the National Debt. London, 1772.

"Farther Proofs of the Insalubrity of Marshy Situations." *Phil. Trans.*, LXIV, Part I, 96–98. London, 1774.

Calculations and Observations relating to the Scheme of the Laudable Society, London, 1774.

"Observations on the Difference between the Duration of Human Life in Towns and in Country Parishes." *Phil. Trans.*, LXV, Part I, 424–45. London, 1775.

"Short and Easy Theorems...." *Phil. Trans.*, LXVI, Part I, 109–28. London, 1776.

Observations on the Nature of Civil Liberty. London, 1776.

Additional Observations on the Nature and Value of Civil Liberty. London, 1777.

A Free Discussion of the Doctrines of Materialism and Philosophical Necessity. London, 1778.

Two Tracts on Civil Liberty. London, 1778. "Introduction" and "Essay on the present state of population in England and Wales." In W. Morgan, *The Doctrine of Annuities and Assurances*. London 1779. [Price's essay was published separately in 1780.]

Fast Sermon ... 10 February 1779. London, 1779.

Facts Addressed to the Landholders .... London, 1780.

An Essay on the Population of England. London, 1780.

Fast Sermon ... 21 February 1781. London, 1781.

The State of the Public Debts. London, 1783.

Postscript to a Pamphlet by Dr. Price on the State of the Public Debts and Finances. London, 1784.

"Directions for Using Tables", (in) Francis Maseres, *The Doctrine of Annuities.* London, 1783.

A Letter to Lieut. Col. Sharman (in) *A Collection of the Letters ... Addressed to the Volunteers of Ireland.* London, 1783.

Observations on the Importance of the American Revolution. London, 1784.

Plans for Annuities. Edinburgh, 1784.

Postscript to Mr G.C. Morgan's "Observations on the Light of Bodies in a State of Combustion". *Phil. Trans.*, LXXV, Part 1, 211. London, 1785.

Letter Introducing Dr Clarke's "Observations on some Causes of the Excess of Mortality of Males above that of Females." *Phil. Trans.*, LXXVI, Part 2, 349. London, 1786.

[Prefatory Letter to] *A Statute of Virginia.* London, 1786.

Letters in Acland *A Plan for Rendering the Poor Independent.* Exeter, 1786.

Sermons on the Christian Doctrine. London, 1787.

The Evidence for a Future Period of Improvement in the State of Mankind. London, 1787.

A Discourse on the Love of our Country. London, 1789.

Additions to Dr. Price's Discourse ... containing Communications from France. London, 1790.

Preface and Additions to the Discourse on the Love of our Country. London, 1790.

Sermons by Richard Price and Joseph Priestley. London, 1791.

"Three Plans communicated to Mr. Pitt" in W. Morgan, *A Review of Dr. Price's Writings on the Subject of the Finances ....* London, 1792.

Sermons on Various Subjects. ed. W. Morgan. London, 1816.

For details of the various editions and impressions of Price's works see (forthcoming) *A bibliography of the works of Richard Price*, compiled by D.O. Thomas, John Stephens, and P.A.L. Jones, to be published in the St Paul's Bibliographies.

A Chronology of Richard Price's Life for the Period Covered by This Volume

1778 *Two Tracts.*
A Free Discussion of the Doctrines of Materialism, and Philosophical Necessity.
6 February: Franco-American treaties signed in Paris.
6 October: American Congress invite Price to become a Citizen of the United States.

1779 "An Essay on the Present State of Population in England and Wales."

1780 *Facts.*

1781 24 April: LL D at Yale.

1782 30 January: Elected to a Fellowship of the American Academy of Arts and Sciences at Boston.
July: Shelburne becomes First Lord of the Treasury and William Pitt becomes Chancellor of the Exchequer.

1783 *State of the Public Debts.*
Fourth edition of *Observations on Reversionary Payments.*
20 January: Preliminary articles of Peace signed at Versailles.
February: Shelburne resigns.
April–December: Fox–North Coalition.
December: William Pitt becomes First Lord of the Treasury and Chancellor of the Exchequer.

1784 *Observations on the Importance of the American Revolution.*

1785 28 January: Elected a member of the American Philosophical Society at Philadelphia.

1786 29 March: William Pitt's Sinking Fund Bill introduced in the House of Commons.

The Correspondence of Richard Price

From A. Turgot

M. Franklin m'a remis, Monsieur, de votre part, la nouvelle edition de vos *observations sur la liberté civile*, etc. Je vous dois un double remerciement 1° de votre ouvrage, dont je connais depuis longtemps le prix, et que j'avais lu avec avidité, malgré les occupations multipliées dont j'etait assailli, lorsqu'il a paru pour la premiere fois; 2° de l'honnetete que vous avez eue de retrancher l'imputation de mal adresse que vous aviez mêlée au bien que vous disiez d'ailleurs de moi dans vos notes additionnelles.

J'aurais pu la meriter, si vous n'aviez eu en vue d'autre mal adresse que celle de n'avoir pas su demêler les ressorts d'intrigues que fisaient jouer contre moi des gens beaucoup plus adroits que je ne le suis que je ne le serai jamais et que je ne veux l'etre. Mais il m'a paru que vous m'imputiez la mal adresse d'avoir choqué grossierement l'opinion generale de ma nation: et, a cet egard je crois que vous n'avez rendu justice ni a moi, ni a ma nation ou il y a beaucoup plus de lumieres qu'on ne le croit generalement chez vous, et ou peut-être il est plus aisé que chez vous meme de ramener le public a des idées raisonnables.

J'en juge, par l'infatuation de votre nation sur ce projet absurde de subjuguer l'amerique, qui a duré jusqu'a ce que l'aventure de Burgoyne ait commence a lui desiller les yeux. J'en juge, par le systeme de monopole et d'exclusion qui regne chez tous vos ecrivains politiques sur le commerce (j'excepte Mr Adam Smith et le doyen Tucker), systeme qui est le veritable principe de votre separation avec vos colonies. J'en juge, par touts vos ecrits polemiques sur les questions qui vous agitent depuis une vingtaine d'années, et dans lesquels, avant que le votre eut paru, je ne me rappelle presque pas d'en avoir lu un ou le vrai point de la question ait été saisi. Je n'ai pas concu comment une nation qui a cultivé avec tant de succes toutes les branches des sciences naturelles a pu rester si fort au-dessous d'elle même dans la science la plus interessante de toutes, celle du bonheur public; dans une science ou la liberté de la presse, dont elle seule jouit, aurait du lui donner sur toutes les autres nations de l'Europe un avantage prodigieux. Est ce l'orgueil national

ORIGINAL: Service Historique de l'Armée, Serie M (Mémoires), Carton 1045, pièce 10. The MS bears the note: 'Copie'. I have not been able to trace the original manuscript. PRINTED: *Œuvres de Turgot*, ed. G. Schelle (Paris, 1913–23), Tome 5ième, 532–40. TEXT: Original, with the kind permission of the Ministère des Armées, Vincennes. The two italicized passages beginning and ending with * were omitted from the printed version of the French text published in *Observations on the Importance of the American Revolution* (London, 1785) but, strangely enough, they were included in the English translation which was published in the same volume. These passages do not appear in the English translation that was published with the first American edition printed at Boston in 1784.

qui vous a empeches de mettre a profit cet avantage? Est-ce parce que vous etiez un peu moins mal que les autres, que vous avez tourné toutes vos speculations a vous persuader que vous etiez bien? Est-ce l'esprit de parti, et l'envie de se faire un appuy des opinions populaires qui a retardé vos progrès, en portant vos politiques a traiter de vaine methaphysique toutes les speculations qui tendent a etablir des principes fixes sur les droits et les vrais interets des individus et des nations? Comment de fait-il que vous soyez presque le premier parmi vos ecrivains qui ayez donne des notions justes de la liberte et qui ayez fait sentir la faussete de cette notion, rebattue par presque touts les ecrivains les plus republicains, que la liberté consiste a n'etre soumis qu'aux lois, comme si un homme opprimé par une loi unjuste etait libre. Cela ne serait pas meme vrai, quand on supposerait que toutes les lois sont l'ouvrage de la nation assemblée; car enfin, l'individu a aussi ses droits, que la nation ne peut lui oter que par la violence et par un usage illegitime de la force genérale. Quoique vous ayez eu egard a celle vérité et que vous vous en soyez expliqué, peut-être meritait-elle que vous la developpassiez avec plus d'etendue, vu le peu d'attention qu'y ont donné meme les plus zélés partisans de liberté.

C'est encore une chose etrange que ce ne fut pas en Angleterre une vérité triviale de dire qu'une nation ne peut jamais avoir droit de gouverner une autre nation; et qu'un pareil gouvernement ne peut avoir d'autre fondement que la force qui est aussi la fondement du brigandage et de la tyrannie; que la tyrannie d'un peuple est de toutes les tyrannies connues la plus cruelle et la plus intolerable, celle qui laisse le moins de ressources a l'opprimé; car enfin, un despote est arrêté par son propre interet; il a la frein du remords, ou celui de l'opinion publique mais une multitude ne calcule rien, n'a jamais de remords, et se decerne a elle-même la gloire lorsqu'elle merite le plus de honte.

Les evenements sont pour la nation anglaise un terrible commentaire de votre livre. Depuis quelques mois ils se precipitent avec une rapidité tres accelerée. Le denoument est arrivé par rapport à l'amerique. La voila independante sans retour. Sera-t-elle libre et heureuse? Ce peuple nouveau, situé si avantageusement pour donne au monde l'exemple d'une constitution ou l'homme jouisse de toutes ses droits, exerce librement toutes ses facultes, et ne soit gouverné que par la nature, la raison et la justice, saura-t-il former une pareille constitution. Saura-t-il l'affermir sur des fondements eternels, prevenir toutes les causes de division et de corruption qui peuvent la miner peu a peu et la detruire?

Je ne suis point content, je l'avoue, des constitutions qui ont été redigées jusqu'a présent par les differents etats américains. Vous reprochez avec raison à celle de pensylvanie le serment religieux exigé pour avoir entree dans le corps des representants. C'est bien pis dans les autres; il y en a une, je crois que c'est celle de Jerseys, qui exige *qu'un croye a la divinite de J.Ch.* Je vois dans le plus grand nombre l'imitation sans objet des usages de l'Angleterre. Au lieu de ramener toutes les autorités a une seule, celle de la nation, l'on etablit des corps differents, un corps de representants, un conseil, un gouverneur, parce que l'Angleterre a une Chambre des communes, une Chambre haute et un roi. On s'occupe a balancer ces differents pouvoirs; comme si cet equilibre de forces, qu'on a pu croire necessaire pour balancer l'enorme preponderance de la royauté, pouvait etre de quelque usage dans des republiques fondées sur l'egalité de tous les citoyens, et comme si tout ce qui etablit differents corps n'etait pas une source de divisions! En voulant prevenir des dangers chimeriques, on en fait naitre de réels; on veut n'avoir rien a craindre du clergé, on le réunit sous la banniere d'une proscription commune. En l'excluant du droit d'eligibilité, on en a fait un corps, et un corps etranger a l'Etat. Pourquoi un citoyen qui a le meme interet que les autres a la defense commune de sa liberté et de ses proprietés, est-il exclu d'y contribuer de ses lumieres et de ses vertus, parce qu'il est d'une profession qui exige des lumieres et des vertus? Le clergé n'est dangereux que quand il existe en corps dans l'etat, que quand il croit avoir un corps des droits et des interets; que quand on a imaginé d'avoir une religion etablie par la loi comme si les hommes pouvaient avoir quelque droit ou quelque interet a regler la conscience les uns des autres; comme si l'individu pouvait sacrifier aux avantages de la société civile les opinions auxquelles il croit son salut eternel attaché; comme si l'on se sauvait ou se damnait en commun. Là ou la vraye tolerance, c'est-a-dire, l'incompetence absolue du gouvernement sur la conscience des individus est etablie, l'ecclesiastique, au milieu de l'assemblée nationale, n'est qu'un citoyen, lorsqu'il y est admis; il redevient ecclesiastique lorsqu'on l'en exclut.

Je ne vois pas qu'on se soit assez occupé de reduire au plus petit nombre possible les genres d'affaires dont le gouvernement de chaque etat sera chargé; ni à separer les objets de legislation de ceux d'administration particuliere et locale; a constituer des assemblées locales subsistentes qui, remplissant presque toutes les fonctions de detail du gouvernment, dispensent les assemblées generales de s'en occuper, et otent aux membres de celles-ci tout moyen et peut-etre tout desir d'abuser d'une autorité qui ne peut s'appliquer qu'a des objets generaux, et par la même etranger aux petites passions qui agitent les hommes.

Je ne vois pas qu'on ait fait attention a la grande distinction, la seule fondée sur la nature, entre deux classes d'hommes, celles des proprietaires des terres et celle des non-proprietaires, a leurs interets et par consequent à leurs droits differents, relativement a la legislation, a l'administration de la justice et de la police, a la contribution aux depenses publiques et a leur emploi.

Nul principe fixe etabli sur l'impôt: on suppose que chaque province peut se taxer a sa fantaisie, etablie des taxes personelles, des taxes sur les consommations, sur les importations, c'est-a-dire se donner un interet contraire a l'interet des autres provinces.

On suppose partout le droit de regler le commerce; on autorise même les corps executifs, ou les gouverneurs, a prohiber l'exportation de certaines denrées dans de certaines occurrences; tant on est loin d'avoir senti que la loi de la liberté entiere de tout commerce est un corollaire du droit de propriété; tant en est encore plongé dans les brouillards des illusions européennes!

Dans l'union generale des provinces entr'elles, je ne vois point une coalition, une fusion de toutes les parties, qui n'en fassent qu'un corps *un* et homogene. Ce n'est qu'une aggregation de parties toujours trop separées, et qui conservent toujours une tendance a se diviser, par la diversité de leurs loix, de leurs moeurs, de leurs opinions; par l'inegalité de leurs forces actuelles, plus encore que l'inegalité de leur progrès ulterieur. Ce n'est qu'une copie de la republique hollandoise; et celle-ci même n'avait pas a craindre, comme la republique americaine, les accroissements possibles de quelques-unes de ses provinces. Tout cet edifice est appuyé jusqu'a present sur la base fausse de la tres ancienne et tres vulgaire politique, sur le prejugé que les nations, les provinces, peuvent avoir des interets, en corps de provinces et de nations, autres que celui qu'ont les individus d'etre libres et de defendre leur proprieté contre les brigands et les conquerants: interet pretendu de faire plus de commerce que les autres, de ne point acheter des marchandises de l'etranger, de forcer l'etranger a consommer leurs productions, et les ouvrages de leurs manufactures; interet pretendue d'avoir un territoire plus vaste, d'acquerir telle ou telle province, telle ou telle île, tel ou tel village; interet d'inspirer la crainte aux autres nations, interet de l'emporter sur elles par la gloire des armes, par celle des arts et des sciences.

Quelques-uns de ces prejugés sont fomentés en Europe, parce que la rivalité ancienne des nations et l'ambition des princes oblige touts les etats a se tenir armés pour se defendre contre leurs voisins armes, et a regarder la force militaire comme l'object principal du gouvernement.

L'amerique a le bonheur de ne point avoir, d'ici a bien longtemps, d'ennemi exterieur a craindre, si elle ne se divise elle-même ainsi elle peut et doit apprecier a leur juste valeur ces pretendus interets, ces sujets de discorde, qui seuls sont a redouter pour sa liberté. Avec le principe sacre de la liberté du commerce, regarde comme une suite de droit de la proprieté, tous les pretendus interets de commerce disparaissent. Les pretendus interets de posseder plus ou moins de territoire s'evanouissent par le principe que le territoire n'appartient point aux nations, mais aux individus proprietaires des terres; que la question de savoir si tel canton, tel village doit appartenir a telle province, a tel etat, ne doit point etre decidée par le pretendu interet de cette province ou de cet etat, mais par celui qu'ont les habitants de tel canton, ou de tel village, de se rassembler pour leur affaires dans le lieu ou il leur et le plus commode d'aller; que cet interet, etant mesuré par le plus ou le moins de chemin qu'un homme peut faire loin de son domicile, pour traiter quelques affaires plus importantes, sans trop nuire a ses affaires journalieres, devient une mesure naturelle et physique de l'etendue des jurisdictions et des etats, et etablit entre touts un equilibre d'etendue et de forces qui ecarte tout danger d'inegalité, et toute pretention a la superiorité.

L'interet d'etre craint est nul quand on ne demande rien a personne, et quand on est dans une position ou l'on ne peut etre attaqué par des forces considerables avec quelque esperance de succès. La Gloire des armes ne vaut pas le bonheur de vivre en paix.

La gloire des arts, des sciences, appartient a quiconque veut s'en saisir; il y a dans ce genre a moissonner pour tout le monde; le champ des descouvertes est inespuisable, et touts profitent des decouvertes de touts.

J'imagine que les Americains n'en sont pas encore a sentir toutes ces verites, comme il faut qu'ils les sentent pour assurer le bonheur de leur posterité. Je ne blame pas leurs chefs. Il a fallu pourvoir aux besoins du moment pour une union telle quelle, contre un ennemi present et redoubtable; on n'avait pas le temps de songer a corriger les vices des constitutions, et de la composition des differents etats, mais ils doivent craindre de les eterniser et s'occuper des moyens de reunir les opinions et les interets, et de les ramener a des principes uniformes dans toutes leurs provinces.

Ils ont a cet egard de grands obstacles a vaincre. En Canada, la constitution du clergé romain, et l'existence d'un corps de noblesse.

Dans la nouvelle angleterre l'esprit encore subsistant du puritanisme rigide, est toujours, dit-on, un peu intolerant.

Dans la Pensylvanie un tres grande nombre de citoyens etablissant en principe religieux, que la profession des armes est illicite, et se refusent par consequent aux arrangements necessaires pour que le fondement de la force militaire de l'etat soit la reunion de la qualite de citoyen avec celle d'homme de guerre et de milicien; ce qui oblige a faire du metier de la guerre un metier de mercenaire.

Dans les colonies meridionales, une trop grande inegalité de fortunes; et surtout le grand nombre d'esclaves noirs, dont l'esclavage est incompatible avec une bonne constitution politique, et qui même en leur rendant la liberté embarrasseront encore en formant deux nations dans le même etat.

Dans toutes, les prejugés, l'attachement aux formes etablies, l'habitude de certaines taxes, la crainte de celles qu'il faudrait y substituter, la vanité des colonies qui se sont crues les plus puissantes, et un malheureux commencement d'orgueil national.

Je crois les americaines forcés a s'agrandir, non par la guerre, mais par la culture. S'ils laissaient derriere eux les deserts immenses qui s'etendent jusqu'a la mer de l'ouest, il s'y etablirait, du mêlange de leurs bannis et des mauvais sujets echappés a la severité des lois, avec les sauvages, des peuplades de Brigands qui ravageraient l'amerique commes les Barbares du Nord ont ravagé l'empire romain de là un autre danger, la necessité de se tenir en armes sur la frontiere, et d'etre dans un etat de guerre continuelle. Les colonies voisines de la frontiere seraient en consequence plus aguerries que les autres, et cette inegalité dans la force militaire serait un aiguillon terrible pour l'ambition. Le remede a cette inegalité serait d'entretenir une force militaire subsistante, a laquelle toutes les provinces contribueraient, en raison de leur population; et les americains qui ont encore toutes les craintes que doivent avoir les Anglais redoutent plus que toute chose une armée permanente. Ils ont tort. Rien n'est plus aise que de lier la constitution d'une armée permanente avec la milice, de facon que la milice en devienne meilleure, et que la liberté n'en soit que plus affermie; mais il est mal aisé de calmer sur cela leurs allarmes.

Voila bien des difficultés; et peut-etre les interets secrets des particuliers puissants se joindront-ils aux prejugés de la multitude pour arreter les efforts des vrays sages et vrais citoyens.

Il est impossible de ne pas faire des voeux pour que ce peuple parvienne a toute la prosperité dont il est susceptible. Il est l'esperance du genre humain. Il peut en devenir le modèle. Il doit prouver au monde par le fait que les hommes peuvent etre libres et tranquilles, et peuvent se passer des chaines de toute espece que les tyrans et les charlatans de toute robe ont pretendu leur imposer sous le pretexte du bien public. Il doit donner l'exemple de la liberté politique, de la liberté religieuse, de la liberté du commerce et de l'industrie. L'asile qu'il ouvre a toutes les opprimés de toutes les nations, doit consoler la terre. La facilité d'en profiter pour se derober aux suites d'un mauvais gouvernement forcera les gouvernements d'etre justes et de s'eclairer; le reste du monde ouvrira peu a peu les yeux sur le néant des illusions dont les politiques se sont bercés. Mais il faut pour cela que l'amerique s'en garantisse, et qu'elle ne redevienne pas comme l'ont tant repété vos ecrivains ministeriels, une image de notre Europe, un amas de puissances divisées, se disputant des territoires ou des profits de commerce, et cimentant continuellement l'esclavage des peuples par leur propre sang.

Touts les hommes eclairés, touts les amis de l'humanité devraient en ce moment reunir leurs lumieres, et joindre leurs reflexions a celles des sages americains, pour concourir au grand ouvrage de leur legislation. Cela serait digne de vous, Monsieur; je voudrais pouvoir echauffer votre zele, et si, dans cette lettre je me suis livré, plus que je ne l'aurais du peut-être a l'effusion de mes propres idées, ce desir a été mon unique motif, et m'excusera a ce que j'espere, de l'ennuy que je vous aurai causé. Je voudrais que le sang qui a coulé, et qui coulera encore dans cette querelle ne fut pas inutile au genre humain.

Nos deux nations vont se faire reciproquement bien du mal, probablement sans qu'aucune d'elles en retire aucun profit reel. L'accroissement des dettes et des charges, *peut etre la banquerote de l'etat*, et la ruine d'un grand nombre de citoyens en seront probablement peut-être l'unique resultat. L'angleterre m'en parait plus près encore que la france. Si, au lieu de cette guerre, vous aviez pu vous exécuter de bonne grâce des le premier moment; s'il etait donné a la politique de faire d'avance ce qu'elle sera infailliblement forcée de faire plus tard; si l'opinion nationale avait pu permettre a votre gouvernement de prevenir les evenements, en supposant qu'il les eut prévus, s'il eut pu consentir d'abord a l'independance de l'amerique, sans faire la guerre a personne, je crois fermement que votre nation n'aurait rien perdu a ce changement. Elle y perdra aujourd'huy ce quelle a depensé, ce qu'elle depensera encore; elle eprouvera, une grande diminution pour quelque temps dans nos commerce, de grands bouleversements interieurs, si elle est forcée a la banqueroute; et, quoiqu'il arrive, une grand diminution dans l'influence politique au dehors. Mais ce dernier article est d'une bien petite importance pour le bonheur réel d'un peuple, et je ne suis point du tout de l'avis de l'abbe Raynal dans votre epigraphe. Je ne crois pas que ceci vous mene a devenir une nation meprisable et vous jette dans l'esclavage.

Vos malheurs seront peut-être au contraire l'effet d'une amputation necessaire; ils sont peut-être le seul moyen de vous sauver de la gangrene du luxe et de la corruption. Si, dans vos agitations, vous pouviez corriger votre constitution en rendant les elections annuelles, en repartissant le droit de representation d'une maniere plus egale et plus proportionnee aux interêts des représentés; vous gagneriez peut-être autant que l'amerique a cette revolution: car votre liberté vous resterait, et vos autres pertes se repareraient bien vite avec elle et par elle.

Vous devez juger, Monsieur; par la franchise avec laquelle je m'ouvre a vous sur ces points delicats, de l'estime que vous m'avez inspiré, et de la satisfaction que j'eprouve a penser qu'il y a quelque ressemblance entre nos manieres de voir.

Je compte bien que cette confidence n'est que pour vous. Je vous prie même de ne point me repondre en detail par la poste; car votre response serait infailliblement ouverte dans nos bureaux de poste, et l'on me trouverait beaucoup trop ami de la liberté pour un ministre et même pour un ministre disgracié.

J'ai l'honneur &c.
Turgot

Translation

Paris, 22d March 1778

Sir,

Mr Franklin by your desire has put into my hands the last edition of your *Observations on Civil Liberty*, &c. for which I think myself doubly indebted to

---

PRINTED: Richard Price, *Observations on the Importance of the American Revolution* (London, T. Cadell, 1785), pp. 107–27. TEXT: *Observations* (1785). A copy of this letter in the original French was first

you. In the first place, for the work itself, of which I have long known the value and read with great avidity, notwithstanding the multiplicity of my engagements, when it was first published: And in the next place, for the politeness you have shewn in leaving out the imputation of *want of address*,[a] which you

a. What is here said refers to the following account of M. *Turgot's* administration in the *second* tract on *Civil Liberty and the War with America*, p. 150, &c. "A new reign produced a new minister of finance in *France*, whose name will be respected by posterity for a set of measures as new to the *political* world, as any late discoveries in the system of nature have been to the *philosophical* world – Doubtful in their operation, as all untried measures must be, but distinguished by their tendency to lay a solid foundation for endless peace, industry, and a general enjoyment of the gifts of nature, arts and commerce – The edicts issued during his administration exhibit indeed a *phaenomenon* of the most extraordinary kind. An absolute King rendering a voluntary account to his subjects, and inciting his people to *think*; a right which it has been the business of all absolute princes and their ministers to extinguish. – In these edicts the King declared in the most distinct terms against a bankruptcy, &c. while the minister applied himself to increase every public resource by principles more liberal than *France*, or any part of *Europe*, ever had in serious contemplation. – It is much to be regretted, that the opposition he met with and the intrigues of a court should have deprived the world of those lights, which must have resulted from the example of such an administration."

[In the three editions of *Additional Observations* and the first edition of *Two Tracts* there follows the passage which gave offence to Turgot and which Price suppressed in the second edition of the latter work; it reads, "It is much to be regretted that the intrigues of a court, want of address, or perhaps want of due regard to that degree of public conviction, which must influence more or less in a despotic as well as free state should have deprived the world of those lights which must have resulted from the example of such an administration." The amended version reads: "It is much to

published by Price in *Observations on the Importance of the American Revolution*. The earliest intimation that he was thinking of publishing it occurs in his letter to Arthur Lee of 18 Jan. 1779, in which he indicates that he might publish it together with some observations of his own. But some time was to elapse before he completed his manuscript and he was uncertain as to whether publication was permissible. Turgot had asked him not to communicate it to others for fear of political repercussions, but after Turgot's death Price felt that publication need not be prevented by the fear that it might be damaging to his, or to his family's, interests. Nonetheless some anxiety remained and Price sought Franklin's advice (R.P. to Benjamin Franklin, 12 July 1784). Franklin responded by securing permission to publish from Turgot's literary executor, Dupont de Nemours (Benjamin Franklin to R.P., 2 Aug. 1784). Although the letter had been set up in type Price assured Franklin that it would not be printed until it was quite clear that it was right to do so. Franklin's reply thus made it possible for Price to include a copy of Turgot's letter in French in the first edition of *Observations on the Importance of the American Revolution*, but since not all of the copies of the pamphlet include the letter, it is possible that some were run off before Price received permission to publish.

Price's original intention was to publish the pamphlet exclusively for sale in America and to accompany it with a translation of Turgot's letter as well as a copy of the original. But it is clear from his letter to Jonathan Trumbull, the elder, dated 8 Oct. 1784, that he did not include a translation of it in the first edition. He was, however, looking forward to receiving one from the hand of Mirabeau. From his letter to Trumbull it would also seem that Price was not aware that Powars and Willis, the Boston publishers, had substituted a translation of Turgot's letter (not Mirabeau's) for the copy of the original that Price had sent, when the pamphlet was reprinted by them in 1784. Mirabeau's translation was available in 1784 because he included a copy of it together with a translation of the whole of Price's pamphlet and lengthy comments thereon in a work published in London in that year under the title *Considérations sur l'Ordre de Cincinnatus*.

Early in 1785 fears of piracy led Price to change his mind about publishing the pamphlet only in America and to produce an edition for the British market in which he included Mirabeau's translation of Turgot's letter.

Price's notes (shown above) are preceded by letters of the alphabet in lower case.

intermixed with the handsome things you said of me in your additional observations.[2] I might have merited this imputation, if you had in view no other *want of address* than incapacity to unravel the springs of those intrigues that were employed against me, by some people who are much more expert in these matters than I am, or ever shall be, or indeed ever desire to be: But I imagined you imputed to me *a want of address* which made my opinions grossly clash with the general opinions of my countrymen; and in that respect I thought you neither did justice to *me* nor to *my country*, where there is a degree of understanding much superior to what you generally suppose in England, and where it is more easy perhaps, than even with you, to bring back the public to hearken to reason.

I have been led to judge thus by the infatuation of your people in the absurd project of subduing America, till the affair of Burgoyne[3] began to open their eyes; and by the system of monopoly and exclusion which has been recommended by all your writers on Commerce, (except Mr Adam Smith[4] and Dean Tucker[5]); a system which has been the true source of your separation from your Colonies. I have also been led to this opinion by all your controversial writings upon the questions which have occupied your attention these twenty years, and in which, till your observations[6] appeared, I scarce recollect to have read one that took up these questions on their proper ground. I cannot conceive how a nation which has cultivated every branch of natural knowledge with such success, should have made so little progress in the most interesting of all sciences, that of the public good: A science, in which the liberty of the Press, which she alone enjoys, ought to have given her a prodigious advantage over every other nation in Europe. Was it national pride which prevented you

be regretted, that the opposition he met with and the intrigues of a court should have deprived the world of those lights, which must have resulted from the example of such an administration.'] In this passage I had, in the first edition, mentioned improperly Mr *Turgot's want of address* among the other causes of his dismission from power. This occasioned a letter from him to inform me of the true reasons of his dismission, and begun that correspondence, of which this letter is a part, and which continued till his death. – It may not be improper to add here, that his successor was Mr Necker[1], author of the interesting Treatise on the Administration of the Finances of France just published [J. Necker, *De l'Administration des Finances de la France* (Paris, 1784)]; and that in the passage just quoted, the following notice is taken of this appointment. – "After a short interval, a nomination, in some respects still more extraordinary, took place in the Court of *France*. A court, which a few years since was distinguished by its bigotry and intolerance, has raised a *protestant*, the subject of a small but virtuous republic, to a decisive lead in the regulation of its finances. It is to be presumed that so singular a preference will produce an equally singular exertion of integrity and talents."

1. Jacques Necker (1732–1804), Director General of the Treasury of France (1776–77); Director General of Finance (1777–81, 1788–90).

2. Richard Price, *Additional Observations* (London, 1777). See Vol. I, 251; Peach, pp. 125–175.

3. On 17 Oct. 1777 General John Burgoyne (see Vol. I, 238) surrendered with his army to General Horatio Gates at Saratoga. This victory proved to be a turning point for the American rebels, for it facilitated the Franco-American alliance.

4. Adam Smith (1723–90), economist, philosopher.

5. Josiah Tucker, see Vol. I, 249.

6. Richard Price, *Observations on the Nature of Civil Liberty* (London, 1776), see Vol. I, 237; Peach, pp. 63–123. The first edition of this work was published in Feb. 1776.

from profiting by this advantage? Or was it, because you were not altogether in so bad a condition as other nations, that you have imposed upon yourselves in your speculations so far as to be persuaded that your arrangements were compleat? Is it party spirit and a desire of being supported by popular opinion which has retarded your progress, by inducing your political writers to treat as vain Metaphysics[b] all those speculations which aim at establishing the rights and true interests of nations and individuals upon fixed principles. How comes it that you are almost the first of the writers of your country, who has given a just idea of liberty, and shewn the falsity of the notion so frequently repeated by almost all Republican Writers, "that liberty consists in being subject only to the laws," as if a man could be free while oppressed by an unjust law.[7] This would not be true, even if we could suppose that all the laws were the work of an assembly of the whole nation; for certainly every individual has his rights, of which the nation cannot deprive him, except by violence and an unlawful use of the general power. Though you have attended to this truth and have explained yourself upon this head,[8] perhaps it would have merited a more minute explanation, considering how little attention is paid to it even by the most zealous friends of liberty.

It is likewise extraordinary that it was not thought a trivial matter in England to assert "that one nation never can have a right to govern another nation"—"that a government where such a principle is admitted can have no foundation but that of force, which is equally the foundation of robbery and tyranny"—"and that the tyranny of a people is the most cruel and intolerable, because it leaves the fewest resources to the oppressed."[9] A despot is restrained by a sense of his own interest. He is checked by remorse or by the public opinion. But the multitude never calculate. The multitude are never checked by remorse, and will even ascribe to themselves the highest honour when they deserve only disgrace.

What a dreadful commentary on your book are the events which have lately befallen the English nation?—For some months they have been running head-long to ruin.—The fate of America is already decided.—Behold her independent beyond recovery.—But will She be free and happy? Can this new people, so advantageously placed for giving an example to the world of a constitution under which man may enjoy his rights, freely exercise all his faculties, and be governed only by nature, reason and justice—Can they form such a Constitution? Can they establish it upon a neverfailing foundation, and guard against

b. See Mr Burke's Letter to the Sheriffs of Bristol. ["I do not pretend to be an antiquary, a lawyer, or qualified for the chair of profess in metaphysicks. I never ventured to put your solid interests upon speculative grounds." *The Works of the Right Honourable Edmund Burke* (London, 1808), III, 177].

7. See Peach, pp. 51, 70.
8. See Peach, pp. 72–73.
9. See Peach, pp. 75–81, 154.

every source of division and corruption which may gradually undermine and destroy it?

I confess that I am not satisfied with the Constitutions which have hitherto been formed by the different States of America. It is with reason that you reproach the State of Pensylvania with exacting a religious test[10] from those who become members of the body of Representatives. There are much worse tests in the other States; and there is one (I believe the Jerseys) which requires[c] a declaration of faith in the *Divinity* of Jesus Christ.[12]—I observe that by most of them the customs of England are imitated, without any particular motive. Instead of collecting all authority into one center, that of the nation, they have established different bodies; a body of representatives, a council, and a Governour, because there is in England a House of Commons, a House of Lords, and a King.—They endeavour to balance these different powers, as if this equilibrium, which in *England* may be a necessary check to the enormous influence of royalty, could be of any use in Republics founded upon the equality of all the Citizens; and as if establishing different orders of men, was not a source of divisions and disputes. In attempting to prevent imaginary dangers they create real ones; and in their desire to have nothing to fear from the clergy, they unite them more closely by one common proscription. By excluding them from the right of being elected into public offices they become a body distinct from the State. Wherefore should a Citizen, who has the same interest with others in the common defence of liberty and property, be excluded from contributing to it his virtue and knowledge? Is it because he is of a profession which *requires* knowledge and virtue? The clergy are only dangerous

c. It is the Constitution of *Del[a]ware* that imposes the test here meant.[11] That of the *Jerseys*, with a noble liberality, orders that there shall never in that Province be any establishment of any one religious sect in preference to another, and that all Protestants of all persuasions shall enjoy equal rights and privileges.[12]

10. In his "General Introduction" to *Two Tracts* Price writes, "The new constitution for Pennsylvania (in other respects wise and liberal) is dishonoured by a religious test. It requires an acknowledgement of the divine inspiration of the Old and New Testament as a condition of being admitted to a seat in the House of Representatives directing however, at the same time, that no other religious test shall for ever hereafter be required of any civil officer." See Penn. Const. art. 2, sec. 10 (1776), Benjamin Perley Poore, ed., *The Federal and State Constitutions, Colonial Charters, and other Organic Laws of the United States*, pt. 2 (Washington, DC, 1875), p. 1543, cited in Peach, pp. 54–55.

11. See Del. Const. art. 22 (1776). The relevant passage reads: "Every person who shall be chosen a member of either house, or appointed to any office or place of trust, before taking his seat, or entering upon the execution of his office, ... [shall] make and subscribe the following declaration, to wit: 'I A B, do profess faith in God the Father, and in Jesus Christ His only Son, and in the Holy Ghost, one God, blessed for evermore; and I do acknowledge the holy scriptures of the Old and New Testament to be given by divine inspiration.'" *Federal and State Constitutions*, pt. 1, p. 276, cited in Peach, p. 200.

12. New Jersey Const. art. 18 (1776). See *Federal and State Constitutions*, pt. 2, p. 1313, cited in Peach, p. 218.

when they exist as a distinct body in the State; and think themselves possessed of separate rights and interests and a religion established by law, as if some men had a right to regulate the consciences of other men, or could have an interest in doing this; as if an individual could sacrifice to civil society opinions on which he thinks his eternal salvation depends; as if, in short, mankind were to be saved or *damned* in *communities*—Where *true* toleration, (that is, where the absolute incompetency of civil government in matters of conscience, is established); there the *clergyman*, when admitted into the national assembly, becomes a *simple citizen*; but when excluded, he becomes an *ecclesiastic*.

I do not think they are sufficiently careful to reduce the kind of business with which the government of each State is charged, within the narrowest limits possible; nor to separate the objects of legislation from those of the general administration, or from those of a local and particular administration; nor to institute local permanent assemblies, which by discharging almost all the functions in the detail of government, make it unnecessary for the general assemblies to attend to these things, and thereby deprive the members of the general assemblies of every means, and perhaps every desire, of abusing a power which can only be applied to general objects, and which, consequently, must be free from the influence of the little passions by which men usually are agitated.

I do not find that they attend to the great distinction (the only one which is founded in nature between two classes of men), between landholders; and those who are not landholders; to their interests, and of course to their different rights respecting legislation, the administration of justice and police, their contributions to the public expence, and employment.

No fixed principle of taxation is established. They suppose that each State may tax itself according to its own fancy, by establishing either *personal* taxes, or taxes on *consumption* and *importation*; that is, that each State may assume to itself an interest contrary to the interest of the other States.

They also every where suppose that they have a right to regulate commerce. They even delegate authority to executive bodies, and to Governors, to prohibit the exportation of certain commodities on certain occasions. So far are they from being sensible that the right to an entire liberty in commerce is the consequence of the right of property. So much are they still involved in the mist of European illusions.

In the general union of the States I do not observe a coalition, a fusion of all the parts to form one homogeneous body. It is only a jumble of communities too discordant, and which retain a constant tendency to separation, owing to the diversity in their laws, customs and opinions; to the inequality in their *present* strength; but still more, to the inequality in their advances to *greater* strength. It is only a copy of the Dutch republic, with this difference, that the *Dutch* republic had nothing to fear, as the *American* republic has, from the future possible increase of any one of the Provinces.—All this edifice has been hitherto supported upon the erroneous foundation of the most ancient and vulgar policy; upon the prejudice that Nations and States, as such, may have an interest distinct from the interest which individuals have to be free, and to defend their property against the attacks of robbers and conquerors: An interest, in carrying on a more extensive commerce than other States, in not purchasing foreign merchandise, and compelling foreigners to consume their produce and manufactures: An interest in possessing more extensive territories, and acquiring such and such a province, island or village: An interest in inspiring other nations with awe, and gaining a superiority over them in the glory of arts, sciences, and arms.

Some of these prejudices are fomented in *Europe*, from the ancient rivalship of nations and the ambition of Princes, which compel every State to keep up an armed force to defend itself against the attack of neighbours in arms, and to look upon a military force as the principal object of government. *America* is likely in no long time to enjoy the happiness of having no external enemy to dread, provided she is not divided within herself. She ought, therefore, to estimate properly those pretended *interests* and causes of discord which alone are likely to be formidable to her liberty. On that sacred principle, "liberty of commerce considered as a natural right flowing from the possession of property," all the pretended interests of commerce must vanish.—The supposed interest in possessing more or less territory disappear on this principle, "that a territory does not belong to nations, but to the individuals who are proprietors of the lands". The question, whether such a canton or such a village belongs to such a Province or such a State, ought not to be determined by the interest in it pretended by that Province or that State; but by the interest the inhabitants of the canton or village have in assembling for transacting their affairs in the place most convenient for them. This interest, measured by the greater or less distance that a man can go from his home to attend to important affairs without injuring his private concerns, forms a natural boundary to the jurisdiction of States, and establishes an equipoise[d] of extent and strength between them, which must remove every danger of inequality, and every pretence to superiority.

There can be no interest in being feared when nothing can be demanded, and when men are in a situation not to be attacked by a considerable force with any hope of success.

The glory of *arms* is nothing to those who enjoy the happiness of living in peace.

The glory of arts and sciences belongs to every man who can acquire it, There is here ample scope. The field of discovery is boundless; and all profit by the discoveries of all.

d. This seems to be a particular of much consequence. The great inequality now existing, and which is likely to increase, between the different States, is a very unfavourable circumstance; and the embarrassment and danger to which it exposes the union ought to be guarded against as far as possible in laying out future States.

I imagine that the Americans are not as sensible of these truths, as they ought to be, in order to secure the happiness of their posterity. I do not blame their leaders. It was necessary to provide for the necessities of the moment, by such an union as they could form against a present and most formidable enemy. They have not leisure to consider how the errors of the different constitutions and States may be corrected; but they ought to be afraid of perpetuating these errors, and to endeavour by all means to reconcile the opinions and interests of the different provinces, and to unite them by bringing them to one uniform set of principles.

To accomplish this they have great obstacles to surmount.

In Canada, an order of Roman Catholic Clergy, and a body of Nobles.

In New England, a rigid puritanical spirit which has been always somewhat intolerant.[e]

In Pensylvania, a very great number of inhabitants laying it down as a religious principle, that the profession of arms is unlawful, and refusing to join in the arrangements necessary to establish the military force of the State, by uniting the character of the Citizen with that of the Soldier and Militiaman, in consequence of which the business of war is made to be the business of *mercenaries*.

In the Southern Colonies, an inequality of fortune too great; and what is worse, a great number of Blacks, whose slavery is incompatible with a good political constitution; and who, if emancipated, would occasion great embarrassement by forming two distinct people in one State.

In all of them, various prejudices, an attachment to established forms, a habit of paying certain taxes, and a dread of those which must be substituted for them; a vanity in those colonies which think themselves most powerful; and a wretched beginning of national pride. I imagine that the Americans must aggrandize themselves not by war, but by agriculture. If they neglect the immense desarts which are at their backs, and which extend all the way to the western sea, their exiles and fugitives from the severity of the laws, will unite with the Savages, and settle that part of the country; the consequence of which will be that bodies of Banditti will ravage America, as the Barbarians of the North ravaged the Roman Empire, and subject the States to the necessity of keeping the frontiers always guarded, and remaining in a State of continual

e. This has been *once* true of the inhabitants of *New-England*, but it is not so *now*. See p. 47 [of the *Observations on the Importance of the American Revolution*, 1785 ed.][13]

---

13. In *Observations on the Importance of the American Revolution* Price applauded the growth of toleration in Massachusetts and welcomed the legal recognition, embodied in the Constitution of Massachusetts, of the individual's right to worship God in the manner he thinks fit. See op. cit. in Peach, p. 199, and Mass. Const. pt., art. 3 (1780). The relevant passage reads: "And every denomination of Christians, demeaning themselves peaceably and as good subjects of the commonwealth, shall be equally under the protection of the law; and no subordination of any one sect or denomination to another shall ever be established by law." *Federal and State Constitutions*, pt. 1, pp. 957–58, cited in Peach, pp. 199–200.

war. The Colonies next to the frontier will of course be better disciplined than the rest; and this inequality of military force will prove a dreadful incentive to ambition. The remedy for this inequality would be to keep up a standing army, to which every State should contribute in proportion to its population; but the Americans, who have the fears that the English *ought* to have, dread nothing so much as a standing army. In this they are wrong. There is nothing more easy than to combine a standing army with a militia, so as to improve the militia, and gain additional security for liberty. But it is no easy matter to calm their apprehensions on that head.

Here are a number of difficulties; and perhaps the private interests of powerful individuals will unite with the prejudices of the multitude, to check the efforts of true Philosophers and good Citizens.

It is impossible not to wish ardently that this people may attain to all the prosperity of which they are capable. They are the *hope* of the world. They may become a *model* to it. They *may* prove by fact that men can be free and yet tranquil; and that it is in their power to rescue themselves from the chains in which tyrants and knaves of all descriptions have presumed to bind them under the pretence of the public good. They may exhibit an example of *political* liberty, of *religious* liberty, of *commercial* liberty and of industry. The *Asylum* they open to the oppressed of all nations should console the earth. The ease with which the injured may escape from oppressive governments, will compel Princes to become just and cautious; and the rest of the world will gradually open their eyes upon the empty illusions with which they have been hitherto cheated by politicians. But for this purpose *America* must preserve *herself* from these illusions; and take care to avoid being what your ministerial writers are frequently saying she *will* be—an image of our *Europe*—a mass of divided powers contending for territory and commerce, and continually cementing the slavery of the people with their own blood.

All enlightened men — All the friends of humanity ought at this time to unite their lights to those of the *American* sages, and to assist them in the great work of legislation. This, sir, would be a work worthy of you. I wish it was in my power to animate your zeal in this instance. If I have in this letter indulged too free an effusion of my sentiments, this has been my only motive; and it will, I hope, induce you to pardon me for tiring you. I wish indeed that the blood which has been spilt, and which will continue for some time to be spilt in this contest, may not be without its use to the human race.

Our two nations are about doing much harm to each other, and probably without the prospect to either of any real advantage. An increase of debts and public burthens, (perhaps a national bankruptcy), and the ruin of a great number of individuals, will prove the result. England seems to me to be more likely to suffer by these evils, and much nearer to them, than France.—If instead of going to war, you had at the commencement of your disputes endeavoured to retreat with a good grace; if your Statesmen had then consented to make those concessions, which they will infallibly be obliged to make at last; if the national opinion would have permitted your government to anticipate events which might have been foreseen; if, in short, you had immediately yielded to the independence of America without entering into any hostilities; I am firmly persuaded your nation would have lost nothing.— But you will *now* lose what you have already expended, and what you are still to expend; you will experience a great diminution of your commerce for some time, and great interior commotions, if driven to a bankruptcy; and, at any rate, a great diminution of weight in foreign politics. But this last circumstance I think of little consequence to the real happiness of a people; for I cannot agree with the *Abbe Raynal*[14] in your motto.[f]

I do not believe all this will make you a contemptible nation or throw you into slavery.—On the contrary; your misfortunes may have the effect of a necessary amputation. They are perhaps the only means of saving you from the gangrene of luxury and corruption. And if they should terminate in the amendment of your constitution, by restoring annual elections, and distributing the rights of suffrages for representation so as to render it more equal and better proportioned to the interest of the represented, you will perhaps gain as much as America by this revolution; for you will preserve your liberty, and with your liberty, and by means of it, all your other losses will be speedily repaired.

By the freedom with which I have opened myself to you, sir, upon these delicate points, you will judge of the esteem with which you have inspired me; and the satisfaction I feel in thinking there is some resemblance between our sentiments and views. I depend on your[g] confining this confidence to yourself. I even beg that you will not be particular in answering me by the Post, for your letter will certainly be opened at our Post-Offices, and I shall be found much too great a friend to liberty for a minister, even though a discarded minister.

> I have the honour to be with all possible respect,
>
> Sir,
>
> Your most humble,
>
> and obedient Servant,
>
> TURGOT.

f. This refers to the following words (taken from Mr Justamond's translation of the *Abbe Raynal's* History of the European Settlements [G.T.F. Raynal, *A Philosophical and Political History of the Settlements and Trade of the Europeans in the East and West Indies*, trans. J. Justamond (London, 1776). This translation is from Raynal's *Historie Philosophique et Politique des Établissements de Commerce des Européens dans les Deux Indes* (Amsterdam, 1770); see Peach, 148]) in the Title-page to the Second Tract on Civil Liberty—"Should the morals of the English be perverted by luxury— should they lose their colonies by restraining them, &c. they will be enslaved. They will become insignificant and contemptible; and Europe will not be able to shew the world *one* nation in which she can pride herself."

g. In compliance with Mr *Turgot's* desire, this letter was kept private during his life. Since his

14. Guillaume Thomas Francois Raynal (1713–96), political writer.

death I have thought the publication of it a duty which I owe to his memory, as well as to the United States and the world. I can add, with much satisfaction, that my venerable friend and the excellent Philosopher and Statesman whose name introduces this letter; and also, that some intimate friends of Mr *Turgot*'s, who have been consulted on this subject, concur with me in this sentiment. [See note under TEXT, above.]

From Thomas Greaves

Rotterdam March. 24: 1778

Reverend Sir,

I have taken the liberty of sending a Line to ask your opinion about the present distracted state of the British Nation, or rather to desire you would inform me by the first return of the Post, if Money, that is; Principal and interest be safe in your Publick Funds and if there is any danger of a rupture, supposing America to be irrecoverably lost, a French War to Commence and the reduction of the West Indies to succeed.

Your answer will have much influence on my own Conduct and that of many others on this side the water, to whom in the political Line you are a perfect oracle. Excuse this trouble and believe me to be with unfeigned respect on account of your sterling merit and rare endowments of mind.

Reverend Sir,
Your most obedient servant,
Th^s. Greaves

ORIGINAL: American Philosophical Society.   PRINTED: Original, with the kind permission of the American Philosophical Society.

To Benjamin Franklin

May 10th [1778]

Dr P[rice] is very sorry the bearer of this has any reason for giving Dr Franklin[1] any farther trouble; but he doubts not but Dr F[rankli]n will receive him with his accustomed goodness.

Is there any truth in the stories propagated here that the Congress is divided; that General Washington is grown unpopular; that his army deserts

ORIGINAL: American Philosophical Society.   TEXT: Original, with the kind permission of the American Philosophical Society.   PRINTED; *Franklin: Papers*, XXVI, 432

1. See Vol. I, 41 n. 1.

in great numbers; and that the sufferings of the Americans are excessive? The Commissioners are gone assured, that the terms they are impowered to offer by the conciliatory Bills, tho' much short of Independence will be accepted,[2] Is there any reason to expect this? Any notice which Dr F[rankli]n may take of these questions to Mr P[ ]r,[3] or any intelligence which he can give with propriety, will be gratefully accepted by Dr P[rice] who indeed, in these times is extremely anxious. He wishes his particular remembrances may be delivered to Mr L[ee][4] and Dr B[ancroft].[5] Mr Curteis[6] and Mr Webb[7] are both broken and ruined. Many events of the same kind have lately happened and there is reason to fear they are but the beginning of sorrows.

A family[8] in which Dr F[ranklin] used to be very intimate, and particularly the amiable Miss G[eorgian]a,[9] are very inquisitive about him, and wish him to know they are all well, and that they always remember him with particular affection and regards. The Society of Whigs at the L[ondon Coffee House] never forget him.

[No signature]

---

2. On 13 Apr. 1778 the Earl of Carlisle was appointed Chief of a Commission to 'treat, consult and agree upon the means of quieting the disorders' in the American colonies. The Commission also included George Johnstone, former Governor of West Florida, William Eden, later Lord Auckland, Sir William Howe, and Lord Howe. (D.N.B.) Adam Ferguson was Secretary to the Commission.

3. Possibly Joseph Parker, see R.P. to Shelburne, 20 Nov. 1782.

4. Arthur Lee, see Vol. I, 253.

5. Edward Bancroft (1744–1821), MD, FRS, who, during the War of American Independence, was a double agent serving both the British and the Americans. (D.A.B.)

6. The editors of Franklin Papers (XVI, 224) suggest that this was William Curtis (1746–99), a Quaker physician and botanist, a translator of Linnaeus, and an expert on the flora of London.

7. Probably Benjamin Webb, a merchant, who until 1774 was a director of the London Assurance Co. (see Franklin Papers, XXV, 353).

8. During his stay in England, Benjamin Franklin became very friendly with Jonathan Shipley, the Bishop of St Asaph, and his family. Shipley (1714–88) became Dean of Winchester and Rector of Chilbolton in 1760, Bishop of Llandaff in 1769, and Bishop of St Asaph later in the same year. It was at Twyford, Shipley's home in Hampshire, that Franklin composed portions of his autobiography, (see The autobiography of Benjamin Franklin, ed. Leonard W. Labaree et al. [New Haven and London, 1964], p. 22).

9. On the outbreak of the War of American Independence, Shipley stopped writing to Benjamin Franklin, and asked his family to do the same. This his daughter Georgiana refused to do. See Brown, pp. 332–33 and 468.

To Joseph Priestley

Newington-Green, May 14, 1778.

Dear Sir,

I am obliged to you for sending me your last replies.[1] I have read them with a desire to be as open as possible to conviction; and even not without wishing for an opportunity of shewing candour by retracting any mistakes into which I may have fallen. But more perhaps through a fault in me, than in you, my views and sentiments continue the same.

I must leave you to manage the publication as you please. You must be sensible that my first remarks were written without the most distant view to publication; and this, I hope, will be an excuse for the incorrectnesses and want of order which will be found in them. There is also, in some parts of these first remarks, a turn of expression which carries an appearance not sufficiently respectful; and which I should have avoided had I written them with a view to publication, and been more on my guard. I know your candour has engaged you to overlook this, but I cannot reflect upon it without some concern.

I shall be very happy should this publication answer any valuable ends; but I am afraid the discussion it contains will be too dry and metaphysical to be generally acceptable. Some good ends, however, it may probably answer. It will afford a proof that two persons may differ totally on points the most important and sacred, with a perfect esteem for one another; and it may like

---

PRINTED: *A Free Discussion of the Doctrines of Materialism, and Philosophical Necessity, in a Correspondence between Dr Price and Dr Priestley* (London, 1778), pp. xxxv–xxxix. TEXT: *A Free Discussion, etc.*

1. In 1777 Joseph Priestley published *Disquisitions relating to Matter and Spirit* and *The Doctrine of Philosophical Necessity Illustrated*. These works, which defend many positions that were unacceptable to Price, provoked him to address a series of questions to Priestley. Priestley answered these, whereupon Price submitted further comments and questions to which Priestley again replied. These exchanges took place during the period May to October 1778, and although initially neither of the authors intended anything more than a private discussion, it was subsequently decided to publish the whole. The book in which these exchanges appear, *A Free Discussion of Materialism, and Philosophical Necessity, in a Correspondence between Dr Price and Dr Priestley*, is divided into three sections: the first part is entitled, "Concerning the penetrability of matter"; the second, "Of the human mind, the mortality of the soul, and the essence of the deity"; and the third, "Of the doctrine of necessity". In these sections Priestley defended a monistic materialism and a form of necessarianism or determinism, while Price defended a mind–body dualism and a form of libertarianism. Price did not make any claims to originality with respect to the arguments used by Priestley and himself—the position he defended on the nature of liberty, he readily admitted, derived from Samuel Clarke, while Priestley's objections derived very largely from Anthony Collins's *A Philosophical Inquiry concerning Human Liberty and Necessity* (see *A Free Discussion*, p. 351n.), but both authors believed that the book would be of interest if only because of the way in which the controversy had been conducted. Priestley, who wrote the introduction to the work, claimed, "This work ... exhibits an uncommon, if not a singular spectacle, viz. that of two persons discussing, with the most perfect freedom and candour, questions which are generally deemed of the greatest consequence in practice, and which are certainly so in theory." (Ibid., p. i.)

wise give a specimen of a proper manner of carrying on religious controversies. There is nothing that offends me more than that acrimony of spirit with which controversies in general, and particularly religious ones, are commonly conducted. In religion there is nothing so essential as charity, candour, and benevolence.[2] How inexcusable then is that cruel zeal which some religious people indulge; and how melancholy is it to see them, in the very act of contending for religion, losing what is most valuable in religion? Will you give me leave, Sir, here to add, that your opinions give a striking proof of a truth, which, could it be stamped on every human mind, would exterminate all bigotry and persecution; I mean the truth, that worth of character, and true integrity, and consequently God's acceptance, are not necessarily connected with any particular set of opinions. Many think yours to be some of the most dangerous possible; and yet the person who holds them is known to be one of the best men in the world; and I ardently wish my soul may be united to his at the time when *all that are in their graves shall hear the voice of the son of man, and come forth; they who have done some good to the resurrection of life, and they who have done evil to the resurrection of damnation.*[3] Our agreement in expecting this awful period makes it of little consequence in what we differ.

With great respect and affection, I am, Dear Sir,
ever yours,
Richard Price.

2. Unlike Priestley, Price had no love of controversy. This was partly due to his temperament for by disposition he was averse to publicity. He published his work because he felt that he had a duty to do so, but once he had stated his views he preferred not to enter into public argument, and wherever possible he avoided replying to his critics and becoming embroiled in controversy. Another reason was that he found the manner in which many debates were conducted distasteful. However wide his disagreement with an opponent, he saw no reason for a personal attack, no justification for abuse or vilification. He firmly believed that all controversy should be conducted with respect for the opponent and that it should be devoted exclusively to the merits and weaknesses of his argument. He valued his controversy with Priestley as much for the way in which it was conducted as for its content; they were giving their contemporaries an exemplar of the way in which a debate on metaphysical and theological topics should be conducted.

3. See John 5. 28, 29: All that are in the graves shall hear his voice. And shall come forth; they that have done good, unto the resurrection of life; and they that have done evil, unto the resurrection of damnation.

To Joseph Priestley

Newington-Green, Sept. 19, 1778.

Dear Sir,

The desire you have expressed that I would give you my sentiments of the Controversy between us, *on a view of the whole of it as now printed,* has induced me

PRINTED: *A Free Discussion of the Doctrines of Materialism, and Philosophical Necessity, in a Correspondence between Dr Price and Dr Priestley* (London, 1778), pp. 321–5. TEXT: *A Free Discussion, etc.*

once more to apply my thoughts to it. I have done this with care and attention; but am not sure that any thing which you will judge of great importance has occurred to me. I might, therefore, have been right to resolve to say no more; and indeed, I am so much afraid of perplexing by a multiplicity of words, and of giving disgust by too many repetitions, that this would have been my resolution, had I not thought, that the *Additional Observations* which you will receive with this letter, contain some *new* matter; and place several of the arguments already insisted on, in a light that may render them to some persons more intelligible and striking.[1] I have now said the best I can; and I leave our readers to judge between us, hoping that whether they decide in your favour or mine, they will be candid, and believe that we are both of us governed alike by a sincere love of truth and virtue. I feel deeply that I am in constant danger of being led into error by partial views, and of mistaking the suggestions of prejudice for the decisions of reason; and this, while it disposes me to be candid to others, makes me ardently wish that others would be candid to me.[2]

I am, in a particular manner, sensible of my own blindness with respect to the nature of matter and spirit, and the faculties of the human mind. As far as I have gone in this dispute I am pretty well satisfied; but I cannot go much further. You have asked me some questions (and many more may be asked me) which I am incapable of answering.

I cannot help taking this opportunity of repeating to you, what I dislike more than I can easily express, the malevolence expressed by most of the writers against you. I have myself, as you well know, been long an object of abuse for a publication[3] which I reckon one of the best actions of my life, and which events have fully justified. The consciousness of not deserving abuse has made me perfectly callous to it; and I doubt not but the same cause will render you so.

It is certain that, in the end, the interest of truth will be promoted by a free and open discussion of speculative points. Whatever will not bear this must be superstition and imposture. Instead, therefore, of being inclined to censure those who, with honest views, contribute to bring about such a discussion, we ought to thank and honour them, however mistaken we may think them, and however sacred the points of discussion may be reckoned. I wish I could see more of this disposition among the defenders of religion. I am particularly sorry to find that even Mr Whitehead[4] does not perfectly possess this temper.

---

1. With this letter Price enclosed a paper entitled "Additional Observations by Dr. Price" which was included in *A Free Discussion*, pp. 327–59.

2. On Price's attachment to candour, see D.O. Thomas, pp. 99–101.

3. I.e., *Observations on the Nature of Civil Liberty* (1776). In *Additional observations* (1777) Price referred to the many who have published "virulent invectives" against him, "I will not attempt to give any list of them. They are without number." See Peach, p. 134.

4. John Whitehead (1740–1804), Quaker, physician, and biographer of John Wesley. In 1778

Had he avoided all uncandid insinuations, and treated you constantly with the same just respect that he does in general, his book in my opinion would have done him much honour.

Dr Horsley[5] is, I fancy, the only person who, in opposing your opinions, has discovered a just liberality. This is worthy of an able Philosopher; and you have, therefore, very properly distinguished him from your other antagonists, by addressing him, in your letter to him, with particular respect. His method of arguing agrees very much with mine. There is, likewise, an agreement between some of Mr Whitehead's arguments and those I have used. But this agreement has been accidental; for our correspondence was begun and finished long before I knew anything of either Dr Horsley's or Mr Whitehead's publications.

Wishing you every possible blessing, I am, with the most affectionate respect,

Yours,
Richard Price.

---

he published *Materialism Philosophically Examined; or, the Immateriality of the Soul asserted and proved, on Philosophical Principles, in answer to Dr. Priestley's Disquisitions on Matter and Spirit.* Priestley's letter to Whitehead was published in *A Free Discussion*, pp. 197–211.

5. Samuel Horsley, see Vol. I, 166. Priestley's letter to Horsley dated June 1778 was published in *A Free Discussion*, pp. 213–28; in it Priestley answered criticisms which Horsley had made of the necessarians (although without naming Priestley) and suggested that the differences between Horsley's determinism and his own position are merely verbal. For Horsley's criticism of the necessarians see Samuel Horsley, *Sermons* (London, 1839), pp. 232–48.

From Joseph Priestley

Calne, Oct. 2, 1778.

Dear Sir,

With this letter you will receive a few remarks on your *Additional Observations*,[1] which I have read with that *attention* which every thing from you demands. That it has not been with *conviction*, your candour, I know, will not impute to any peculiar *obstinacy*, but to my unavoidably seeing the subjects of our discussion in a light different from that in which you see them. We have not the same idea of the nature of the human mind, or of the laws to which it is subject, but we are both sufficiently aware of the force of *prejudice*, and that this

---

PRINTED: *A Free Discussion of the Doctrines of Materialism, and Philosophical Necessity, in a Correspondence between Dr Price and Dr Priestley*, (London, 1778), pp. 407–15. TEXT: *A Free Discussion, etc.*

1. See R.P. to Joseph Priestley, 19 Sept. 1778. Priestley's replies to Price were published in *A Free Discussion*, pp. 361–405.

Joseph Priestley (1733–1804). Portrait by Ellen Sharples. Reproduced by kind permission of the National Portrait Gallery, London.

may equally throw a bias on the side of the *long established*, or of *novel* opinions. Also, equally respecting the christian maxim of *doing to others as we would that others should do to us*, we are each of us ready to give to others that liberty which we claim ourselves; while we equally reprobate those rash sentiments which proceed from a decision without a previous discussion of the reasons for and against a question in debate.

I am not a little proud of your commendation of me for my "fairness in the pursuit of truth, and following it in all its consequences, however frightful, without attempting to evade or palliate them" (p. 352). It is a conduct that I hope I shall always pursue, as the first of duties to that God who has given me whatever *faculties* I possess, and whatever *opportunity of inquiry* I have been favoured with; and I trust I shall continue to pursue this conduct at all risks. As he is properly no christian, who does not *confess Christ before men*, or who is *ashamed* of his religion in an unbelieving age, like the present; this maxim, which the author of our religion inculcates with respect to christianity in general, the reason of the thing requires that we extend to every thing that essentially affects christianity.

So long, therefore, as I conceive the doctrine of a *separate soul* to have been the true source of the grossest corruptions in the christian system, of that very *antichristian system* which sprung up in the times of the apostles, concerning which they entertained the strongest apprehensions, and delivered, and left upon record, the most solemn warnings, I must think myself a very lukewarm and disaffected christian if I do not bear my feeble testimony against it.[2]

With respect to the private conduct of individuals, as affecting our happiness after death, I do not lay any stress upon this, or upon *any opinion whatever*, and there is no person of whose christian temper and conduct I think more highly than I do of yours, though you hold opinions the very reverse of mine, and defend them with so much zeal; a zeal which, while you maintain the opinion at all, is certainly commendable. But with respect to the *general plan of christianity*, the importance of the doctrines I contend for can hardly, in my opinion, be rated too high. What I contend for leaves nothing for the manifold corruptions and abuses of popery to fasten on. Other doctrinal reformations are partial things, while this goes to the very root of almost all the mischief we complain of; and, for my part, I shall not date the proper and complete downfall of what is called *antichrist*, but from the general prevalence of the doctrines of materialism.

---

2. As a sequel to his *Disquisitions relating to Matter and Spirit*, and included within the same volume, Priestley published "The History of the Philosophical Doctrine concerning the Origin of the Soul, and the Nature of Matter; with its Influence on Christianity, especially with respect to the Doctrine of the Pre-existence of Christ." In it he traced the origins of the soul/body dualism, the belief in the immortality of the soul, and the doctrine of the pre-existence of Christ, all of which he believed to be alien to the teaching of the Gospels and due to the intrusion of elements from Greek, Egyptian, Persian, and Indian sources.

This I cannot help saying appears to me to be that fundamental principle in true philosophy which is alone perfectly consonant to the doctrine of the scriptures; and being at the same time the only proper deduction from natural appearances, it must, in the progress of inquiry soon *appear to be so*; and then, should it be found that an unquestionably true philosophy teaches one thing, and revelation another, the latter could not stand its ground, but must inevitably be exploded, as contrary to *truth and fact*. I therefore deem it to be, of particular consequence, that philosophical unbelievers should be apprized in time, that there are christians, who consider the *doctrine of a soul* as a tenet that is so far from being *essential* to the christian scheme, that it is a thing quite *foreign* to it, derived originally from heathenism, discordant with the genuine principles of revealed religion, and ultimately subversive of them.

As to the doctrines of *necessity*, I cannot, after all our discussion, help considering it as *demonstrably true*, and the only possible foundation for the doctrines of a *providence*, and the *moral government of God*. Continuing to see things in this light, after the closest attention that I have been able to give to them, before, or in the course of our friendly debate (and you will pardon me, if I add, feeling this in a stronger light than ever) you will not be displeased with the *zeal* that I have occasionally shewn; as I, on my part, intirely approve of yours, who consider yourself as defending important and long received truth, against fundamental and most dangerous innovations.

We are neither of us so far blinded by prejudice as not to see, and acknowledge, the wisdom of constituting us in such a manner, as that every thing *new* respecting a subject of so much consequence as *religion*, should excite a great alarm, and meet with great difficulty in establishing itself. This furnishes an occasion of a thorough examination, and discussion of all new doctrines, in consequence of which they are either totally exploded, or more firmly established. The slow and gradual progress of christianity, and also that of the reformation, is a circumstance that bids fairer for their perpetuity, than if they had met with a much readier reception in the world. You will allow me to indulge the hope of a similar advantage from the opposition that I expect to this article of reformation in the christian system, and that the truth I contend for will be the more valued for being dearly bought, and slowly acquired.

As to the *odium* that I may bring upon myself by the malevolence of my opposers, of which, in your letter to me, you make such obliging mention, I hope the same consciousness of not having deserved it, will support me as it has done you, when much worse treated than I have yet been, on an occasion on which you deserved the warmest gratitude of your country, whose interests you studied and watched over, whose calamities you foresaw, and faithfully pointed out; and which might have derived, in various respects, the most solid and durable advantages from your labours. But we are no christians, if we have not so far imbibed the principles and spirit of our religion, as even to *rejoice that we are counted worthy of suffering* in any good cause.

Here it is that, supposing me to be a defender of *christian truth*, my object gives me an advantage that your excellent *political writings* cannot give you. All your observations may be just, and your advice most excellent, and yet your country, the safety and happiness of which you have at heart, being in the hands of infatuated men, may go to ruin; whereas christian truth is a cause *founded on a rock*,[3] and though it may be overborne for a time, we are assured that the *gates of death shall not prevail against it*.[4]

Having now, each of us, defended, in the best manner that we can, what we deem to be this important truth, we are, I doubt not, equally satisfied with ourselves, and shall chearfully submit the result of our discussion to the judgment of our friends, and of the public; and to the final and infallible determination of the *God of all truth*.

I am, notwithstanding this, and every other possible difference in *mere opinion*, with the most perfect esteem,

Dear Sir,
Yours most affectionately,
J. Priestley

---

3. Luke 6. 48.
4. Matthew 16. 18; "the gates of hell shall not prevail against it".

To the Earl of Shelburne[1]

Newington Green Oct 31st 1778

My Lord,

I cannot help sending you these few lines just to thank you for the letter which you honoured me before you left London. When you return I suppose it will be to stay for the winter; and then I shall hope to be restored to my usual opportunities of conversing with your Lordship.

I have been lately informed from very good authority that a notification has been made from the Court of Spain of its resolution to take a decided part in favour of France, if the quarrel between it and this country is not compromised.[2] From the same authority I have been assured, that an Ordinance has been published by the King of the two *Sicilies* granting the free use of his ports and a free trade with his subjects to all American ships; and that the Plenipotentiaries at Paris have been desired by him to give a description of the

---

ORIGINAL: Bowood.   TEXT: Original, with the kind permission of the Marquis of Lansdowne.
1. See Vol. I, 96.
2. In the event Spain did not enter the war against Britain until June 1779.

American flag that due regard may be paid to it and due succour given. Indeed, I am frighten'd when I think of the present state of the nation. Events, however, may turn out better than I fear; and I study to suppress my anxiety and to bring my mind to an acquiescence in whatever may happen feeling no concern about my own personal interest, and knowing that I have born such a testimony as I am capable of bearing, and that little or nothing lies in my power. I have heard a great deal from a variety of places of the slackness of trade. My nephew from Norwich[3] informs me particularly of the distress which prevails there in consequence chiefly of the loss of the trade to the Mediterranean. Forty persons, he says throw themselves every week into their vile workhouse; and the distress is likely to increase as the winter comes on. In Spital-Fields also there is more distress than has been known for many years; and the number of persons in the workhouse is, I am told 400.

Governour Johnstone[4] is come home loaded with infamy. What a despicable figure does he make? His letter to Mr Dana[5] is nothing but a collection of falshoods. But I will not lengthen this letter. My best wishes attend Lord Fitzmaurice.[6] Mrs Price sends her best respects to your Lordship. In hopes of soon seeing you in town; and under a very grateful sense of your Lordship's kind civilities and friendship, I am, with great regard

Your most obedient and Humble servant

Rich*d* Price

---

3. George Cadogan Morgan (1754–98), the second son of William Morgan and Sarah, sister of Richard Price. Born at Bridgend and educated at Cowbridge Grammar School, Jesus College, Oxford, and the Dissenting Academy at Hoxton. In 1776 he received a call to preach at the Octagon Chapel at Norwich, where he remained until 1785 when he moved to Great Yarmouth. In 1783 he married Anne, the daughter of William Hurry, a wealthy Dissenter at Yarmouth. He moved to Hackney in Mar. 1787 to assist his uncle by taking the afternoon service at Gravel Pit Meeting House. Later in the year he assisted his uncle at New College, Hackney, where Price had been appointed to lecture in mathematics, natural science and moral philosophy. During the session 1788/9 Morgan also lectured in classics. He resigned these teaching duties in Apr. 90 and after Price's death in Apr. 1791 he gave up taking services at Gravel Pit and devoted his time and energies to the highly successful school he had established at Southgate. He died in 1798. See D.O. Thomas, "George Cadogan Morgan", *The Price–Priestley Newsletter*, No. 3 (1779), 53–70.

4. George Johnstone (1730–87). After service in the Royal Navy he was appointed Governor of West Florida, a post which he held from 1763 until 1767. Upon his recall he became an MP, sitting successively for Cockermouth (1768–74), Appleby (1774–80), Lostwithiel (1780–84), and Ilchester (1786–87). In Parliament he "at once distinguished himself by his shameless and scurrilous utterances". (*D.N.B*). From 1774 he became clearly identified with the Rockingham party and opposed the Administration's colonial policy, but when the Rockingham party declared in favour of the recognition of American independence in 1778 he joined forces with the government. In the same year he was appointed to Carlisle's Peace Commission, believing that the repeal of the Quebec Act and the Declaratory Act would be sufficient to heal the breach between the colonists and the British government. He returned home earlier than the other Commissioners. (Namier and Brooke, II, 683–85.)

5. Francis Dana, see Vol, I, 200.

6. John Henry Petty, Viscount Fitzmaurice. See Vol. I, 156.

Should your Lordship see Dr Priestley deliver my remembrances to him. I hope soon to write to him. I hear that the Americans are dissatisfied with D'estaing's[7] conduct; and that there has been a tumult at Boston between some *English* sailors who had been taken, and some *French* sailors, in which the Boston people took part with the English sailors, and *D'estaing* himself had been obliged to interpose, and had been wounded. But I do not give much credit to this account. I am afraid it is too true that we are to send a strong reinforcement to America, which is to be replaced in this Kingdom by an army of Russians. But your Lordship best knows whether this is true.

---

7. Charles-Hector, Comte d'Estaing (1729–94), French admiral, who took command of the first French naval force sent to help the American rebels after the conclusion of the Franco–American alliance in 1778.

From Benjamin Franklin, Arthur Lee[1] and John Adams[2]

Passy near Paris Dec*r* 7, 1778

Sir,

By one of the *latest* [late] ships from America, we had the Pleasure of receiving from Congress, an attested Copy of their Resolution of the sixth of October, [conceived] in these words,[3]

In Congress 6 Oct*r* 1778

Resolved

That the Honourable Benjamin Franklin, Arthur Lee, and John Adams Esqrs or any one of them, be directed forthwith to apply to Dr Price, and inform him, that it is the Desire of Congress to consider him as a Cityzen of the united States, and to receive his Assistance in regulating their Finances. That

---

ORIGINAL: Yale University Library. The Adams Papers (Reel No. 93) contains a similar version of this letter, of the same date, signed by John Adams only. In the text printed here square brackets enclose passages that are in the Adams version but not in the Franklin et al. version, and passages in italics indicate passages in the Franklin et al. version that are not in the Adams version. TEXT: Originals, with the kind permission of Yale University Library and the Trustees of the Adams Papers.

1. See Vol. I, 253.
2. John Adams (1735–1826), President of the United States (1796–1800).
3. *Journals of Congress, 1774–1789*, 12 (1908), pp. 984–5.

if he shall think it expedient to remove with his family to America and afford such Assistance, a generous Provision shall be made for requiting his Services
extract from the Minutes

Cha. Thompson Secy[4]

From a great respect to the Character of Dr Price

We have much satisfaction in communicating this Resolution. We request your Answer, *Sir*, as soon as *may be* convenient. If it should be in the Affirmative, you may depend upon us to discharge the *Expence of your Journey and Voyage* [the Expenses of your Journeys and Voyages] and for every Assistance, in our Power to make your Passage agreable, as well as your Reception and Accomodation in our Country. We have the Honour to be with the Highest Esteem and Respect, Sir, your most obedient

and most humble *Servants* [Servant]
B. Franklin
Arthur Lee
John Adams.

---

4. Charles Thomson (1729–1824), was Secretary to the Continental Congress from 1774 to 1789. He retired in 1789 and devoted the remainder of his life to translating the Septuagint and the New Testament. (*D.A.B.*)

From Arthur Lee

Paris Dec*r* 8*th* 1778

Dear Sir,

I cannot express the pleasure I felt, at receiving the vote which accompanies this. I am in the fullest hope, that both your inclination and your circumstances will permit you to gratify our wishes.

You are sensible, how much the future happiness of a People depends upon the proper arrangement of their Finances, how difficult it is to remedy original defects in all Constitutions; and therefore how much ill you will prevent, and how much good promote by giving the assistance that is requested.

It seems that where you are, your aid is not required. Those who conduct that Government, esteem themselves much abler to manage than you can advise. And indeed considering how opposite their end is to ours, I think they are right. Their abilities are exactly shaped to their purpose, the ruin of the Empire.

ORIGINAL: American Philosophical Society. PRINTED: *Memoirs*, pp. 78–79 (an incorrect version). TEXT: Original, with the kind permission of the American Philosophical Society.

Let me therefore beseech you to come where you will be welcome, and be useful. It will be the noblest consolation for the calamities that must fall upon the old People, to promote the happiness of the new. As long as there was any hope of preventing those calamities, your utmost endeavours were not wanting. But the total prevalency of vice and corruption, have not left a probability of amendment.

In this situation the pure and unambitious voice of Congress, has desired your assistance in a manner that bears the most honorable testimony of your merit, and of their wishes to promote the permanent good of the People who have reposed in them the guardianship of their rights and interests.

It is the voice of wisdom which calls you to the noblest of all works: the assisting to form a Government which means to make the principles of equal justice and the general rights the cheif object of its attention. Generations yet unborn will bless the Contributors to this inestimable work, and among them I trust the names of Dr Price will hold a distinguished place.

I am, with the sincerest respect and friendship

Dear Sir your most obedient servant

Arthur Lee

To William Adams[1]

Newington Green Dec: 28*th* 1778

Dear Sir,

Your letters always give me pleasure. I was made particularly happy by your last. In going thro' the correspondence between Dr Priestley and me[2] you will probably wonder that a man of his abilities can reason in the manner he does sometimes. Indeed no two persons can well differ more than we do; but I know the goodness of his heart and his views and we have finished our dispute with the same affection for one another which we possess'd when we begun it. Since I was favoured with your letter, a friend has sent me the first part of Dr Tucker's confutation of Mr Locke.[3] I have read it with some attention; and

---

ORIGINAL: Gloucestershire County Records Office.   TEXT: Original, with the kind permission of the Gloucestershire Records Office.

1. See Vol. I, 83.

2. Joseph Priestley and Richard Price, *A Free Discussion of the Doctrines of Materialism, and Philosophical Necessity* (London, 1778).

3. Probably the first part of *A Treatise on Civil Government* which was published in 1781. In this work Tucker claimed that Price and Priestley both derived their political philosophy from Locke's *Two Treatises* and that the basis of Locke's teaching is to be found in the principle that the right of private judgement is indefeasible. Tucker believed that the following elements in the works of Price and Priestley stem from Locke: that all men have equal political rights; that since the judgement of the individual is indefeasible, government can only be founded in unanimity; that since the individual's responsibility to govern is inalienable, delegation is impossible; that taxes are to be regarded as none other than free gifts or voluntary donations; that the people have the

cannot help thinking it a very injudicious performance. The *matter* of it is liable to some of the strongest objections; but the *manner* is petulant to a degree that must disgust most of his readers. The notice he has taken of me is far from giving me any offence. On the contrary; I think myself much honoured by the company to which he has joyned me. I only wish he could think as well of my intentions as I do of his. The concessions he makes in favour of liberty go, in my opinion, but a little way. Government, he says, is a *trust*.[4] The warmest advocates for despotism will say the same. The great question is whether it is a trust from God, or from the people. If from the people, they must have a right to model it as they please. Taxes must be *their* gifts for supporting it, and all civil governors must be their delegates and servants. But this Dr Tucker seems to deny. He allows indeed a right to resist; but he allows it only when the abuse of power becomes glaring and alarming; that is, when it may be too late to resist. A horse when he is abused will kick, and endeavour to throw his rider. The resistance which Dean Tucker allows seems to be nothing more than this kind of resistance. It is my opinion, that a people ought always to keep a jealous eye over the men to whom they have committed the trust of government, and to resist as soon as they think oppression is beginning. It is owing to their neglecting this and being too abject, that civil government has generally degenerated by degrees into tyranny, and become a greater evil than that which it was intended to remedy.[5]

I wonder at the conclusion which Dr Tucker draws from the comparison I have made between civil and religious liberty. How strange is it he should think, that because a man cannot depute another to make a creed or to settle a mode of worshipping God for him, therefore he cannot depute another to defend his property or to settle any temporal concern for him? He mistakes exceedingly the sense of the maxim *That in a free state every man is his own governor*. Had he consider'd the explanation of it which I have given in Pag. 9 etc of my *Additional Observations* he could scarcely I think have objected to it in the

---

right to change their governors and forms of government; that all political rights are founded in personality; and that the dissolution of government restores men to the state of nature. What is remarkable about Tucker's thesis that Price and Priestley derive directly from Locke is the extent to which he interpreted Locke in the light of what the radicals themselves taught. His thesis is plausible only if we share his assumption that Locke actually did teach what he says that Price and Priestley derived from him. But whatever the shortcomings in his interpretation of Locke and despite his failure to recognize that Price and Priestley introduced elements that would have been unacceptable to their mentor, without doubt Tucker is a shrewd and forceful critic of the positions adopted by Price and Priestley.

4. See *A Treatise on Civil Government*, p. 160. Cf. Richard Price, *Observations on the Nature of Civil Liberty*, "All *laws* are particular provisions or regulations established by COMMON CONSENT for gaining protection and safety. And all *Magistrates* are Trustees or Deputies for carrying these regulations into execution." See Peach, p. 69.

5. See *Observations on the Nature of Civil Liberty*, "He who will examine the history of the world will find, there has generally been more reason for complaining that they have been too patient, than that they have been turbulent and rebellious." See Peach, p. 95.

manner he does.[6] The author of the pamphlet to which I refer in P. 10 is Dr Ferguson Secretary to the Commissioners.[7]

The paper signed *Cassandra* was put into my hands by a Friend sometime ago. I discovered immediately that it was Dean Tucker's.[8] What he says in it of the conduct of the Dissenters and their vast increase since their unsuccessful applications to Parliament, is all news to me and my Brethren. Nothing indeed can be more visionary. The truth is (and it may be some comfort to Dean Tucker to be informed of it) that the Dissenting interest, particularly in and about London, is declining very fast. But I ask your pardon for writing so much on these subjects. Mr Brown[9] did me the favour to call upon me a few days ago, and I am to dine with him next thursday. Admiral Kepple's trial is much talked of and seems to threaten great inconveniencies and commotions.[10] The West-Indies are thought to be in particular danger. A fleet from Brest has been gone thither sometime. D'estaing's fleet is also probably there; and Byron's fleet which should have followed is separated and disabled.[11]

Deliver my kind respects to Mrs Adams and Miss Adams. Wishing you and them the compliments of the season, I am, Dear Sir, with great respect and affection;

Your very humble servant
Rich*d* Price

---

6. See *Observations on the Nature of Civil Liberty*, "In every state every man is his own Legislator." See Peach, p. 69. Cf. Richard Price, *Additional Observations*, "Every independent agent in a free state ought to have a share in the government of it, either by himself *personally*, or by a body of representatives, in chusing whom he has a free vote, and therefore all the concern and weight which are possible, and consistent with the equal rights of every other member of the state." See Peach, p. 140.

7. Adam Ferguson (1723–1816) became Professor of Natural Philosophy at Edinburgh in 1759. In 1764 he relinquished this chair to become Professor of Pneumatics and Moral Philosophy in the same University. In 1778 he was appointed Secretary to the Carlisle Commission which attempted to negotiate a settlement with the Americans. The pamphlet to which Price refers, and which he attributes correctly to Ferguson, is entitled *Remarks, on a Pamphlet lately published by Dr Price ... in a Letter from a Gentleman in the Country to a Member of Parliament* (1776).

8. See Nichols, *Illustrations*, VII, 402.

9. Possibly Isaac Hawkins Browne; see Isaac Hawkins Browne to R.P., 30 Mar. 1780.

10. Augustus Keppel (1725–86), admiral. MP for Chichester, 1775–61; New Windsor, 1761–80; and Surrey, 1780–82. He was court martialled on 7 Jan. 1779 on charges arising out of an engagement with the French fleet off Brest in July 1778. His acquittal won tumultuous popular approval. On Rockingham's accession to power he became first Lord of the Admiralty and was raised to the peerage as Viscount Keppel. In January 1783 he resigned in protest against Shelburne's peace preliminaries but returned to the Admiralty with the coalition ministry and remained in office until Dec. 1783. (Namier and Brooke, III, 7–11.)

11. John Byron (1723–86), vice-admiral, grandfather of the poet. In 1778 he was appointed to the command of a squadron fitting out for the North American Station at Plymouth. Maladministration and storms at sea off the American coast delayed his setting out from Sandy Hook to offer a challenge to d'Estaing.

I am sorry for the death of Dr Worthington. He was writing a reply to Mr Farmer. Is there any probability that it will be published?[12] Mrs Price sends her best respects.

---

12. William Worthington (1703–78), Vicar of Llanrhaiadr, Denbighshire. He wrote two replies to Hugh Farmer's *Essay on the Demoniacs*: *An Impartial Enquiry into the case of the Gospel Demoniacs* (1777), and *A Further Enquiry into the case of the Gospel Demoniacs*, which was published posthumously in 1779.

To Benjamin Franklin

Jan*y* 15*th* 1779

The bearer has been recommended to me; and, I believe, he has no improper views. He has urgent reasons for going abroad, and if Dr F[ranklin]n will be so good as to enable him to get access to the persons he wants to see he will oblige one who is, with great affection and respect his very humble servant and Friend.

R.P.

Original: American Philosophical Society. Text: Original, with the kind permission of the American Philosophical Society.

To Benjamin Franklin, Arthur Lee and John Adams

London Jan: 18: 1779.

Dr Price returns his best thanks to the Honourable Benjamin Franklin, Arthur Lee, and John Adams esquires, for conveying[1] to him the resolution of Congress on the 6th of October last, by which he is invited to become a member of the united states; and to give his assistance in regulating their Finances. It is not possible for him to express the sense he has of the honour which this resolution does him, and the satisfaction with which he reflects on the favourable opinion of him which has occasioned it. But he knows himself

---

Original: Yale University Library. Text: Original, with the kind permission of Yale University Library.

1. See Benjamin Franklin, Arthur Lee, and John Adams to R.P., 7 Dec. 1778.

not to be sufficiently qualified for giving such assistance; and he is so connected in this country, and also advancing so fast into the evening of life, that he cannot think of a removal.

He requests the favour of the honourable Commissioners to transmit this reply to Congress, with assurances that Dr Price feels the warmest gratitude for the notice taken of him, and that he looks to the American States as *now* the hope, and likely *soon* to become the refuge of mankind.

To [Arthur Lee]

Newington-Green Jan*y* 18*th* 1779

Dear Sir

Your most kind and excellent letter, together with the letter conveying the resolution of Congress[1], has made the deepest impression on my mind. I entreat you to accept yourself and to deliver to Dr Franklin and Mr Adams my best acknowledgements. Tho' I cannot hesitate about the reply address'd to the Honourable Commissioners and thro' them to Congress, which accompanies this letter, yet so flattering a testimony of the regard of an Assembly which I consider as the most respectable and important in the world, cannot but give me the highest pleasure, and I shall always reckon it among the first honours of my life.

There is an indolence growing upon me as I grow older which will probably prevent me for ever from undertaking any public employment. When I am in my study and among my books, and have nothing to encumber me I am happy; But so weak are my spirits that the smallest hurry and even the consciousness of having any thing to do which *must* be done, will sometimes distress and overpower me. What I have written on the subject of Finances has been chiefly an amusement which I have persued at my leisure with some *hope* indeed but very little *expectation* of its being useful. Nothing can be more melancholy than to see so many great European states depressed and crippled by heavy debts which have been the growth of ages and which in the end must ruin them, but which a small appropriation faithfully applied might have always kept within the bounds of safety. This is particularly true of this country. Here our debts must soon produce a shocking catastrophe. The new world will, I hope, take warning; and profit by the follies, corruptions and miseries of the old.

ORIGINAL: Boston Public Library.   TEXT: Original, with the kind permission of the Trustees of the Boston Public Library.

1. See Arthur Lee to R.P., 8 Dec. 1778 and the joint letter from Benjamin Franklin, Arthur Lee and John Adams to R.P., 7 Dec. 1778.

My Pamphlets on the principles of Government and the American war[2] were extorted from me by my judgement and my feelings. They have brought upon me a great deal of abuse; but abundant amends have been made me by the approbation of many of the best men here and abroad, and particularly by that vote of Congress to which I suppose they may have contributed. When you write to any of the members of that Assembly be so good as to represent me as a zealous friend to liberty who is anxiously attentive to the great struggle in which they are engag'd and who wishes earnestly for the sake of the world that British America may preserve its liberty, set an example of moderation and magnanimity, and establish such forms of government as may render it an *Asylum* for the virtuous and oppressed in other countries.

Tell Dr Franklin that he is one of the friends in whom, while in this country, I always delighted, and for whom I must ever retain the greatest esteem and affection. We are now separated from one another never probably to meet again on this side the grave. May he be long preserved a blessing to his country. My connexions and state of health and spirits are such, that I must stay in this country and wait its fate. I do this with a painful concern for the infatuation that has brought it to its present danger, but at the same time with indifference as far as my own personal interest is concerned, and a perfect complacency in the consciousness of having endeavoured to act the part of a good citizen and to serve the best of all causes. Will you further mention me particularly to Mr Adams; and inform him that I greatly respect his character?

Some good friends of yours (and mine) are well; but I differ from them at present in opinion.[3]   Under a grateful sense of your friendship, and with great regard, and wishes of all possible happiness, I am, Dear Sir,

Your obliged and very obedient and Humble servant
Rich*d* Price

The interest of mankind depends so much on the forms of Government established in America that I have long thought it the duty of every man to contribute all he can towards improving them. I am possesst of some observations which have been made by a great man[4] with this view, and I may sometime or other take the liberty to communicate them, with a few additional observations.[5] My best wishes to Mr I[ ]g, Dr &c.

---

2. *Two Tracts on Civil Liberty, the War with America, and the Debts and Finances of the Kingdom with a General Introduction and Supplement* (1778), incorporating *Observations on the Nature of Civil Liberty* (1776) and *Additional Observations* (1777).

3. Possibly a reference to Price's disagreement with Shelburne as to whether Britain should acknowledge the independence of the American colonies.

4. See Turgot to R.P., 22 Mar. 1778.

5. The first intimation of Price's *Observations on the Importance of the American Revolution and the means of making it a Benefit to the World.* which was printed in London for publication in America in 1784 and reprinted in Boston in the same year.

To Baron J. D. van der Capellen[1]

Newington-Green, near London
Jany 25th, 1779

Dear Sir,

You may possibly have almost forgotten that on the 14th of December 1777 you did me the honour to write to me.[2] You must undoubtedly be greatly surprised that I have taken no notice of so great a favour; and I am afraid, that for a long time I have been losing ground in your esteem. But the truth is that your letter did not come into my hands till lately. In turning over some papers and parcels lately at our Custom-House in London, your letter dropp'd out, and a Gentleman present who happened to attend to my name in the direction took it up, and conveyed it to me. It appeared plainly when it was brought to me, never to have been opened; and therefore it has arrived safe, tho' a year too late. The *tracts* which accompany'd it, I shall, I suppose, never receive. The reason of this must be that the captain of the ship which brought the letter and the tracts, or the person, whoever he was, to whose care they were committed, neglected them; and that in consequence of this, they were thrown aside at the Custom-House where they continued till they became forfeited, and were order'd to be sold as lumber among other unclaimed papers and parcels. In these circumstances I think myself fortunate that your letter has not been lost as well as the Tracts. Had this happened, I should have lost a very particular satisfaction; for indeed I can scarcely tell you how much I think myself honoured by it, or what pleasure it has given me. How happy am I in having found in your Province so good and able a Friend? What an honour have you done me by translating my Pamphlets and making yourself in the manner you relate an advocate for me?

It is impossible this should not deeply impress me. I am conscious of having wrote my Pamphlets with pure and honest views. Being known to the public, I thought I would try the effect of such a testimony as I could give against a war which in every view of it I consider'd as wicked and detestable.

No work ever proceeded more from the heart; and I have had the satisfaction of seeing the public attention more engaged by it than I could possibly have expected. It has indeed brought upon me a good deal of abuse; but this abuse has been far from giving me any pain. The approbation of my own mind, united to the hope of doing some good and the esteem of such persons as you are, make me abundant amends for all the opposition I can meet with. It is impossible that the interest of mankind should be more served by any thing than by leading them to a just sense of their own rights, and of the importance

---

PRINTED: *Brieven*, pp. 96–100.   TEXT: *Brieven*.

1. See Vol. I, 261.

2. van der Capellen to R.P., 14 Dec. 1777. See Vol. I, ibid.

of civil liberty and public virtue. The smallest degree of success in such work is worth the labours of a life. How melancholy is it to see human beings, crouching, as they do, under the yoke of tyranny, and acting as if they thought themselves only a body of beasts made to be disposed of at the discretion of a set of men who call themselves their *governours*, but who in reality are their own *Delegates* or *servants*. Britain has been long a country happy above all others. A few years ago it was at the head of the world in respect of arts, commerce, science, naval power and liberty. But it seems to be now losing fast its pre-eminence. Increasing corruption and luxury have sapped its liberties, and almost annihilated its excellent constitution of government. The most slavish principles are continually abetted in it. Its trade and opulence are threaten'd with ruin by the separation of America from it; and *France* and *Spain* are likely to rival its naval power. But the worst is, that the people are so enervated and their spirit so sunk that they can see this shocking change without being alarmed. I am sorry to find that Holland is not in a much better state. There it seems, as well as here, a sovereign power dispensing places and employments governs all; and the people either have no idea of their rights or are careless about them. One would indeed have expected that your country would have been the last upon earth where any difference of opinion could have been found about our war with our colonies. On this side the Globe every thing seems to be degenerating. Happy it is for the world, that there is one region where the value of civil and religious liberty is understood, and an Asylum likely to be provided for the virtuous and oppressed among mankind.

I return you many thanks for the account you give me of the transactions about the Scotch brigade, and of your patriotic efforts. They do you indeed the greatest honour. May heaven raise many more such virtuous and able men to stem the torrent of corruption in the world. You intimate that you would be glad to be introduced to an acquaintance with Dr Franklin. I wish I could oblige you in this, but it is scarcely in my power. While in England, he was one of my most intimate friends, but from mutual regard, we have since avoided writing to one another.

Admiral Kepple's[3] trial makes much noise here at present. There is no reason to doubt but that he will be acquitted with honour, and that the disgrace will fall upon his accuser. We are in pain for the West-Indies. The French seem to be bending their force that way, and should they succeed, and our settlements there as well as in North-America, be lost, the measure of our calamities will be full. Will your Sir be so good as to favour me with another letter and to inform me. Should this get safe into your hands? Under a grateful sense of your civility and candour, and with great respect I am

Your very obedient and humble servant,
Richd Price.

---

3. Admiral Keppel, see R.P. to William Adams, 28 Dec. 1778.

Be so good as to excuse any mistake into which I may have fallen in the manner of addressing you, and also my incapacity of writing to you either in French or Dutch.

I have just heard that two of the Tracts which you have done me the honour to send me, have been found, and that I shall be able to recover them.

From Charles Chauncy[1]

Boston May 20th 1779

Reverend and dear Sir,

As the Honourable Mr Temple[2] is going to Holland, and may have it in his power to convey a letter to you with safety, I could not excuse my self from writing by so favorable an opportunity. What I have in view is to assure you, that the situation of our public affairs is not as has been represented by Governor Johnson,[3] and the Commissioners, sent with him to America. They were confined to Philadelphia and New York the whole time of their continuance here, and had, nor could have had, no other information respecting the congress, or the circumstances of these states, than what they received from British officers, and refugees who had taken part with them. The ministry therefore could, by their accounts, have no true knowledge of the state of things in this part of the world; and so far as they might be disposed to act upon principles grounded on these accounts, they must act upon the foot of misrepresentation, not to say direct falsehood. Governor Johnson by his conduct while here has proved himself to be nothing than a ministerial tool, and is universally held in contempt. By his speeches in Parliament, relative to America, he appears to have known nothing of its real state, or to have given a notoriously wrong representation of it. A very great part of what he delivered

---

ORIGINAL: American Philosophical Society.   PRINTED: *M.H.S.P.* (1903), 319.   TEXT: Original with the kind permission of the American Philosophical Society.

1. See Vol. 1, 1, 88.

2. John Temple (1732–98) was born in Boston, the son of Captain Robert Temple who founded a Scotch-Irish settlement on the Kennebec. Through the influence of the Grenville family to whom he was related he became Surveyor General of the Customs of the Northern District of America in 1760, and Lieut.-Governor of New Hampshire in 1761. In 1767 he became one of the Commissioners of the Board of Customs for N. America, a post which he held until 1770. Appointed Surveyor General of the Customs again in 1771, he was dismissed from that post by Lord North in 1774 and remained out of office for ten years. After the Peace of Paris he became Consular General to the United States. On the death of Sir Richard Temple, the seventh baronet, in Nov. 1786 he assumed the baronetcy of Stowe. He married Elizabeth, daughter of James II Bowdoin, in 1767. See Temple Prime, *Some Account of the Temple Family*, 3rd ed. (New York, 1896), pp. 51–53.

3. i.e. George Johnstone, see R.P. to Shelburne, 31 Oct. 1778.

there, as we have had it in the newspapers, is wholly beside the truth, and indisputably so. We pity the man, but much more the ministry in giving so much credit to his accounts as in any measure to govern their conduct by it. Tis indeed acknowledged, our paper-currency has sunk in value to a great degree, which has occasioned the price of the necessaries of life to rise to an enormous height; but this has not been disadvantagious to us *collectively* considered. None have suffered on this account but salary men, those who depended on the value and interest of their money for a subsistence, and the poor among us: As to the rest, whether merchants, farmers, manufacturers, tradesmen, and day-laborers, the rise of their demands has all along been in proportion to the depreciation of the currency and the rise of the necessaries of life thereupon. It may seem strange, but 'tis a certain fact, that the American states, notwith-standing the vast depreciation of their paper currency, and the excessive high price of provisions of all kinds, are *richer* now in *reality*, and not in *name only*, than they ever were in any former period of time, and they are much better able to carry on the war than when they began it. One great fault they are justly chargeable with. It is this; they have almost universally been too atten-tive to the getting of gain, as there have been peculiar temptations hereto since the commencement of the present contest. They would otherwise, I have no doubt, have cleared the land of British troops long before this time; and nothing is now wanting (under the smiles of Providence) to effect this, but such exertions of the King's forces as would generally alarm the Country. There would then appear a sufficiency of strength to do by them as was done by Burgoin[4] and his army. While they suffer themselves to be, as it were, imprisoned in New-York and Rhode-island, and go not forth unless to steal sheep and oxen, and plunder and burn the houses of poor innocent people by surprize, it makes no great noise here, whatever, by pompous exaggeration, it may do in London. Our people want only to be roused, it would then be seen what they could do. I may add here, our freeholders and farmers, by means of the plenty of paper money have cleared themselves of debts, and got their farms enlarged and stocked beyond what they could otherwise have done, and rather than give up their independency, or lose their liberties, would go forth to a man in defence of their country, and would do it like so many lyons. The British administration hurt themselves more than they do us, as a people, by continuing the war, and they must bring it to a conclusion, or they will ruin themselves instead of us. The longer they protract the war, the more difficult it will be to obtain such terms of peace as they might have had, and perhaps may still have. These States will soon lose that little confidence they may now place in the British ministry. None of the minority in Parliament have a worse opinion of them than is generally entertained here. A valuation of the Massa-chusetts-State has lately been made in order to its being properly taxed; and

---

4. i.e. General John Burgoyne, see Vol. 1, 238.

tis found, notw'thstanding the vast number of cattle which have been slain for the Army, as well as inhabitants, that they are more numerous now than in any period of time since the settlement of the country. In the County of Worcester only, which within my remembrance had but a very few inhabitants, there appears to have been more than fourty thousand head of cattle, and sheep in proportion. No longer ago than the year 1721 I rode thro' Worcester, now as well and largely inhabited a town as almost any in this State, and it was in as perfectly wilderness a condition as any spot between Boston and Canada, not an house or inhabitant to be seen there. I have mentioned this only to point out to you the internal source of provision we have, should the war be continued over so long. But I may not enlarge.

Your good friend Mr Professor Wintrop[5] died about 12 days ago. I am also grown infirm as well as old, and very unable to write, for which reason you will excuse the blots, as well as almost illegible writing of the present letter; for I could not transcribe it to send it to you.

If I should live to see a settled state of things, I will, if I should have strength, write you very largely upon our affairs. I am with all due respect,

Your friend and humble servant

[No signature]

P.S. Congress are as firmly united as ever in their attachment to the liberties and independence of America, and the people place as intire confidence in them as from the beginning, notwithstanding all that Johnson and the other commissioners ridiculously (to me) endeavour to make people believe on your side the water. And notwithstanding the depreciation of our Currency, and the high price of provisions, the people are more averse then ever to submission to Great Britain, and would rather die than come into it. Mr Temple has been from New-York to Boston, and from Boston to Philadelphia, and from Philadelphia back again to Boston. He went thro most of the more populous towns between these two places, and as he had opportunity of seeing and conversing with the first and best gentlemen we have in these States, he can, should he go to England, give you a more just and true account of our political affairs than you have yet had. And I believe you may depend upon his giving you an honest account of things among us.

---

5. John Winthrop, Hollis Professor of Mathematics and Natural Philosophy at Harvard (see Vol. I, 93), died on 3 May 1779.

To Baron J. D. van der Capellen

Newington Green near London
May 28th 1779.

Dear Sir,

I am extremely obliged to you for the letter with which you favoured me a few weeks ago. The account you give me in it of yourself has particularly interested me. How absurd and tyrannical is the constitution of your Province? How grievous is it to think that the body of mankind should in almost all countries be so dreadfully debased by oppression and slavery? But you stand forth their protector and friend. What a glorious distinction do you enjoy among your countrymen? What a pity is it that such characters should be so singular? I am impatient to know the issue of the contest in which you are engaged, and I hope you will be so good as to inform me. Should the arm of power succeed against you, I shall be extremely sorry, but you will possess the unspeakable reward inseparable from the satisfaction of your own mind, and the admiration of all the friends of justice and liberty.

I continue an object of much censure, but at the same time I am blest with many friends who joyn with me in deploring the late follies of this country, and in dreading the calamities with which it is likely to be visited, should the present war continue and spread. My feelings drew from me on our public Fast day in February last a sermon[1] in which, contrary to my usual practice in the pulpit, I enter'd a little into politics, and took notice of our public measures and the state of parties among us. This sermon having been misrepresented, I was obliged to publish it; but it did not at all contribute, as you have been

---

PRINTED: *Brieven*, pp. 100–103. TEXT: *Brieven*.

1. Richard Price, *A Sermon delivered to a Congregation of Protestant Dissenters, at Hackney, on the 10th of February last, [1779] being the Day appointed for a General Fast* with *Postscript to Dr Price's Sermon on the fast-Day; containing Remarks on a Passage in the Bishop of London's Sermon preached at the Chapel Royal on Ash-Wednesday last*, (London, 1779).

In this sermon Price holds that the salvation of a country depends upon men of virtuous character and that even where the state becomes corrupt God will stay the hand of retribution as he did at Sodom and Gomorrah for the sake of the virtuous men that remain. The virtuous are those who are loyal to their own country, but, at the same time, jealous of their rights as citizens and careful to supervise the way in which their government discharges its sacred trust. They play their part in keeping "the springs of legislation pure" and in checking all tendencies to oppression. They are righteous in their private as well as in their public lives and delight in discharging the duties of religion.

In the short postscript to the sermon, Price defends himself against the accusation made by Dr Lowth, Bishop of London, that he was one whose "study it has long been to introduce confusion, to encourage sedition and to destroy all rule and authority." Price defends himself by claiming that it is not subversive to hold that all political authority originates with the people, and that a nation is free in the proportion that it enjoys representative government and is secure in that enjoyment.

informed, to produce the tumults which attended Admiral Kepple's acquittal. Mr Dentan, a very agreeable gentleman whom probably you have some knowledge of, undertook, when he left this country lately to go to Holland, to convey to you one of these sermons; and I hope you have received it. You will find in the postscript a proof that we are going backward in this country in our sentiments of government and civil Liberty. The excellent Dr Lowth,[2] mentioned in pag. 43, is the same with the present Bishop of London against whose censure of me I have been obliged to defend myself. I think it proper to intimate this to you, because even here many, for want of knowing this, have not understood the force of that part of my reply; which has obliged me to be more explicit in the third edition.[3]

I hope I have now done with political publications. I have aimed at promoting the best of all causes; and I wish to be able in tranquility to commit the issue to that righteous providence which governs human affairs. There seems at present no danger of the subjugation of America. There, I trust, a government of peace and liberty and virtue will be established. From the late examination[4] before our *House of Commons* of some of the principal commanders of our armies there, it appears, that it is a country wonderfully formed for a defensive war, that the body of the people are unanimously against us, and that no force which it is practicable for us to transport thither can be adequate to the purpose of conquering it. The expedition against Georgia has in a great measure miscarried.[5] The reinforcement for America in the fleet under *Arbuthnot*[6] does not consist of more than about 5000 troops. It has not yet sailed, and probably will not get to New-York before August. We are here in daily expectation of some important news from the West-Indies. More than can be expressed depends on the part Spain will take. Negotiations have been going forward thro' the mediation of Spain, but they have hitherto proved fruitless. Even your country seems to be growing hostile to us. Our late successes in destroying the French trade, and in getting home our own, have kept up our Friends and raised our spirits; and it is well if they do not encourage us too much to go on with a destructive war. You are so good as to say, that you will inform me, should you receive any particular intelligence from America. I

---

2. Robert Lowth (1710–87), successively Bishop of St David's (1766), Oxford (1766), and London (1777). He was elected FRS. in 1765.

3. All three editions were published in 1779.

4. Price refers to the proceedings relating to the conduct of the American war which began in the House of Commons on 29 Mar. and continued until 30 June 1779.

5. Price was misinformed. Following the capture of Savannah by Colonel Archibald Campbell in Dec. 1778, the defeat of the rebels at Briar Creek in the following March and again at Stono Ferry in June, the British gradually succeeded in securing control of Georgia (Boatner, pp. 1034–36).

6. Marriot Arbuthnot (1711–94), Admiral. In the spring of 1779 he was appointed to the command of the North America station for which he sailed on 1 May. He took part with Sir Henry Clinton in the successful expedition against Charleston.

shall think myself greatly obliged to you for this, and for any other News which you may think fit to communicate. You mention a letter to you from Governor Trumbull,[7] written by order of Congress. A copy of it, agreeably to the kind intimation you give, would highly gratify me. I do'nt wonder indeed that you reckon it a greater honour than any monarch can bestow.

I have at last recover'd all the tracts you sent me, and cannot sufficiently thank you for them; but at the same time I regret exceedingly my ignorance of the language in which they are printed. Accept, Dear Sir, my repetition of my thanks to you for your kind attention to me. Wishing you every valuable enjoyment, I am, with particular respect and affection,

Your obliged and most obedient servant
Rich*d* Price.

Postscript.

I cannot wish you to give yourself the trouble of writing in English to me. There is not the least occasion for it. Since this was written, *Arbuthnot*, it is said, has sailed with the fleet for America.

---

7. Jonathan Trumbull, the elder (see Vol. I, 208). Trumbull's letter to van der Capellen dated 27 June 1777, is referred to in *Brieven*, p. 66.

From Baron J. D. van der Capellen

Amsterdam 1 Juillet 1779.

Cher ami!

Mr Dentan m'a remis de votre part le sermon en question.[1] Votre lettre du 28 May m'est parvenue aussi. Je vous ai une obligation infinie de tant de bonté. Les marques d'amitié, dont vous voulez bien m'honnorer, me sont une grande consolation dans ma situation actuelle. Mes affaires sont tellement embrouillées, qu'il est impossible d'en predire l'issue, du moins d'en esperer une heureuse. Je suis le premier que l'on a osé attaquer de cette maniere.[2] Les privileges de la Noblesse ont été respectés jusquici; mais a la fin rien est sacré. L'on persiste a me refuser d'etre jugé selon les loix du Pais, ce qu'auparavant

PRINTED: *Brieven*, pp. 103–106. TEXT: *Brieven*.

1. See R.P. to van der Capellen, 28 May 1779, n.1.

2. In 1778 van der Capellen had been expelled from the States of Overijssel for publishing "an anonymous, defamatory, famous libel". The alleged libel lay in an attack in the name of natural rights upon the continuation of some remnants of feudal dues paid to the headman of the quarter, dues known as 'drostediensten'. See I. Leonard Leeb, *The Ideological Origins of the Batavian Revolution* (The Hague, 1973), pp. 145ff; Simon Schama, *Patriots and Liberators* (London, 1977), 64ff.

mes antagonistes euz meme avoient declaré etre leur intention; mais voiant depuis l'impossibilité de m'ecraser par voie de droit, et qu'en *bonne* justice ils perdroient assurement le proces, dont ils m'ont menacé, ils ont changé de batteries, et inventé l'expedient d'aller a leur but (mon expulsion de l'Assemblée des Etats de ma Province) sans qu'ils soient obligés de me intenter *l'action injure*; ... Mais, pour vous donner une idée claire de ce dont il s'agit, je seroie obligé d'entrer dans des details, qui passeroient les bornes d'une lettre, je prendrai la liberté de vous communiquer, ci apres, une histoire succincte et complete de toute cette affaire qui continue de faire beaucoup de bruit. L'on a publié quantité de brochures en ma faveur, et, chose bien rare, même aucun mercenaire n'a osé entrer en lice pour la defence de mes adversaires. Apres avoir écrit ceci, une brochure vient de paroitre, mais elle est si remplie d'absurdités qu'elle opere directement contre l'intention de son auteur. Elle fait du bien a ma cause. Mais apres tout, je suis perdu, malgré, l'indignation du Public. L'on veut se defaire de ma personne à tout prix et le plan en est formé par ceux, qui possedent assez depouvoir pour l'executer meme à la barbe de tous ceux qui voudroient s'y opposer.

Voici la lettre[3] du G[overnor] T[rumbull] (dont vous avez desiré la copie. J'ai pris la liberté d'y joindre une autre du G[overnor] L[ivingstone][4]) que j'ai recu depuis peu. Une traductione Hollandoise est actuellement sous presse. Ces pieces ont fait une grande impression sur tous ceux, qui les ont lûes. Celle du G[overnor] L[ivingstone], étant de nouvelle date, a convaincu bien de gens, que la desunion, qui regneroit en Amerique et la grande disposition a rentrer sous la domination des Anglois, sont des mensonges, inventés par ceux, qui trouvent leur compte a jetter un voile sur les affaires de l'Amerique. Vous pouvez faire tout l'usage, que vous jugerez a propos, de ces lettres. Vous en étes le maitre. Seulement aiez la bonté de ne pas dire en public que c'est de moi que vous les avez. Je crois que publiées dans quelque News papers elles feroient du bien. Votre sermon sera traduit en Hollandois.[5] Tout ce qui vient de vous est bien reçu ici. L'Amerique est libre et independante. Rien ne me paroit plus certain. Mais je suis faché (comme vous l'étes aussi) de que l'intolerance ait eu tant d'influence, dans la formation de cette nouvelle Republique. J'espere cependant, que, ci apres, l'on tachera d'elargir sa base a cet egard, et que de meme les Americains, si tot qu'ils se verront libres et en sureté, ne perdront pas de vue les interests des pauvres Negres, qui gemissent encore sous le joug de l'Esclavage parmi eux. Il seroit dangereux de leur donner la liberté a la fois, dans les circonstances actuelles; mais de ne la pas faire en tems opportun, et de perpetuer l'esclavage dans les 13 Etats, seroit une

---

3. Price had requested a copy in his letter of 28 May 1779.

4. William Livingstone (1723–90), lawyer, farmer, and politician. After serving as a delegate to the First and Second Continental Congresses and being in command of the state militia, Livingstone became Governor of New Jersey in 1776.

5. No evidence that Price's pamphlet was translated into Dutch has come to light.

conduite, qui donneroit un dementi aux principes dont l'Amerique a toujours fait profession. Un peuple, qui pourroit soutenir la vue de creatures humaines traitées comme des betes, ne meriteroit pas d'etre libre[6]—les Hollandois d'aujourdhui ont cette dureté. Depuis 3 ans les Negres ne sont plus libres, comme ci devant, des qu'ils se trouvent dans cette, ainsi nommée, Republique. Je suis le seul qui ait protesté contre cette Loi revoltante. Que je serois heureux de pouvoir quitter ce continent fatal! Ma nation, cher ami, ne devient pas hostile envers l'Angleterre. Elle ne cherche, elle ne souhaite que la liberté du commerce fondée sur le droit des Gens et les Traités—mais les Traités, l'Angleterre les a violés sans cesse et nonobstant toutes nos representations—ils n'existent donc plus. C'est dorenavant le droit des gens seul qui doit regler la conduite des deux puissances. Les Etats de la Province de Hollande (seule *plus* puissante que toutes les autres ensemble) sont sur le point de prendre des mesures d'éclat *eux seuls*, en cas que les autres Provinces, gouvernées despotiquement par . . . continuent de refuser une protection *illimiteé* a tout commerce licite. Cette Province est en état, quand elle n'est pas contrecarrée par les autres, de mettre en mer une flotte capable de se faire respecter, et elle le fera si l'on continue de gener sa navigation. Ce seroit donc une grande imprudence de la part de l'Angleterre, de pousser sa patience a bout. Soyez persuadé, mon cher Monsieur, que l'animosité est plus grande que l'on s'imagine et quelle pourroit avoir des suites tres serieuses. J'ai fait la connaissance du fameux Mr Stephen Sayre, ci devant Sherif de Londres, et dont l'affaire a fait beaucoup de bruit.[7] Il me paroit homme de coeur et de tete, franc, ouvert, et fait pour les grandes affaires. Aiez la bonté de m'informer si celle-ci vous soit parvenue. Je l'ai envoié par le vaisseau, qui doit partir d'Amsterdam toutes les semaines. Je crois que nous pourrions continuer notre correspondence a meilleur marché par ce moien que par la poste ordinaire où ce pacquet auroit couté bien beaucoup a cause de sa pesanteur. Aiez la bonté d'envoier votre Reponse par le meme vaisseau et de l'adresser chez Mr Jacob Kool, brasseur sur la Kadijk a Amsterdam.

Je suis toujours,
T.T.q.n.

N'approuveriez vous pas de m'ecrire dans ce gout sans signature de *nom?* Je connois votre écriture et Newington-green.

---

6. In *Observations on the Importance of the American Revolution* Price wrote, "I am happy to find the United States are entering into measures for discountenancing it and for abolishing the odious slavery which it has introduced. Till they have done this, it will not appear they deserve the liberty for which they have been contending. For it is self-evident, that if there are any men whom they have a right to hold in slavery, there may be *others* who have had a right to hold *them* in slavery." Peach, p. 213.

7. Stephen Sayre (1736–1818), merchant, banker, and American diplomat. Born at Southampton, Long Island and educated at the College of New Jersey, he came to England when he joined the house of De Berdt. In 1773 he was appointed Sheriff of London, but his activities on behalf of the American colonists led to his being arrested in Oct. 1775 on a charge of high treason. The case was dropped through lack of evidence, and Sayre went to the continent on diplomatic activity on behalf of the colonists. [*D.A.B.* and *Annual Register* (1775), pp. 239–43].

To the Earl of Shelburne

Newington Green July 12th 1779

My Lord,

Having learnt from the Papers on Saturday last that your Lordship is married,[1] I cannot resist my inclination to send a line to congratulate your Lordship, and to express my wishes that you may enjoy all the comfort and happiness that an amiable partner can give. I have heard a high account of Lady Shelburne; and I hope she will also accept my best wishes. I am very desirous of being introduced to her; and your Lordship will, I doubt not, do me this honour. I should have called this day at Shelburne House with this view; but I am afraid of intruding myself; and I am also just setting out for Buckinghamshire to visit a friend there with whom I am to spend the whole week.

With great regard I am your Lordship's
Most obedient and Humble servant
Richd Price.

Mrs Price desires to joyn her congratulations

ORIGINAL: Bowood. TEXT: Original, with the kind permission of the Marquis of Lansdowne.

1. On 9 July 1779, Shelburne married Lady Louisa Fitzpatrick, second daughter of John, the first Earl of Upper Ossory. The children of this marriage were Henry (b. 2 July 1780), who became the third Marquis of Lansdowne, and a daughter (b. 8 Dec. 1781) who died in infancy.

To the Earl of Shelburne

Newington-Green July 24th 1779

My Lord,

I am very sorry I have not met with more success in my enquiries for Mr F[ ]'s son.[1]

I have been with Mr Towgood;[2] but he told me that he had lately discharged one of the persons in his compting-house, and that he had scarcely employ-

---

ORIGINAL: Bowood. TEXT: Original, with the kind permission of the Marquis of Lansdowne.

1. Possibly Edward Fastnedge (1758–1812) who was created Principal Clerk at the Equitable Assurance Office in 1783. See Ogborn, p. 161.

2. Matthew Towgood (1732–91), son of Michaijah Towgood (1700–92). Matthew was educated for the Dissenting ministry at Bridgwater, where he was a minister from 1747 until 1755. He left the ministry to become a merchant and later (from 1773) a banker.

ment enough for those that were left. Mr Rogers[3] also told me that he had by no means employment for any supernumeraries. Having a friend who is one of the partners in the house lately Sir Sam[ue]l Fludger's[4] I went to him and asked him whether he could employ for half a year a young person in writing and accounts. His answer was the same that Mr Towgood had given me. He had parted, he said, with one of his hands; and those that remained were so far from being fully employ'd that one person added would likely to be spoiled.

The truth is, I suppose, that in consequence of the stagnation of trade there is now less to be done than ever. I informed all these gentlemen that the labour of the youth I wished to recommend might be had without pay, because nothing was meant but to get him employ'd for a little time and kept from bad company.

I enquired at Mr Canton's[5] in Spital=Square, and found that he had discontinued the practice of taking boarders; but goes on teaching Mathematics and finishing for business such scholars as chuse to attend him, of whom he has a considerable number. Mr F[ ]'s son might attend him, and lodgings might be found for him in the neighbourhood. In these circumstances, however, there would be no body to superintend him, and he would be unemploy'd a greater part of his time. It would be highly agreeable to me to assist your Lordship in this or any other business; and I wish it was more in my power. Next Monday I go to visit a friend in Surrey where I shall spend the next week. I am to go the following week to the Bishop;[6] and from thence to some other friends in Hampshire. It would give me great pleasure in this excursion to pay my respects to your Lordship at Bowood; but I am doubtful whether I shall not find it impracticable.

I hope Lady Shelburne will accept my congratulations and best wishes. Never was there time in which there was more reason for seeking consolation and relief in such a union as that into which your Lordship is enter'd. May it prove to both of you the foundation of all possible happiness. My kind compliments wait on Lord Fitzmaurice[7] if at home. I hear no particu-

---

3. Thomas Rogers (d. 1793), son of a glass manufacturer at Stourbridge, and father of the poet, Samuel Rogers. He came to London in his youth to work in a warehouse owned by his father and Samuel Radford. In 1760 he married Radford's daughter, Mary, and the following year entered into partnership with his father-in-law. He settled at Newington Green and was treasurer of the meeting place at which Price was minister. He lived next door but one to Price and both families were on intimate terms. In 1765 Rogers joined George and Thomas Welch, the bankers in Cornhill, and laid the foundation of a considerable fortune. He and Price had many interests in common. They were both strong supporters of the American colonists, and it is almost certain that Rogers was the confidant with whom Price discussed the projects for financial reform which he produced for Shelburne.

4. Sir Samuel Fludyer (1705–68), who amassed a great fortune, said to be £900,000, as a merchant in the City of London. He was made a baronet in 1759 and became Lord Mayor of London in 1761. *Gent. Mag.*, XXXVIII (1768), 47.

5. William Canton, a son of John Canton (1718–72), Master of the Academy in Spital Square.

6. Jonathan Shipley, Bishop of St Asaph. See R.P. to Benjamin Franklin, 10 May 1778.

7. See Vol. I, 156.

lar news. I tremble indeed when I think of the State into which we are brought.

Under a very grateful sense of your Lordship's candour and friendship I am, with regard,

Your Lordship's obedient and humble servant
Rich*d* Price

I have just called on Dr Rees[8] who is employ'd in compiling a new edition of Chamber's Dictionary, imagining he might be glad to be informed of a person whom he might employ gratis as a writer. But I have been disappointed. This morning I received a present of Pine=apples which gives me pleasure as a proof of your Lordship's remembrance.

---

8. Abraham Rees (1743–1825), was educated under David Jennings and became a tutor at Coward's Academy at Wellclose Square in 1762. A little later in the same year he became resident tutor when the Academy moved to Hoxton. He entered the ministry as assistant to H. Read at St Thomas's, Southwark where he became pastor on Read's death in 1774. In 1783 he became minister at Old Jewry, an appointment which he retained until his death. He published an edition of Chambers' *Cyclopaedia* in 1778 and a much larger augmented edition in four volumes in the period 1781–86. It is to the work on this project that Price refers. Rees was elected FRS in 1786 and in the same year he was appointed to teach Divinity, Hebrew, Jewish Antiquities and Ecclesiastical History at New College, Hackney.

To the Earl of Shelburne

Newington=Green Augst 21st 1779

My Lord,

I cannot help taking the first opportunity to return to you and Lady Shelburne my best thanks for your kind civility to me at *Bowood*. I got to Newbury to dinner on thursday. After dinner I went to drink tea with Mrs Montagu[1] whom I found not perfectly well. She seemed much alarmed by the News of the combined fleets being in the channel, and read to me accounts which she had received of it from London.[2] She enquired after your Lordship, and joyned

---

ORIGINAL: Bowood.   TEXT: Original, with the kind permission of the Marquis of Lansdowne.
 1. See Vol. I, 96.
 2. In the summer of 1779 the combined fleets of France and Spain entered the Channel to prepare the way for an invasion of England. See A. Temple Patterson, *The Other Armada* (Manchester, 1960). On 15 Aug. Captain Penny of the *Marlborough* sighted the enemy off Scilly, and instructed his first lieutenant, Sir Jacob Wheat, to put into Plymouth and ride to London to give news of the approach of the Franco-Spanish fleet. It was this news that raised the alarm of invasion throughout the Southern counties. In the event the combined fleet abandoned the project and retired to its home ports.

with me in rejoycing in your Lordship's happiness. Yesterday morning I set out early from Newbury, and got home in the evening, which is one of the longest journeys I ever performed on horse-back in a day. I have found Mrs Price and such of my Friends as I have yet seen in a state of much perplexity; and we are all now anxiously expecting to hear of an engagement which may decide the fate of the Kingdom. The combined fleets it seems are off Plymouth, and troops are embarking at *Morlaix* to be transported to Causson Bay near Plymouth in order to make a descent there. But I will not pretend to send your Lordship intelligence. All that I know you will have from others in a better manner.

The present crisis is surely dreadful. It is impossible to think without distress of a kingdom, lately at the head of the world, suffer'd by providence to fall under the direction of infatuated men whose councils are now threatening it with destruction. But whatever happens, those who have opposed these councils and endeavoured to bear a faithful testimony will have reason for satisfaction.

A gentleman at Amsterdam tells me in a letter dated Aug: 6th that the Dutch Provinces strongly favour America and will not enter into any connexion with Britain that may prejudice America, being determined to observe a strict neutrality. He also tells me that Captain Balfour[3] of the Culloden was just arrived at Amsterdam by way of *Statia*, having been permitted to go home on account of bad health, and that he mentioned with tears the distrest and sickly state of the Fleet which had already buried above 1200 men.

Mr [Arthur] L[ee] in a letter to Mr B. uses the following words. *I must beg you would desire Dr P. to make my congratulations to the Earl of Shelburne on his late marriage.[4] He made one of the best husbands I ever saw.*

My best Compliments wait on Lady Shelburne.

Under a very grateful sense of her condescension, and your candour and friendship I am your Lordship's

Most obedient and humble servant
Rich: Price

Aug: 23d I intended to send this letter on Saturday last; but I was not quick enough for the Post here, It is given out today that the combined fleets have disappeared. Perhaps they have gone in quest of Sir Charles Hardy,[5] or to meet the transports from Morlaix. But I have not been in town this morning, and know not what new accounts there may be.

Will your Lordship be so good as to deliver my kind remembrances to Dr

---

3. Captain George Balfour. See *The Private Papers of John Earl of Sandwich*, ed. G.R. Barnes and J.H. Owen, *Navy Record Society Publications*, LXIX, 1932, I, 205.

4. See R.P. to Shelburne, 12 July 1779.

5. Admiral Sir Charles Hardy (1716–80) was brought out of retirement in 1779 to assume command of the Channel Fleet on the resignation of Admiral Keppel.

and Mrs Priestley.[6] I hope the latter had the satisfaction of finding her mother better at Bristol. Mrs Price sends her respectful compliments. I have just seen a friend who has been in the City. There is, he says, no news except that the combined fleets have disappeared. There was a report that the East= India=fleet was arrived, and that the two men of war which convey'd it had joyned Sir Charles Hardy. But he enquired at the India-house and found it was not true. The East=India=fleet is expected, but no account of it has been yet received.

---

6. Mary Priestley, see Vol, I. 115.

To the Earl of Shelburne

Newington=Green Oct 12*th* 1779

My Lord,

I received last Saturday with much pleasure the honor of your Lordship's letter. The question inclosed seems not very difficult. Public credit being founded on public confidence they must rise and fall together; nor can I conceive of any operation of government by which the former can be maintained; and consequently the Funds kept up, when the latter is sinking. In such circumstances all that a government can do is to throw money into the public market or direct its dependents to do so. But they will give only a temporary support. Such management cannot be carried far or continued long; and when withdrawn, if public confidence is wanting, the Funds will fall lower than before. The condition of a kingdom in this respect is not unlike the condition of a crowd in a Playhouse when there is an alarm of fire. None will go in, but all will endeavour to get out at any loss; nor is it possible this should be prevented while the apprehension of danger remains. The necessity of raising money by public loans is, I think, a cause of the fall of public Funds which is in some degree different from the diminution of public confidence. Such a necessity, by increasing the demand for money and leading lenders of money to lay it up or to withdraw it from old funds in order to profit by a public loan, must necessarily raise the rate of interest and sink the Funds. But it is very obvious, that this effect being derived from the want of money by government, cannot be prevented by it. Such are my sentiments on this subject which I submit to your Lordship's judgment and correction. They seem to be abundantly confirmed by experience.

Your Lordship knows much more than I do of the state of public affairs. The late accounts from America have given me no particular pain. The cruelties practised there will provoke and exasperate, and leave us without one friend

---

ORIGINAL: Bowood.   TEXT: Original, with the kind permission of the Marquis of Lansdowne.

on that continent. There has been hitherto a strong moderate party there. The consequence of pushing the war in the manner we now do will be annihilating that party, and rendering all violent. The Congress has threaten'd retaliation and I find it is begun. Indeed, I fancy I see in Tryon's barbarities[1] the conflagration of our own towns, and the commencement of a horrid mode of carrying on war that has seldom been before known. A neig[h]bour of mine returned lately from New-York after spending all last winter and a great part of this summer there. He says that even at *New-York* the majority are not our Friends; and that in *Long Island* we have hardly any friends; that the grand objects pursued by the Army are promotion and plunder, and that the Government there is arbitrary to a degree that gives a shocking specimen to America of what it must expect if conquer'd by us.

Deliver my best respect to Lady Shelburne. Wishing her and your Lordship all possible happiness I am, with great respect, your most obedient

And Humble servant

Rich*d* Price

Many thanks for the Pine apples which I have lately received. Mrs Price sends her respectful compliments. Remember me kindly to Lord Fitzmaurice if at home. Byron,[2] I find, is come home. Paul Jones,[3] with his ships and prizes is got into the Texel. Destaing is gone to St Domingo, and from thence he is, it is said, to go for New-York, but some think he has Jamaica in view. Mr Maseres[4] having declined standing for the Recordership, Mr Adair[5] was just now chosen by a majority of 13 to 12 against Mr Howarth.[6]

---

1. William Tryon (1725–88), became Lieutenant Governor of North Carolina in 1764, and Governor in the following year. He became Governor of New York in 1771, resigning this appointment in 1778 in exchange for a military command with the rank of Major-General. He advocated a vigorous prosecution of the war, and in the summer of 1779 undertook a successful expedition into Connecticut.

2. Admiral Byron (see R.P. to William Adams, 28 Dec. 1778) was in command of a squadron which fought the French off Granada in July 1779, but was unable to recapture the island. After these sea battles his health deteriorated and he returned home, reaching England on 10 Oct. 1779.

3. John Paul Jones (1747–92), alias John Paul, a Scot, who was commissioned as a lieutenant in the American Navy in 1775. From Brest in April 1778 he cruised in the Irish Sea and won a reputation among the British for violent marauding and piracy. In Aug. 1779 he again set sail, this time in the *Bonhomme Richard*—so named as an astute compliment to Franklin—and obtained a desperate victory off Flamborough Head. It was after this engagement that he reached the Texel in Holland on 3 Oct. 1779 (Boatner, 565–68).

4. See Vol. I, 99–100.

5. James Adair (?1743–98) lawyer. MP for Cockermouth (1775–80), and Higham Ferrers (1793–98). In 1779 he was appointed Recorder of London, a post which he retained until 1789. He was a Dissenter and a formidable supporter of Wilkes and of the American rebels.

6. Howorth, Henry (c.1746–83), son of Henry Robert Howorth of Maesllwch, KC, MP for Abingdon (Dec. 1782–May 1783). Drowned in a boating accident. See Namier and Brooke II, 650–51; and *Gent. Mag.*, LIII (1783), I, 458. I am indebted to Mr P.A.L. Jones for these references.

To Benjamin Franklin

Newington=Green, Oct 14th 1779

Dear Sir

Will you be so good as to get the inclosed letter convey'd to Mr A[rthu]r Lee, if he is near you and it can be done easily? If not, be so good as to burn it. Being obliged for particular reasons to avoid politics, it is a short acknowledgement of the favour he did me by a letter I received from him at the beginning of last summer, and contains nothing of much importance.

I received the greatest pleasure from the note which you sent me by Mr J[one]s[1] and Mr P[aradi]se.[2] They were much gratified by your kind notice of them. Dr Priestley is well, and much engaged in prosecuting his Experiments on air. Dr Ingenhouz,[3] by whose hands this is convey'd has lately been warmly employ'd in the same pursuit. He will tell you what great success he has met with.

The Society of honest whigs[4] which you used to honour with your company, are soon to renew their meetings for the winter; and you will undoubtedly be one of the first subjects of our conversation. I spent in August sometime with

ORIGINAL: American Philosophical Society. TEXT: Original, with the kind permission of the American Philosophical Society.

1. Sir William Jones (1746–94), linguist, orientalist and lawyer, was educated at Harrow and University College, Oxford. From his early youth he showed exceptional brilliance as a scholar. In 1765, while he was still at Oxford, he was appointed tutor to Lord Althorp. In 1772 he was elected FRS and in 1773 became a member of Dr Johnson's Literary Club. He was called to the bar at Middle Temple in 1774, and, after a distinguished career as an advocate, was appointed Judge of the High Court in Calcutta in 1783. He was knighted in the same year. In May 1779, together with John Paradise (see below) for whom he was acting as legal adviser, he went to Paris to seek Benjamin Franklin's advice. They returned to England on 5 June. (Cannon, I, xlvii–xlix, 297.)

2. John Paradise (1743–95), linguist, was educated at Padua and Oxford. Elected FRS in 1771. Well known in literary circles, he became a member of the club which Dr Johnson began at the Essex Head in 1783. He had married a wealthy American whose income from her Virginian estate had been collected and retained by the authorities. Together with William Jones, his legal adviser, he went to see Franklin in the hope that the latter might suggest ways in which confiscation of the property might be averted. See Garland Cannon, *Oriental Jones* (London, 1964), 57.

3. Jan Ingenhousz (1730–99), physician and physicist, was born at Breda and educated for the medical profession. He came to London to practise medicine in 1764. In 1768 was sent by Sir John Pringle to Vienna to inoculate members of the Austrian Royal Family against smallpox and became physician to Joseph II and Maria Theresa. He returned to London in 1779 and was elected FRS in the same year. He was a frequent visitor to Bowood, the seat of the Earl of Shelburne, and like Joseph Priestley was long engaged in experiments on the constitution of air. In 1779 he published *Experiments on Vegetables, Discovering their Great Power of Purifying the Common Air in Sunshine, but Injuring it in the Shade or at Night*. The success to which Price refers—if indeed he was not sharing a private joke with Franklin—may have been Ingenhousz's discovery that plants give off oxygen in sunshine, and carbonic acid in shade.

4. See Vol. I, 42n.

an amiable family near Winchester.[5] The house in the garden, that you used to frequent often brot you to our remembrance. You can scarcely imagine with what respect and affection you are talked of there. I have heard with particular concern of the death of Dr Winthrop.[6] To this we are all destined; but the virtuous will be happy in better regions. The clouds gather frightfully over this country. I am waiting for the issue with anxiety, but at the same time with much complacency in the reflexion, that at this most important period I have endeavoured to act the part of a faithful and good citizen. Accept, my dear Friend, these lines as a testimony of my very affectionate remembrance. May heaven preserve you and grant you the best enjoyments

With great regard, I am ever yours
R. Price

---

5. The family of Jonathan Shipley, Bishop of St Asaph, at whose home at Twyford Franklin had frequently been a guest during his stay in England.

6. i.e. John Winthrop. See R.P. to Benjamin Franklin, 20 May 1779.

To [John Temple]

Newington=Green Oct 18*th* 1779

Dear Sir,

You have been indeed very good to me in sending me the account in the letter which I received from you last Saturday. You cannot imagine with what emotions I read it. I shall be in Pallmall on thursday to take leave of a friend there who is going abroad, and I intend to give myself the pleasure of calling upon you about eleven; but don't wait on this account if any business calls you from home.

I have received a letter from Dr Gordon[1] dated *Jamaica=plain* Aug. 3d, which I will shew you when I see you; but it contains no particular intelligence. Under the grateful sense of your civility, and with great regard,

I am your obliged and humble servant
Rich*d* Price

ORIGINAL: Massachusetts Historical Society.   TEXT: Original, with the kind permission of the Massachusetts Historical Society.

1. See Vol. I, 207.

To Baron J. D. van der Capellen

Newington=Green near London, Oct. 26th 1779.

Dear Sir,

I cannot help taking the opportunity which now offers itself of conveying a few lines to you by a friend who is going for Amsterdam. I wrote to you a few months ago,[1] and have been for some time wishing to hear from you, and to be informed how the dispute in which you were engaged, when you favoured me with your last letter, had proceeded and terminated. But I have lately learnt by a letter from Mr Neufville[2] to a correspondent of his in London, that you have been so good as to write to me, and to send me by the captain of a ship copies of Governor Trumbull's letters. I think myself much obliged to you for your attention; but it is a little mortifying to me that these papers have been lost in the way. When you favour me again with any letters or papers, be so good as to direct them to *Mr Morgan at the office for Equitable Assurances near Black-Fryars Bridge London.* They will in this way be less in danger of miscarrying. Mr Morgan is my nephew, and I have taken the liberty to send you a book lately published by Mr Morgan.[3] The *Introduction* and the concluding Essay are mine. The rest, being for the most part *mathematical*, few will read except Mathematicians, and such persons as are interested in the society for equitable assurances, and wish to know how its calculations are made.

Our affairs are growing more and more embarrassed. The war is by no means supported in a manner suitable to the pride with which we begun it. We are reduced to the necessity of making it in a great measure a defensive war, May Heaven give it a happy issue; and I shall think any issue happy that preserves us from the convulsion with which we are threaten'd, and secures that independence and liberty for America in which all mankind are interested. *Ireland* is now demanding a free trade, and menacing a rebellion, if it is not granted; but I do not see how it can be granted without the danger of a rebellion among ourselves. Such is the shocking dilemma into which our government has brought itself. We are impatient to know what determination the States-general are likely to come to in answer to the demand, made by our

---

PRINTED: *Brieven* pp. 106–108. TEXT: *Brieven*.

1. Price wrote to van der Capellen on 28 May. His letter was acknowledged by van der Capellen in his letter of 1 July, but it would appear that Price had not received the latter before he wrote on 26 Oct.

2. D. Neufville, a banker in Amsterdam.

3. William Morgan (see Vol. I, 239) published his *The Doctrine of Annuities and Assurances on Lives and Survivorships Stated and Explained* in 1779. The concluding essay written by Price is entitled "Essay containing an account of the progress from the Revolution and the present state of the population." This essay was published separately in 1780 under the title, *An Essay on the Population of England and Wales from the Revolution to the Present Time.*

court, of succours, and of the restoration of the ships carried by Paul Jones to the Texel. Accept my ardent wishes that your happiness and usefulness may be long continued; and permit me, sir, to renew the assurances of the great esteem with which I am your oblig'd and

most obedient servant,
Rich. Price

To William Eden[1]

Newington=Green Jany 4th 1780

Sir

Mr Lee[2] having convey'd to me your letter to him, I cannot make myself easy without sending you my thanks for the candour with which you have received my remarks; a candour which I wish to imitate. What I said of the quantity of tea paying duty consumed in the kingdom was too hasty. My only *datum* for determining this was the produce of the Customs and Excise on tea; but had I attended to this with more care, I might have concluded that the quantity of tea paying duty must have been nearly as you give it.[3] Still, however, I must think that any estimate of the tea smuggled which makes it greater than or near so much as the tea that pays duty, exceeds too much all the bounds of credibility.[4]

With respect to the decrease in the gross receipt of the Customs, I reckon that somewhat more than a million of it has been derived from the cause you

---

ORIGINAL: The British Library, Add. MSS 34,417 f.12.   TEXT: Original, with the kind permission of The British Library Board.

1. In 1779 William Eden (see Vol. I, 123) published *Four Letters to the Earl of Carlisle*. When the third edition of this work appeared in the following year he added a fifth letter in which he criticized some of the arguments on the state of the economy and the decline of the population that Price had put forward in *Observations on Reversionary Payments* and in the "Essay" which had been published in William Morgan's *The Doctrine of Annuities and Assurances* (see R.P. to van der Capellen, 26 Oct. 1779). Since Eden's fifth letter is dated 17 Jan. 1780, the letter published here must have been part of a correspondence that took place before the published exchanges. Price replied to Eden's criticisms in an appendix attached to his essay when it appeared separately under the title *An Essay on the Population of England*. The preface to this publication is dated 8 May 1780. In all these exchanges, Eden, in defence of the government's policy, attempted to counter Price's pessimistic claims that the economy and the state of the population were in serious decline.

2. John Lee (see Vol. I, 123).

3. In his fifth letter (3rd ed., p. 214) Eden claimed that the annual produce of the "neat duties" on the consumption of tea was about £700,000 per annum.

4. The Abbé Raynal claimed that the annual consumption of tea in Great Britain at this time was 12 million pounds per annum, at least half of which, he conjectured, was smuggled. Eden cites the 1775 edition of Raynal's *Histoire Philosophique et Politique* (Vol. I, p. 384) which was published in Maestricht.

mention, or a decrease in the importation of tobacco, and the remainder from a decrease in our other importations but in both cases it equally proves a decrease of trade; for the produce of such Tobacco as was imported and not consumed in the Kingdom was drawn back on exportation, and formed a valuable branch of trade, particularly to France, from whence, I have been told, the returns were chiefly made in specie.[5] But I am afraid I am taking an undue liberty with you by thus addressing you directly. I should not have done this, had not Mr Lee been gone to Bath. Under a grateful sense of your civility, and with much respect, I am,

Sir, your most obedient
and humble servant
Rich*d* Price

---

5. In his fifth letter Eden acknowledged that in the years 1776–9 the annual produce of the tax on imported tobacco had fallen from its average for the years 1765–75 of £1,231,051 to £176,825. But he maintained that the loss was not as damaging to Britain's prosperity as it might appear because the shortfall of £1,054,236 was nearly equalled by the amount repaid on drawbacks in the years prior to hostilities when the tobacco was re-exported. Price points out that nonetheless the loss of the re-exports was damaging because it meant a loss of the gold coin that was received in payment for the re-exported tobacco.

From Benjamin Franklin

Passy, Feb. 6, 1780.

Dear Sir,

I received but very lately your kind Favour of Oct. 14[1]—Dr Ingenhousz who brought it having staid long in Holland— sent the enclosed directly to Mr L[ee]. It gave me great Pleasure to understand that you continue well. Take care of yourself. Your Life is a valuable one. Your writings, after all the Abuse you and they have met with, begin to make serious Impressions on those who at first rejected the Counsels you gave; and they will acquire new Weight every Day, and be in high Esteem when the Cavils against them are dead and forgotten. Please to present my affectionate Respects to that honest, sensible and intelligent Society,[2] who did me so long the honour of admitting me to share in their instructive Conversations. I never think of the Hours I so happily spent in that Company, without regretting that they are never to be repeated. For I see no Prospect of an End to this unhappy War in my Time. Dr

---

ORIGINAL: Library of Congress, Franklin MSS. PRINTED: *Franklin*: Bigelow (London, 1904), VIII, 173. TEXT: The Franklin MSS.

1. See R.P. to Benjamin Franklin, 14 Oct. 1779.
2. The Club of Honest Whigs.

Priestly you tell me continues his Experiments with success. We make daily great Improvements in *Natural*—there is one I wish to see in Moral—Philosophy; the Discovery of a Plan that would induce and oblige Nations to Settle their Disputes without first Cutting one another's Throats. When will human Reason be sufficiently improv'd to see the Advantage of this! When will Men be convinc'd that even successful Wars at length become Misfortunes to those who unjustly commenc'd them, and who triumph'd blindly in their success, not seeing all its Consequences. Your great Comfort and mine in this War is, that we honestly and faithfully did every thing in our Power to prevent it; Adieu, and believe me ever, my dear Friend,

Yours most affectionately
B F

To Isaac Hawkins Browne, the Younger[1]

March 30th, 1780

Dear Sir,

I received your letter last night with much pleasure. Lord Shelburne is pretty well.[2] His wound is almost healed, and he goes about as usual. He has indeed had a narrow escape, for had not the ball spent its force in passing thro a parcel of letters in his wastecoat pocket, it would most probably have proved fatal to him. I heartily lament with you the absurd and barbarous custom of the world in this instance; But I do not see that it was possible for Lord Shelburne to avoid conforming to it, without discrediting himself to a degree that would have almost destroy'd his consequence and usefulness. Thro' the

---

ORIGINAL: Trinity College Library, Cambridge. TEXT: Original, with the kind permission of the Master and Fellows of Trinity College Cambridge.

1. Isaac Hawkins Browne, the Younger (1745–1818). He inherited an estate in Shropshire and lived the life of a leisured country squire until 1784, when he entered politics. He was MP for Bridgnorth (1784–1812). In 1773 he received the D.C.L. at Oxford. Price and Browne had been acquainted for some time; in his *London Diary for 1773* (ed. R.S. Walker [Aberdeen, 1946]) James Beattie notes that Browne was present at a dinner given by Price at Stoke Newington on 24 May 1773.

2. Shelburne fought a duel with William Fullarton in Mar. 1780. On 20 Mar. Fullarton, who was MP for Plympton Erle at the time, made an attack upon Shelburne in the House of Commons. He complained that Shelburne had sarcastically called him a *commis*. Being called to order in the House, and unable to complete his speech, he published it in the *Public Advertiser*, and delivered a copy at Shelburne House. Shelburne then challenged him to a duel the following morning in Hyde Park. In the encounter Shelburne received, a slight injury in the groin (see Fitzmaurice, II, 52ff.). Fitzmaurice notes that after the affair "numerous addresses were sent to Shelburne; several towns conferred their freedom upon him, and the Common Council of London sent to inquire how he did."

whole affair he has acted, as far as I know, with great manliness and dignity; and the result has proved favourable to him by leading the public to look more to him and exciting a general concern for him.

I am unwilling to lose this post, and therefore cannot write to you a longer letter, There are few I respect so much. Happy would the nation be were all the gentlemen of fortune in it endued with your principles and virtues. Deliver my respectful compliments to Mrs Brown. I hope she is restored to her former health. Wishing her and you all possible happiness, I am, Dear Sir

Your oblig'd and most obedient and humble servant,

Rich*d* Price

Mrs Price sends her respects. I have just seen Lord Shelburne. He has desired me to deliver his respects to you and thanks you for your kind enquiries. He hopes, he says, he shall always merit your good opinion.

To Granville Sharp[1]

Chatham=Square M*ch* 30*th* 1780

Dear Sir

Mr Belfour,[2] one of the candidates for the place of Clerk to the Surgeons company, has been long one of my friends. He was partner in business with Mr Crutenden[3] the late clerk, and must be well known to the company. I believe him to be a very worthy man; nor can I doubt but that he is upright, diligent and able in his profession as a lawyer. Will you be so good as to mention this to

---

ORIGINAL: Hardwicke Court MSS Box no. 54. TEXT: Original, with the kind permission of Col. Arthur B. Lloyd-Baker.

1. Granville Sharp (1735–1813), scholar and philanthropist. He devoted much time and energy to the promotion of political reform in England and Ireland and in 1774 published *A Declaration of the People's Natural Right to a Share in the Legislature*. He defended the American rebels, canvassed the introduction of an episcopate in America, assisted in founding the British and Foreign Bible Society, and crusaded against the practice of pressing for service in the navy. But his name is probably most closely associated with the movement for the abolition of slavery. In 1767 he began a struggle for the liberation of slaves in England which culminated in the famous case of James Sommerset, and in 1787 he founded the Society for the Abolition of Slavery.

2. Okey Belfour was appointed Clerk to the Company of Surgeons in April 1780, and continued as Secretary to the Royal College of Surgeons from 1800 to 1811. See Cecil Wall, *The History of the Surgeon's Company, 1745–1800*, (London, [1937]), p. 169 and Zachary Cope, *The Royal College of Surgeons of England: a History* (London, 1957), p. 254.

3. Joseph Cruttenden, an attorney at law, was clerk to the Company of Surgeons from 1745 to 1780. In March 1780, he tendered his resignation following the discovery of irregularities in his administration of the company's finances. His resignation was accepted in April when the Court moved to appoint Okey Belfour (see n. 2 above) to his place. See Cecil Wall, pp. 43, 166–69. I am indebted to Mr Robin Price for the references in this and in the preceding note.

your Brother?⁴ Such is my regard for Mr Belfour, that I wish much to be able to serve him. Permit me to assure you, Dear Sir, of my sincere esteem. There are few of whose principles and character I have so high an opinion. You have done much towards promoting the interest of public liberty and virtue; and, tho' none of us meet with the success we wish for, yet as far as we mean well and do our best, we cannot fail of our reward. I do not much expect that the present efforts of the people will terminate in any thorough reformation. We must, I am afraid, suffer more before we are brought to this. The Wiltshire Committee which met at Devizes last tuesday, resolved to instruct their deputies should they hereafter chuse any, to confine themselves to the single object of Oeconomy.⁵

Wishing you all possible happiness I am truly and affectionately

Yours

Rich*d* Price

---

4. Probably William Sharp, a surgeon at Fulham.

5. This letter preceded the foundation of the Society for Constitutional Information, of which both Price and Sharp were members, in April 1780. In March the deputies from the Freeholders of the Counties had declared support for a programme of economic and political reform which included demands for a hundred additional members for the counties and annual parliaments. But the Wiltshire Committee which had been summoned to meet at Devizes on 27 and 28 March 1780 to consider the Plan of Association sent to them by the General Meeting of the Deputies of the Freeholders, decided to restrict their participation in the reform movement to issues of public economy. They resolved: "That if the Committee shall hereafter think it advisable to send any of their members to meet Gentlemen sent from other Counties, that the Persons so sent be restrained to promoting the Prayer of the Petition—Public Oeconomy." See H. Butterfield, *George III, Lord North, and the People, 1779–80* (London, 1949), p. 293.

To David Hartley, the Younger¹

Newington=Green May 30th 1780

Sir

I am afraid I am now going to take an improper liberty with you; but the strong desire I feel to recommend to your vote and interest a friend whom I highly value urges me to it. The person I mean is Mr Jones, who is offering himself a candidate to represent the University of Oxford at [the] next general election.² He is well known to be one of the first scholars in the world; but his

---

ORIGINAL: Mr Derek Hartley Russell. TEXT: Original, with the kind permission of Mr Derek Hartley Russell.

1. David Hartley (1730–1813), son of David Hartley (1705–57), the philosopher. MP for Hull, 1774–80, and 1782–84.

2. In 1780, the Parliamentary election for the University of Oxford was won by Sir William Dolben and Francis Page. William (later Sir William) Jones and William Scott tried to contest the seat but were compelled to withdraw before the election because support for the Whigs at Oxford was inadequate. See Namier and Brooke, I, 360.

principal recommendation on the present occasion is the excellence of his public principles which are those of a zealous and decided Whig. I may safely say that in this respect he is far from having an equal among his competitors. Hoping for your indulgence, and wishing you all possible success in your endeavours to serve the public at this very important period, I am, with great respect,

Your most obedient and humble servant
Rich<i>d</i> Price

From Lord Monboddo[1]

Edinburgh. 11 July 1780

Sir,

When I had the pleasure of seeing you, I thought you was only a Political Arithmetician. But since I have returned to Edinburgh, there has fallen into my hands a Book,[2] containing a correspondence betwixt you and Dr Priestley, which shows me that you are a Philosopher, and a Philosopher of the highest kind—a Metaphysician. You have combated very well, Dr Priestley's strange system of Philosophy, and stranger still of Christianity. But you have made some Concessions to him which, though supported by an authority which I very much respect—the authority of Dr Clarke,[3] are, I think, dangerous to Theism.

You admit that Mind, tho' immaterial is extended, and even the Supreme Mind, you say, has this property; and the only Difference in this respect betwixt the two is that our mind, being finite, the extension of it is only finite, whereas the Supreme Mind being infinite is infinitely extended: the consequence of which, I think, necessarily is that our Mind must be both figured

ORIGINAL: National Library of Scotland. PRINTED: Knight, pp. 109–114. TEXT: Original, with the kind permission of the National Library of Scotland.

1. James Burnett, Lord Monboddo (1714–99). In 1737 he was admitted to the Faculty of Advocates, and, after a successful career at the Bar, became an Ordinary Lord of Session in 1767, assuming the title of Lord Monboddo. See E.L. Cloyd, *James Burnett, Lord Monboddo* (Oxford, 1972). The work referred to in this letter is *Antient Metaphysics*, a six volume work which was published at the following times: Vol. I, 1779; Vol. II, 1782; Vol. III, 1784; Vol. IV, 1785; Vol. V, 1797; Vol. VI, 1799.

2. Richard Price and Joseph Priestley, *A Free Discussion of the Doctrines of Materialism, and Philosophical Necessity* (London, 1778).

3. Samuel Clarke (1675–1729) became Rector of St James's, Piccadilly in 1709. His publications include *A Discourse concerning the Being and Attributes of God, the Obligations of Natural Religion, and the Truth and Certainty of the Christian Revelation* (1705–6), and *The Scripture-Doctrine of the Trinity* (1712). Monboddo had a very high opinion of Clarke's abilities. In *Antient Metaphysics* he refers to him as "the greatest metaphysician that ever was in England." Vol. I, p. 235.

and Divisible into aliquote parts,[4] such as a *half*, *third*, or *fourth*; and these parts must at least in idea be separable or discerptable; and the Divine Mind, tho' it cannot be figured, must be conceived as having aliquant parts,[5] if not aliquote, though they may not be separable from one another; for I cannot conceive what is extended, not to have parts; and *figure* I think is nothing else but extension limited and circumscribed. Accordingly I *observe* that Dr Priestley has laid hold of these Concessions[6] of yours to draw these inferences; and he draws this further inference, that if the Deity be extended, and our minds also extended; and if at the same time they be not solid and impenetrable, then they must necessarily penetrate one another as they exist in the same space: so that here will be a strange confusion of Divine and human natures; whereas, (if we ... but) I hold that nothing is extended except Body, for *to be extended* is to occupy *space*, from which the extended is certainly different. Now I can conceive nothing different from space, yet occupying space, and extending over it, except what is material. Mind therefore being immaterial, cannot occupy space, or be extended; any more than it can be solid impenetrable or Divisible.

What makes the difficulty in the case is that Mind must be *somewhere*, and the Supreme Mind it is said is *everywhere*; now whatever is *anywhere* must have a local Position, and therefore must be extended. But to this I answer that Mind no doubt acts or energises in *some* part of space; and the Supreme Mind in *every* part. And I allow that nothing can act except where it is. Mind therefore exists *in* space. But as it is a substance of a nature quite different from Body, it is impossible that it can exist in the same manner, that is, extended and filling up space as Body does; so that there is no vacuum where it is. In short as Mind is immaterial, that is not matter, I hold all its qualities to be a negation of the qualities of matter; therefore it does not occupy space, is unextended, indivisible, not solid, not resisting; for as we do not know the substance of either, we cannot distinguish them but by denying the qualities of the one to the other.

I am not satisfied neither with Dr Clarke's notion that infinite space and duration are properties of the Supreme Being;[7] and much less am I pleased with what Sir Isaac Newton has said, that space is a kind of *organum* for the

---

4. In aliquot part = contained in another, dividing it without remainder. Thus 2 is an aliquot part of 6. (*O.E.D.*)

5. In aliquant part = contained in another, but not dividing it equally. Thus 3 is an aliquant of 7. (*O.E.D.*)

6. For Priestley's contention that Price's discussion of the nature of space implies that it is discerptible, see *A Free Discussion*, pp. 69, 169; and for his claim that Price's position implies that the Divine mind and the human mind interpenetrate, see ibid., pp. 58–59.

7. Infinite Space and Infinite Duration are, according to Clarke, both "modes of an essence or substance incomprehensible to us." See Samuel Clarke, *Works*, 4 Vols. (London, 1738), II, 538. On Clarke's own awareness of the difficulties of conceiving of space and duration as qualities or properties see Des Maiseaux's introduction to the 1720 ed. of the Leibniz–Clarke Correspondence, cited by H.G. Alexander (ed.), *The Leibniz–Clarke Correspondence* (Manchester, 1956), pp. xxviii–xxix. See also note 6 to Monboddo to R.P., 15 Sept. 1780.

Deity.[8] I hold that neither space nor duration is the property of any thing: for space considered by itself is a mere nonentity, and has no existence except in relation to Body. So that if there was no Body there could be no space: therefore it is improperly applied to mind; for, tho' it may be said that mind acts in space, in that expression space is only considered as the interval betwixt Bodies, the Boundary of Bodies, or the Capacity of Receiving them. Even of Body it is no property, but only related to it in the three respects I have mentioned; far less is it a property of Mind. To be convinced that it is only a relation, you may suppose that nothing existed, neither Body nor Mind. What then would space be? or would it be anything? for I deny that space is extended, extension being only a property of what is in space. It is true that space may be measured, but that is only when it is the interval betwixt Bodies, or the Boundary of them, and when Body is applied to it; so that without Body it is truly nothing.

As to Duration, whether it be infinite duration, or that which is limited and known by the name of *Time*, it is no property neither of any thing, and is only a kind of adjunct to Being; so that if we suppose nothing to exist, neither Mind nor Body, we could not conceive any such thing as duration, which is nothing but the continuation of [the] Existence of some one thing or another. If the Being is without change either in Substance, Qualities, or Energies, such as we conceive the Supreme Being to be, then duration only is applicable to it, without limit or measure; and such a Being is properly said not to exist in *in time*. But if the Being be liable to Changes, then limited duration is applied to it, to measure the interval betwixt its changes and such a Being is said to exist in *time*.

These things I have explained in my Metaphysics, in two chapters, one upon the subject of *space*, and the other upon the subject of *Time*, to which I refer you;[9] and if you have not a copy of the Book, I hope you will accept of it as a present from me, and I will desire Mr Caddel[10] to give it you, if you think it worth your while to call for it.

As to *Free Will* and *Necessity* I have likewise a chapter upon that subject, which Dr Horsley has read, and intirely approves of. As Dr Priestley makes a machine of *Man*, such as a clock, the necessity of our determinations and actions which he maintains is a material necessity. This I have distinguished

---

8. See the famous passage in Query 31 of Newton's *Opticks*, where he speaks of God, "who being in all places, is able by his will to move the bodies within his boundless uniform sensorium." See *Opticks* (London, 1931), p. 403. On the question whether the reference to God's sensorium is to be taken metaphorically see R.P. to Monboddo, 11 Dec. 1780; Alexander, pp. xv, xvi; and Frank E. Manuel, *The Religion of Isaac Newton* (Oxford, 1974), pp. 77–78.

9. In the first volume of *Antient Metaphysics* Monboddo devotes the first three chapters of Book IV (pp. 347–72) to a discussion of space. The third of these is devoted to a criticism of Clarke and Leibniz. He deals with Priestley's conception of body in Vol. II, pp. 296–310.

10. i.e. Thomas Cadell (see Vol. I, 248).

from the necessity of Intelligence being determined by the most powerful motive.

Upon these subjects, which are of the greatest consequence in Philosophy I should be very glad to have your thoughts, and as you seem to be very well acquainted with Dr Priestley, I should be glad you would ask him the following particulars:

1st.   Whether Man being a Machine, the parts of which that Machine is [?] composed, were put together by divine wisdom, or whether they came together by material necessity, and by the operations of the particles of matter upon one another.

2d.   After he has informed you how the Machine was made, I should be glad if he would tell you how the motions of it are carried on; whether the several parts of it are moved by themselves, whether there be any external Cause of their motion, or whether they be not moved by divine power; and if by divine power whether they be moved by a force originally impressed upon them, as Sir Isaac Newton supposes the Planets are moved, or by the constant and unceasing operation of Deity.

3d.   I should be glad to know what Dr Priestley means when he says [p. 256][12] that tho' a Body be perfectly organised, yet it will not have thought or sensation without Life; but as soon as Life is added to it, then it has immediately both sensation and thought. He says that this Life, is the Cause of Respiration and the Circulation of the Blood. Now I desire to know what it is that produces these effects. He plainly considers it as distinct from the organised Body. But I should wish that he were more explicit, and told us whether it was substance or mode, material or immaterial.

These questions, I think, ought to be answered by a man who says we have no soul.

If you will favour me with [an] answer, a letter addressed to Lord Monboddo in Edinburgh will find me: and I have sent you two franks in case you should not have a Member of Parliament at hand.

[No signature]

---

11. Free will and necessity are discussed in Vol. I, pp. 296–310 of *Antient Metaphysics*.
12. *A Free Discussion*.

To Lord Monboddo

Newington Green Aug*st 2d* to 12*th* 1780

My Lord,

I think myself much honoured by your Lordship's letter.[1] When I received it I was going a journey into the country. Being now returned, and this being the time of year when I throw off study and enjoy myself in excursions to visit distant friends, I am setting out again, and shall not probably be at home till near the middle of next month. But I cannot omit for so long a time taking notice of your Lordship's favour.

I have been lately so much talked of as a Politician, that I do not wonder you should have taken me for nothing else. But the truth is, that the study of politics has been a late deviation into which I have been drawn by the circumstances of the times and the critical situation of our public affairs. Of this study I am now almost sick; and I am continually resolving to confine my attention for the future to moral, metaphysical, mathematical and theological subjects. With these I begun, and they have always been my favourite and most delightful studies. I am glad to find that your Ideas and mine on metaphysical subjects are so much alike. I was always a warm admirer of Plato among the antients, and of Cudworth[2] and Clark among the moderns. This you may learn from my *Review of the principal Questions and difficulties in morals*,[3] which, tho' my first work and that which has been least read, is not in my own opinion my worst. This book I have desired Mr Cadell to convey to you when he has an opportunity of sending to Edinburgh; and I hope you will accept it as a small return for your book on *Antient Metaphysics* which, in consequence of the encouragement given me in your letter, I have called for and received from Mr Cadell. I am ashamed that I had not long before this time read this book. The journey which I have in view will not allow me at present to read the whole of it. I have however read with much attention a good deal of it, and particularly what you say on the subjects of liberty and space and time. I agree so entirely with Dr Clark in my notions of liberty that where you differ from him I find myself obliged to differ from you. But perhaps, as your Lordship observes in Pag. 307, there may be no other difference than arises from a different use of words.[4] I think you extremely right in asserting that *will* implies *liberty* in the

---

ORIGINAL: The National Library of Scotland. PRINTED: Knight, pp. 119–123. TEXT: Original, with the kind permission of the National Library of Scotland.

1. See Monboddo to R.P., 11 July 1780.
2. See Vol. I, 193.
3. See Vol. I, 49.
4. "So that I am persuaded what difference there is betwixt the Doctor and me is more in words than in reality." *Antient Metaphysics*, I, 307.

Idea of it, and in laying a stress on the distinction between *sensations* and *Ideas*, and between *moral* and *natural necessity*. These are distinctions of great importance; but I think that it is also highly proper to distinguish between the *active* and *passive* faculties of the soul. Did we *act* by the same necessity by which we believe the truth of a proposition upon attending to its evidence, or *judge* two and two to be equal to four, we could not, I think, be said to be free. There seems to be the same difference between these that there is between *seeing* the way upon directing our eyes to it, and *walking* along it. In the one case, we only receive an *impression*, in the other, we exert a *power*.

I am much obliged to you for the remarks you have made on my concession to Dr Priestley, that the soul is extended. But I have not explicitly made this concession. The truth is, that I am much at a loss how to frame my Ideas on this subject. All I am satisfied about is that the soul, as well as every thing else, does exist in place as well as time; but *how* I know not. If it is extended; that is, if it exists in space as matter does, it must one would think be as you say *figured* also; but Dr Clark has observed that it will not follow that it must be *divisible*, for space, as he says, is extended, but cannot be conceived to be divided, without a contradiction;[5] and the same is true of *time*. The present moment is omnipresent; but it is the *same* every where and cannot be divided, nor indeed, tho' it co=exists with every point of immensity, does it consist of parts some of which exist in one place and some in another, but the *whole* of it exists in *every* place. There are, therefore, ways of occupying place which do not imply *divisibility* or even a diffusion of parts thro' space. But, perhaps, I may be now talking very incorrectly; and probably there is some great impropriety in our modes of thinking and speaking on this subject.

I am sorry that I cannot assent to your account of space and time. The former you call *A relation of bodies to one another, and an adjunct* of *bodies*;[6] and without body, you say in your letter, it is truly nothing, so that *where* body is not *there* is no space. Are not these last words the same as to say that there is no space in the part of space where body is not? and does not this sound like a contradiction? But not to insist on this. Body, you acknowledge, exists *in* space. But does not this imply that it is something independent of body? How can any thing exist in its adjunct? The visible world supposing it bounded might be moved directly forwards with any velocity. But if there is no space where body is not, it would always remain in the same place. Was there no such thing as space *before* body? If so, there was no place for body, and it could not exist. Similar observations are applicable to Duration. The world, if it began to exist, might have been created sooner or later. But this implies a contradiction if before the world there was no duration. *Time* I consider the same with *duration*. They may however be distinguished, by considering *time* as

---

5. See Clarke's "Third Reply to Leibniz", Alexander, p. 31.
6. *Antient Metaphysics*, I, 364–65.

that *part* of infinite duration which is commensurate with the existence of the world. But tho' this may be a proper distinction, it is not easy to speak always agreeably to it. In short, space and duration offer themselves to me as necessarily existing and boundless and the foundation of the possibility of all other existence. I think them therefore to be nothing but the Divine *immensity and eternity*. In like manner. That infinity of *possibles* which I find I cannot in idea destroy, I think to be the *Divine omnipotence*. That infinity of *abstract* truth and of *knowables* which I see to be necessary and eternal, I think to be the *Divine eternal mind*. And that *nature* to which Atheists ascribe all things and which they say contains in itself a principle of order, I consider as only the Divine agency and wisdom preserving, conducting and governing all things according to certain fixed rules or laws. I have touched these subjects in a [Ch]apter in my Review of morals,[7] but I cannot properly explain them; and I [think] that your sentiments are very different. [I am] happy however in thinking that with respect to the [mo]st important parts of this speculation I have on my side Plato, Newton, Clark and Cudworth. I differ from Cudworth only in his notion of Plastic Natures, and I have given my reasons in a Note in my Dissertation on Providence;[8] and this is another instance in which I have the mortification of finding that I differ greatly from your Lordship.

Dr Priestley lives in Wiltshire[9] at a great distance from me, and he is in much trouble being himself very ill and likewise his wife ill. I cannot therefore at present put to him the questions you propose at the end of your letter, but I know so well his sentiments that I have no doubt but he would say in answer to the first of them, that the parts of the machine which he calls man were put together by Divine wisdom; and in answer to the second, that the motions of this machine are produced not by the matter itself that composes the machine, but by the constant operation of the Deity whom he makes the only agent in nature. As your Lordship has honoured the correspondence between him and me with your perusal, you must be sensible that I differ extremely from him. Indeed no two persons can differ much more on most Theological and Metaphysical subjects, and yet we respect and love one another. I have enclosed a Note for Dr Webster.[10] May I give your Lordship the trouble of getting it convey'd to him? I am acquainted with Dr Robertson,[11] Dr Smith, and Mr Stewart[12] the

---

7. See particularly, Ch. I, sect. ii, and Ch. V. of *Review*.

8. For Price's criticisms of Cudworth's notion of plastic natures as advanced in the first book of *The True Intellectual System of the Universe* see Richard Price, *Four Dissertations*, 2nd ed., pp. 46–49n.

9. i.e. at Calne; at this time Priestley was Shelburne's librarian and had a house at Calne near to Shelburne's seat, Bowood.

10. Alexander Webster, see Vol. I, 104.

11. William Robertson, see Vol. I, 39.

12. Dugald Stewart (1753–1828), mathematician, and philosopher. He was invited by his father Matthew Stewart, to assist him in teaching mathematics at Edinburgh, where in 1775 he became joint-Professor, a post which he held until 1785 when he succeeded Adam Ferguson as Professor of Moral Philosophy.

Mathematical Professor, and I have also corresponded with Dr Erskine.[13] Should any of them happen to come in yo[ur] way at Edinburgh, deliver my respectful [remembran]ces to them.

With great regard and the best [respects,] I am, my Lord,

Your Lordship's most obedient and humble servant

Rich*d* Price

I have been interrupted in writing this letter by the sudden death in my house of a most amiable and excellent Friend. This has thrown me and my wife into a state of bitter grief; and obliged me to postpone my journey. But being now recovered a little; I intend to set out in a few days.

---

13. John Erskine (1721–1803), a celebrated preacher. He was minister successively at Kirkintilloch (1744), Culross (1753), New Greyfriars (1758), and Old Greyfriars, Edinburgh (1767). DD (1766). He was a prominent member of the Society for the Propagation of Christian Knowledge, and an editor of several religious works, including those of Jonathan Edwards and Samuel Stoddart. His preaching at Old Greyfriars Church is described by Scott in *Guy Mannering*. See *A Biographical Dictionary of Eminent Scotsmen*, ed. Thomas Thomson (London, 1875), half-vol. II, pp. 550–54.

From A. Turgot

A Paris le 22 Aout 1780[1]

Je profite, Monsieur, d'une occasion pour vous remercier de votre essay sur la population de l'Angleterre[2] que Mr Franklin m'a fait passer de votre part. tout ce qui sort de votre plume a droit d'interesser et me devient encore plus precieux quand je le tiens de vous. receves en je vous prie tous mes remercimens. la matiere que vous traités est encore bien peu connue—malgré le grand nombre d'auteurs qui en ont parlé. on manque presque partout d'elemens suffisamment exacts pour constater les faits, et on est peut etre encore plus loin de connaitre l'influence des differentes causes qui concourent a faire varier ces faits. je ne suis pas au reste eloigné de penser que cette science approfondie seroit plus interessante pour les philosophes qu'importante pour les politiques, dont les operations seroient beaucoup mieux dirigées par les

---

ORIGINAL: Cyfarthfa Castle Museum, Merthyr Tydfil. TEXT: Original, with the kind permission of Cyfarthfa Castle Museum.

1. This letter did not leave Turgot's hands until 9 Oct. 1780; see postscript.

2. *An Essay on the Population of England from the Revolution to the Present Time, with an Appendix containing Remarks on the Account of the Population, Trade and Resources of the Kingdom, in Mr Eden's Letters to Lord Carlisle* (London, 1780).

principes très simples d'une legislation fondée sur la seule justice, que par les resultats de faits assés incertaines et qui fussent-ils connus avec precision, seroient toujours le produit très compliqué d'une foule de causes, les unes entierement ignorées les autres malconnues. je suis bien loin malgré cela de ne pas sentir combien vos recherches ont de prix, je veux seulement dire que les gouvernemens ont des chemins plus courts pour parvenir a rendre les nations heureuses et riches en veritables richesses, et aussi riches en argent, aussi puissantes et aussi nombreuses qu'elles doivent l'etre à raison de leur territoire, pour etre heureuses et vraiment riches.

Je presume que je ne vous dis là, Monsieur, que ce que vous savés mieux que moi.

Je ne vous parle plus des Américaines;[3] car quelque soit le denouement de cette guerre, j'ai un peu perdu l'esperance de voir sur la terre une nation vraiment libre et vivant sans guerre. ce spectacle est reservé a des siecles bien eloignés.

Le Docteur Ingenhousz m'a remis dans le tems une lettre par laquelle vous me reassurés sur un papier dont Mr de Peyer avoit parlé. je n'ai plus aucune inquietude d'après ce que vous m'aves marqué. comme je souffrois beaucoup de la goute lorsque votre lettre m'est parvenue, je crains de n'y avoir repondu et je vous en fais mes excuses.

J'ay l'honneur d'etre avec la plus sincere estime, Monsieur, votre très humble et très obéissant

Serviteur
Turgot

Cette lettre est ecrite depuis assés longtems, la personne qui devoit la porter n'etant point partis pour l'Angleterre. Mrs Jones et Paradise veulent bien s'en charger aujourdhui, 9 Octobre.

---

3. See Turgot to R.P., 22 Mar. 1778.

From Lord Monboddo

15th Sept. 1780

Sir,

I had the favour of your Letter,[1] and am very desirous of the Continuance of the Correspondence; for from what I have seen of your Communications with

---

ORIGINAL: The National Library of Scotland.　PRINTED: Knight, pp. 124–37.　TEXT: Original, with the kind permission of the National Library of Scotland.
1. See R.P. to Monboddo, 2 Aug. 1780.

Dr Priestley, I think you are both wellbred men and of good temper and Disposition; having never seen a Controversy managed with more temper and good breeding. Altho' I differ from Dr Priestley almost in every thing and from you in some things, yet I hold you both to be Men of Genius who not contented with Experiments, Facts of Natural History and Mathematics, have aspired to the knowledge of the Causes and Principles of things; for tho' I hold Physics to be the groundwork of all good Metaphysics, and Mathematics an excellent Handmaid to Philosophy of every kind I have always thought him a man of low Genius, and little elevation of Mind above the Vulgar, who rested satisfied with the inferior Sciences—among which I reckon even Geometry and Astronomy—and could not raise his mind to the *first Philosophy*, which explains the Principles of them all, and enquires concerning the Universe and the first Causes of all things. But as this Philosophy is the highest of all, so I hold it to be the most difficult, and which it has been the labour of many ages to bring to any degree of perfection. Whoever therefore thinks he can excell in this Philosophy without being taught by the very best Masters, deceives himself most egregiously, and will be apt to fall into the most dangerous errors of which we have seen of late several Examples.

You say the Masters from whom you have learned your Metaphysics are Cudworth and Clarke among the Moderns and Plato among the Antients. Cudworth I think is the best of the Moderns you could have applied to; for he was thouroughly learned in the Antient Philosophy. As to Dr Clarke, he was an excellent Greek and Latin Scholar, but not at all learned in the Antient Philosophy as I think I have shown very clearly, p. 213,² and indeed is evident to any man learned in Antient Philosophy who reads his works. As to Plato, he was certainly a great genius and a Philosopher truly Divine. But he was not so learned in Metaphysics as his Scholar Aristotle, nor does it appear to me that Metaphysics any more than Logic was formed into a Science in Greece in his time. It was reserved for his Scholar Aristotle to make a Science of both but you are not to suppose that he invented either; for that exceeded the Abilities of any one Mortal Man: but he was so happy as to get hold of some writings of the Pythagoreans of which he made excellent use; and from what is yet preserved of these Books, I think I do him no injustice when I say that he took his whole Philosophy, of Logic and Metaphysics from them. If it be asked from whence the Pythagoreans got these Sciences, the Answer is Obvious, that their Master Pythagoras brought them with him from Egypt, where all Sciences had been cultivated for Thousands of years, by a long Succession of Philosophers from father to son, in the several Colleges of Priests. It is therefore to Aristotle that I

---

2. *Antient Metaphysicks*, I, II, xvii, 213 where Monboddo attacks Clarke for confusing perception and consciousness, and for allegedly using thought, intelligence, consciousness, perception and knowledge as synonymous terms. Monboddo complains that Clarke was not sufficiently versed in ancient Greek philosophy and notes that had he been he would have been able to distinguish "ψυχν and νους, betwixt mind that only moves and mind that like wise understands."

have chiefly applied myself as my master in Metaphysics as well as in Logic; for Aristotle decides what Plato only disputes about; nor is there any thing more true than the Common saying that *Disputat Plato, docet Aristoteles*.[3] And he has made a compleat Science of it by inventing terms of Art, which he has defined, and by using them saves a great many Circumlocutions with which Plato abounds. With Aristotle I have joined the study of his Commentators of the Alexandrian School, without whose Assistance, his Acroamatic works,[4] or works of abstruse Philosophy are not to be understood. If therefore I am mistaken in my Metaphysical Notions, you are to lay the blame upon Aristotle if you suppose that I rightly understand him. As to Dr Priestley, he does not appear to me to be much Conversant in the Antient Authors; and the only man from whom he professes to have learned his Metaphysics, is one Dr Hartley,[5] of whom I never heard so much as the name till I was last in London. But I ask from whom did he learn his Metaphysics?

As to the first question you mention concerning Free Will and Necessity, I have had no assistance at all from the Antients that I have studied, who appear to me not to have had the least doubt but that the Will was necessarily determined by what appeared the strongest Motive or reason; and indeed whoever has been taught the Antient Philosophy, and has learned to distinguish betwixt Sensations and Idea, and to know the nature of Intellect and Will, cannot in my Apprehension have any doubt in the matter. And the whole Controversy appears to me to have arrisen from Modern ignorance, and the neglect of Antient Philosophy. There is one most obvious distinction in this matter which however Dr Clarke does not seem to have made, and that is betwixt the determination of the Mind to act, and the Action itself. The Action is certainly not necessary for we may not have it in our power to perform it; or we may alter our Mind, as we frequently do, and come to a Contrary determination. But the determination both first and last is of Absolute Necessity, being the necessary Consequence of a Proposition to which we have given our Assent that the thing is fit to be done, that it is good and profitable, useful, etc. This is a Proposition as much as any in Euclid and I can make no distinction betwixt the Assent I give to such a practical Proposition, and the Assent I give to a Speculative one. They are both equally necessary; but is a necessity perfectly different from Material Necessity. Nor ought we to call it *Necessity*, if we would speak with the accuracy of antient Philosophers; for in that most valuable piece of Pythagorean Philosophy which Proclus has preserved to us, I mean Timaeus *De Anima Mundi*,[6] to be found in all the editions of Plato, the

---

3. [Plato disputes, Aristotle teaches.]

4. An allusion to the fact that the works of Aristotle that we have were lecture courses delivered to his pupils. Whatever Monboddo may have thought Aristotle was not propounding an occult philosophy confined to initiates.

5. David Hartley, see Vol. I, 44.

6. Proclus (AD 410–485) wrote a commentary on Plato's *Timaeus* in AD 437 See A.E. Taylor,

distinction is expressly made in the very beginning of it, betwixt Intellect and Necessity, which as he explains the word is only Material or Bodily Necessity; or if we will call the determination of the will necessary, it is that necessity by which every thing is what it is, and has essential Properties belonging to its nature; the same necessity by which the three angles of a triangle are equal to two right ones. There is no doubt, as you say, a difference between seeing the way, and walking in it; but suppose I have determined to walk in it, for Reasons which appear to me convincing; is not that determination necessary and will not the Action necessarily follow if I do not change my Mind, and nothing happens to hinder me.

As to Mind being extended, and having the three dimensions; if you have not made that Concession intirely, I hope you will now intirely deny it, as a most absurd position. Indeed till I read your Controversy with Dr Priestley I did not imagine that Dr Clarke had been so intirely ignorant of Antient Philosophy and indeed of the Nature of things as to have maintained that an immaterial substance could have that essential property of Matter, or to speak more properly, of Body, and which makes it what it is, I mean the property of being extended. And when this Notion is carried to the Deity as it must necessarily be, and he is said to be infinitely extended, it is a most impious as well as a most Absurd notion. With respect to our Minds, you allow that, if they are extended, as the extension is not infinite, they must be figured; but you say Dr Clarke will not allow that they are divisible and discerptible. But I say they must be both, tho' Space be neither; for they certainly must be something different from Space, for they are something that is in Space; and if they likewise be extended they must also be divisible and discerptible like every thing else that is extended. Now what a strange kind of Mind is this that has length, breadth and depth, and may be cut and carved like a piece of Meat. It is however true that our Minds must exist somewhere, as the Divine Mind exists everywhere; but it does not from thence follow that they must exist in the same manner that Body does, that is with the three dimensions; but on the Contrary as Mind is a substance of a nature quite different from Body it follows of necessary consequence that it must exist in a manner altogether different. This manner we cannot explain; but we ought to be contented to know as much of Mind, as we do of Body with which we are so much Conversant. Now Extension is but a Property of Body, an essential Property indeed, but not Body itself as the Cartesians would make it. There is something therefore which is extended; for extension is not a mere ideal Abstraction, such as Length from Breadth, but Body is really something without its dimensions or

---

A Commentary on Plato's Timaeus (Oxford, 1928), 36. In the first century AD a treatise On the Soul of the World and Nature was forged in the name of Timaeus of Locri. Taken to be a genuine document by the neo-Platonists, it is now seen to be merely a summary of Plato's Timaeus. See F.M. Cornford, Plato's Cosmology (London, 1937), p. 3.

bounds, so that we are obliged, whether we will or no, to come back to the Antient Notion of a ὕλυ or *first Matter*, which has been attempted to be so much ridiculed. Now if any Man can tell me how he can conceive that this first Matter can exist without Dimensions, I will tell him how I can conceive that Mind exists and exists in a place without having either Length, breadth or depth. The fact truly is that we know nothing either of Mind or Body, but by their Operations and we know that both Mind and Body operate in place, and therefore exist in place; but as to their manner of Existence, we can say nothing with any Certainty, because we do not know their Substance or Essence; and therefore all we can say is that we know certainly that their Substances are different, and therefore that their Manner of Existence must be different.

As to Space, what it is, or whether it be any thing, is a matter, no doubt, of difficult and abstruse Speculation. One thing is certain that if it be a Being at all, it is a being eternal self-existent, necessarily existent indivisible, and immoveable; and this being the case, it is no wonder that the Atheists have set it up as a Rival to Divinity, and have rejected all the Arguments used to prove that God is the only eternal self-existent, necessarily existent, independant, indivisible and immoveable being. On the other hand it is as little to be wondered that Dr Clarke, and other Theists supposing it likewise to be a Being, have contended that it was a quality or property of the Supreme Being, that it is an *Accident* of which the *Substance* of God is the *Substratum*; so Dr Clarke has expressed himself on his Answer to the third Letter of the Glocestershire Gentleman.[7] And because Space the Accident is of necessary Existence there-fore the Substance God must *a fortiori* be of necessary Existence. And Sir Isaac Newton has carried this notion of Space, or infinite Space, for so it must be with respect to the Deity being an Attribute of Divinity, so far as to assert that it is as it were the Sensorium of the Deity.[8] So that according to Sir Isaac it is a most necessary attribute of God, without which, it would seem, he thought he could have no perception or Intelligence any more than we could have without our Sensorium. The Glocestershire Gentleman Observes—I think very justly—that if infinite Space be a property of the Divinity, finite Space must be a property of inferior Minds such as ours.[9] The Doctor's answer to this in his third Letter to that Gentleman, is to me altogether unintelligible; and I find a great deal of that kind in the Doctor's metaphysical writings, being the necess-ary Consequence of a Man writing upon the most difficult and abstruse of all

7. See *Several Letters to the Reverend Dr Clarke, from a Gentleman in Glocestershire [Joseph Butler]* in Samuel Clarke, *The Works* (London, 1738), II, 745: "*Space*, is a Property [or *Mode*] of the Self-existent Substance; but not of any other Substances. All other *Substances* are IN *Space*, and and are *penetrated by it*; but the Self-existent Substance is not IN *Space*, nor *penetrated by it*, but is itself (if I may so speak) the *Substratum* of *Space*, the *Ground* of the Existence of *Space and Duration itself*."

8. See Monboddo to R.P., 11 July 1780, n. 8.

9. "*Space*, I own, is *in one Sense*, a property of the Self-existent Substance, but, *in the same Sense*, 'tis also a property of all other Substances." Samuel Clarke, *Works*, II, 744.

Sciences without having learned it from good Masters; for tho' I think the Doctor was a man of very good parts yet I deny that it was possible for him, or for any one Mortal Man to have invented such a Science. Here therefore we have certain portions of Space that are common Property betwixt the Deity and inferior Minds, and Body must also be a Sharer in this property so far as it occupies Space; for if Space be a property of the Mind, I think it is impossible but that it must be likewise a Property of Body, which we are sure it occupies in a manner we very well understand, whereas Mind occupies it in a manner we cannot so well explain.

These are strange Notions; and if they be well founded, they may be set down among the other great discoveries that we moderns are supposed to have made in Philosophy. The Antients disputed very much, whether such a thing existed as a vacuum which we mean by the word Space; and in Aristotle's fourth Book of Physics there is a very long and subtile Disputation upon the Subject.[10] But none of them appear to have had the least Notion that Space was either a Substance by itself or the quality of any other Substance. It is therefore I think a matter of great Curiosity, and also of great importance to the Doctrine of Theism to enquire whether the Antients or the Moderns are in the right in this matter.

The Modern Philosophers, both Theists and Atheists agree in this, that Space is a being; whereas I agree with the Antients and say that it is no being itself, however necessary it may be for the Existence of other beings.

And in the first place I say that if it be a Being, it must be either Substance or Accident, for no Man can conceive a Being that is not either the one or the other. Now it is certainly not Substance; for if it were Substance it must be either Body or Mind, that is material or immaterial because betwixt these two it is impossible there can be any third Substance. Now no body will say that it is Body for it is Space without Body: and no Philosopher that ever I heard of maintained that it was Mind. The Atheists therefore are certainly mistaken, when they make a Substance of it.

The only Question then is whether it be an Accident. Now the Accidents are reduced to nine Classes, as they are arranged by Aristotle in his book of Categories,[11] which I hold to be the foundation of the Metaphysics—or the Science of Generals, and is I believe as Antient a piece of Philosophy as any in the world, being taken by Aristotle from the School of Pythagoras and brought by Pythagoras, as I believe, from Egypt. Now I would desire to know to which of these nine classes Space belongs? Is it quantity? Dr Clarke as he makes it an Attribute of the Deity, will certainly say that it is not. Is it quality? If it be I desire to know what Quality it is, whether Colour, figure, hardness softness

---

10. Aristotle, *Physics*, trans. R.P. Hardie and R.K. Gaye, (Oxford, 1930), Bk. IV, chs. 7–9, 213a–217b. Against the atomist tradition Aristotle rejects the existence of a genuine void.
11. See *Categories*, especially ch. 4.

etc. Is it doing or suffering [?] I need not go thro' them all in this way and I shall only mention one more to which it seems to be more akin than to any other, and that is *Relation* or προς τι, as Aristotle expresses it, and which very well denotes the nature of it; for it is alwise betwixt two things at least, and it must denote an Idea, which arrises from comparing the two things together. Now I desire to know what two things compared together produces in us the idea of Space?

But there is one argument which to me is demonstration that it is neither substance nor accident: and it is this that it has no place; for every thing existing whether substance or accident must exist in some place, the substance primarily occupying the place, and the accident secondarily as being in the substance. In short every thing existing, must exist somewhere. Now I desire to know where or in what place does Space exist? And I say it has no place itself, tho' it be the place of every thing else; but it is impossible that there can be a place of a place for that would go on *in infinitum*; from whence I conclude that space having no place is no real being, because every being, whether Mind or Body, or the Accidents of Mind or Body, must be somewhere.

To make this matter still clearer if possible, let us suppose that nothing existed neither Mind nor Body; I should desire to know what Space would be upon that supposition; or whether it would be any thing; and whether it would not be strictly true, what every man would say, who has not confounded his head with Modern Metaphysics, *that nothing existed*, for if any thing has a real Existence by itself, it would exist if nothing else in the Universe existed.

I know it may be said that there would be in the case I suppose a capacity of containing Body; and that this may be considered as something. But I deny that this Capacity merely will make space a Being; for there is no being existing nor indeed can we conceive such a being, which is only Capacity and Nothing else; for tho' beings have many properties in Capacity only, or δυναμει not ευεργεια, as Aristotle expresses it they are alwise something besides mere Capacity, and I deny that we have any Conception of a Being that exists only δυναμει, and not at all ενεργεια.

It is however true that nothing could have existed without Space; and it was for that reason that Democritus and after him Epicurus, made Space or a Vacuum one of the Principles of Nature; for the same reason Aristotle has made privation one of his three principles of Natural Things, Matter and Form being the other two.[12] But the Privation of one form be no doubt necessary, before Matter can receive another as a piece of Wax or Clay cannot receive the form of a Globe before it loses the form of a square or any other form it might have had before, yet Aristotle never dreamt that the Privation of the Square was any property of the Globe; or that privation was to be reckoned a

---

12. For Aristotle's demonstration that the fundamental principles are three in number (matter, form, and privation) see *Physics*, Bk I, chs. 7–9; 189b30 192b4.

Being. On the Contrary both he and his Commentator Simplicius[13] tell us that it is a no-being, or a τò μιǒν, and is not the presence of any thing but the Absence, tho' that Absence be absolutely necessary for the Existence of any particular thing. (*See* Aristotle's *Phys. cap. ult.*)[14] In this way we may if we please consider Space, and say it is the Privation of fullness, or of Body, which it certainly is with respect to Body, which cannot exist where another Body is. As to Mind, we cannot exactly tell how it exists—only we are sure that it exists in Space and even in the same Space where Body is; for that is the case of Mind animating Body.

You will perhaps be surprised when I tell you that I think space is not extended; for I hold Extension to be a property of Body and of Body only. A body therefore in Space is extended but not Space by itself, so that when we speak of measuring Space if we rightly understand what we say, we mean only measuring the Body that is in Space. For we cannot otherwise measure Space but by a Body that is in it or supposed to be in it. It is however natural enough that in common Language we should apply to Space that Extension and measure which can be properly predicated only of the Body that is in it.

What I have said therefore in the first part of my Metaphysics I am still of opinion, upon the strictest review is true, that Space is no being by itself but only exists in relation to Body in the threefold view I have mentioned so that it is absolutely nothing when Body, or, if you will, Mind, does not exist in it. It may be true what you observe that I have used an improper word, when I said it was an adjunct of Body;[15] but from what I have here said, and even from what I have there said, I think my meaning is abundantly clear.

If you should think that in Consequence of what I have said of the threefold relation of Space to Body, that at least it falls under the Category of Relation, and therefore is *Something*, I would have you consider that when two things are said to be related, they are so by quantity or quality, or doing or suffering, or some other of the Categories, But two Bodies in Space at whatever distance from one another, cannot be said to have any such relation. It is true we give a name to the distance and call it interval; and we likewise measure it; but that is as I said by puting Body in it or supposing it to be put. If however you chuse to rank Space under the Category of Relation, I have no Objection, provided you agree that it is not Substance nor any property of Substance, and least of all of the Divine Substance.

As to Duration, I still think it is absolutely impossible to conceive it without something that exists, and continues to exist or to endure. But how it should be a property of the thing existing is to me inconceivable. One thing, I think, is

---

13. Simplicius was a neo-Platonist scholar of the 6th century AD who wrote commentaries upon Aristotle's *De coelo, Physica, De anima*, and *Categoriae*.

14. *Physics*, Bk I, ch. 9, 192a.

15. See R.P. to Monboddo, 2 Aug. 1780.

absolutely certain that if Eternal duration be a property of the Supreme Being Duration limited must be a property of inferior Beings; so that we have here more Common Property. I find you agree with Dr Clarke in considering Time and Duration as the same.[16] But this is an error that Dr Clarke has fallen into by not being learned in the Antient Metaphysics; for there he would have learned that time is only the measure of Motion. It therefore could not exist but with the material world; so that if we could suppose nothing existing but the Supreme Mind, which is immoveable, there would be in that case be duration, or αιον, as the Greek Philosophers call it, but not χϱϕνος or Time. And the Doctor should not have rejected the Common Distinction made by all Philosophers and Divines before him betwixt Time and Eternity without assigning better reasons than he has done.

I have only to add something concerning my Queries to Dr Priestley. Your answer to the first Query, I expected, because I do not reckon the Doctor an Atheist, tho' I think his Opinions have a very dangerous Tendency that way. But I own your Answer to the second surprises me. And I cannot at all reconcile it to the Doctor's words or Arguments; for if our machine of Intellect does not go on of itself when once set agoing like a Clock, but is carried on by the immediate agency of God, then I think it is not properly a Machine, or if you will call it so, it is a Machine, such as a Pipe upon which a Musician plays; and we can be no more answerable for our thoughts and actions, nor indeed are they ours any more than the Time is the Pipe's and not the Musician's. The Doctor says somewhere that our reasoning Machine is a kind of superstructure upon that part of us by which we breathe, and our Blood Circulates.[17] Now I should desire to know of the Doctor, whether that part of our Composition likewise be a kind of Pipe, which is played upon by the Supreme Being and I would ask the same question concerning the Scientific part of our Nature also, if the Doctor had learned to distinguish the three natures of which we are composed: the Intellectual, the Sensitive and the Vegetable. If they are all moved immediately by the Deity and have no Principle of Motion in themselves, then God is literally speaking *All in all*, and there is properly speaking neither Man, nor Brute, nor Vegetable in this world. These are questions which the Doctor should certainly be ready to answer before he publishes any more on the Subject of Philosophy.

As you say you delight so much in speculations of this kind, I need not make any appology for the Length of this Letter which has swelled into a Dissertation. Whether I shall convince you of the Truth of my opinions I know not; but

---

16. Although Price notes a way in which it might be useful to distinguish them (R.P. to Monboddo, 2 Aug. 1780), he is content to interchange the terms time and duration; see, for example, *A Free Discussion*, p. 55. In this he followed Clarke who also interchanged the terms eternity and infinite duration; see Samuel Clarke, *Works*, II, 536–39, and Alexander, xxix.

17. Cf. *A Free Discussion*, p. 256: '... sensation and thought do necessarily result from the organization of the brain, when the powers of mere *life* are given to the system.'

I am sure I shall profit by the Correspondence either by being convinced of my Errors or by being confirmed in the Truth of my Opinions, by finding that even you cannot make any Objection to them that I think is solid. This is all the Profit I have reaped by my Publications and it is a profit with which I am very well satisfied. I have had a great deal of correspondence upon the subject of the Origin of Language[18] by which I have been much instructed. But you are only the second Correspondent that I have had upon the subject of my Metaphysics.[19]

Your note to Dr Webster I forwarded to him, and shall make your Compliments to the persons you mention when I see them.

I am, with great regard and Esteem

Your most obedient and humble servant

[No signature]

---

18. See James Burnett, Lord Monboddo, *Of the Origin and Progress of Language*, 6 vols. (London, 1773–92). The first three vols. of this work had appeared before Monboddo wrote this letter to Price.

19. Samuel Horsley.

To [John Temple]

Sept. 18*th* 1780

Dear Sir,

On Saturday night I received with much satisfaction the favour of your letter. I have been wandering in the country ever since I had the pleasure of seeing you. At present I am with a friend at Richmond,[1] and cannot return to Newington Green before saturday. It is not, therefore, in my power to be at your house on friday. On tuesday sen=night I shall be disengaged and glad to dine with you, and to meet your Brother[2] and governor Trumbull's son.[3] I had heard of their being in town before I received your letter, and I wished greatly for the pleasure of seeing them. Should you have any engagements for tuesday, any subsequent day in next week except friday will be equally convenient to

---

ORIGINAL: Massachusetts Historical Society.   TEXT: Original, with the kind permission of the Massachusetts Historical Society.

1. Possibly, Mr Pritchard, George Street, Richmond. See R.P. to Shelburne, 16 Sept. 1782.

2. Robert Temple (1728–82), John Temple's elder brother. A Mandamus Councillor, he became a Loyalist refugee.

3. John Trumbull (1756–1843), son of Jonathan Trumbull, Governor of Connecticut. After military service under Gates and Sullivan, and with the help of John Temple, he succeeded in obtaining permission to come to London to study painting under Benjamin West. He left America in May 1780, but on 19 Nov. he was arrested on suspicion of treason and imprisoned in Tothill Fields, Bridewell. (Boatner, pp. 1119–121).

me. A line from you on this subject directed to Newington=Green will find me on saturday.

I am afraid that what you say of the reason of the dissolution of Parliament is too good to be true. I do not think that our present rulers will humble themselves so far as to treat with the Americans as independent states and not subjects; but probably even this would be now too late unless France and Spain were made parties in the treaty. So dreadfully are our affairs embroiled.

With much regard and the best wishes

I am, your most obedient and humble servant

Rich*d* Price

To [Francis Dana]

Newington Green Sept. 26, 1780

Dear Sir,

Two of my friends' are just setting out for Paris, and I cannot make myself easy without embracing the opportunity their journey offers me to convey to you a few lines to express my gratitude for a very kind letter with which you favoured me some time ago. I received particular pleasure from the proof it gave me that I am remember'd by you and have a place in your good opinion. I am a very anxious spectator of the struggle in which your country has been for some time engaged. The part I have taken in it, tho' it has brought upon me a vast deal of abuse and ill-will, I reflect upon with the greatest satisfaction. May God grant it a happy issue. The ardent wish of my heart is that every country under heaven may enjoy the blessings of liberty and independence. We are continually amused here with accounts of the disposition of the Americans to return to a connexion with this country, their sufferings, and their weariness of the war, and of the Government of Congress. These accounts are greedily swallowed, and since the taking of *Charles=town*² the common expectation has been that America will soon be ours again.

But I must not enlarge. With this you will probably receive the second

---

ORIGINAL: Massachusetts Historical Society. TEXT: Original, with the kind permission of the Massachusetts Historical Society.

1. It is likely that the two friends who deliver'd Price's letters to Benjamin Franklin and Francis Dana together with copies of *An Essay on the Population of England* were William Jones and John Paradise. See Benjamin Franklin to R.P., 9 Oct. 1780. But if this is true Price must have made a mistake in dating this letter, as William Jones left London for Paris on 18 Sept. 1780 (Cannon, I, 438).

2. On 12 May 1780 General Clinton captured a large army of American troops at Charlestown in South Carolina. (Boatner, p. 212.)

edition of a pamphlet³ which I published at the beginning of this summer. Tho' of little value I hope you will accept it as a testimony of the Author's respect. May you, Dear Sir, enjoy every blessing that can make you happy. With great esteem I am your obliged and very obedient and

humble servant

R P

---

3. *An Essay on the Population of England.*

To [John Temple]

Chatham=Square Oct 5th 1780

Dear Sir

I shall be much oblig'd to you for committing the care of these two parcels to Mr Appleton, delivering to him my best wishes: The parcels for Governor Tr[umbu]ll and Mr Bowdoin¹ contains only my Political Tracts and Fast Sermon;² and the note inclosed in the former is the same that I read to you. The parcel for Mr *Bowdoin* is accompany'd with a note to inform him, that I have been encourag'd by you to hope that he will accept it as a testimony of my respect. It contains also a letter to Dr Chauncy³ in which I have given my sentiments freely about that part of the new constitution which I mentioned to you; and I have repeated what I said in a former letter concerning your endeavours. The News=papers say that Mr Lawrens⁴ is in town and has been examined. Will you be so good as to inform me, should you hear anything particular of him, or of any intelligence that may be learnt from him? Wishing you as happy as possible, I am, Dear Sir, with much regard.

Your very obedient and humble servant

Rich: Price

ORIGINAL: Massachusetts Historical Society.   TEXT: Original with the kind permission of the Massachusetts Historical Society.

1. James Bowdoin, see Vol. I, 232.
2. *A Sermon Delivered to a Congregation ... at Hackney,* see R.P. to van der Capellen, 25 May 1779.
3. Charles Chauncy, see Vol. I, 88.
4. Henry Laurens (1724–92). In September Laurens was taken prisoner by the British from a ship which was captured off Newfoundland. Before being taken he attempted to dispose of papers which included the Lee-Van Berkell draft of a projected treaty with Holland, but failed. This draft served as a pretext for the British to declare war on the Dutch (20 Dec. 1780). Laurens was confined in the Tower of London from 6 Oct. 1780 until 31 Dec. 1781. Upon his release he went to Bath (see R.P. to Benjamin Franklin, 7 Jan. 1782), and, subsequently, had conversations with Shelburne. He returned to America in August 1784.

From Benjamin Franklin

Passy, Octbr 9th 1780

Dear Sir,

Besides the pleasure of their Company, I had the great satisfaction of hearing by your two valuable Friends, and learning from your letter, that you enjoy a good state of Health.[1] May God continue it as well for the good of Mankind as for your Comfort. I thank you much for the second Edition of your excellent Pamphlet.[2] I forwarded that you sent to Mr Dana, he being in Holland. I wish also to see the piece you have written, (as Mr Jones tells me) on Toleration.[3] I do not expect that your new Parliament will be either wiser or honester than the last. All projects to procure an honest one, by Place Bills, &c appear to me vain and impracticable. The true cure I imagine is to be found only in rendering all places unprofitable, and the King too poor to give Bribes and Pensions. 'Till this is done, which can only be by a Revolution, and I think you have not virtue enough left to procure one, your nation will always be plundered; and obliged to pay by Taxes the plunderers for Plundering and Ruining. Liberty and Virtue therefore join in the Call, *Come out of her, my People!*[4]

I am fully of your opinion respecting Religious Tests; but though the people of Massachusetts have not in their new Constitution kept quite clear of them;[5] yet if we consider what that people were 100 years ago, we must allow that they have gone greater lengths in Liberality of Sentiment, on Religious Subjects: and we may hope for greater Degrees of Perfection when their Constitution some years hence shall be revised. If Christian Preachers had continued to teach as Christ and his Apostles did, without Salaries, and as the Quakers now do, I imagine Tests would never have existed: For I think that they were invented not so much to secure Religion itself, as the Emoluments of it. When

---

ORIGINAL: Franklin MSS, Library of Congress. PRINTED: *Franklin*: Bigelow, VIII, 310. TEXT: Original.

1. See R.P. to [Francis Dana], 26 Sept. 1780.

2. *An Essay on the Population of England.*

3. See R.P. to Benjamin Franklin, 22 Dec. 1780.

4. "And I heard another voice from heaven, saying, Come out of her, my people, that ye be not partakers of her sins, and that ye receive not of her plagues." (Rev. 18. 4.)

5. In the General Introduction to *Two Tracts* Price notes that in Massachusetts the "civil authority interposes no further in religion than by imposing a tax for supporting public worship, leaving to all the power of applying the tax to the support of that mode of public worship which they like best." (Peach, p. 53.) In *Observations on the Importance of the American Revolution* Price warmly admired the provision in the Constitution of the State which gave an equal protection to all sects of Christians, but he disapproved of the article which required members of the House of Representatives and the Senate to declare "their firm persuasion of the truth of the Christian religion." (Peach, pp. 199, 200.)

a Religion is good, I conceive that it will support itself; and when it cannot support itself, and God does not take care to support it, so that its Professors are obliged to call for the help of the Civil Power, 'tis a sign, I apprehend, of its being a bad one. But I shall be out of my depth if I wade any deeper in Theology, and I will not trouble you with Politics, nor with News which are almost as uncertain: But conclude with a heart-felt wish to embrace you once more, and enjoy your sweet Society in Peace, among our honest, worthy, Friends at the *London*,[6]

Adieu, &c.
B.F.

---

6. i.e. the London Coffee House, where the Club of Honest Whigs met.

To the Earl of Shelburne

Newington=Green Oct 16*th* 1780

My Lord,

I think it so long since I have had the pleasure of seeing your Lordship, that I cannot help sending you these few lines. Mr Jervis[1] has told me that Lady Shelburne and your Lordship are well, which has given me much pleasure; and I have also been made happy by the proof of your remembrance of me which your Lordship's kind present of Pine=apples has given me. August and September being my usual time for excursions into the country, I have lately been at Norwich[2] and some other places; but I am now settled for the winter at home. The hot weather in August relaxed and sunk me a good deal, but the weather being now cool I feel myself much relieved. The Parliament being to meet the week after next, I suppose your Lordship will be soon coming to town. I have no hope from the new Parliament; nor while the representation of the kingdom continues such a mockery as it is, and subject both in its appointments and deliberations, to such an undue influence, is it to be expected that we should ever have any Parliaments that will be more than instruments of the crown. Mr Fox's triumph at Westminster[3] and Admiral

---

ORIGINAL: Bowood. TEXT: Original, with the kind permission of the Marquis of Lansdowne.
  1. Thomas Jervis, see Vol. I, 145.
  2. Price's nephew, George Cadogan Morgan, was at this time living in Norwich.
  3. At the General Election in Oct. 1780, Sir George Rodney and Charles James Fox defeated the Earl of Lincoln, the Government nominee, at Westminster. Price was encouraged by this result because at this stage in his career Fox was in favour of shorter parliaments, an increase in the number of representatives for the counties, and an enfranchisement of hitherto unrepresented interests. See John W. Derry, *Charles James Fox* (London. 1972), 94–98. Fox had been appointed Chairman of the Westminster Committee of Correspondence on 2 Feb. 1780.

Kepple's in Surry[4] I have enjoy'd much; and likewise Sir Harbord Harbord's at Norwich;[5] but the changes in favour of opposition have, I am afraid, been much less numerous than the changes in favour of the ministry. My friend Mr Rogers has been engaged in a sad scuffle at Coventry.[6] The outrages committed by the Court candidates there will, I hope, be exposed and punished. There must be a new election, and then probably Mr Rogers will be chosen, but I wish he had a more respectable partner than Sir Thomas Hallifax.[7] The defeat of General Gates[8] seems to have revived the ministry; but I expect no other effect from it than the prolongation of war and bloodshed. Happy are those who at the present juncture are out of power. Lord North, I think, if he had a due sense of his own situation, would tremble. A few more loans of 12 or 14 millions will probably leave him without the power of borrowing. In order to draw money into the Treasury he sent last week to the Bank to inform the subscribers to the last loan, that if they would make the two payments still due *immediately*, they should in two or three days afterwards receive the three quarters interest due at Michaelmas last. But this expedient did not succeed to his wishes, and it was probably one cause of the fall of stocks last friday and saturday. To-day the stocks are risen again, in consequence of a report that Mr Cumberland[9] is returned with some proposals of peace from Spain.

The payment of Navy Bills has been brought down to Christmas 1778, but the board of Ordnance, I am told, is so much behind=hand in its payment that there are debentures which have been due ever since August 1778, and the Proprietors of these Debentures are now about petitioning the Board for

---

4. On 27 Sept. 1780 Sir Joseph Mawby and Admiral Keppel defeated Thomas Onslow, the Government nominee, in the contest in Surrey.

5. Sir Harbord Harbord (1734–1810), MP for Norwich from Dec. 1756 until his elevation to the peerage in Aug. 1786. His victory in 1780 delighted Price because Harbord had the support of the Dissenters and because he was in favour of parliamentary reform.

6. Thomas Rogers and Sir Thomas Hallifax, stood for the Corporation at Coventry against Edward Yea and Lord Sheffield, both Government nominees, in one of the most turbulent Parliamentary contests of the century. The election was so violent that the sheriffs closed the poll without a return. The Commons ordered a new election and Rogers and Hallifax were returned. They were, however, later unseated.

7. Sir Thomas Hallifax (d. 1789) founded a Banking House in partnership with Joseph Vere and Richard Glyn. He was Lord Mayor of the City of London in 1776 and 1777. Price's aversion to him might have been due to his standing against Wilkes in 1772 as Court candidate for the Mayoralty of London.

8. Horatio Gates (1728–1806). Early in his career Gates saw service with the British Army in America and was wounded at Fort Duquesne in 1755. He emigrated to Virginia in 1772 and was commissioned in the Continental Army in 1775. He was in command of the American Army of the North at Saratoga in 1777. The defeat to which Price refers was the battle of Camden on 16 Aug. 1780, in which Gates's forces were routed by Cornwallis.

9. Richard Cumberland (1732-1811), dramatist. When Lord George Germaine became Colonial secretary in 1775, Cumberland was appointed Secretary to the Board of Trade in succession to John Pownall. In 1780 he went on an unsuccessful secret mission to Spain to try to persuade the Spanish authorities to conclude a separate treaty.

quicker payments, and an allowance of interest. Your Lordship, I think, knows Captain Sterling.[10] He is just appointed to the command of the Gibraltar, a Spanish 80 Gun ship, and order'd in a great hurry to the West-Indies. One of his sons,[11] tho' not of age, is made a captain of a frigate.

But I ask pardon for writing this to your Lordship. Deliver my very respectful compliments to Lady Shelburne. No one can wish more ardently your Lordship's increased honour and happiness. Under a grateful sense of your kind attention and candour I am, My Lord, your Lordship's

Most obedient and humble servant

Rich*d* Price

Your Lordship gave me leave to direct some papers which I wanted from a correspondent at Edinburgh to be sent to me under cover to your Lordship in Berkeley Square. I am informed that they have been sent; But I shall not want to receive them till your Lordship comes to town. After writing thus far I received the letters from Scotland from Mr Fombelle. I am much obliged to your Lordship for wishing to see me at Bowood, but it has been scarcely possible for me to come.

---

10. Sir Walter Stirling (1718–86), a captain in the Navy, was appointed to the *Gibraltar* in 1780 and sent to the West Indies with Sir Samuel Hood. After the capture of St Eustatius he came home with despatches and was knighted.

11. Charles Stirling (1760–1833), the younger son of Sir Walter Stirling, was promoted to the rank of Commander in May 1780. On 6 Sept. 1781 while serving in the *Savage* he was captured by the American privateer *Congress*. He became a Vice-Admiral on 31 July 1810. See *D.N.B.* and *Gent. Mag.*, CIV (1834)), part 1, 330.

From Benjamin Franklin

Nov. 27. 1780

Dear Friend,

I thank you much for the Pamphlets, you have sent me from time to time. They contain much important Information, and are written in that true Publick spirit and sincere zeal for the Welfare of Mankind, by which your Character has ever been distinguished. I rejoice to hear that your Health is better, I hope it will enable you long to continue your usefulness. I have lately had a severe Fit of the Gout which confined me six Weeks, but I think it has done me much Good. Please to present my respects and best Wishes to Dr Priestly, and beli[e]ve me to be with the sincerest esteem and affection.

Your ever

[No signature]

ORIGINAL: Franklin Papers, Library of Congress. TEXT: Original.

To the Earl of Shelburne

Newington=Green Dec: 4*th* 1780

My Lord,

I feel most sensibly your Lordship's great candour and kindness express'd in the two letters with which you have lately favoured me, and particularly the last. There was much malice in distributing the hand=bills on Sunday which gave notice that on the following morning there would be a letter published in the Morning Post from me to the American Congress. This raised painful apprehensions in the minds of many of my friends; but knowing that there could be nothing genuine of that kind which could do me any harm or bring upon me any discredit I felt myself perfectly easy. I expected it would be the very letter which appeared afterwards in the papers.[1] Your good opinion I highly value, and I am very glad that you do not think that there is any thing in that letter which can be a disadvantage to me. Indeed I think I ought to be allowed some merit for refusing an offer flattering to my ambition in order to stay in a country where I am continually abused. The hopes entertained by our ministers of conquering America are now revived, but possibly the events which encourage them may only be the means of producing a more certain and dreadful ruin. The war is grown hotter than ever, and there seems to be some danger that it may at last end in a general carnage.

There is, a forgery of Bank notes which is now much talked of and gives a considerable alarm. These are chiefly £40 and £20 notes; and they are so well executed that it is impossible for any person who is not skillful to detect them. The most serious consequences must follow should such forgeries become frequent. The currency of Bank notes will be destroy'd as soon as it becomes necessary to examine them before they can be received with safety.

I have just learnt that the Navy debt on the 31st of September last was £9,794,125, which is near four millions more than it ever was in the last war.

I am at present very busy in preparing a new Edition of a book which I have had the honour of inscribing to your Lordship. I mean, my Treatise on Reversionary Payments.[2] I am anxious about making it as complete as I can, and the alterations and additions I have in view will employ me all this winter.

ORIGINAL: Bowood.   TEXT: Original with the kind permission of the Marquis of Lansdowne.

1. The *Morning Post and Daily Advertiser* for 27 Nov. 1780 published the following extract from Benjamin Franklin's letter to the Committee of Congress for Foreign Affairs dated Passy, 26 May 1779, "Dr Price, whose assistance was requested by Congress, has declined that service, as you will see by the copy of his letter enclosed." [The enclosed letter was R.P. to Benjamin Franklin, Arthur Lee and John Adams, 18 January 1779].

2. *Observations on Reversionary Payments*. Price refers to the fourth edition which was subsequently published in 1783.

Mrs Price has been sometimes unhappy about me from the apprehension of my being in danger; but she is now easy. She sends her respectful compliments. May your Lordship and Lady Shelburne enjoy all the blessings this world can give, and at last enjoy the better blessings reserved for the virtuous. With much gratitude for your Lordship's freindship and great regard

I am your much obliged
and very humble servant
Rich*d* Price

To [John Temple]

Newington=Green Dec:8th 1780

Dear Sir,

I have for some time been wishing to hear of you, but have avoided calling lest in the present time of suspicion and jealousy an improper interpretation should be put upon it.

I am extremely grieved for the hard fate of Mr Trumbull.[1] Should you ever see him I request the favour of you to deliver to him my kind remembrances, and to inform him that I am obliged, by the advice of my friends, to do violence to my feelings by not visiting him. I feel very tranquil under all the censure and abuse and threatenings which are thrown out against me. There is nothing in the course of my life that I reflect upon with more satisfaction than the part I have taken in the present struggle with America. May God grant it an issue favourable to the cause of public liberty and justice. Should you ever favour me with any letters be so good as to send them to my Nephew's or Mr Morgan's at the Assurance Office near Black=Fryars=Bridge.[2] Wishing you all that can make you happy I am, Dear Sir,

Your very obedient and humble servant
Rich*d* Price

Have you heard from Mr D. Neuville since he has been gone? The intercepted letters have had a great effect in leading the people to conclude that America cannot go on with the contest and that it will be soon brought under our government again.[3]

ORIGINAL: Massachusetts Historical Society.   TEXT: Original, with the kind permission of the Massachusetts Historical Society.

1. John Trumbull was arrested on 19 Nov. 1780 "on suspicion of treason".
2. William Morgan.
3. See R.P. to [John Temple], 5 Oct. 1780, n.4.

To Lord Monboddo

Newington Green Dec: 11*th* 1780

My Lord,

I think myself much obliged to your Lordship for the honour you do me by desiring the continuance of the correspondence between us; and I am sorry I have been so long without answering your last letter.[1] This delay has been occasioned by my own slowness joyned to a particular business which has for some time occupied almost my whole attention, and which will continue to employ me during the greatest part of this winter.[2]

I am glad your Lordship approves the manner in which the controversy between Dr Priestley and me has been conducted. I wish indeed all controversies were carried on in the same amicable manner. I differ, as your Lordship says *you* do, from Dr Priestley in almost everything, and consider his system as most dangerous in its tendency; but at the same time I honour him as an upright and able man.

I have received pleasure from the account which you give me of your sentiments of Cudworth, Clarke, Plato and Aristotle. The three first of these writers I have read, studied, and admired; but, in consequence of some early prejudices, I have been but little conversant in Aristotle's writings. This, perhaps, may have been a great disadvantage to me; but it is now too late for me to begin the study of Aristotle, and I must content myself with such opinions as I have formed, preserving however a mind always open to any new arguments, and a desire to be influenced by them as far as I can see their force.

I am afraid we must be willing to continue to differ about most of the points which are the subjects of your Lordship's letter. I offer'd what I thought of most weight with respect to them in my last letter, and I have consider'd carefully your replies. The determinations of the mind, your Lordship says, are of absolute necessity; but yet you acknowledge we may alter our minds and come to a contrary determination. This last assertion seems evidently true, but scarcely consistent with the former. Determination, you add, is the necessary consequence of our assent to the proposition that a thing is fit to be done. I would ask how then we ever come to do things that we are conscious at the time to be *unfit* to be done? Every one to his sorrow knows that he often does such things, or that he determines against his convictions and judgement; and if this is never done, there is no such thing as guilt or sin in the world. The assent of

ORIGINAL: The National Library of Scotland. PRINTED: Knight, pp. 141–46. TEXT: Original, with the kind permission of the National Library of Scotland.

1. See Monboddo to R.P., 15 Sept. 1780.

2. At this time Price was kept very busy on the revision of *Observations on Reversionary Payments*, the fourth edition of which eventually appeared in 1783. See R.P. to Shelburne, 4 Dec. 1780.

the understanding is in my opinion a totally different thing from the determination of the will. Your Lordship asks, supposing I have determined to walk in a way for reasons that appear to me convincing, will not the action necessarily follow? I answer, by no means; because I may change my mind. If I do not change my mind the action will indeed follow if there is no physical impediment; but this is only saying that I will do a thing if I continue to chuse to do it. I would observe farther, that if by *determination* is meant the same with actual *volition*, saying that it is necessary is begging the question or asserting the very thing that is deny'd. On the contrary; if by *determination* is meant the *intention* or *resolution* to act, saying that it is necessary seems wrong because we have a controuling power over our intentions or resolutions. Your Lordship distinguishes between *determination* and *action*, and make[s] the former *necessary* and the latter *free*. But I do not feel the force of this distinction. If our *determinations* are necessary the actions that follow them must be equally so. I assent entirely to what you say about *material* necessity, and think that it is of the last importance that no such necessity, or any other inconsistent with the power of self-determination, should be ascribed to the operations of the mind.

I have the happiness to agree with your Lordship almost entirely about the extension of spirit. It exists and operates in place; but, as your Lordship says, it cannot be concluded from hence that it is long, broad and thick, or that it occupies space in the same manner with body. Time, truth, the first matter, Ideas etc. exist in place, or have a *presence* here and everywhere; but without dimensions. Why, therefore, as you very properly ask, may not mind likewise so exist?

I wish I could agree as much with your Lordship on the subject of space. What Sir Isaac Newton has said concerning space, that it is *As it were* the *sensorium* of the Deity, has, I think, been much misunderstood. He seems to me to have meant principally to make use of a strong figure or comparison. As *we* see things, by being present in our *sensoria* and there perceiving the images of things convey'd thither by the organs of sense, so the Deity sees all things by existing in every part of infinite space, and there perceiving not the images of things but the things themselves by being intimately present with them and their existing in him. Nothing, according to my Ideas, can be more just than all that he says on this subject at the end of his *Principia* and *Opticks*.[3]

I do not chuse to call space a *being*; nor am I able to give any satisfactory answer to the question, whether it is a substance or accident. But I am satisfied in general that it is *something*. Were it *nothing*, it would not be what your Lordship says it is, *necessary to every thing*. It seems a manifest absurdity to assert that what is itself nothing is necessary to any thing; or that the *sine qua non* of all existence has itself no existence. Every thing, your Lordship says, "must exist in place or somewhere, but where can place itself exist? If it be anything must

---

3. See "General Scholium", *Principia*, II, 390–91; and *Opticks* (London, 1931), pp. 403–404.

there not be previously a place for it, and a place for that place and so on for ever?'' This argument your Lordship reckons a demonstration. How different in this instance are our conceptions? This argument seems to me the same as if I was to attempt to prove that there was no room for any more books in a Library by saying that if there was, there must be room for that room and so on *in infinitum*; or as if I was to prove, that there was no such thing as *time* by saying that time being necessary to the existence of every thing, time itself cannot exist because if it did it must exist in itself and there must be time for time and so on.

To your question, supposing neither body nor mind to exist what would exist? I would answer, the *possibility* of body and mind, that is *time* and *place* would still exist. These are so real that they cannot be even *supposed* not to exist; and this *necessity* of their existence is, according to my Ideas, the same with the necessity of the first eternal and omnipresent nature.

Your Lordship says (p. 13)[4] that space is not extended. I know not how to understand this. Supposing it true it will still follow that space is *something*; for of nothing, nothing can be either affirmed or denied. It will also follow that saying infinite space or immensity is an attribute of the Deity is not the same with saying that he is infinitely extended, which would indeed be a most improper expression.

The difference between us about duration is less than about space. Your Lordship says, that duration cannot be conceived without something that exists, and yet you deny that it is a property of anything that exists. I do not see how anything can justly be said to *endure*, and yet that *enduring* not be a property of it. Is there not a sense in which whatever can be rightly affirmed of a thing is a property of it? If infinite duration, you say, is a property of the Deity, limitted duration is likewise a property of inferior beings. I find no difficulty in this. Intelligence, Power, goodness etc. are properties of the Deity, and also of inferior beings. But they are properties of the Deity in a peculiar manner. He possesses them necessarily and independently. Inferior beings possess them by derivation from him. He is that infinite truth by which all minds know, and all beings are intelligent. The question whether there is a just distinction between *duration* and *time* appears to me to be chiefly a question about words.

I am much surprised as you can be at some of Dr Priestley's opinions. He does indeed assert that the Deity is the *only agent* in nature, and that we have in ourselves no principle of motion or action;[5] the consequence of which is, as

---

4. See Monboddo to R.P., 15 Sept. 1780.
5. In *A Free Discussion* Price asks: "Can Dr Priestley believe easily that in all those crimes which men charge *themselves* with, and reproach *themselves* for, God is the agent; and that (speaking philosophically) *they*, in such instances, are no more *agents*, than a *sword* is an agent when employed to commit murder?" (pp. 158–59). Priestley replies: "It does require *strength of mind* not to startle at such a conclusion; but then it requires nothing but strength of mind" (p. 161). Cf. pp. 219, 233. See also Priestley, *The Doctrine of Philosophical Necessity Illustrated*, pp. 108, 112.

your Lordship says, (and Dr Priestley in effect acknowledges it) that we are not properly responsible for our actions, that they are not really *ours*, and that the machine called man is only a kind of pipe (to use your Lordship's comparison) which is play'd upon by an invisible hand, his actions being no more his own than the tune is the pipe's.

I have been afraid in writing this of repeating too [much] of what I said in my former letter, and this has made me less particular in my replies than I should otherwise have been. These are subjects which are hardly capable of being elucidated by a multiplicity of words, and long discussions. I think for myself as well as I can; and if, after employing myself in laying my thoughts before others with the reasons of them, they do not receive them, I endeavour to make myself easy and to content myself with the improvement (often perhaps imaginary) derived from the attention bestowed in proposing them. It would, indeed, have given me great pleasure to be able to tell your Lordship that your arguments have convinced me on all the points in debate between us. The reason of the difference between us may be my ignorance of that first Philosophy and those antient Metaphysics with which your Lordship is so deeply conversant. I am afraid you discern in me much of this ignorance; but I rely on your candour. My delay in sending this letter I reflect upon with pain. In hopes that it will be excused and with great respect I am, my Lord,

Your Lordship's obliged and most obedient servant
Rich*d* Price

To Benjamin Franklin

Dec*r* 22 1780

Dear Sir

I have received with particular pleasure your letter[1] by Dr H[2] and I cannot help returning by him a few lines to thank you for remembering me and to express the satisfaction with which I have heard, that you are recover'd from a fit of the gout which you think has been of service to you. May your life be preserved to do good to the world, and to see the end of the present struggle. I cannot describe to you the feeling with which I view the progress of it. God grant that the issue may prove favourable to public liberty and the general rights of mankind. You cannot imagine how much I have been lately abused and threatened. My enemies by their charges against me make me of much

---

ORIGINAL: American Philosophical Society. TEXT: Original, with the kind permission of the American Philosophical Society.

1. See Benjamin Franklin to R.P., 9 Oct. 1780.
2. Possibly Dr Hamilton, see R.P. to Benjamin Franklin, 18 Nov. 1782.

more consequence than I am. I feel easy. There is nothing in the conduct of my life that I reflect upon with more satisfaction than the part I have taken in the dispute with A[meric]a and the endeavours I have used to warn and serve my country, and to communicate right sentiments of Government and civil and religious liberty. On the subject of *Toleration* I have writ a good deal; but the friend who told you that I had published on this subject was mistaken. When you see Mr T[urgo]t deliver my best respects to him and my thanks for a kind letter[3] with which he has lately obliged and honoured me. Dr P[riestley] lives at Bir[mingha]m and has lately been invited to preach in the afternoon to a congregation there.[4] His health is better, but he was last week alarmed by some symptoms of a return of his bilious disorder. He has just finished another volume upon air.[5] With the greatest respect and affection I am, my dear Friend, ever yours

[No signature]

Dr Fothergill[6] is relapsed into the disorder [a suppression of urine] which brought him to the brink of the grave last winter, and lies now dangerously ill. I shall take care that the letter to Mr I[genhouz]s be safely delivered. He is now in the country. The war spreads. What will become of us.

---

3. See Turgot to R.P., 22 Aug. 1780.

4. In September 1780 Joseph Priestley, having ceased to be Shelburne's librarian, moved to live at Fair Hill, Birmingham. Not long after his arrival there he received an invitation to become a minister at New Street Meeting House. *Autobiography*, p. 120–1; Gibbs, p. 135.

5. The first volume of *Experiments and Observations relating to various Branches of Natural Philosophy* (vols. 4,5, and 6 of *Observations on Different Kinds of Air*) appeared in 1779, the second (which is probably the one to which Price refers) appeared in 1781 and the third in 1786. See Crook, p. 153; Gibbs, p. 106.

6. John Fothergill (1712–80), physician and botanist. He was elected FRS in 1763. A close friend of Franklin who said of him, "I can hardly conceive that a better man has ever existed." He died on 26 Dec. 1780. (*D.N.B.*)

From Lord Monboddo

Edinburgh 5 Feb*y* 1781

Dear Sir,

I am very much obliged to you for the trouble you have taken to read the sheets I sent to you, and to give me your thoughts upon them.[1] I know the

---

ORIGINAL: The National Library of Scotland. PRINTED: Knight, pp. 147–155. TEXT: Original, with the kind permission of the National Library of Scotland. The MS cover bears the following note: Letter to Dr Price/5 Feb*y* 1781/On the Newtonian Philosophy—In answer to his Observations upon Book 4 of Ant[ient] Metaph[ysics], vol. 2.

1. The letter to Monboddo in which Price discusses Book 4 of Volume 2 of Monboddo's *Antient Metaphysics* does not seem to have survived.

prejudice is so great in favour of the Mechanical Philosophy at present, that I did not expect you was to be convinced by any thing I have said against it. At the same time I was very desirous to know what a Man so ingenious as you could say against the Principles of the Antient Philosophy which I have endeavoured to defend. It is well in the present state of Philosophy if a Man will allow that motion was at first begun by mind; which even Des Cartes admitted, but I am affraid many of our present Philosophers do not. But that they should admit that [it] is not only begun but carried on by mind, is not to be expected; at least not till the Antient Philosophy be revived, of which I have some hopes in England where the Language of it is understood.

I have so far profited by your remarks as to perceive that there are some things I have not sufficiently explained in the sheets I sent to you; referring too much to the Dissertation at the end of my first volume.[2] There I am perswaded I have obviated the Objection you urge against my system that I make Body stop itself. This indeed would be as contrary to my Notions, as to the Notions of the Newtonians, and it would be most absurd to maintain that Body can neither begin to move itself, nor continue to move itself, and yet could stop itself. But I no more believe that any Body organized or unorganized, can stop itself, than I believe that our Body can stop its own Motion. It is Mind according to my Philosophy, that makes Body both move and cease to move; at least it is one of the Causes of the Cessation of Motion, for Body by its impenetrability and Resistance, will also make the Motion of another Body cease.

The great difference I observe betwixt the Antient and Modern Philosophy, with respect to the doctrine of Motion is that we moderns have applied most successfully geometry and mechanics to it, and have measured and calculated very exactly, but we have not inquired concerning the Cause of it as the Antients did, at least concerning the immediate Cause of it; for tho Sir Isaac Newton has calculated most accurately the Motions of the Celestial Bodies, and shown by what Laws they are moved, yet he has not said a word in his *Principia* of the Cause of those Motions. He has only told us that their Motion is combined of Projection and Gravitation. But what it is that gives the projectile Motion, whether Body or Mind, he has not said. And as to Gravitation it is well known that he desired at least to account for it by Bodily impulse. What makes me inclined to believe, that he supposed that the Projectile Motion was produced in the same Manner, is *first* that it would make the system more consistant, both Motions being produced in the same way, and secondly that otherways his first Law of Motion, which he makes the basis of his whole system, would not apply for it is only Bodies moved by impulse of

2. "Dissertation on the principles of the Newtonian philosophy". *Antient Metaphysics*, I, 497–555. According to Monboddo, Newton supposed that there are two kinds of motion—the projectile and the gravitational—and that both are produced by impulse (pp. 501–502).

other Bodies, that continue their Motion after the impulse ceases; for that Bodies, moved by Mind, do not continue their Motion in that way, we know with as great certainty as we know anything; I mean from Consciousness of the Motion of our own Body: and this is more to be attended to that it is only from thence that we have any idea of Mind moving Body. Now I am sure we are conscious first that our Mind does not move our Body in the same way that Body moves Body, that is by impulse: and indeed it is impossible when we consider the nature of Mind and Body, that it should; for Body acts upon Body by its surface; and what we call impulse is the impression that the surface of the one Body makes upon the surface of the other; and which is the necessary consequence of the resistance and solidity of Matter. But how is it possible that a substance, that has neither surface, resistance, nor solidity, can act in that manner? It is manifest therefore that Mind must move Body in a manner quite different, and it is in the way that Dr Clarke says Gravitation operates, by Acting not upon the surface of the Body only, but upon every the most inmost particle of it; that is in one word, by animating it.[3]

2do, we learn from Consciousness not only negatively that Mind does not move Body by impulse, but we know positively that it moves it by constant and incessant Energies, in the same way that Dr Clarke says that God Almighty, or some inferior Mind, moves the Celestial Bodies.[4] Now I am very desirous to know, whether you think it is possible that Sir Isaac's first Law of Motion can be applied to the Celestial Bodies, if we suppose them to be moved immediately by Mind, and not by Bodily impulse.

You admire Dr Clarke, as a Metaphysician; and so do I. But I wonder his Authority has no more influence with you, with respect to the manner in which Mind moves Body, and with respect to the Motion of the Celestial Bodies in particular, which, he says most expressly, cannot be accounted for by one original impression or impulse made upon them, nor otherwise except by the Constant Agency of Mind; and I am also surprised that you are not moved by the Authority of Sir Isaac himself, who in the only part of his works, where I think he has philosophised, that is, enquired concerning the Cause of Motion, has said in so many words, that neither the beginning, nor continuance of Motion, can be accounted for otherwise than from an active principle in

---

3. See Clarke's note in his translation of Rohault's *System of Natural Philosophy* (London, 1723), I, 54n., cited in Alexander Koyré, *Newtonian Studies*, (London, 1965), p. 171: "Gravity is always in proportion to the Quantity of solid Matter, and therefore must of Necessity be ascribed to some cause that penetrates the very inward Substance it self of Solid Matter."

4. See Clarke, *Works*, II, 601: "It [the world] depends every Moment on some superior Being, for the *Preservation* of its Frame; and that all the great Motions in it, are caused by *some* Immaterial Power, not having *originally* impressed a *certain Quantity of Motion upon Matter*, but *perpetually and actually* exerting itself every Moment in every part of the World." For Price's reply and his acceptance of Clarke's teaching on this point see R.P. to Monboddo, [April, 1781].

Matter.[5] Now that active Principle is what I call Mind; and Sir Isaac did certainly believe that it was something different from the Matter in which he says it is inherent, for otherwise he must have believed that Matter moves itself, which no body can believe but an Atheist; and certainly Sir Isaac was no Atheist, though by following too much the Mechanical Philosophy of Des Cartes, he has laid down Principles which have a tendency that way.

Thus you see I am not destitute of Authorities, modern as well as antient, in support of my system, and among these of Modern times, I reckon Dr Horsley one of the greatest. He is a Mathematician, Scholar and Philosopher; such a Man may be common with you; but I do not know a single Man in Scotland such as Dr Horsley. As to his Philosophy, I can assure you I have learned more Philosophy in conversation with him than I have done by reading Dr Clarke's works; and he has fallen into no error so gross as that of Dr Clarke's concerning *Extended Spirit*.

As to the Change in Motion; it appears to me impossible to deny that there is one Change constantly going on in Motion; I mean Change of Place. And the last Change of Place, I think can no more be without a Cause, than the first Change. That this was the Philosophy of Aristotle is evident from his Definition of Motion;[6] and that he was so ignorant as not to know what you call an Axiom, that all the several Changes of the Place of Body are produced by one single impulse, is also evident from the passage that I have quoted from his Physics: and Dr Clarke, it would appear, was as ignorant, at least with respect to the Motion of the Celestial Bodies. And even Sir Isaac Newton, whatever he may have thought when he wrote his Principia, appears to have changed his Mind when he published his Optics in which he has said in so many words that Motion can not be continued any more than begun without a Principle of Activity in Matter. This I think is plainly giving up his first Law of Motion.

Motion to be sure is not such a Change of a Body as the Alteration of its Figure; but still it is a Change. The Sun when he goes from East to West is certainly changed with respect to his situation, tho' he is not changed as to his Figure. If there be an increase of the Velocity of the Motion as in the case of falling Bodies, I think it cannot be denied that there is a Change in Motion. And what is this Change? It is nothing else but the Body changing its place oftener, in the same time so that this Change is no more, than a Mode or Quality of Change of Place.

You say that Motion or passing from one point of Space to another is no more a Change of the State of the Body than passing from one instant of Time

---

5. See Newton, *Opticks*, Query 31, "The *vis inertiae* is a passive principle by which bodies persist in their motion or rest, receive motion in proportion to the force impressing it, and resist as much as they are resisted. By this principle alone there never could have been any motion in the world. Some other principle was necessary for putting bodies into motion; and now they are in motion, some other principle is necessary for conserving the motion."

6. *Physics*, Bk. III, ch. 1, 201a9–16.

to another. But this is comparing two things quite different, viz. the Motion of the Body, and its Duration measured by *time*, that is by the Motion of other Bodies, such as the Sun or the Moon; for the Motion is in the Body and belonging to it; whereas the Motion of other Bodies is extrinsic to it, and only applied by the Mind to measure the duration of a Body or of its motions. Of this no Man can have the least doubt that has studied the doctrine of *Motion* and *Time* in the Antient Books.[7] As to *Existence* and *Motion*, they are certainly Ideas quite different, for tho' everything in Motion must exist, yet a thing certainly may exist that is not in Motion.

To conclude, there are but three ways possible, in which the Celestial Bodies can be moved; for either they must move themselves by a *vis insita*, or Power essential to the Body; or, if they do not move themselves, they must be moved either by impulse of other Bodies, or by Mind; καὶ παρὰ ταυτὰ οὐδεν as Aristotle says.[8] Now as to the first Alternative, Sir Isaac has said that one of the two Motions by which he makes the Planets to be moved, viz. Gravitation, is not essential to Matter,[9] and for the same reason I think we cannot doubt, but that he believed the projectile Motion likewise not to be of the Essence of Matter. And indeed whoever believes that Body can move itself, and with so much constancy too, and regularity, as the Planets are moved, must be an Atheist whether he knows it or not. As to the second Alternative, I think it is evident from what I have said that he supposed the projectile motion to be produced immediately at least by Bodily impulse, otherwise his first Law of Motion would not apply; and it is certain he desired to account for the Motion of Gravitation in the same way; and indeed it was necessary, in order to make his system Uniform and Consistant. But whatever Sir Isaac may have thought, you seem to be clearly of Opinion that the last Alternative is the truth, and that the Planets are moved immediately and directly by Mind. But you do not agree with Dr Clarke and Dr Horsley, that they are moved by the Constant Agency of Mind; but you say, they are first projected by Mind, and then go on of themselves in the Line of Projection by Sir Isaac's first Law of Motion but are bent by the power of Gravitation into the Curve, which power, if I understand you right, operates not as the projectile force does, by one original impulse, but constantly and incessantly. So that here there are two operations of Mind concurring to produce this Single Motion, and the one of these operations different from the other.

---

7. For Aristotle's definition of time as the number of motion, see *Physics*, Bk. IV, ch. 11, 219b1–2.

8. [and nothing beyond these]

9. See the preface to the second English edition of *Opticks* (1717), cxxiii: "To shew that I do not take Gravity for an essential property of Bodies"; and R.S. Westfall, *Force in Newton's Physics* (New York), 1971), p. 392. In *Letters to Bentley* Newton enjoined Bentley not to ascribe to him the notion that gravity is essential to matter; see *Opera Omnia*, ed. S. Horsley (London, 1782), IV, 437, cited in Alexander Koyré, *Newtonian Studies*, 149, 202n.

This must appear at first sight a system very complex and not at all probable; and indeed, I think, impossible to be true, unless it could be demonstrated that it was impossible that Mind could move Body in a Circle or Elipsis, otherwise than in this round about way; for I lay it down as a Postulatum that cannot be refused me, that Mind, intelligent or directed by supreme Intelligence, will move these Bodies in the most simple and direct way possible. If indeed they were moved by Bodily impulse it were impossible that they should be moved otherwise than by a double Motion. But there is no such necessity when Mind is the Mover.

In order to prove that there is such a necessity, it must be proved that there can be no motion, not even by Mind, except in a straight Line; and it appears to me that Sir Isaac has proceeded upon that hypothesis. But if the Difference betwixt the manner in which the Mind moves Body, and that in which Body moves Body is attended to it will be evident that Mind may move Body in a Curve, as well as in a streight Line; for as Mind moves Body not by impulses, which carry on the Body in a streight Line for some time after the impulse has ceased, but by incessant Energies and Exertions in every instance, it is plain that the direction may be altered in every instant of the Motion, and so the Curvilinear Motion be produced. And this is not a matter of speculation only, but a matter of fact for the truth of which every man may convince himself by describing a Circle with his hand, upon the Table. If Sir Isaac had attended to this difference betwixt the Motion of Body by Mind, and Motion by another Body, and had believed, as you seem to think he did, that the Motion of the Planets was produced immediately by Mind, I cannot have the least doubt, but that he would have agreed with me in opinion.

As to what you say of Sir Isaac's demonstration of the fourth Proposition of the Seventh Book,[10] I do not deny the force of it; but then it proceeds intirely upon the hypothesis of the Combined Motion of the Moon. For Sir Isaac has certainly not demonstrated that the motion of the moon must necessarily be combined, and could not have been produced by one single power. But he supposed (and the possibility of the supposition must be admitted) that the motion of the Moon might have been produced in the same manner as the Motion of Projectiles upon Earth. And from the similarity he has observed betwixt the Motion of these projectiles and the Motion of the Planets, he has demonstrated that the same power which makes a stone fall to the earth will be necessary to keep the Moon in her orbit, and prevent from going on in the Line of Projection. And here it may be observed that Sir Isaac's whole system is founded not upon the actual Existence of the Motions of Projection and Gravi-

---

10. The reference to a seventh book presents difficulties, for neither the *Opticks* nor the *Principia* runs to seven books. As Price's letter is not available we can only conjecture. Perhaps Monboddo was referring to the fourth proposition of the *third* book of *Principia*, namely, "That the moon gravitates towards the earth, and by the force of gravity is continually drawn off from a rectilinear motion and retained in its orbit." *Principia*, II, 215.

tation in the Celestial Regions, but upon the analysis of the Motion of the Planets into these two motions in the same manner as the Motion in a Streight Line is analyzed into two lateral Motions, of which therefore the Rectilineal Motion is said to be compounded: and accordingly the Demonstration of this Composition of Motion is a fundamental Proposition in the *Principia*.

Thus I have given you at great length, much greater than I first proposed, my Answers to your Objections, by which if I have not convinced you I have at least given you the Pleasure of being more confirmed in your own Opinion by seeing the frivolousness of the Reasons urged against it. In return for this Pleasure, I hope you will take the trouble to let me know, how you have convinced yourself of the fallacy of my reasoning that so I may either come over to your Opinion; or have the pleasure, in my turn, to be more confirmed in my own. Which ever of the ways our Correspondence ends, we shall both profit by it: and we have already so far profited that we are both clear as to that more important Distinction betwixt Body and Mind, that the one is extended, the other not; and you seem now to be of Opinion that Space cannot be set up as a Rival to Deity, or held out as a Being eternal, independant, immoveable, as well as Deity. And I hope upon further Reflexion you will be convinced that it is truely no Being at all, but only the Capacity of Containing Being; which must no doubt be previous, or at least concomitant, to all Being; for no Being could exist, if there was *No where*, that it could exist.

[No signature]

To William Adams

Newington=Green M*ch* 19*th* 1781

Dear Sir,

With this you will receive a sermon¹ which I have resolved to publish partly in compliance with the desire of several friends and partly on account of what I

ORIGINAL: Gloucestershire County Records Office.   TEXT: Original, with the kind permission of the Gloucestershire Records Office.

1. *A Discourse addressed to a Congregation at Hackney on February 21, 1781, being the day appointed for a Public Fast* (London, [1781]). This sermon is Price's apologia for publishing his views on political questions, particularly his condemnation of the Administration's policy regarding America. The rewards that the virtuous are entitled to expect are not to be found in this world, but in the heaven that Christ will create for them. But although these rewards are to be found in another world, we must not forget that our probation is on this earth, that we have duties here, and that we ought to cultivate the virtues and discharge the duties of citizenship, by being vigilant in preventing corruption, and in defending liberty and our natural rights. In the course of this sermon Price reminded his congregation of the prophecies he had made in his pamphlets, *Observations on the Nature of Civil Liberty* and *Additional Observations*: that if Britain went to war with the colonies there was a danger that they would form an alliance with France, that a general war would ensue, and that this might end in a catastrophe "never before known among nations." Price's sermon was reviewed in *The Monthly Review* for April 1781 (Vol. LXIV (Jan.–June, 1781), 315–16. Noting that

say of my own conduct at the end of it; but, I am afraid, it will require to be read with a great deal of candour. I reflect, particularly, that into what I call the Post=script I have introduced some things that are too unsuitable to a sermon. But it is out of my hands and now too late to repent. Six years ago I little thought of engaging in Politicks; but, always auguring ill of the quarrel with America, I was drawn into it by my feelings in a manner that I now think of with surprize. I may have been wrong in some particulars and perhaps I carried my apprehensions too high. Upon the whole, however, I reflect with much satisfaction on what I have done; and those of my friends who may differ from me will not, I hope, on this account withdraw from me their favourable opinion. You are one of those friends whose good opinion I most value. The state of public affairs has been long such as has disposed me more than ever to look higher than this world, and to recur to that source of consolation under all evils on which I have insisted in the discourse I now send you. Many think that at present our affairs look promising, and that we are likely soon to triumph over all our enemies. A little time will shew how far this expectation is just.

Negotiations for peace are much talked of; and may heaven soon grant such a peace as may be most favourable to the true interest of this nation and the general rights of mankind.

The greatest part of my time is at present employ'd in preparing for the Press a new edition in two volumes of my Treatise on Reversionary Payments.[2] This work having been for some time out of print and having gone thro' three editions and been well received I am anxious about making it as perfect and complete as I can; and with this view I am composing a great variety of New Tables and collecting as many new Observations as I can procure. I think it a long time since I have had any communication with you. A few lines from you when you are most at leisure would give me much pleasure. Deliver my kind respects to Mrs Adams[3] and Miss Adams.[4] Wishing you and them all possible happiness, I am, Dear Sir, with the truest respect and affection,

Your very obedient and humble servant
Rich*d* Price

Mrs Price sends her best respects.

---

the course of the war had confirmed Price's predictions the reviewer commented: "They were ridiculed when they were first published, as the dreams of a splenetic visionary; or execrated as the malignant effusions of a heart that only wished what it pretended to foresee. But however divided the world may be about Dr Price's motives, there is something which all must agree in, what *was* speculation, is now a *fact.*"

2. *Observations on Reversionary Payments*, see Vol. I, 97.

3. See Vol. I, 86.

4. Ibid.

To Lord Monboddo

[April?, 1781]

My Lord,

I am very sorry I have so much reason for again entreating your Lordship's forgiveness of my dilatoryness in the correspondence with which you honour me. For the last seven weeks I have resided in London and had my time and attention taken almost entirely from all my usual employments and persuits. Had I continued at my quiet home and my thoughts been less dissipated by London engagements, you would undoubtedly have heard from me much sooner. I am now returned to Newington=Green and having for some time reflected with pain on the debt I owe your Lordship, I have resolved to make the discharge of it my first employment. I have not however much to say; and I believe we must be contented with the differences of our opinions. I have read with care the Dissertation at the end of your Lordship's *antient Metaphysics*; but without seeing reason to alter my sentiments of Sir Is. Newton's first law of motion. A body, you acknowledge, cannot stop itself. Must it not then, after being once moved, *whether by mind or any other cause*, continue to move for ever unless some foreign action upon it stops it, and in the same direction too, unless some cause alters that direction?

Your Lordship seems (in P. 3d of your letter) to acknowledge that this law may hold with respect to motion produced by the impulse of other bodies, but at the same time, intimate, if I understand your Lordship, that it cannot be applied to motion produced by the action of mind. To me it appears to be equally applicable to both; nor can I conceive how this can be denied without maintaining that a body once moved needs no action upon it to stop it, but will stop itself. For if it does not stop itself, and nothing else stops it, it is self-evident that it will *never* be stopp'd; or, in other words, that it will continue to move for ever. Mind, let us suppose, has moved a body. If that body afterward ceases to move, it must be in consequence of being stopp'd either by its own action upon itself, or by the action of another body, or by the action of mind. Let there then be no such action, and it will move for ever. I must think that this is as clear a demonstration as can be given of any point. When I describe a circle with my finger on a table, there is a constant action of my mind on my finger to keep it in the circle; and were it to be separated instantly from my hand, or, as your Lordship speaks, to cease to be animated, it would go off in a tangent and never stop till *something* (that is, either body or mind) stopp'd it.

ORIGINAL: The National Library of Scotland.   PRINTED: Knight, pp. 176–79.   TEXT: Original, with the kind permission of the National Library of Scotland.

What Sir Is: Newton says of the prejectile and centripetal forces by which the planets are kept in their orbits is no more than this.

Your Lordship (in the fourth page of your letter)[1] tells me that you desire I would inform you whether I think it possible to apply Sir Is: Newton's law of motion to the celestial bodies, if we suppose them to be moved immediately by mind and not by bodily impulse. Your Lordship has my answer in what I have just said. It makes no difference with respect to the truth of this law, by what cause bodies are moved.

You intimate (P. 5) that I differ from *Dr Clark*, who thought that the motions of the celestial bodies could not be accounted for by one original impulse upon them without the constant agency of mind; and also from *Sir I. Newton*, who has said that *neither the beginning nor the continuance of motion can be accounted for otherwise than from an active principle*. But in this your Lordship has mistaken me. I agree entirely with Dr Clark in thinking that no original impulse will account for the motions of the planets without the action of gravity continually turning them out of their rectilineal direction; and gravity, as well as all the other active principles in nature, must, in my opinion, be derived either mediately or immediately from the power of the creator constantly exerted. This I have maintained with some zeal in my Dissertation on Providence.[2] When Newton says that neither the beginning not the continuance of motion in nature can be accounted for, except from the active principles in nature, he means that as (according to him) the quantity of motion in the world is always diminishing by the collisions of bodies, there must be active powers such as gravity, electricity etc., which keep it up; and these active principles, I also think with him, must be resolved into powers not mechanical.

In P. 9 your Lordship says that Sir Is. Newton must have supposed that the projectile motion of the planets is produced by bodily impulse. I cannot think that he supposed this; nor do I believe that he has said any thing that implies it. But *whatever cause* produced the projectile motion his first law of motion is *equally* applicable to it.

These remarks will shew your Lordship what reply I would make to those parts of your letters of which I take no explicit notice. Were I to reply to them in the manner to which I am inclined by the respect due to your Lordship, I should probably only make myself tiresome without being able to say any thing that your Lordship would think of much consequence. I will, however, just observe concerning space with which your Lordship's letter concludes, that tho' it may not be proper to call it either a *being* or a *mode of being* yet being (as your Lordship seems to acknowledge) *some what* that is *eternal, independent,*

---

1. Monboddo to R.P., 5 Feb. 1781.
2. See "On Providence", *Four Dissertations*. 4th ed. (London, 1777). In sections II and III (pp. 22–87), Price argues that the Creator exercises a continuous superintending influence upon his creation: "The cause from which the general laws that govern the material world are derived is, the immediate power of the Deity exerted everywhere." (p. 72.)

infinite and *necessary to the existence of everything*, it cannot, in my opinion, but be related to that nature whose attributes these are.

I have inclosed a sermon which I have lately published.[3] Will your Lordship be so good as to accept it merely as a token of respect? I did not think it worth the sending to you before publication.

Sir John Pringle[4] is lately removed to Edinburgh. Should he come in your way be so good as to deliver to him my very respectful remembrances. I have been very happy in his friendship.

Relying on your Lordship's candour, I am with great regard,

Your Lordship's most obedient and humble servant,

Rich*d* Price

---

3. Richard Price, *A Discourse addressed to a Congregation at Hackney on February 21, 1781*. See R.P. to William Adams, 19 Mar. 1781.

4. See Vol. I, 136.

From Lord Monboddo

8 June 1781

Dear Sir,

You have made me ample amends for your long silence by the Pamphlet,[1] which you have sent me. I heard of you in London as one of the sons of Party, that I was not very desirous to be acquainted with; but having read some of your Works upon Political Arithmetic, which I was much pleased with, I desired Dr Garthshore[2] to introduce me to you, which accordingly he did as you will remember. I thought I discovered by your conversation that you was not that tool of Party, which you had been represented to me; but I am now fully convinced you are not, by the sermon you have sent me, and by the Postscript you have added to it, containing some things that you had formerly published concerning the American War. I think you may say what Cicero says of himself, *Se nunquam de Republica nisi divine sensisse.*[3] You really have

---

ORIGINAL: National Library of Scotland.   PRINTED: Knight, pp. 181–85.   TEXT: Original, with the kind permission of the National Library of Scotland. The cover bears the following note: Letter/to/Dr Price/8 June 1781.

1. See R.P. to Monboddo [April, 1781]. The pamphlet was Price's *A Discourse addressed to a Congregation at Hackney on February 21, 1781*.

2. Maxwell Garthshore (1732–1812), physician. In 1764 after practising in Uppingham for eight years he settled in London where he acquired a large practice as an accoucheur. In the same year he graduated MD at Edinburgh (*D.N.B.*).

3. This passage presents several difficulties both as to the location of the passage in Cicero from which Monboddo quotes and as to the interpretation which he thought Dr Middleton gave of it. Monboddo appears to be quoting rather freely from *Letters to Atticus*, X, 4. In Ernesti's edition (Halis Saxonum, 1775, Vol. III, part 2, p. 823) the relevant passage reads: "Quum cogito de me republica aut meruisse optime, quum potuerim; aut certe numquam, nisi divine cogitasse." "Nisi

written of our affairs with the spirit of Divination (for that is the true meaning of the Passage in Cicero. tho' I see Dr Middleton[4] has mistaken it) and I am very sorry, and I am persuaded so are you, that you have been so true a prophet. But I will say no more of politics, of which I hate to speak, write, or even think.

I come now to Philosophy. I admire very much your ingenuity in maintaining the most violent paradox that ever was maintained by any Philosopher since the beginning of the world, that a Body once set in motion, will continue in motion for ever, that is, will continue to change its place an infinite number of times, by virtue of one impulse as slight as can be imagined given to it so many millions of years ago, without any other Cause moving it; and with this considerable addition, as I think, to the Paradox, that tho' the velocity of the motion will be affected by the greater or less violence of the impulse, that has not the least effect upon the duration of it. This Proposition, if it can be maintained, is the greatest triumph that ever was obtained by Philosophy over Common sense and the apprehensions of the vulgar; and it is also I think the greatest discovery, that has been made in modern times. I only wish that the Glory of it had belonged to our great Sir Isaac Newton, and not to the French Dreamer Des Cartes, who certainly invented it for a purpose that you will not approve of, to support his Mechannical Philosophy; for which I think it is absolutely necessary, but not at all necessary for Sir Isaac Newton's Astronomy, and directly contrary to Dr Clarke's notion of the Cause of the Motion of the Celestial Bodies, which he says is produced by the constant agency of Mind, and not by any original impulse. This I see you would apply only to one part of the combined motion of the Planets as you suppose it, viz. Gravitation; but certainly Dr Clarke's Words will not bear that meaning; for in the first place it does not appear to me that he supposed a Motion produced by the Agency of a single power, and that power Mind to be combined; and

---

divine" also occurs in an edition published by Nicolaus Ienson in Venice in 1470 and in Lallemand's edition published in Paris in 1768, whereas several modern editors, for example Winstedt (1953) and Shackleton Bailey (1961), read: "nisi pie". In claiming that Middleton's interpretation was mistaken Monboddo may have been referring to *The Life and Letters of Marcus Tullius Cicero* (London, 1840), p. 737, in which the relevant passage is translated: "When I reflect that I have either rendered the greatest services to my country when it was in my power; or certainly have never thought of it but with reverence." The difficulty with this conjecture however is that although the life of Cicero in this volume was contributed by Middleton, the letters were translated by Heberden. Alternatively, Monboddo may have been thinking of a passage in Middleton's *A Vindication of the Free Inquiry into the Miraculous Powers* in which the ascription to Polycarp of the power of divination is contrasted with Cornelius Nepos attributing Cicero's powers of foretelling the future to his prudence, and in which Middleton appears to prefer explanations of the latter kind to those which presuppose divine inspiration. See Conyers Middleton, *The Miscellaneous Works* (London, 1752), I, p. 311n.

4. Conyers Middleton (1683–1750). Educated at Trinity College, Cambridge, where he became a Fellow in 1706. His publications include *The History of the Life of Marcus Tullius Cicero* (1741) and *A Free Enquiry into the Miraculous Powers* (1749).

secondly if he had supposed it to be combined, he would certainly have distinguished as all the Newtonians now do, betwixt the two Motions, and said that the one Motion, viz. Gravitation, was produced by the Constant Agency of Mind, whereas the other of Projection was produced by an original impulse, instead of which he has said of the Motion in General that it is produced by the constant agency of Mind, and has denied expressly that it is produced by an Original impulse; and as to Sir Isaac Newton in his Queries, I have not the book before me at present, but I do not think that Sir Isaac is there speaking at all of the Decrease of Motion in the Universe; or if he were, you might acknowledge that he speaks much to[o] generally and very inaccurately upon the supposition of the truth of his first Law of Motion, when he says that by the *vis inertiae* alone, by which Bodies continue in their motion or rest, this continuance in Motion cannot be accounted for; which I think is giving up in so many words his first Law of Motion.

There is one argument you mention which I agree with you would be perfect Demonstration, if the enumeration upon which it was founded were compleat. You say that a Body in Motion cannot cease to move unless it be stopped either by itself, by another Body, or by Mind; therefore if it does not cease its Motion one or other of these ways, it must continue to move for ever. This would indeed, as you say, be demonstration, if there was not a fourth way by which a Body might cease to be moved but which you have not mentioned, viz. the ceasing of the moving power to act. And I think there is no more natural way of Motion ceasing; for as Body is by its nature absolutely inert and incapable of moving itself, which you admit, the consequence necessarily is that as soon as the moving power ceases to act, the Body ceases to be in Motion, and returns to its natural state of inertness. That this is the case when Mind moves Body I think we have dayly experience in the Motions of our own Bodies, for I have no Idea that our Mind stops our Bodies; nor indeed have I the least conception how an immaterial and unresisting substance can act in that way upon Bodies, but it makes their Motions cease by discontinuing its action upon them: and not only does Motion cease in that way when Mind moves the Body, but also when Body moves Body by trusion or Pressure; for as soon as the Pressure is withdrawn the Motion ceases. I think therefore that this kind of Motion by Body should be an exception to the general rule as well as the Motion by Mind.

I have two very ingenious friends in Edinburgh with whom I converse frequently on this subject, and who are as zealous as you for the honour of Sir Isaac, and of Modern Philosophy, and therefore desire very much to support this first Law of Motion. The one in answer to my argument from the Motion of our own Bodies denies that our Mind moves them, and in this I suppose your friend Dr Priestley will agree with him; but he goes farther than Dr Priestley, I believe, would be inclined to go, for he says that our Bodies move themselves and stop themselves; and indeed I have always thought that Sir

Isaac's first Law could not well be defended except upon the hypothesis of Body moving itself; and if we allow it to move itself, I think we cannot well deny it the power of likewise stopping itself. The other Gentleman foreseeing the Consequence of admitting that Motion by Pressure ceases when the Pressure Ceases, denies that there is any such thing as Motion by Pressure, *in vacuo*, but such Motion can only be where there is Friction or Resistance in the medium. Now I should be glad to know your opinion on this matter whether you are satisfied with the answer given by these two Gentlemen to my Arguments, or whether you think any better can be given.

[No signature]

To Joseph Willard[1]

London. July 21st 1781

Dear Sir,

I think myself much honoured by the favour of your letter dated the 28th of February last which I received about a month ago. I am made very happy by the information it contains that, in the midst of war and the most important struggle that a people were ever engaged in, a new Academy for promoting arts and sciences has been established at Boston. In compliance with your desire I have communicated the incorporating Act and list of members to the President and Secretaries of the Royal Society, attended with a letter of my own stating the contents of your letter to me, and the hopes which the American Academy entertains that the Royal Society, governed by the neutrality of Philosophy, will favour it with its encouragement. I do not yet know what notice will be taken of these communications. The reply that has been reported to me from the President is that it has not been customary to lay before the Royal Society notices of the institution of any societies whatever.

I am obliged to be cautious in communicating the inaugural oration of your honourable and worthy President[2] on account of some political passages in it. For my own part, I not only approve but admire these passages; and I request the favour of you to deliver my best respects to the author.

ORIGINAL: Collection of the American Academy of Arts and Sciences at the Boston Athenaeum (duplicate). PRINTED: *M.H.S.P.* (1909–10), 609. TEXT: Original with the kind permission of the American Academy of Arts and Sciences. The postscript in *M.H.S.P.* concludes with the following sentence which does not appear in the Boston Athenaeum MS: "A copy of this letter was sent by another conveyance."

1. Joseph Willard (1738–1804), classicist, mathematician, and astronomer. He served for several years as Corresponding Secretary and Vice–President of the American Academy of Arts and Sciences. Became President of Harvard in December 1781.

2. James Bowdoin, *A Philosophical Discourse, addressed to the American Academy of Arts and Sciences ... in the presence of a respectable audience assembled at the Meeting-house in Brattle Street in Boston, on the eighth of November M,DCC,LXXX, after the Inauguration of the President into office* (Boston, 1780).

I have deliver'd your letters to Dr Morell[3] and Mr Maskelyne.[4] I have have likewise got a Friend to communicate to the Society of Arts and Commerce the copy of the incorporating Act which you intended for them.

I am at present busy in preparing for the Press a 4th Edition of my Treatise on Life-Annuities and Reversionary payments. I shall enlarge it to two Volumes;[5] and when out of the Press (which I am afraid will not be till the beginning of next summer) I shall endeavour to get it convey'd to you in hopes of the honour of its being accepted as a testimony of my respect for the American Academy. This work having been of some use I am anxious about making it as complete as I can. With this view I am collecting all the observations I can get on population, the increase of mankind and the duration of human life in different situations.

All that can be worth communicating to you in the Philosophical and Astronomical way is published in the numbers of the Philosophical Transactions of the Royal Society which come out every half-year. What has lately most engaged attention is the new star discover'd near *Auriga* by Mr Herschel[5] a gentleman at Bath who has for sometime been very curious and diligent in watching the heavens. This star was at first taken for a comet; and the Astronomer Royal once expected that it would have passed over the disk of the Sun at the beginning of last month; but he has since told me that it is doubted whether it may not be a planet never before discover'd moving at a much greater distance from the Sun than Saturn. It has been for sometime hid by the Sun's rays. Should it appear again, something more certain will probably be determined concerning it.

Dr Priestley never went farther in his History of Philosophy than Electricity[6] and Optics.[7] He has been for some years wholly employ'd in making experiments on different sorts of air. In this branch of Philosophy he has made several very important discoveries, an account of which he has given in five Octavo volumes, the last published within this month.[8] One of the most important facts which he has discover'd is the effect of vegetation, aided by the action not of *heat* but of *light*, in purifying preserving and restoring common air constantly injured and diminished by the breathing of animals, the burning of fires, putrefaction, and other causes. In the day time, and particularly in sun

3. Thomas Morell (1703–84), Rector of Buckland, Hertfordshire. A distinguished classical scholar, he supplied the libretti for some of Handel's oratorios, including Judas Maccabeus. Elected FRS in 1768. In 1776 he published *Notes and annotations on Locke on the human understanding*.

4. Nevil Maskelyne, see Vol. I, 153.

5. Sir William Herschel (1738–1822), astronomer. The "new star" to which Price refers was in fact the planet Uranus; it was discovered on 13 Mar. 1781 (*Phil. Trans.*, LXXI, 492). Initially, Herschel intended to name the new planet Georgium Sidus. Elected FRS on 6 Dec. 1781.

6. *The History and Present State of Electricity*, see Vol. I, 37.

7. *The History and Present State of Discoveries relating to Vision, Light and Colours*, see Vol. I, 103.

8. Vol. 2 of *Experiments and Observations relating to Various Branches of Natural Philosophy*, and vol. 5 of *Observations on Different Kinds of Air*. See R.P. to Benjamin Franklin, 22 Dec. 1780.

shine, the purest kind of air is emitted by the leaves of trees and all vegetables; and this emission is more or less copious in proportion to the vigour of the vegetation and the force of the Sun's light. In the night and in the dark it entirely ceases. Dr Priestley is going on with these experiments, and very probably another volume will be published in a little time.

If you think that my best respects and wishes will be acceptable to the members of your Academy, I beg you would deliver them. No one can observe with a more earnest attention than I do all that is now passing in America. With much gratitude and the greatest regard I am,

Sir, your most obedient and humble servant,
Rich*d* Price

Deliver my very respectful remembrances to the venerable Dr Chauncy. Dr Winthrop *was* my correspondent. With pain, I think, that he is no more in this world to promote virtue and science. But we are all following him. God grant that we may leave the world wiser and better for us.

To Lord Monboddo

Newington=Green Aug*t* 6*th* 1781

My Lord,

Having been lately in a state of health and spirits that has been rather languid, I have been advised to go to the seaside for a change of scene and air. I am, therefore, preparing to go for Brighthelmstone, where I intend to stay till some time in next month; but I cannot set out without first acknowledging the favour of your Lordship's letter,[1] and sending you the remarks which have occurred to me on some passages in it. I still think that when Dr Clark says that the motion of the planets is produced by the constant agency of the Deity he means only their curvilineal motion, or their motion in their orbits, which certainly could not be produced by any original single impulse or projection without the constant action of gravity, which gravity he makes to be the agency of the Deity.

I cannot find, that Sir Isaac Newton has any where asserted that by the *vis inertiae* alone the continuance of bodies in motion cannot be accounted for. Had he said this, he would indeed, as you say, have given up his first law of motion. All he could mean is, that the continuance of motion in the Universe cannot be thus accounted for, on account of the many causes which are continually diminishing it.

ORIGINAL: The National Library of Scotland. PRINTED: Knight, pp. 185–87. TEXT: Original, with the kind permission of the National Library of Scotland.

1. See Monboddo to R.P., 8 June 1781.

The proposition which your Lordship represents as a triumph over common sense and the most violent paradox that was ever started, namely, that a body once in motion will for ever continue in motion till some cause stops it, appears to me no more a paradox than the proposition, that a body once at rest will for ever continue at rest till some cause moves it. Both amount to no more than that an effect once produced will for ever remain till some cause destroys it; and this I look upon as one of the fundamental principles of human knowledge.

I have said that if a body in motion is stop'd it must be stopp'd either by itself, or by the impulse of other matter or by some spiritual agency; and that consequently if none of these causes operate it must go on moving for ever. To this you answer, that there is another cause which may stop it; and that is, the *ceasing* of the action of the power that moves it. The reply I shall make seems to me clear and decisive. The stopping of motion once produced requires, like all other effects, some *action* or the positive exertion of some power. But the *ceasing* of action is not action; and it would be a contradiction to say that it can do anything, for it would be the same with saying that a power acts when it ceases to act, or that a body may be stopp'd, not by any action upon it, but by the negation of action. Upon the whole, it seems wonderful to me that it should be possible there should be any difference between us on this point. It has a tendency to teach me the utmost candour with respect to those who differ from me in other instances the most widely, and to impress me with a deep sense of the frailty of our faculties.

As for *trusion*,[2] it differs in nothing from *impulse*. It is only a succession or repetition of impulses either to accelerate motion, or to overcome some resistance that is continually destroying motion after it has been produced; and, therefore, your friend who at the conclusion of your Lordship's letter you say asserts that there can be no such thing as trusion in *vacuo* (except to accelerate) appears to me to be very right. The assertion of your other Friend, that our bodies move and stop themselves is quite unintelligible to me. Certainly our bodies cease to move after the action of the will ceases only in consequence of some resistance they meet with.

Accept my best thanks for the candour with which your Lordship speaks of me at the beginning of your letter. Nothing indeed can be more unjust than to charge me with being a tool of party. But I am willing to submit to such censures having a consciousness in my own breast that makes me insensible to them.

Wishing you, My Lord, all happiness I am, with great respect,

Your Lordship's most obedient and humble servant
Rich*d* Price

---

2. The action of pushing or thrusting (*O.E.D*).

Should Sir John Pringle ever come in your way deliver my very respectful remembrances to him; and should you favour me with another letter inform me, if you easily can, how he is.

To the Earl of Shelburne

Newington=Green Aug 6th 1781

My Lord,

   Having been advised lately to go to the seaside for the sake of the benefit of the sea air and sea bathing, I am to set out tomorrow for Brighthelmstone where I intend to stay till some time in September; but I feel that I shall be much easier there in consequence of having first writ to your Lordship to express my respect and gratitude. I have received the pine=apples which your Lordship has order'd me, and think with pleasure of these tokens of your remembrance of me. My nephew[1] informs me from Norwich that Lord Fitzmaurice did him the honour to call upon him about a fortnight ago, and that he admired much his agreeable manners. Every thing was shewn him that could be seen, and instruction given him in every branch of the manufactory; Mr Morgan's friends, he says, being so eager in their civilities to him as to make him fearful he must have found them troublesome. My nephew adds perhaps too warmly that he reflects with pain that so fine a young man should be under a necessity of finishing his education in an university which is only another name for a nursery of folly and wickedness; there being, in his opinion, few greater evils in this kingdom than that dissipation, folly and vice should have usurped the places where virtue, discipline and science should reign. He supposes that Lord Fitzmaurice may have informed you what melancholy scenes the manufacturing houses in Norwich now are. Their mills, he tells me, are rotting for want of employment, and only a few scatter'd people to be seen where formerly multitudes were busy and happy; twenty empty looms to one that is in motion, and not a crowd to be seen save in the workhouses, the last refuge of idleness, want and distress.

   We have in London been alarmed lately by several considerable bankruptcies. The debts of Mr Marler[2] (a West=India merchant who has suffer'd much by the capture of St Eustatius) amount to £300,000. Mr Peach[3]

ORIGINAL: Bowood.   TEXT: Original, with the kind permission of the Marquis of Lansdowne.
   1. George Cadogan Morgan.
   2. John Marlar, a merchant in Iremonger Lane, London. His bankruptcy was reported in *Gent. Mag.*, LI (1781), 396 and 492.
   3. Samuel Peach, a merchant in Bread Street, London. His bankruptcy too was reported in *Gent. Mag.*, LI (1781), 492.

also and Mr Roberts[4] (two East=India Directors) are broken for considerable sums. A third East=India Director is just broken whose name I cannot learn; and it is feared that more bankruptcies will follow. Some of my friends are likely to suffer by Mr Peach. He has been a foolish and venal man; and had, it is said, made a bargain with Lord North who was to introduce him to Parliament next winter. He made two grand entertainments every week, one at his house in town, and another at his country house; and a little before he broke had begun driving with his coach and four. He has been lately supporting himself by what they call accommodation paper; and his stopping has been partly occasioned by the refusal of the Bank to discount this paper. There is reason, however, to apprehend that the Bank has been too partial to some of these bankrupts; for Mr Marler, I am told, owes them near £100,000. Support by accommodation paper has been always a neverfailing forerunner of ruin; and is not this at present too much the support of the kingdom itself?

Many people are disposed to look upon the failures among the East=India Directors as a prelude to the failure of the company itself. Affairs, indeed, in the East Indies look very dark. The same is true of our affairs almost everywhere and our ministers seem at present to have nothing to console then except that they are doing infinite mischief in Virginia. A letter from Amsterdam tells me,[5] that it will not be found *in the end* that the Dutch are such a low people as we represent them; and that it is certain that at least the majority of the people would not now easily make up the quarrel with us. Mr Smith has called upon me with your Lordship's note, and I reckon myself much obliged to him for his civility. Deliver my best respects to Lady Shelburne. May she and you enjoy all possible happiness. With many thanks for your Lordship's kind attention and candour I am your Lordship's obliged and most obedient servant

Rich*d*Price

Mrs Price presents her very respectful compliments to Lady Shelburne and your Lordship.

Since writing this letter I have been told that Mr Roberts's affairs are likely to be made up without a bankruptcy, and that the report of the bankruptcy of a third East=India director is a mistake. Mr Peach, it is said, has for some years carried on little or no trade, and his principal business has been coining and negotiating fictitious bills. Mr Jarvis's[6] Brother was one of his clerks.

I have heard it said, but I don't know how truly, that Lord North's indisposition is a stroke of the palsy.

---

4. John Roberts, a contractor, had been since 1779 a partner in the firm of James, Smith, Roberts and Atkinson. He was a director of the East India Company, and in 1777 was Chairman of the Court of Directors (Baker, pp. 34, 219, 220). Tried, unsuccessfully, to enter Parliament as a member for the City of London in 1773 and 1774 (Namier and Brooke, I, 329).

5. Probably from D. Neufville and Son, see R.P. to [John Temple], 7 Aug. 1781.

6. i.e. Thomas Jervis.

To [John Temple]

Dear Sir,

I have been lately very glad to hear by Mr H[artley] and Mr [Parker] of your safe arrival at Amsterdam. You intend, I find, to return as soon as you can to America. May you be blest with a prosperous voyage and a happy meeting with Mrs Temple[1] and your friends. I was favoured a few weeks ago with a letter from Mr Willard, the corresponding Secretary of the American Academy of Arts and Sciences. I have inclosed as answer to it which I beg the favour of you to deliver.[2] Will you be so good also as to deliver my best respects to Mr Bowdoin and Dr Chauncy. I have writ to the latter more than once since your arrival in England. Tell him that I truly venerate him, and am waiting with great anxiety for the issue of the present war. God grant it may terminate in the advancement of the interests of truth and liberty, and the *reformation* rather than *ruin* of this country. Be so good also as to convey my gratitude to Dr G[ordo]n for a letter I lately received from him. He is indeed very kind to me, and I derive much instruction from his letters. It is not possible for me at present to write to him. Were I to write, it would be only to thank him, and to express my wishes of his happiness, and this I hope you will be so good as to do for me.

I received last week some lines from Mr De N[eufvi]lle which gave me great pleasure. Deliver my very respectful compliments to father and son. I can hardly tell them how much satisfaction their civility and good opinion give me. Remember me also with great regard to Mr Tr[umbul]l,[3] if now at Amsterdam. He was exceeding kind in calling upon me before he left this country. I think with much pleasure of the share of your company and attention which you allowed me while in L[ondo]n. Accept, Dear Sir, of the best wishes of your obliged and very obedient servant

Rich*d* Price

I am just now sett[ing out] with all my family for Brighthelmston to enjoy there for some weeks the benefit of sea-air and sea-bathing. I have writ this, therefore, in a great hurry.

ORIGINAL: Massachusetts Historical Society.   TEXT: Original, with the kind permission of the Massachusetts Historical Society.

   1. Elizabeth Temple (née Bowdoin). See Charles Chauncy to R.P., 20 May 1779.

   2. R.P. to Joseph Willard, 21 July 1781.

   3. John Trumbull. See R.P. to [John Temple], 18 Sept. 1780. On his release from Tothill Fields he went to Amsterdam to negotiate a loan for Connecticut with De Neufville and Son.

To Sir Charles Gould[1]

Newington Green Dec. 17. 1781

Sir,

I have received with much pleasure your obliging letter; and I feel very sensibly the favourable manner in which you and the Directors and Members of the Equitable Society for Assurances on Lives and Survivorships are pleased to receive my endeavours to serve them. No one can rejoice more than I do in the prosperous state of the Society, or wish more to promote its usefulness and stability. The new tables[2] by which its business is for the future to be conducted will contribute greatly to this end; and, together with the advantage it enjoys in being honoured with so excellent a President, will probably soon raise it to the highest credit, and render it an object of particular importance to this Kingdom.

ORIGINAL: General Court Meetings Minute Book, 18 Dec. 1781, Equitable Life Assurance Society. TEXT: Original, with the kind permission of the Equitable Life Assurance Society.

1 Sir Charles Gould (1726–1806), after 16 Nov. 1792 known as Sir Charles Morgan. Married Jane, daughter of Thomas Morgan of Tredegar in 1758. Appointed Judge Advocate General in 1771. MP for Brecon (1779–87) and Breconshire (1787–1806). Knighted in 1779 and created a baronet in 1792. For many years he was closely associated with the Equitable Life Assurance Society, becoming its President in 1773, a position which he held until his death (Ogborn, 98, 138–41).

2. One of the more important contributions Price made to the development of life assurance in general and to the prosperity of the Equitable Life Assurance Society in particular lay in the construction of the Northampton Tables of Mortality. He had drawn attention to the need for these tables in the introduction he contributed to William Morgan's *The Doctrine of Annuities and Assurances on Lives and Survivorships Stated and Explained* (London, 1779). At this time Morgan was Actuary to the Equitable. The Northampton tables were based on the bills of mortality for the parish of All Saints in Northampton, initially for the period 1735–70, and subsequently including also the years 1771–80. Equipped with these, William Morgan and his assistant, Thomas Cooper, spent the better part of the year 1781 preparing sets of tables which exhibited the values of different annuities and assurances. On 5 Dec. 1781, Sir Charles Gould reported to the General Court of the Society that he had presented these sets of tables to Price for his inspection and approval, and that Price had examined them and certified his approbation. The Court then asked the President to thank Price on their behalf. Gould did so, and received in reply the letter which is published here, and which he communicated to the General Court on 18 Dec. 1781. On 20 Dec. the General Court further resolved that Price be requested to accept some form of present as a testimony of their respect and of their gratitude for the many services which he had rendered on this and on other occasions. Gould apparently had some difficulty in persuading Price to accept a present at all, for on 17 Jan. 1782 he had to report to the General Court that he had not been able to get him to indicate what form of present would be acceptable. At the same time he asked permission to offer Price a hundred guineas, a present which was eventually accepted. See Ogborn, pp. 110–11, and Minutes of the General Court Meeting of the Equitable Life Assurance Society.

Under a grateful sense of your kind attention, and with great respect, I am, Sir

> Your most obedient and humble servant,
> Richard Price

To Per Wilhelm Wargentin[1]

Newington=Green near London Dec 24*th* 1781

Sir,

In addressing these lines to you I am afraid that I am taking an improper liberty. I must, therefore, refer myself to your candour, in hopes that you will not be unwilling to excuse me. My Friend Mr Howard[2] is just returned to *London* after employing the summer in visiting the prisons in *Sweden, Denmark, Russia* &c. When at *Petersburgh* he wrote to Mr *Keene* at *Stockholm*, and sent him a letter he had received from me requesting that an application might be made to you for information with respect to the Bills of Mortality in *Sweden*, in consequence of which I understand that you have been so obliging as to tell Mr *Keene* that papers containing this information shall be convey'd to *London* in January next. I write this to express my gratitude to you for your readiness to oblige Mr Howard and me in this instance, and also to acquaint you that what has led me to make this application to you is the particular instruction which I have derived from a memoir of yours in a collection of the Memoirs of the Royal Academy of Sciences at *Stockholm* published at Paris in 1772. The accounts in this memoir, and the Observations on human mortality in your country are more curious than any I have ever met with; and *Sweden* in this instance enjoys an advantage and distinction which are peculiar to itself. I cannot help, therefore, feeling myself very happy in the prospect of being favoured by you with a continuation of these accounts; but I wish to give you as

---

ORIGINAL: Kungl. Vetenskapakademiens Bibliotek, Stockholm. PRINTED: N.V.E. Nordenmark, *P. W. Wargentin* (Uppsala, 1939), 261. TEXT: Original with the kind permission of the Vetenskapakademiens Bibliotek, Stockholm.

1. Per Wilhelm Wargentin (1717–83), the Swedish demographer. In his paper to the Royal Society entitled "Observations on the difference between the duration of human life in towns and in country parishes and villages", (*Phil. Trans.*, LXV, 424–45) Price paid a special tribute to Wargentin's work. He had used Wargentin's mortality tables extensively, "because they fully verify most of the observations in the preceding paper, and contain more distinct and authentic information in the subject of human mortality than I have ever before met with." This information Price derived from a memoir on the state of the population in Sweden which had been published in Stockholm in 1766, translated into French by de Keralio, and published in *Mémoires de l'Académie Royale des Sciences de Stockholm* (Paris, 1772).

2. John Howard, see Vol. I, 92. On his many travels Howard was of considerable help to Price in the collection of data on demographical and other matters.

little trouble as possible. The particulars of one or two of the last enumerations of *Sweden* and Stockholm; the Births, Burials and marriages; the numbers of males and females living at every period of life, together with the ages at which all have died for the last seven or eight years, would satisfy my curiosity. But should an account of these particulars be more than can be easily obtained, *any* account of such of them as you may think proper to communicate will be very gratefully received.

I am the more sollicitous about this, because now employ'd in calculating Tables of the values of annuities on lives from the accounts in your memoir. These Tables I am to insert in my Treatise on Reversionary payments published some years ago. There is now a demand for a fourth edition of this Treatise; and having been of use in this kingdom, I wish to make it as complete as possible.[3]

Permit me, Sir, to assure you of my best wishes and particular respect. Hoping that you will not be displeased with me for giving you this trouble I am

Your most obedient and humble servant

Richard Price

Should you favour me with any communications they may be directed to be left for me at the Office for Assurances on Lives and Survivorships[4] near Black=Fryars Bridge London.

---

3. *Observations on Reversionary Payments*. For details of the information supplied by Wargentin which Price included in the fourth (1783) edition of this work, see R.P. to Per Wilhelm Wargentin, 9 June 1783.

4. i.e. The Equitable Assurance Society, now the Equitable Life Assurance Society.

To Benjamin Franklin

Newington=Green Jan*y* 7*th* 1782

Dear Sir,

The Bearer of this is the son of a widow [Mrs Curtould] who belongs to my congregation at Hackney. He is going over to Am[eri]ca not intending to return; and *any* notice that you may be so good as to take of him will be well bestowed and gratefully received.

I rejoyce heartily in the security which an object which has been long a favourite one with me, seems lately to have received; but wishing ardently for the liberty happiness and independence of both countries, and indeed of every

---

ORIGINAL: American Philosophical Society. TEXT: Original, with the kind permission of the American Philosophical Society.

country under heaven I lament that lust of power and tenaciousness of dominion which still influence the councils of this country, and seem to threaten the continuance of a destructive and cruel war.

I heard with pleasure not long ago that you are well. May your usefulness be continued and as many year added to your life as are consistent with its happiness. Sir John Pringle is breaking fast, and not likely to live long. The society of Whigs at the L[ondo]n Coff[ee Taver]n continue the same, and never meet without drinking your health. I can never forget the many happy hours which in better times we have spent together.

With all possible good wishes and the greatest regard and affection, I am, my dear Friend,

ever yours
R P

If Dr B[ancrof]t is with you deliver my respects to him I have heard with great concern of the death of Mr Turgott. Mr Lawrens[1] was discharged last week, and yesterday went for *Bath*, his health having been much impaired by his confinement and sufferings.

In July last *Heckingham* Workhouse in *Norfolk* was fired and in danger of being destroy'd by lightening tho' defended by eight pointed conductors each above half an inch in Diameter and continued without interruption to a *drain*. Mr Wilson[2] triumphs in this fact, and has carried it lately to his convert the King, and to the board of Ordnance; in consequence of which this board, apprehensive of danger to the magazine at Purfleet from the pointed conductors there, has again apply'd to the Royal Society for advice; and a Committee is just appointed by the Society to examine into the facts. The lightening did not appear to have enter'd at the points; but, avoiding them, struck into the building within a few yards of one of them. A similar event happen'd sometime ago at *Purfleet*. These events have a tendency to discredit conductors; but Mr Wilson's triumph seems improper, because there is no reason for believing the same or worse would not have happened had the conductors been blunt.

---

1. Henry Laurens.
2. Benjamin Wilson, see Vol. I, 38. He conducted a long controversy with Benjamin Franklin on the question whether lightning conductors should be round or pointed at the top; he favoured the former, Franklin the latter. Wilson was elected FRS in 1751, and awarded the Copley medal in 1760. See *The Papers of Benjamin Franklin*, IV, 391n.

Re John Vaughan[1]

Newington Green Jany. 10 1782

I concur entirely with Dr Priestley in the Account he has given in this paper of the family of Mr J. Vaughan which I have long loved and honoured as one of the worthiest in the Country. Mr J. Vaughan in particular I believe to be what Dr Priestley has represented him and the opinion I have of his unexceptionable character and attachment to civil and Religious liberty, together with the Respect I bear his excellent parents interest me deeply in his happiness and make me wish that I could by this declaration recommend him to the notice and friendship of any worthy persons.

Rich*d* Price

ORIGINAL: Madeira—John Vaughan MSS, Vaughan Papers, William L. Clements Library, The University of Michigan, Ann Arbor.   TEXT: Original, with the kind permission of the William L. Clements Library.

1. John Vaughan (1756–1841), son of Samuel Vaughan (see Vol. I, 87). He entered Warrington Academy in 1771. In 1782 he settled in Philadelphia as a merchant and a land speculator, taking with him, as this note indicates, letters of introduction from Joseph Priestley and Price. He was a luminary of the American Philosophical Society, to which he was elected in 1784 becoming Secretary (1789–91). Treasurer (1791–1841) and Librarian (1803–41) He was a Unitarian preacher. See Rutt, I, 59; Schofield, pp. 371–72; *Mon. Rep.*, IX, 390; and *Catalogue of Portraits...in the possession of the American Philosophical Society* (Philadelphia, 1961), 95–96.

To the Earl of Shelburne

Chatham Square M*ch* 26*th* 1782

My Lord,

Having had long experience of your Lordship's candour, and being anxious to improve the present moment, I take the liberty to offer to your consideration the following sentiments on the subject of the new administration which your Lordship is now employ'd in arranging.[1]

The leaders of the late opposition have made great promises. They have led the public to expect that the new administration will be a strong administration into which will be collected all the ability and integrity that can be got

ORIGINAL: Bowood.   TEXT: With the kind permission of the Marquis of Lansdowne.

1. In Rockingham's ministry which was formed on 27 Mar. 1782, Shelburne became Secretary of State for Home and the Colonies.

without regarding any other qualifications. They have declared in the warmest language against the *American* and *Dutch* wars, the extravagance that has prevailed in the expenditure of public money, the enormous influence of the crown, and that system of corruption by which our late ministers have supported themselves. This has raised the expectations of the people high; and they now think they see the dawnings of peace at home and abroad, of Oeconomy in our finances and virtue in our councils. By former oppositions they have been grievously disappointed; and should they be disappointed on the present occasion there will be an end of all confidence, in public men; no credit will be hereafter given to any pretensions to patriotism, and the new ministers will be more detested than the old.

So distracted is the state of our affairs, and so great are the difficulties to be encounter'd, that the courage of new ministers in being willing, from a desire to save the nation, to take the direction of affairs and to expose themselves to the consequences of a mischief done by others, cannot be sufficiently admired. In my humble opinion the only plan on which such persons can come into office with the least danger to themselves and the most advantage to the public is the following.

Their first object should be to secure the *salvation* of the country by a *general* Peace. In order to accomplish this, it is indeed necessary that the nation should be *let down* and some humiliating concessions made. *France* yielded to this at the end of the last war, and has since recover'd itself. The same, I hope, may happen to Britain. But, in our present circumstances, with a load of debt so heavy, taxes so multiplied, and resources so strained, it is impossible to continue the war much longer without producing either total ruin or a horrid convulsion by which the men then in power will be the greatest sufferers. I have mentioned a *General Peace*, because I am persuaded that the notion of the possibility of a *separate* peace with *America* is a sad delusion.

Secondly. In order to a general peace the first thing necessary is the acknowledgement of the independence of America.[2] I mention this with pain; nor can I enough regret the difference of opinion between us about it. So different are our opinions in this instance, that what your Lordship reckons a calamity will, I think, be a blessing to America, to us and to the world. There is no worse slavery than the subjection of countries to one another. I wish, therefore, all the countries upon earth independent, and bound to one another by no other ties than alliances founded on mutual benefits and render'd firm by a common interest. When this war is over the colonies will be at liberty to enter into an alliance with us, and they will rejoyce in a family compact which will give us greater advantages than can be derived from any dominion over them. The shadow of dominion, or a dependence merely nominal cannot surely be worth

---

2. See R.P. to Shelburne, 21 Mar. 1778 (Vol. I, 273–75) in which Price urged upon Shelburne the wisdom of concluding a peace and recognizing the independence of America.

the struggling for. It would be no less foolish than cruel to spend money or to spill blood to obtain it.

Thirdly. Something should by all means be done to purify the fountain of legislation among us, and to reform the representation of the kingdom. The opposition has pledged itself for this, and it cannot I suppose be omitted. The Bill for restricting the civil list, the exclusion of Contractors from the House of Commons and depriving Revenue officers of votes at elections will not be sufficient to satisfy the public. The representation of the kingdom is little better than a mockery. Let new men give us a *real* represent[at]ion. This is the grand reformation we want, and this is the time for accomplishing it. If it is put off to a time of tranquility, it will never be done. The people of Ireland are now acting under this conviction; and new ministers, instead of opposing them, ought to assist them, and to grant them all they want to render their constitution of government as well as their trade perfectly free.

Should new ministers act on this plan and *succeed*, they will fix themselves in the hearts of the friends of humanity and liberty and make themselves objects of the admiration of future ages. Should they *attempt* it and *fail*, they will enjoy a satisfaction greater than any the emoluments of power can give in the approbation of their own minds and in the grateful esteem of all the honest and worthy part of the nation.

Such, My Lord, are my sentiments in this hour of general expectation and hope. I have no favour to ask, except that you would, with your usual goodness, excuse the liberty I have taken in sending them to you. Perhaps I have been too presumptuous. Your Lordship has in your own mind and in your excellent friends Colonel Barre[3], Mr Dunning [4] &c much abler advisers. I have the honour to be, with great respect, your Lordship's

most obedient and humble servant,
Rich*d* Price

I have written this letter this morning in some haste. On reviewing it I feel pain least I should be thought to act impertinently but the attention and friendship by which your Lordship has always done me great honour encourages me to resolve to send it; and I shall call soon in hopes of finding that your Lordship is not offended.

A West=India merchant from the City has this moment called upon me and informed me that Nevis, Montserrat, and St Kitts are taken and that Sir Samuel Hood[5] has retired to Antigua.

---

3. Isaac Barré, see Vol. I, 146.
4. John Dunning, see Vol. I, 146.
5. Sir Samuel Hood (1724–1816) had been appointed in 1780 to a command sent out to reinforce Rodney in the West Indies. Price's informant may have been referring to the retreat from Basseterre on St Christopher's on 13 Feb. 1782.

To the Earl of Shelburne

Chatham=Square Ap:3d 1782

My Lord,

   I begin to fear that the event by which so many are now gainers, and which, I hope, is likely to be a blessing to the nation will prove a loss to me by depriving me of an intercourse from which I have for many years derived much pleasure. I have called at different times at Shelburne=house, but found your Lordship so engaged, that it would have been very improper for a person who

---

ORIGINAL: Bowood.   TEXT: Original, with the kind permission of the Marquis of Lansdowne. An earlier draft, now in the Bodleian, was written on 2 Apr. 1782. I have printed the final version, the changes from the first draft being as follows (the final draft being quoted first):

line
2   begin to fear/begin to be afraid
     event/change
4   from which...pleasure/which has for many years given great pleasure
5   but found ... himself/but found that it would be very improper to intrude myself
7   My chief design was...sent/My chief business was to remove the anxiety I have felt about
     the letter I sent to your Lordship
10   your success/your Lordship's success
13   Some of my acquaintance/Some persons
     presuming ... think/presuming on the interest they suppose
14   by their/with
17   conveying to your Lordship/conveying
20   desired/requested
     Friends/of my Friends
21   able/ ingenious
22   some shocking/the shocking
     Ordnance/Board of Ordnance
28   in abuse ... friendship/in abuse and many unjust imputations, but disdaining all preten-
     tions to any advantage for myself or connexions from the power your Lordship now possesses,
     I hope I may be allow'd to give my opinions of the manner in which it ought to be employ'd
     for the public advantage, without giving offence or losing the regard and attention with which
     your Lordship has hitherto honoured me.

The composition of this letter evidently caused Price a great deal of anxiety, as may be seen from the difficulty he had in writing it, particularly in deciding what to say in the last paragraph. On the MS of the first draft he jotted the following notes in shorthand:

   I hope it cannot be considered unreasonable in me to wish that notwithstanding the distance between us, I may still retain a place in your Lordship's regard and estimation.
   That the regard and estimation with which your Lordship has hitherto honoured me may be continued.
   Having shared largely with your Lordship in abuse and submitted to some hard imputations I hope it will not be thought unreasonable in me to request that now your Lordship is possessed of power I may not be denied a small recompense I ask. I mean that I may be allowed the liberty to convey to your Lordship sometimes my ideas on public points and public matters, and that as long as I do not impute to you ... and that our differences of opinion and the increased distance between us may remove me from the place I have hitherto held in your Lordship's attention.

had no particular business to intrude himself. My chief design was to satisfy myself whether I had offended your Lordship by the letter I sent on tuesday in last week,[1] and also to express my wishes of your success and happiness in the office on which you are enter'd.

Some of my acquaintance, presuming too much on the interest they think I have with your Lordship have distress'd me by their sollicitations; but nothing shall engage me to add to the trouble which *suitors* now give your Lordship. There is, I hope, nothing inconsistent with this resolution in conveying to your Lordship the inclosed paper. It comes from two wine=merchants one of whom I am intimately acquainted with. It should have been sent to the Treasury; but I am desired to put it into your Lordship's hands. Another Friend (Mr Blackbourn a very able surveyor)[2] seems to wish for an opportunity of giving an account of some shocking abuses in the Ordnance office. But having had no communication with the Duke of Richmond[3] for a long time, I know not how to mention this to him.

Mr Pepys tells me he has called at Shelburne=house, and I have promised to inform your Lordship that he wishes for an opportunity of paying his compliments to you.

Having shared largely with your Lordship in abuse and submitted to some hard imputations I hope it cannot be thought unreasonable in me to request that, now your Lordship is possessed of power, I may not be deny'd the only recompense I ask for, I mean, that I may be allowed the liberty of conveying to your Lordship, when I may think it necessary, my Ideas on public points and public measures; and that our differences of opinion and the increased distance between us may not remove me from the place I have hitherto held in your Lordship's friendship.

With great respect I am your Lordship's most obedient and Humble servant

Rich*d* Price

---

1. See R.P. to Shelburne, 26 Mar. 1782.

2. William Blackburn (1750–90), surveyor and architect. In 1781 the Commission which was appointed to advise on the administration of the 1779 Act for the provision of penitential houses, and which included Sir Gilbert Elliott, Sir Charles Bunbury and Thomas Bowdler, gave Blackburn a prize for the plans for a penitentiary. Blackburn was subsequently appointed architect and surveyor.

3. See Vol. I, 130.

From George Jeffery

Reverend Sir,

Presuming as well as hoping that you will be consulted on the subject of the Publick Finances, I take the liberty of suggesting to you an idea which I have long had respecting the Public Expenditure, which tho foreign to the department that you will be so useful in, yet as you are so connected with the heads of the different Offices, if you approve my Plan and think proper you can communicate it to them, particularly to the Duke of Richmond.

The thing is simply this, that all Publick Contracts should be paid in ready money, that is by Issuing paper, not payable by any certain time, but always provision to be made for the payment within the Year, the paper bearing interest at 5 per cent from the day it is issued, and allowing the Contractor the Discount which the said paper would be at in the Market on that day which in fact is paying the Contractor in Ready Money.

I know it will be urged that such a quantity of paper in the Market will increase the Discount but if Government take care to pay it off within the Year the Discount will be very moderate, which they may as well do as keep an unfunded debt so long; and I think it matters not what the Discount is for Government must pay it first or last, either in the Discount or in the prices of the Contracts and if in the latter case, as it is now, with an immense additional profit to the Contractor to secure him from a possible loss.

The advantage of such a scheme appears to me to be very great to the Publick, as every Contractor would then know for a certainty his profit, and would be in that certain state of Payment content with a very moderate profit, as I should hope in the present reform, all Contracts would be open and for a short duration and be advertised as the Navy Contracts generally are. One thing, I have to observe on that subject that the tenders given in should never be suffer'd to be amended, but that the different Boards should always either accept of the first lowest offer or reject them all.

This scheme of allowing the Discount is sometimes done in the Navy Contracts for Hemp and I cannot see why it should not be universally adopted. The Idea first struck me in a case of my own, some time ago, an Ordnance Contractor applied to me for a parcel of Goods but could give me no other payment than ordnance Debentures, as my Trade is [kept] at a small profit for ready money or a short Credit. I at first declined the order as being contrary to my mode of business, but being pressed to make a price in proportion to the length of Credit, I did it and sold the Goods, tho it was at such an

---

ORIGINAL: Bowood. TEXT: Original, with the kind permission of the Marquis of Lansdowne.

exorbitant profit I was ashamed to ask it. However I found I was still lower than other People.

I am told that the Ordnance paper cannot now be disposed of even at 30 per cent Discount. What are Contractors to do!

The Navy is not so bad, but still in that as well as every other office, if this Method was to be adopted, I cannot help thinking that a prodigious saving would be made.

If you are of my opinion and think it worth attention I shall be very happy; if not, I am persuaded I shall meet with your approbation in having made an effort to serve the Publick.

Permit me, Sir, to congratulate you on the happy change in the affairs of this Country and to thank you for the considerable part you have had in it, by your steady attachment to the cause and by the excellent advice and information you have so frequently given.

I am with the greatest respect

Reverend Sir,
Your Most Obedient Servant
George Jeffery

To Mr Brown[1]

Newington=Green Apl 20th, 1782

Dear Sir,

I am sorry I cannot give the information you desire in the letter with which you have favoured me and which I received last night. I do not know where Mr Laurens is at present. He has been for some time out of town, and, I believe, is so still. I shall probably hear of him when he returns, and I will take care to inform you as soon as I know myself. Deliver my kind respects to Mrs Brown.

I am with sincere regard, your obliged and very obedient and humble

servant
Rich<i>d</i> Price

ORIGINAL: Mr Derek Hartley Russell.   ADDRESS: Mr Brown, No: 35 Grace=Church=Street (in Price's hand).   TEXT: Original, with the kind permission of Mr Derek Hartley Russell.

1. Possibly Isaac Hawkins Browne.

To the Earl of Shelburne

Newington=Green Ap: 24th, 1782

My Lord,

I have been requested to convey to your Lordship the inclosed letter.[1] It contains an account of a gross violation of the freedom of Election at Yarmouth, and is signed with the names of several respectable gentlemen and merchants of credit and character who reside there and some of whom I am acquainted with. They confide in the virtue of the present administration, and this has encouraged them to make the representation contained in this letter.

I have the honour to be your Lordship's
most obedient and humble servant
Rich*d* Price

ORIGINAL: Bowood. TEXT: Original, with the kind permission of the Marquis of Lansdowne.

1. The enclosed letter complained of the power which the Townshend–Walpole group derived from the exercise of patronage in the Corporation of Yarmouth and sought Shelburne's help to break it. Similar representations were made to Shelburne by George Walker, to Rockingham through Lord Chedworth and to Fox through William Windham. See R.P. to Shelburne, 21 May 1782. For a detailed account of this complaint see Ian R. Christie, "Great Yarmouth and the Yorkshire Reform Movement," *Myth and Reality* (London, 1970), pp. 284–95.

From Henry Laurens

Dover 14th May 1782

The Rev'd Dr Price,

You will recollect, my Dear Sir, that I was to have devoted last Friday Evening to reading the papers which you had put into my [hands in] the [morning], the same Evening I received the additional favor from you of a Note and present of your pamphlets, but being surrounded by Visitors could not turn away without breach of hospitality and good Manners it was impracticable for me to read that night, my friends detained me to my usual bedtime. I was fatigued broke down body and Mind and obliged in the first Moment of respite to fly to the pillow as well to seek repose as to escape. [ ] the next Morning was unavoidably engaged in Visits [ ] these were not finished 'till near 3 o Clock, from that time I had work enough to adjust [ ] accounts, force thro a Crowd, and to begin my journey when the Sun had nearly finished his. All that day I honestly confess Dr Price's papers safe in my pocket were out of

---

ORIGINAL: Mrs Henry P. Kendall's Collection of Laurens Papers, Massachusetts Historical Society. TEXT: Original, with the kind permission of the Massachusetts Historical Society.

my Mind, nor did the remembrance of them return there till I had passed upwards of twenty Miles on Sunday, otherwise I have returned them unfolded in preference to bringing them out of town. A profound calm at Dover having afforded leisure, I have perused them with much Satisfaction, and they shall be sent by tomorrow's coach under cover directed to the care of Mr Bridgen,[1] and I must rely upon your goodness to excuse me for a transgression which is altogether the effect of accident and inadvertence not of presumption or mere negligence. I think Mr Turgot wanted better information in particular points,[2] nevertheless I am pleased with his generous sentiments in general, and not less with the contents of your letter to Dr S and I should regret the injunction against copying, but that I flatter myself with hopes of your committing the whole with improvements and very soon to my countrymen. I had read the Tracts on Civil Liberty[3] and Appeal to the public[4] in America and the fast Sermons when[5] I was confined in the Tower, and I believe have copies of the whole among my books. My best thanks however are not less due for this additional Mark of your friendship and affection which I shall acknowledge with gratitude and embrace every opportunity of testifying the [ ] assurance that I am with the highest esteem and respect, Dear Sir

Your much obliged and obedient humble servant

[No signature]

---

1. Edward Bridgen (d. 1787), a wealthy London merchant who had married as his second wife Martha, the daughter of Samuel Richardson, the novelist. He was a frequent contributor to the *Gentleman's Magazine*, a collector of antiquities, a Fellow of the Royal Society, and Treasurer to the Society of Antiquaries. See *Gent. Mag.*, LVII (1787), part 2, p. 646.

2. See A. Turgot to R.P. 22 Mar. 1778.

3. *Two Tracts*.

4. *An Appeal to the Public on the Subject of the National Debt.*

5. *Fast Sermon . . . 10 February, 1779*; and *Fast Sermon . . . 21 February 1781.*

To Benjamin Franklin

Newington Green May 20th 1782

Dear Sir,

May I take the liberty to introduce to you the two gentlemen who will attend upon you with this note? Any notice, however slight, that you will take of them they will reckon an honour. One of them Mr Milford is a young gentleman of good character, the son of a considerable merchant at *Exeter*, whose views are to amuse himself by an excursion on the continent. His companion Mr Brown

---

ORIGINAL: University of Pennsylvania. TEXT: Original, with the kind permission of the University of Pennsylvania.

has different views. He is quitting this country entirely and going over to America. His Brother set the example four or five years ago, and has been for sometime a surgeon in the army under General Washington. You kindly assisted him, but this probably you may not recollect. A great Revolution has at last taken place in this country. The opposers of the late measures have now the direction of our affairs. God grant they may succeed in extricating this country and shew themselves the friends of public liberty and justice; and may the bloodshed and havock of this war be soon terminated by an equitable and general peace. I am afraid I am too often troublesome to you, but I rely on your friendship, and am, with the greatest regard and affection,

Ever yours,
Rich*d* Price

To the Earl of Shelburne

Newington=Green May 21*st* 1782

My Lord,

Your Lordship may remember that about three weeks ago[1] I put into your hands a representation from some Gentlemen at Yarmouth complaining of an oppression of that Corporation by Mr Charles Townshend.[2] Similar representations were presented to the Marquis of Rockingham by Lord Chedworth,[3] and to Mr Fox by Mr Windham.[4] I have since received another letter from the same Gentlemen to inform me that, in compliance with your Lordship's circular letter,[5] the inhabitants have met and determined to associate

ORIGINAL: MS M.3803, Archive Department, Library Services, London Borough of Hackney.
TEXT: Original, with the kind permission of the Archive Department, Library Services, London Borough of Hackney.

1. See R.P. to Shelburne, 24 Apr. 1782.

2. Charles Townshend (1728–1810), MP for Great Yarmouth from 1756 to 1784 and from 1790 to 1796. A close friend of Lord North, whom he consistently supported. At the general election of 1784, Townshend and Richard Walpole were replaced by Henry Beaufoy and Sir John Jervis whose victory was hailed as a success for the reform movement.

3. John Howe (1754–1804), fourth Lord Chedworth.

4. William Windham (1750–1810), MP for Norwich from 1784 to 1802.

5. In May 1782, Shelburne sent out to the mayors of all the large towns proposals for the creation of a new militia. His scheme was based on the plan presented by H.S.Conway to Parliament in 1757. (See J.R. Western, *The English Militia in the Eighteenth Century* (London, 1965), p. 217.) Infantry battalions were to be raised in each town. The officers were to have property qualifications and be appointed on the recommendation of the chief magistrates of the town. The men were to be exercised in the evenings and on Sundays and holidays with arms furnished by the government. See *Parl. Hist.*, XXIII, 1–14, and *Considerations on Militias and Standing Armies. With some Observations on the Plan of Defence suggested by the Earl of Shelburne* (London, 1782).

and to learn the use of arms under Captain Hurry, but only on the plan of being Volunteer companies and without *accepting commissions*. If they are encouraged on this plan they are likely to form a considerable body and will be glad to act in concert with the military at Yarmouth for the defence of the town and the support of government. They suppose the Mayor has given this account; but fearing that the hostility of the Corporation to the new ministry may occasion some misrepresentation, they have, they say, explained the whole in a letter to your Lordship; and they have also thought proper to send the same explanation to me. Your Lordship may well wonder they should thus distinguish me, but it is owing to a few leading Gentlemen there who look upon me as your Lordship's Friend and think me of more importance than I am. I cannot help taking this opportunity to express to your Lordship the particular satisfaction that has been given me by your Lordship's late declaration that you are for an equal representation of the kingdom,[6] and by the just and liberal concessions that have been made to Ireland. I can scarcely say how much I admire the conduct of the people in that country.

With great respect I am, my Lord, your Lordship's
most obedient and humble servant
Rich*d* Price

---

6. In Jan. 1782 in concert with Barré, Dunning and Pitt, Shelburne had prepared a parliamentary motion which embodied demands for shorter parliaments, additions to the county representation and the abolition of rotten boroughs (see Norris, 162ff.).

To Mr Manning

Newington Green, May 25*th*, 1782

Dear Sir,

I have received with much pleasure your second letter, and communicated the contents of it to Lord Shelburne, who has desired me to assure you and the other gentlemen, "that he will shew every possible attention to whatever comes from them; and also to acquaint you, that the answers from the several towns to his circular letter are laid before the King as they come in, and that after comparing and considering them some general resolution will be taken respecting them." What this resolution will be cannot at present be known; but for *for my own part*, I cannot help heartily approving the determination of the Gentlemen and inhabitants of Yarmouth to associate and learn the use of arms for their own defence and the defence of the kingdom, as Volunteer

ORIGINAL: Cardiff Public Library. ADDRESSED: To/Mr Manning/Yarmouth/Norfolk TEXT: Original, with the kind permission of Cardiff Public Library.

companies without taking commissions.[1] The right to do this is an essential right of *Englishmen*; and all good governors who mean nothing but public liberty and happiness will encourage the exercise of it.

Should you communicate this letter to any of the Gentlemen deliver my best compliments to them; and particularly to Captain Hurry[2] who, if I mistake not, in company with his Brother, breakfasted with me one morning some time ago at *Black:Fryars* Bridge.

Under a sense of your civilities and with sincere respect and affection, I am, Sir, your very obedient and Humble servant

Rich*d* Price

1. See R.P. to Shelburne, 21 May 1782.
2. Members of a numerous, wealthy and influential family of Dissenters at Yarmouth. "Early in the eighteenth century, Thomas Hurry and his son, [also a Thomas Hurry] with some members of his family established themselves at Great Yarmouth, as Hemp and Iron Merchants ... They were also ship agents, agents for Lloyd's and Vice-Consuls for Prussia and other foreign powers." Thomas Hurry-Houghton, *Memoirs of the Family of Hurry of Great Yarmouth, Norfolk...* (Liverpool, 1926), p. 9.

To the Earl of Shelburne

Newington Green June 1*st* 1782

My Lord.

Accept many thanks for the two kind notes with which your Lordship has favoured me. I wrote immediately to the Gentlemen at Yarmouth and gave them the information your Lordship directed. The second Note I did not receive till Yesterday. I have known Mr Hazlett[1] ever since he first set out as a dissenting minister. I believe him to be a very honest man; but his great zeal as a liberty=man and his enmity to the late administration have sometimes

ORIGINAL: Bowood. TEXT: Original, with the kind permission of the Marquiss of Lansdowne.
1. William Hazlitt (1737–1820), Dissenting minister and father of William Hazlitt, the essayist. Educated at Glasgow University, he entered the Dissenting ministry, and from 1770 to 1780 was a minister at Maidstone. It was during this period that he became friendly with Price and Joseph Priestley. In 1780 he became a minister at Bandon, near Cork, where he remained until emigrating to America in March 1783. It was while he was at Bandon that he attempted to relieve the plight of some American prisoners of war who were being ill treated at the prison at Kinsale. According to his biographer, Hazlitt wrote to John Palmer and to Price seeking their assistance. Shelburne, at Price's request, forwarded a letter written by Hazlitt to Colonel Fitzpatrick, then Commandant at Kinsale, and the plight of the prisoners was, for a time at least, relieved. See W. Carew Hazlitt, *Four Generations of a Literary Family*, 2 vols. (London and New York, 1897), I, 17. In 1783 he settled in Philadelphia, and was one of the earliest if not the first to preach the Unitarian doctrine of the Divine unity in America. He returned to Britain in 1786 and settled at Wem in Shropshire.

brought him into difficulties by making him too open in his declarations and too imprudent in his conduct. I shall perhaps, in compliance with his request, take the liberty to give Col. Fitzpatrick[2] a line about him, and I am much obliged to your Lordship for so kindly offering to convey the letter. I must however first consult Dr Kippis[3] and one or two more of his friends. I called yesterday at *Shelburne*=house, and heard with pleasure that your Lordship's indisposition was so far abated as to admit of your going out. My best respects wait on Lady Shelburne. May your Lordship's health be long preserved to be a happiness to her and to the kingdom. I have the honour to be ·

Your Lordship's most obedient and humble servant

Rich*d* Price

---

2. Richard Fitzpatrick (1748–1813), a brother of Shelburne's second wife; MP for Okehampton from 1770 to 1774, and for Tavistock from 1774 to 1807. In April 1782 he went to Ireland as Secretary to the Duke of Portland, and in April 1783 became Secretary of War in the Fox–North coalition. (Namier and Brooke, II, 433–35.)

3. See Vol. I, 140.

From Benjamin Franklin

Passy June 13: 1782[1]

Dear Sir,

I received a few Days since your kind letter of the 27th.[2] past by Messrs Milford and Brown. It gave me great Pleasure to hear of your Welfare. All that come with a Line from you are welcome.

I congratulate you on the late Revolution in your Public Affairs. Much good may arise from it, though possibly not all that good Men, and even the new Ministers themselves, may have wished or expected. The Change however in the Sentiments of the Nation, in which I see evident Effects of your Writings, with those of our deceas'd Friend Mr Burgh,[3] and others of our valuable Club, should encourage you to proceed. The ancient Roman and Greek Orators could only speak to the Number of Citizens capable of being assembled within the Reach of their Voice: Their Writings had little Effect, because the Bulk of

---

ORIGINAL: American Philosophical Society. Another version is held in the Franklin MSS at the Library of Congress.   PRINTED: William Temple Franklin, *Memoirs of the Life and Writings of Benjamin Franklin*, 2nd ed., (London, 1818), II, 116 (incomplete); *Franklin*: Bigelow, IX, 220 (incomplete); *Memoirs*, pp. 95–97 (incomplete).   TEXT: Original, with the kind permission of the American Philosophical Society. The version in the Franklin MSS has some minor differences, and the following passages are lined through: lines 2–5 (Dear Sir . . . are welcome) and lines 21–27 (I suppose . . . B. Franklin).

1. This letter was conveyed to Price by Dr Dimsdale. See R.P. to Shelburne, 26 June 1782.

2. Probably an inaccurate reference to R.P. to Benjamin Franklin, 20 May 1782.

3. James Burgh, see Vol. I, 241.

the People could not read. Now by the Press we can Speak to Nations; and good Books, and well-written Pamphlets, have great and general Influence. The Facility with which the same Truths may be repeatedly enforc'd by placing them daily in different Lights, in Newspapers which are every where read, gives a great Chance of establishing them. And we now find that it is not only right to strike while the iron is hot, but that it is very practicable to heat it by continual Striking.

I suppose we may now correspond with more Freedom, and I shall be glad to hear from you as often, as may be convenient to you. Please to present my best Respects to our good old Friends of the London Coffee House.

I often figure to myself the Pleasure I should have in being once more seated among them. With the greatest and most sincere Esteem and Affection, I am, my dear Friend,

Yours ever
B. Franklin

To the Earl of Shelburne

Newington=Green June 26*th* 1782

My Lord.

The multiplicity of your Lordship's present engagements, and my fear of breaking in improperly upon you, induce me to take this method of conveying a few things which I wish to mention to your Lordship.

I spoke sometime ago to Mr Jervis on the subject you mention'd to me, and urged as well as I could without offending, the particular necessity of his utmost diligence at this time: and I cannot but believe that he is sensible of this, and resolved from a regard to his own future credit, the happiness of his pupil and your Lordship's comfort, to discharge his important trust will all the fidelity prudence and attention he is capable of.

The Foreigner (Mr Chanal) whom your Lordship did me the honour to refer to me, has been with me several times. He made me a present of the book he has printed; but being written in Italian I could not read it. He, therefore, composed a kind of abstract of his scheme in *English*, and he has since sent me another paper containing farther explanations. But in neither of these papers, nor I fancy in the book itself does he enter into such an account of the particulars of his scheme as to make it possible for me to understand it or to form any judgment of it. The design of it is, by what he calls lotteries of production, by Tontines and loans and the establishment of a grand society for improving

ORIGINAL: Bowood.   TEXT: Original, with the kind permission of the Marquis of Lansdowne.

agriculture, to pay off the public debts, accumulate treasure and render the waste lands of the kingdom fruitful. Finding that I was giving him a vast deal of trouble, and he not understanding my language nor I his, and suspecting at the same time that little was to be expected from this scheme, I thought it best in the most respectful manner I could to put him off. Last week, therefore, I writ a letter to him with this view, and returned to him his papers imagining that he might chuse to shew them to some other person. I am afraid this may have offended him, but indeed I was afraid of being drawn in to spend my time very unprofitably on a visionary and impracticable scheme.

I am much obliged to your Lordship for transmitting my letter[1] to Colonel Fitz=patrick. He has been so polite and obliging as to send me an answer to it. When you see him will you be so good as to deliver to him my best thanks.

Some of the Dissenting ministers are a little alarmed by your Lordship's recommending Sunday as a proper day for learning the use of arms.[2] I cannot say I entirely agree with them. They have had a private meeting on this occasion, and I have promised to speak to your Lordship. Should such a measure be carried into execution they will probably deliver a remonstrance against it.

I once mentioned to your Lordship that Mr Fastenedge[3] had chosen to quit his place at the *Assurance office* on the marriage of my nephew.[4] This makes it proper for me to inform you that he is, on account of the imperfection in his sight, an object of compassion; and that having about a month ago desired to be restored to his place, Mr Morgan has consented to take him again.

I received on Saturday a letter of congratulation on the change of ministry from Dr Franklin brought by Dr Dimsdale.[5] Much good, Dr F[rankli]n says may arise from this change; tho' possibly (he adds) not all that good men, or even the new ministers themselves, may have wished or expected.

My best regards wait on Lady Shelburne. I have the honour to be, with great regard,

Your Lordship's most obedient and humble servant
Rich*d* Price

1. See R.P. to Shelburne, 1 June 1782,

2. See R.P. to Manning, 25 May 1782.

3. Edward Fastnedge (see R.P. to Shelburne, 24 July 1779) became blind with cataract but was cured by the operation known as "couching". Ogborn, p. 161.

4. William Morgan, Actuary to the "Equitable", who married Susannah Woodhouse in 1781.

5. Possibly Thomas Dimsdale (1712–1800), physician. Educated at St Thomas's Hospital. In 1768 he was invited to St Petersburg to inoculate the Empress Catherine and her son. MP for Hertford, 1780–1790.

To the Earl of Shelburne

Newington=Green July 18*th* 1782

My Lord,

Your Lordship having been so good as to desire I would put you in mind of the friend in whose favour I took the liberty to speak to you on Saturday last, I write this to inform you that his name is *Adam Jellicoe*,[1] and that he is now the head=clerk in the Navy pay office in which office he has been an able and faithful servant for more than thirty years. It gives him great concern to lose so good a master as Mr Barre.[2] I have, however, made him easy with respect to the change that is to take place, by telling him that your Lordship has been so good as to promise to recommend him to Mr Barre's successor in order to prevent any danger of his being displaced. Indeed there are few who deserve more to be recommended, or whose integrity and abilities in his place can be more depended on. He has a large family and the loss of his place would be severely felt by him. Mr Barre would probably confirm in some measure the account I have given of him, and between him and Mr *Goodenough*[3] (who, I understand, is made one of your Lordship's Secretaries) there is a family connexion. I admire your Lordship's desire to be recommended to honest men capable of giving you information and assistance in your High office. I have recollected that the person I mentioned to you some time ago was Mr Blackburn, a very able surveyor. He has been with the Duke of Richmond to give him an account of some abuses in the Ordnance office. I do not know that he could give your Lordship any information with respect to the Treasury; but, I believe, there are few equal to him in his line of business, and a sufficient proof of this is, that in consequence of having gained the prize offer'd to the artist who should produce the best plan and drawings of the new Penitentiary house, he is to direct and superintend the building of it and has been lately employ'd in drawing an estimate of the expence, which I find, will amount to near £150,000.[4]

ORIGINAL: Bowood.   TEXT: Original, with the kind permission of the Marquis of Lansdowne.

1. According to the *Journals of the House of Commons* (XXXVIII, 717) Adam Jellicoe had been First Clerk in the Office of Paymaster to the Treasurer of the Navy for more than forty years. He died in August, 1789 overcome, Price thought, by the failure of some enterprise in which he had invested heavily. He was a close friend of Price, a Dissenter, and a member of the Committee of New College, Hackney. See "Journal", pp. 391, 411.

2. In July 1782, Isaac Barré relinquished his appointment as Treasurer of the Navy to become Postmaster-General, an appointment which he held until April 1783. In January 1784 he became Clerk of the Pells.

3. George Goodenough, who was appointed Secretary of the Board of Taxes in 1782 (Binney, p. 182).

4. See R.P. to Shelburne, 3 Apr. 1782.

As for myself, in consequence of weak health and spirits, I am obliged to avoid everything that has any tendency to encumber me. Tranquillity is the great blessing I desire, and I am happy when I have nothing to do but to pursue at my leisure some object of speculation or enquiry in my study. I have lately been almost wholly employ'd in preparing a fourth edition of the Treatise inscribed to your Lordship, which has been for some time out of print, I mean the Treatise on Annuities, population, public credit &c.[5] I have been enabled to improve it by some materials which have been sent me from *Sweden* and *Germany*. It will be increased into two volumes; and if it was ever of any value, it will now be of much more value. I mention these particulars because I have entertained some thoughts of desiring your permission to change the inscription into a short letter of dedication. The greatest part is printed off, and probably I shall publish this work in the beginning of the winter.

Some of my friends, who are likewise your Lordship's friends tremble for the edge on which your Lordship now stands. They are afraid of the consequences of continuing the war. The country cannot bear much more. The last loan lies very heavy, and they apprehend that the difficulties and dangers attending another and a larger loan will be dreadful.

But I am taking up too much of your Lordship's time. The remainder of the summer I am to spend at *Brighthelmston*, and in visits to friends in the country. But I hope to have the pleasure of seeing your Lordship before I go, I remain, with great regard,

Your Lordship's most obedient and humble servant
Rich*d* Price

---

5. *Observations on Reversionary Payments*. Price did not pursue the idea of substituting a letter of dedication for the inscription to Shelburne which he had included in the third edition.

To the Earl of Shelburne

Newington-Green July 29th 1782

My Lord,

I have been applied to again by the Yarmouth people, and desired to convey to your Lordship the following proposals. In a letter from them to your Lordship which I had the honour of conveying some time ago,[1] they have given an account of the state of oppression in which for several years they have been held by Mr Charles Townshend, who, during the late ministry owed his power

---

ORIGINAL: Bowood. TEXT: Original, with the kind permission of the Marquis of Lansdowne.
  1. See R.P. to Shelburne, 24 Apr. and 21 May 1782.

among them to the disposal of the places in the town and posts held under government. The Act² lately pass'd for taking away the votes of Revenue officers has not sufficiently relieved them, for still by expectations, quarterings and an improper application of public money Mr Townshend maintains an influence which overpowers the independent electors. But did it appear that the disposal of places went now in a different channel and that Mr Townshend's influence no longer existed, the whole system of corruption at Yarmouth would fall, and the independent inhabitants would be able to introduce any members they best liked. They have, therefore, desired me to signify to your Lordship that *provided Mr Townshend is deprived of his patronage*, they will undertake to bring into Parliament at the next election any independent men and sound whiggs your Lordship will recommend to them; Capt. L[eveso]n Gower³ has been mentioned to them but nothing has pass'd between him and them, nor does he know that he has been mention'd; and their choice is to refer all to your Lordship's determination.

The popularity of a minister in the County of Norfolk will, I am told, depend greatly on what is done in this affair. Were only one particular man, a creature of Mr Townshend's, displaced; or were the first place that shall become vacant disposed of at the recommendation of the members for the County, it would be concluded that Mr Townshend had lost his patronage, the independent interest would gain the ascendant, and the town would be emancipated.

I have promised to inform the Gentlemen at Yarmouth of your Lordship's sentiments as soon as possible. I shall, therefore, call on wednesday morning in hopes of learning them, not doubting but that the candour and attention with which you have honoured [me] in other instances will be continued to me in this. To morrow sen=night, I intend to make my escape from London for the remainder of the summer. With great regard

I am your Lordship's most obedient and humble servant

Rich*d* Price

---

2. Crewe's Act, an act for disfranchising revenue officers (22 Geo. III, c. 41) received the Royal Assent on 19 June 1782. For an account of this act and its effects, see Betty Kemp, "Crewe's Act", *Essays in Eighteenth Century History*, arranged by R. Mitchison (London, 1966), pp. 195–200.

3. Hon. John Leveson-Gower (1740–92), sixth son of the first Earl Gower, was MP for Appleby from 1784 to 1790 and for Newcastle-under-Lyme from 1790 to 1792. He was Lord of the Admiralty from Jan. to Apr. 1783 and from Dec. 1783 until 1787.

To the Earl of Shelburne

Newington=Green Aug 6th 1782

My Lord,

I now return the Manuscript your Lordship deliver'd to me, with remarks.[1] The author desired I would send my remarks first to him; but being afraid this might engage me in a dispute, I have chosen to refer him for them to your Lordship. Some other remarks offer'd themselves to me on incidental passages which appear'd to me to be wrong, but it is not worth while to trouble you with them. I did not understand Sir George Colebrook's explanation of the scheme for raising money by loans.[2] The author has it in writing and I will consider it if your Lordship pleases, but I cannot say I expect much from it.

I feel a high respect for Mr Pitt. He does me great honour by supposing me capable of being of any use to him. I shall be happy should I ever find this to be the case.

Your Lordship will probably soon receive an application about the Penitentiary houses[3] from an interested person who wishes to overthrow the scheme. I am informed he has already made some impressions on one of the Secretaries of State. Will you pardon me if I say, that no regard should be paid to him without consulting Mr Howard from whom the Act of Parliament which establishes the scheme took its rise; and also the three supervisors Sir Charles Bunbury,[4] Sir Gilbert Elliot[5] and Dr Bowdler,[6] who

ORIGINAL: PRO 30/8/169   TEXT: Original, with the kind permission of the Public Record Office.

1. With this letter Price enclosed a paper entitled "Observations on a scheme for paying off 200 millions of the National Debt in 99 years" in which he commented upon a manuscript sent to him by Shelburne (PRO 30/8/275). The author of this manuscript was a M. de Herrenschwand, probably J. Frederic de Herrenschwand, an economist who published *De l'Économie Politique Moderne. Discours Fondemental sur la Population* (London, 1786), and *De l'Économie Politique et morale de l'Espece Humain* (London, 1796).

2. Sir George Colebrooke (1729–1809), a London banker. MP for Arundel from 1754 to 1774. In 1767 he was appointed a Director of the East India Company. He ran into financial difficulties and his bank was closed in 1773. In 1774 he was forced into liquidation and in 1778 he retired to Boulogne. See Namier and Brooke, I, 235–37. The Shelburne Papers, now in The William L. Clements Library, The University of Michigan, contain a paper entitled "Essay on a new system for raising the public loans", dated May 1781 which is probably the paper to which Price refers.

3. In 1779 *An Act to Explain and Amend the Laws relating to the Transportation, Imprisonment and other Punishment of Certain Offenders* (19 Geo. III, c. 74, sect. 5) provided for the erection of two penitentiary houses. John Howard was appointed to the Board for putting the scheme into effect, but he resigned in 1781.

4. Sir Charles Bunbury (1740–1821) was MP for Suffolk from 1761 to 1784 and from 1790 to 1812.

5. Sir Gilbert Elliott (1751–1814). MP for Morpeth, 1776–77; Roxburghshire, 1777–84; Berwick-upon-Tweed, 1786–90; and Helston, 1790–95. He was created Baron Minto in 1797 and first Earl Minto in 1813.

are so disinterested as to intend to give up their time and attention to this business without any pay.

I intend soon to write to one of the principal dissenting ministers at Dublin with the view your Lordship mentioned to me.[7] I will also mention to Dr Priestley your Lordship's wishes.

I am at this moment setting out for Brighthelmston. I hope your Lordship's cold is by this time entirely removed. Wishing you all the happiness that the use of power to establish peace and liberty can produce, I am, with great respect, your Lordship's most obedient and humble servant

Rich*d* Price

I have just received a letter from Mr Nicholas in which he is very particular in expressing his grateful sense of your Lordship's politeness, attention and goodness to him on a late occasion.

I am oblig'd to Col. Barre for the *Report*.[8] It belongs I find to Mr Townshend,[9] and I will take great care of it.

Mr Howard has just now called upon me. He is going again to Ireland, and I have mention'd to him my wishes that he would take such opportunities as may come in his way to conciliate the minds of the people there to the administration of Lord Temple[10] by representing him as a Nobleman of liberality who is likely to make it his study to oblige and serve them. I find Mr Howard expects that more discontents are rising there, and that Lord Temple may have hard work to do.

---

6. Dr Thomas Bowdler (1754–1825), physicist, philanthropist and the editor of Shakespeare whose puritanical zeal brought a new verb into the language.

7. S. Thomas. See S. Thomas to R.P., 14 Oct. 1782.

8. Probably "The report from the committee appointed to enquire into the amount of the sums raised, by annuities, towards the supply granted to His Majesty between 5 January 1776 and 5 April 1782", *Reports from Committees of the House of Commons*, Vol. XI, Miscellaneous Subjects (1782–99), (1803). See R.P. to Shelburne, 30 Aug. 1782.

9. Thomas Townshend (see Vol. I, 204n.) who had become Secretary of State (for home affairs) in Shelburne's administration.

10. George Nugent-Temple-Grenville (1753–1813), became the second Earl Temple in 1779. On 31 July 1782 he was appointed Lord-Lieutenant of Ireland in succession to the Duke of Portland. At the time Price wrote this letter Temple had not taken up his duties in Ireland; he eventually did so on 15 September. He became Marquis of Buckingham in December 1784.

To the Earl of Shelburne

Brighthelmston Aug*st* 30*th* 1782

My Lord,

It gives me pain that I cannot well avoid complying so far with the sollicitations of some of the Gentlemen at Yarmouth, as again to trouble your Lord-

---

ORIGINAL: Bowood.   TEXT: Original, with the kind permission of the Marquis of Lansdowne.

ship about their affairs.[1] The following is an extract from a letter which I received from thence last night.

"A vacancy in one of the Revenue offices has happen'd here this morning by the death of Mr John Hurry[2] one of the Brothers of Messrs Hurrys. He has for more than forty years had the employment of collecting the Duties for the Stamp-office, and should have declined it this year in favour of his son (who has been made acquainted with the business) had not his death prevented it. Should this office be otherwise disposed of, it will be interpreted as done in opposition to their interest. Messrs Hurrys are, therefore, anxious, and their friends wish much, on that account more than from the emolument arising from the employment, to have his son *James Hurry*[3] deputed to this business. The appointment comes from the Commissioners of the Stamp Office London. If you would therefore, be so obliging as to request Lord Shelburne to name Mr James Hurry to the Commissioners for this office, it would be a particular obligation. For to establish the Idea of his having this power and disposition in filling two or three of the first vacancies is what we are principally anxious for as the means of securing an election for any of his friends.

The Officer is stiled *Distributor of the Stamps* at Yarmouth, and is paid solely by the Commission on the amount of what he disposes of."

To the account in this extract I will only add that I am acquainted with and have a great respect for Messrs Hurrys, and that they are some of the leading and most active and respectable men at Yarmouth in the Whig=interest.

Should your Lordship think fit to enquire of Lord Keppel I believe he would be able to give some account of them. Relying on your Lordship's usual indulgence and candour I am, with great respect, your most obedient and Humble servant

Rich*d* Price

In consequence of being at Brighthelmston the letter from Yarmouth did not reach me till nine days after it was written, and this has occasioned a delay which I am sorry for. I feel myself recruited and strengthen'd by the change of scene and air, sea=bathing and riding about these downs, but at present I am confined by a dreadful kick which I received yesterday from a horse on the side of my Ankle=bone. I hope, however, I shall be well again in a few days and able to set out for home on thursday next.

Since I have been here I have been amusing myself with considering the Report of the Committee appointed by the House of Commons for taking an account of the national debt and the state of the Finances which Colonel Barre

---

1. See also R.P. to Shelburne, 3 Sept. 1782.

2. John Hurry (1724–82), third son of Thomas (1696–1780) and Elizabeth Hurry. He married Sarah Winn in 1746.

3. James Hurry (1763–1842), second son of John and Sarah Hurry (see n. 2 above).

was so good as to borrow for me from Mr Alderman Townshend.[4] I have been led by it to some thoughts on the best methods in the present state of our finances, of raising money by loans,[5] which, if I can mature them to my own satisfaction, I shall be glad, before another loan comes, to be allowed to lay before your Lordship and Mr Pitt. The Duke of Manchester[6] is one of my nearest neighbours here. I was glad to be informed by him yesterday that he had seen your Lordship and that you were well. Lady Dartrey[7] is also here, and Mr Ord's child is very near me. My best respects wait on Lady Shelburne.

---

4. See R.P. to Shelburne, 6 Aug. 1782, n.8.

5. In 1783 Price published *The State of the Public Debts and Finances at Signing the Preliminary Articles of Peace, in January 1783, with a Plan for Raising Money by Public Loans and for Redeeming the Public Debts.*

6. George Montagu (1737–88), fourth Duke of Manchester. He was Ambassador to France from Apr. to Dec. 1783.

7. Lady Dartrey (1740–1826), second wife of Lord Dartrey of Dawson's Close.

From Henry Laurens[1]

Nantes 31*th* August, 1782

Dear Sir,

I should not have been near two months indebted for your very obliging favor of the 21st June had I been possessed of that Constitution which certain late ministers contrived to break down. I was very ill in Bed 130 Posts from the place when it reached me, on a visit to my brother[2] and our distressed family at Vigan, fifteen days never able to go out of the House till I entered the chaise and forced myself down to the salt Water. Bathing in the Mediterranean helped me, but I could not, or thought I could not afford time to take enough of it. I came forward in order to be in the way of Duty, sick the whole journey and upon my arrival here reduced to Bed and the Chamber till about twenty days

---

ORIGINAL: From a private collection in Massachusetts, USA   TEXT: Original, with the kind permission of the Director of the Kendall Whaling Museum, Sharon, Massachusetts.

1. Henry Laurens was released from the Tower of London on 31 Dec. 1781. Some four months later he was exchanged for General Cornwallis who was then technically a prisoner of war in American hands. In May he journeyed to Amsterdam to offer his aid to John Adams and thence he went to Vigan near Nismes in the South of France to visit his sick brother James who with his wife was looking after Henry's daughters, Martha and Mary Eleanor. From Vigan he went to Bordeaux and eventually reached Nantes in July where he hoped to embark for America. Perhaps because he feared recapture he changed his mind and returned to England to demand a safe return to America. See Wallace, pp. 388, 395.

2. James Laurens (1728–84), a merchant. In 1778 he and his wife, Mary, together with Henry Laurens's two daughters (see preceding note) retired to Vigan in the South of France and remained there until the end of the war. At this time James was in failing health (Wallace, p. 226.)

ago, the Cause of my Complaints, provoked most probably by [bouts?] of starvation, bleeding, evacuatives etc., suddenly took leave of me. I went to Bed as usual, heavy and grunting and rose in the Morning chearful and easy, except weakness, extreme weakness in the knees and Ankles. I keep close to my Regimen and shall not too hastily quit it, convinced, by what I feel at this moment, that a small blast would overset me. Within 6 or 7 days past I have been much troubled by Head-Ach the constant attendant upon every exertion to write or read, and which at this instant compells me to take the couch.

2 September. It appeared clear to me that the new great Minister[3] had flattered himself with hopes of winning the United States, by proposing to them terms equal to those which had been extorted by Ireland, for I am intirely of your opinion Sir, in this article. His Lordship also entertained an overweening opinion of his influence in that country, which the people there knew nothing of, hence he was beguiled to make a fresh trial by tampering with Congress and with individuals, the result as it was certainly disgr[ace]ful— must have been mortifying, but that it has produced conversion is doubtful—it does not yet clearly appear that he is in earnest to pursue the only line wh[ich] promises to lead to permanent peace. A sensible man, one who will have something to do in framing a Treaty, if there is to be one formed, entertains jealousies of [a] latent design on the part of Great Britain, not to treat directly with the Commission of the U.S. to effect nevertheless a General Peace and keep in reserve a plan for securing the subjection when Europe shall be in repose; the grounds for this suspicion I confess app[ear] to me extremely remote and my sentiments have been signified to my friend accordingly, ne[ver]theless as there is a possibility and as even such an attempt would produce no extraordinary proof of weakness or madness [I] have taken occasion to write to one of your active politicians, who has sent me a crafty spi[rited] scheme for pacification in terms which I shall take the liberty to lay before you, req[ues]ting the whole may be entre nous.

"I saw your notorious" etc. down to "our [?] ditch"

From this transcript may be collected that as far as Mr L knows, we are in a state of unce[r]tainty; that no solid or serious steps toward peace have yet been made. I am persuaded nevertheless th[at] all the contending parties earnestly wish to put an end to the War, but each has its selfish views, one in particular is buoyed up by hopes of gaining those "few more victories" and of being en-abled [there]by to give the Terms. Mean time even that one is in a state of fear and trembling, from a consciousness of the dangerous leak in the Bottom. Were I to hazard an opinion it would be, that, barring such [?] a suspension of hostilities will take place before Christmas. Having found some difficulties in providing a proper embarkation at this place, a friend suggested that I was certainly entitled to a safe d[el]ivery in one of the United States by the Govern-

---

3. Shelburne.

ment of Great Britain, in return for the safe delivery of Lord Cornwallis[4] at [h]is own House. I took the hint—it seemed to be well founded—and im[m]ediately requested friends in London to apply in my behalf to the proper authorities for leave [to] return to England and to embark in one of the packets for New York from whence I may ob[tain] a passport to Philadelphia. I am now waiting the result of their representations, if we succeed I shall once more have the happiness of assuring you in person how much and with how much Esteem and Respect I am, Dear Sir,

Your obliged humble servant
[No signature]

---

4. Charles Cornwallis (1738–1805), became Earl Cornwallis on the death of his father in 1762. In Feb. 1776 he sailed for America as a major-general to serve under Clinton, and in April 1778 he became second-in-command. He was in command of British troops at the surrender at Yorktown in 1781. In Feb. 1786 he succeeded Warren Hastings as Governor General in India. When Laurens was a prisoner in the Tower it was suggested that he should be exchanged for Cornwallis who was then held by the Americans. At this time Cornwallis was Constable of the Tower of London, so Laurens was his prisoner; but at the same time Cornwallis was the prisoner of Laurens's son, John, who was Captain General of the prisoners in American hands. Thus, Cornwallis was the prisoner of the son of his own prisoner. (See Wallace, p. 395.)

To the Earl of Shelburne

Brighthelmston Sept 3d 1782

My Lord,

The inclosed letter addressed to your Lordship I received last night from the Gentlemen at Yarmouth by an express. It was accompany'd with a *second* letter

---

ORIGINAL: Bowood. TEXT: Original, with the kind permission of the Marquis of Lansdowne. Enclosed in this letter was the following letter from the Gentlemen of Yarmouth:

Yarmouth 19th Aug*st* 1782

My Lord,

The death this morning of Mr John Hurry Distributor of the Stamps occasions us to trouble your Lordship at this time to request the favor of you to nominate his son Mr James Hurry to the Office in his room.

The deceased possessed the office with great satisfaction to the Commissioners of the Stamp Duties and the public for more than forty years, and growing old, he had come to a determination to ask leave to resign in favor of his son but a sudden fit of illness carried him off unexpectedly and left not the opportunity.

We beg leave to assure your Lordship, that the son by having been used to the business of the office for sometime past is every way qualified for it, and we presume that your Lordship will think him under these particular circumstances to have a prior claim to your Lordship's patronage

We are My Lord

Your Lordship's Obedient Servants

Tho: Scratton	Samuel Hurry	D.H. Urquhart
John Fowler	Tho*s* Hurry	Ja*s*. Walker
Edmund Cobb	John Bell	Tho*s* Dage
John Drake	George Hurry	Will*m* Hurry
	Edm*d* Laron	

to me occasioned by a supposed miscarriage of their first letter. There is no difference between this and the former letter[1] than that in this they insist a little more on the effect which the appointment of any other person than Mr James Hurry will have in discourageing the friends of liberty at Yarmouth, and in leading them to conclude that the influence of the old ministry is still prevalent there. I respect so much those of the gentlemen who make this application that I am acquainted with, and particularly the family of the *Hurries* whose interest is in some measure concerned, that I cannot help heartily wishing them success. It grieves me to be troublesome to your Lordship in this business, and hoping to be excused I am, My Lord,

Your Lordship's most obedient and humble servant
Rich*d* Price

The accident I have met with has thrown me sadly back, but I hope to be well enough to get home before the end of the week.

---

1. See R.P. to Shelburne, 30 Aug. 1782.

To the Earl of Shelburne

Newington Green Sept 7th 1782

My Lord,

When I came home last night from Brighthelmston I found another letter from Yarmouth to inform me, that Mr Charles Townshend had been with your Lordship to sollicit the vacant place there for the son of one of the common=council men, and that he had acquainted his friends there that he was encouraged to hope for success. This has alarmed the gentlemen for whom I have wrote to your Lordship, and occasions this third trouble which I am obliged to give your Lordship. I wish, indeed, they had put this business into the hands of a fitter person, but having trusted me with it, I am not willing they should suffer by any omissions I can avoid. Will your Lordship allow me to say in what light it appears to me?

Mr James Hurry, the son of the late Distributor of Stamps and a person used to the business, seems to have so much reason to expect a preference, that the appointment of him could not justly bear a *party* interpretation. On the contrary, his rejection would be marking him and punishing him in order to gratify a very venal party, which has all along supported the measures of the late ministry, and therefore would be a decided declaration in their favour. It is obvious what effect this will have on the opinions of people in that town and country.

I have the honour to be your Lordship's most obedient and humble servant

Rich*d* Price

ORIGINAL: Bowood. TEXT: Original, with the kind permission of the Marquis of Lansdowne.

To the Earl of Shelburne

Newington=Green Sept 10*th* 1782

My Lord,

Immediately after sending my last letter to Shelburne=House I received the favour of your Lordship's letter and when I think of the multiplicity and importance of your present engagements I cannot but feel myself obliged by such instances of your Lordship's attention.

I have nothing to add to what I took the liberty to say in my last letter[1] on the appointment to the vacant place at Yarmouth. All must be referr'd to your Lordship's judgment and determination. May your administration be crowned with blessings to the kingdom and honour to yourself and find its support among the honest and independent rather than among the people who have supported a ministry which has degraded the nation, but who, I suppose are ready to offer their support to any ministry.

I am busy in endeavouring to digest my thoughts on the subject I mentioned to your Lordship. My best respects wait upon Lady Shelburne. I am now under the care of Mr Watken, and the wound in my leg, tho' much better, is far from being healed.[2] Wishing your Lordship an agreeable time at Bowood, I am, with great regard, your most obedient and humble servant

Rich*d* Price

Mrs Price sends her best respects. Just as I had finish'd this letter, I received your Lordship's Note desiring me to inform you of the Name of the Presbyterian minister at Plymouth.[3] His name is Mr Reynel; and I am told he is a worthy man who with a small income is oblig'd to maintain a large family.

ORIGINAL: Bowood.   TEXT: Original, with the kind permission of the Marquis of Lansdowne.

1. See R.P. to Shelburne, 7 Sept. 1782.

2. See R.P. to Shelburne, 30 Aug. 1782. In his will Price left £10 to a Mr Watkin, Surgeon "as a small testimony of the respect and gratitude due to him for many kind attendances on myself and particularly my late Wife." (MS American Philosophical Society; "Journal", p. 402). A Daniel Watkins appears in "A list of the Master, Wardens, Courts of Assistants, and other members of the Corporation [of Surgeons]" in *Medical Register* for 1779, 1780 and 1783. He also appears in *Medical Register* for 1783 as a surgeon of the Royal Navy, having received his warrant on 16 Apr. 1777. But there is no conclusive evidence that this is the Watkin[s] who treated Price and his wife.

3. John Reynell (1736–1800) was born at Newton Abbott. Educated at the Academy at Daventry, he became Pastor of the Presbyterian Congregation in Treville St., Plymouth in 1762. In May 1784 he moved to Thorverton, near Exeter, where he ministered to a Presbyterian congregation until his death in Sept. 1800. See W.J. Odgers, *A Brief History of the Plymouth Unitarian Congregation* (1850), p. 16. I am indebted to the Revd Derek Smith of Mansfield and Mr W. Sam Burgess of Plymouth for this reference.

This instant a Gentleman (Mr Houlton Harries)[4] has called upon me and brought me a letter from his father,[5] who is a dissenting minister of the best character at Swansea in Glamorganshire with whom I have been intimately acquainted from my youth. The design of the letter is to beg a recommendation of the son who brings me the letter and who is just returned from the West=Indies after being taken by the French at St Eustatius. He has been for some years a surgeon in the general Hospitals in America, but is at present a surgeon in the 13th Regiment reduced by death and other causes almost to nothing. He has his father, Brother, and sister to help; complains of having been disappointed by Lord Lisburne,[6] and seeing other surgeons, promoted over him; and says his wishes are to get interest enough *to be placed on the general staff of the Hospitals either at home or abroad.*

I am often distressed by such applications and sometimes almost tempted to wish I could put myself into your Lordship's station for a few minutes only.

---

4. Houlton Harries (d. 1793), surgeon. Harries first saw service in the warrant rank of hospital mate. He was commissioned as Surgeon to the 13th Foot on 25 Mar. 1779, and admitted to the Corporation of Surgeons in the same year. It is not known whether Shelburne intervened on his behalf, but it is not unlikely, for on 22 Oct. Harries succeeded in obtaining a place as a surgeon on the Hospital Staff. Subsequently, he served in Barbados and afterwards at the Garrison of Dominica. See W. Johnston, *Roll of Commissioned Officers in the Medical Services of the British Army . . . 1727 Medical Register*. I am indebted to Mr Robin Price at the Wellcome Institute for the History of Medicine for the references in this note and in note 2 above.

5. Solomon Harries (1726–85), a Dissenting minister, was born at Cilgwyn, Cardiganshire. He studied at Carmarthen Academy from 1746 until 1750, and was ordained a Presbyterian minister at Swansea in 1751. When the Academy moved from Carmarthen to Swansea in 1784 he was appointed Principal Tutor. Throughout his career his theological views became more liberal, and it is said that by 1776 he had become an Arian. See *Yr Ymofynydd* (1900), pp. 258–59.

6. Wilmot Vaughan (1730–1800), MP for Cardiganshire, 1755–61 and 1768–96; and for Berwick on Tweed from 1765 to 1768. He was created Earl of Lisburne in July 1776.

To the Earl of Shelburne

Newington Green Sept: 16*th* 1782

My Lord,

Since my last letter[1] I have recollected that possibly your Lordship, when you desired to know the name of the dissenting minister at Plymouth, might mean, not Mr Reynel who is the minister of the *Presbyterian* denomination, but

---

ORIGINAL: Bowood. TEXT: Original, with the kind permission of the Marquis of Lansdowne.

1. See R.P. to Shelburne, 10 Sept. 1782.

one of the ministers of the *independent* denomination. Of these there are three at Plymouth, and their names are Mr Mence,[2] Mr Heath[3] and Mr Kinsman.[4]

Your Lordship has been so good as to tell me, that you will not determine in the Yarmouth business till you have returned to town and talked with me. Last Saturday I received another application from the Gentlemen there requesting me to inform your Lordship that they beg a suspension of the appointment till you have heard once more from them. They hope to be able to apply thro' such a channel and to communicate such information, as will convince your Lordship that much may be lost by deciding in favour of Mr Ch[arle]s Townshend, an avowed friend to corruption, one of the most servile in Lord North's train, and, as I am told, a virulent enemy to everything free and liberal. The gentlemen who are so urgent in this business are some of the first merchants and inhabitants of Yarmouth, and the leaders of the whig interest there; and your Lordship may find probably that they are abetted by Mr Coke,[5] Sir Edward Astley,[6] Sir Harbord Harbord, Sir John Rous[7] &c.

I am to go on wednesday to a friend at Richmond and I shall stay there till the end of next week. Should your Lordship chuse to see me before that time I could easily take a ride to London and be at Shelburne=House at any time after ten any morning. A line sent by the general Post would soon reach me if directed to me at Mr Pritchard's, George=street Richmond Surry.

Many thanks to you for the Pine apples. The proof they brought of your remembrance of me was very agreeable.

---

2. Probably Christopher Mends (1724–99), a Calvinist Methodist who was the Pastor of Batter Street Presbyterian Chapel in Plymouth from 1760 to 1798. Prior to this appointment Mends had been a minister to an Independent Congregation at Brinkworth in Wiltshire.

3. Robert Heath (1741–1800), Calvinist Methodist preacher, a member of Andrew Kingsman's congregation at Plymouth until he became a minister at Wotten under Edge in Gloucestershire in 1789. From 1790 until his death he was minister at Rodborough Tabernacle near Stroud. He played a prominent part in relieving the distress of American internees imprisoned in Mill Prison during the war years 1775 to 1783. See "Memoir of the late Robert Heath", *Theological Magazine* (May, 1801), 161–62, and Sheldon S. Cohen, "The Mill Prisoners and the Englishman who continued in the light", soon to be published in *Enlightenment and Dissent*.

4. Andrew Kinsman (1725–93) was a minister to the Calvinist Methodists at Plymouth and Devonport. He was born at Tavistock where he became a grocer. He is said to have been converted to Methodism by reading Whitefield's sermons. In 1745 he moved to Plymouth and married Ann Tiley. It was on a site given to the Methodists by his wife that the Tabernacle at Plymouth was built. Although he assumed the leadership of the Society at the Tabernacle it was not until after Whitefield's visit to Plymouth in 1749 that Kinsman began his ministerial career. He preached the gospel in the streets of Devonport and in 1753 registered a house there as a Dissenting Meeting House. In 1763 he was ordained a Minister of the Calvinist Methodists. see C.E. Welch, 'Andrew Kinsman's Churches at Plymouth', *Transactions of the Devonshire Association* (1965), 212–35. I am indebted to Mr J.R. Elliott for drawing my attention to this account.

5. Thomas William Coke of Holkham Hall (1754–1842), the celebrated farmer. MP for Norfolk, 1776–1784, 1790–1807, 1807–32; and for Derby Feb.–Apr., 1807.

6. Sir Edward Astley (1729–1802), fourth Baronet. MP for Norfolk. 1768–90.

7. Sir John Rous (1750–1827), sixth baronet. MP for Suffolk, 1780–96.

My best compliments wait on Lady Shelburne.

With all best wishes I remain, My Lord,
your Lordship's most obedient servant
Rich. Price

Mr Will: Lee,[8] brother to Mr Arthur Lee, in a letter which the gentleman who received it last Saturday has shewn me, gives a copy of a letter just received there from *Madrid* containing an account that Prince Masserano[9] was arrived at Madrid express from Gibraltar with the news that the Hanoverians had revolted, and that the Duke de Crillon[10] had got possession of the advanced batteries and expected every hour the Garrison to surrender.[11] Mr Lee's letter is dated Sept. 10th. Your Lordship best knows what regard is due to this intelligence.

---

8. William Lee (1739–95), brother of Richard Henry and Arthur Lee. He came to London in 1768 to begin a business career; he and his brother Arthur were staunch supporters of John Wilkes. In 1773 he was elected Sheriff and in 1775 Alderman of the City of London. In June 1777 he crossed over to France to act as a commercial agent for the colonies at Nantes. He then became engaged in diplomatic activity and negotiated a commercial treaty between the colonies and Holland. At the time Price received this letter Lee was living in Brussels.

9. Carlo Ferrero-Fieschi, Prince Masserano (d. 1837), a Spanish diplomat, was a member of an ancient Piedmontese family that had settled in Spain. (*N. Biog. Gén*).

10. Crillon-Mahon, Louis de Berton des Balbes de Quiers (1718–96), Duc de, (*N. Biog. Gén*).

11. In June 1782 the Duc de Crillon was appointed commander of the forces that were to attempt to capture Gibraltar. Price's gloomy prognostications were not fulfilled, for the garrison successfully withstood siege until hostilities were suspended in Jan. 1783. See J. Drinkwater, *A History of the Siege of Gibraltar 1779–1783* (London, 1905); and George Hills, *Rock of Contention* (London, 1974), pp. 306–44.

To the Earl of Shelburne

Richmond Sept. 18th 1782

My Lord,

After leaving your Lordship this morning I recollected with pain that I had been deficient in faithfulness to my Friends at Yarmouth by not repeating the request from them which I mentioned in my last letter,[1] that the appointment may be suspended till they have had time to apply to your Lordship in another way. This will not probably produce a delay of more than a few days, and it is not I hope, too great a favour for them to expect. This will be the last trouble

---

ORIGINAL: Bowood.   TEXT: Original, with the kind permission of the Marquis of Lansdowne.

1. See R.P. to Shelburne, 16 Sept. 1782.

which I shall give your Lordship about this business. Hoping to be excused and wishing ardently your Lordship's true honour and happiness, I am,

Your Lordship's most obedient and humble servant

Rich*d* Price

I hope it will not be understood that I wish in this instance to destroy the corruption of Tories by substituting that of whigs. I detest both alike. But this need not be the effect of emancipating the Burrough of *Yarmouth* except it be a minister's own fault. In so large a town as Yarmouth extending the right of voting to one or two of the adjoyning hundreds as your Lordship proposed would not destroy corruption there; but it would be done by extending this right to the inhabitants and House=keepers at large, instead of confining it to a set of freemen who, under Mr Townshend's direction, are always nominating one another; and in such an extension the Gentlemen there would rejoyce. It would favour much the plan of Parliamentary reform which your Lordship mentioned, and which I rejoyce to find your Lordship has in view.[2]

---

2. Ian R. Christie maintains (*Myth and Reality*, p. 295) that throughout the struggle the Yarmouth reformers had not proposed any radical change in the spoils system. "Their object was to capture the system for themselves." This letter shows that Price was keenly aware of the danger that the only result of change might be to substitute one corrupt party for another; it also shows that he believed that it was possible to prevent abuses by reforming the electoral system.

To the Earl of Shelburne

Newington=Green Oct 4th 1782

My Lord,

It is probable that Mr *Herrenschwand* will repeat his applications to the Treasury about the scheme for paying off the national debt which your Lordship desired me to examine and therefore, I think it necessary to send you the inclosed copy of answers which I have given to some questions which he lately sent me.[1] He does not chuse that I should keep these questions, but your Lordship will be able easily to judge of them by the answers I have given. He has desired a personal interview with me, but I have declined it knowing that it would answer no end and being unwilling to enter into any disputes with him.

When I can have the pleasure of seeing your Lordship, I shall take the

---

ORIGINAL: Bowood. TEXT: Original, with the kind permission of the Marquis of Lansdowne.
1. See R.P. to Shelburne, 6 Aug. 1782 for details of Price's paper on Herrenschwand's scheme. Price now sent Shelburne a paper entitled "Answers to questions to Dr Price by Mr Herrenschwand." (Bowood.)

liberty to propose two or three taxes which I have been desired to mention to your Lordship, and which seem to be very proper ones because they would operate as useful regulations as well as bring additions to the revenue. Having heard since I came home a sad report of Mr Barre,[2] I called yesterday in *Charles=Street* in order to enquire after him; but found he was removed. I afterwards called at Shelburne=House, and was informed that the report was true. Will your Lordship have the goodness to mention to him my concern. I love him, and my feelings for him on this occasion are such as I cannot express.

My best respects wait on Lady Shelburne. I have the honour to be your Lordship's most obedient and humble servant

Richd Price

Mrs Price desires your Lordship's acceptance of her best respects.

---

2. In the autumn of 1782 Isaac Barré was struck by an attack of the blindness which was eventually to terminate his political career. See Brown, p. 221; Norris, p. 244.

From S. Thomas

Rathmines road Dublin 14th Octr 1782

Dear Sir,

Confession of Sins and Supplications for Pardon are no longer confined to devotional Exercises, but make a constant part of my correspondence with those friends who are so good as to write to me. It is really a burden on my Mind, that I have so long omitted acknowledging the Favour of your last Letter. I hope you will be assured, that I receiv'd your obliging Communications[1] relating to our new Lord Lieutenant[2] with the truest Satisfaction, and lost no time in making the proper use of them among my Brethren and friends in this Country. I need not tell you in what Estimation we hold your Sentiments, and the favourable opinion which you express of Lord Temple has added much to the pleasing Expectations which we had been taught to entertain from his Lordship's Character. The deputation from the Dissenters who waited on his Excellency with their Congratulatory address thought ourselves receiv'd with great Cordiality, and I am happy to believe that there is a very general prepossession in favour of his administration. The Duke of Portland[3]

ORIGINAL: Bowood.   TEXT: Original, with the kind permission of the Marquis of Lansdowne.

1. See R.P. to Shelburne, 6 Aug. 1782.

2. Lord Temple, see R.P. to Shelburne 6 Aug. 1782.

3. William Henry Cavendish Bentinck (1738–1809), third Duke of Portland, who was twice Prime Minister (Apr. to Dec. 1783, and 1807–09). When the Marquis of Rockingham came to power in Apr. 1782, Portland went to Ireland as Lord Lieutenant and was recalled in July 1782. He became Prime Minister in April 1783, with Charles James Fox and Lord North as Secretaries of State.

paved the way for his Successor with much advantage, by speaking of him to all his friends in very handsome Terms, and you know his Grace was very popular among all descriptions of Men in this Kingdom. In every Community some Malecontents will be found, and we have some persons among us who profess to be dissatisfied with all the advantages which we have obtain'd, and who will raise objections to any Measure which Government can propose for the public Welfare. The number and influence of these men are visibly declining, and I hope Lord Temple's administration will be easy and honorable to himself, and conducive to the real Interests of Ireland.

I shall be much obliged by a Line whenever you have a Leizure hour from the various important Avocations which employ your time. I beg my best Compliments to Mrs Price. I shall be glad to hear that your visit to Brighthelmstone has answered your wishes in regard to your health.

I am with the truest Esteem, dear [Sir]

your affectionate and respectfull humble servant
S. Thomas

Mr Taylor begs the return of his Compliments.

To Henry Laurens

Newington=Green Oct 22d 1782

Dear Sir,

This letter will be deliver'd to you by Mr Retford, the friend whom I have mentioned to you as having resolved to remove to America in order to settle there for life with his fortune. He is to go over to the continent in a few weeks, from whence he intends to remove to America in the spring. I have great confidence in him as a man of sense, ability and integrity who is likely to make a valuable addition to the citizens of America. He has requested me to introduce him to you; and he will think himself obliged and honoured by any notice you will take of him.

I heard with pleasure from Mr Bridgen, when I called upon him last week, that you were better. May you continue to grow better, and may Bath be the means of restoring to you that health of which you have been so cruelly deprived by your confinement in the tower. Do not give yourself any trouble about writing to me. I shall know from Mr Retford how you are; and when you return to London I shall hope for the pleasure of an interview with you.

ORIGINAL: Richard Price Misc. Papers, Rare Books and Manuscripts Division, The New York Public Library, Astor, Lenox and Tilden Foundations. TEXT: Original, with the kind permission of the New York Public Library.

Dr Franklin, I find continues in a bad state of health; and I am afraid he is not likely to obtain his wish to live to see the end of the present contest. With great respect and affection, I am, Dear Sir, your obliged and very humble servant

Rich*d* Price

To the Earl of Shelburne

Newington Green Oct 25*th* 1782

Dr Price presents his respectful compliments to Lord Shelburne, and acquaints him that he has received his note, and writ to Mr Smith to tell him that he will wait upon him in Albemarle Street about one=o=clock on tuesday next.

Dr Price has inclosed a letter which he has just received from Mr Thomas, one of the principal dissenting ministers at Dublin,[1] because he imagines it may be agreeable to Lord Shelburne to see one or two passages in it.

ORIGINAL: Bowood.   TEXT: Original, with the kind permission of the Marquis of Lansdowne.
   1. See S. Thomas to R.P., 14 Oct. 1782.

To the Earl of Shelburne

Newington=Green Oct 31*st* 1782

My Lord,

I have called on Mr Motteaux, and in consequence of the conversations I had with him, I sent him a copy of the inclosed paper on Mr *Herrenschwand's* scheme,[1] which he is to convey to Mr Her[renschwan]d. Indeed, I should not have thought this scheme worth so much attention, had I not been told that Lord North and even Lord John Cavendish[2] had express'd a high opinion of it, and that the former had lamented that his resignation had render'd him incapable of carrying it into execution.

ORIGINAL: Bowood.   TEXT: Original, with the kind permission of the Marquis of Lansdowne.
   1. "Comparison showing the Inefficiency of Herrenschwand's Scheme for Paying off the National Debt." MS Bowood.
   2. Lord John Cavendish (1732–96), Chancellor of the Exchequer in Rockingham's administration from Mar. to July 1782. On Rockingham's death he refused to serve under Shelburne. In the Fox–North coalition he returned to the Exchequer from Apr. to Dec. 1783.

With the paper on this scheme I have sent another on the *Extraordinary expence* of the war, to which I beg the favour of your Lordship's attention. I mentioned it to you when I had the pleasure of seeing you at *Streatham*. In two or three days I shall send your Lordship another paper containing a proposal of a scheme for the next loan.[3]

I admire much your Lordship's intention to prevent as far as possible the farther increase of the unfunded debt. It will appear from one of the inclosed papers that if the war must continue (which God forbid) seventeen millions at least will be necessary to be borrowed and funded every year in order to accomplish this end. I went on tuesday to Mr Smith, and found reason to be pleased with his good sense and candour. I thought most of his Ideas very right, particularly, those relating to taxes of regulation, and the necessity of looking to the redemption of debts at the time of contracting them and putting the Navy debt into a more fixed and regular course of payment. He proposed several taxes of regulation; but we agree'd that much could not be expected from them as additions to the Revenue, and that many of them are too hazardous to be trusted as funds for a loan at a time like the present.

My best respects wait on Lady Shelburne, I am, My Lord,

Your Lordship's most obedient and humble servant

Rich*d* Price

I have sent copies of these papers to Mr Pitt

---

3. See R.P. to Shelburne, 7 Nov. 1782.

To The Earl of Shelburne

Newington=Green Nov 7*th* 1782

My Lord,

I send you herewith a scheme for the next loan.[1] I shall convey a copy of it to Mr Pitt; but I wish nothing may be determined with respect to it, till I have

---

ORIGINAL: Bowood.   TEXT: Original, with the kind permission of the Marquis of Lansdowne.
    1. See "Proposal of a scheme for raising money for the service of 1782", MS Bowood. Price proposed that a loan should be raised on the following terms: £10 million to be raised on an irreducible stock bearing an initial interest of 6 per cent and an extra 1/4 per cent each year on that portion of stock which remained unredeemed; £250,000 each year from a Sinking Fund to be devoted to the redemption of the loan; the basic interest of 6 per cent to be met by fresh taxation, the additional interest to be met either from taxation or from the Sinking Fund; Parliament to guarantee that the interest would be irreducible and that no greater redemptions would be made in any one year than those specified in a table written into the Act; the administration of the loan and its redemption to be in the hands of Commissioners or Trustees. Price realized that the ten millions raised by this loan would not be adequate to meet existing needs. He himself would have preferred to meet the excess by additional taxation, but, if this were not feasible, additional money could be raised by offering for every £150 subscribed £100 of the new stock, £50 of a 5 per cent stock irredeemable for 21 years, and a long annuity of 10*s.* for 77 years.

laid before your Lordship another scheme[2] which may possibly be thought to deserve a preference. Your Lordship will receive it in a few days together with some account of taxes proposed by Mr Smith[3] and others who have writ and talked to me on this subject.

I have bestowed much attention on the two schemes and shall be happy should they prove of any use; But should they not, I hope they will be accepted as proofs of my desire to oblige your Lordship and to serve the public. With all good wishes I am Your Lordship's

most obedient and humble servant
Rich*d* Price

Mr Smith,[4] a friend of Lord Dartrey's,[5] has just called upon me. He intends to offer himself a candidate for the direction of the East=India company. I have been long intimately acquainted with him, and always entertained a high opinion of the worth of his character.

---

2. A paper entitled: "A second proposal for raising money by a loan for the service of 1783" was forwarded to Shelburne on 20 Nov. 1782.

3. See R.P. to Shelburne, 25 Oct. 1782.

4. Probably Samuel Smith (1755–93), son of Samuel Smith who founded the banking house of Samuel Smith and Son in 1776. MP for Ilchester, 1780–84, Worcester, 1784–90, and Ludgershall, 1791–93. Became a director of the East India Company in 1783.

5. Thomas Dawson (1725–1813) was created Baron Dartrey of Dawson's Close in 1770, and Viscount Cremorne in 1785.

To Benjamin Franklin

Newington=Green Nov: 18th 1782

Dear Friend,

I have for some time been intending and wishing to write to you; and I now embrace with great pleasure the opportunity of doing this which offers itself by Mr Laurens,[1] now in deep affliction occasioned by the loss of his son,[2] but happily restored in some measure to health after his long and hard and cruel confinement in the Tower. He is, I understand, going on an important commission to *Paris*, to which may God grant success. One of the chief obstacles to Peace, is I hope, now removed by the acknowledgement of the independence of

---

ORIGINAL: American Philosophical Society.   TEXT: Original, with the kind permission of the American Philosophical Society.

1. See R.P. to Henry Laurens, 19 Nov. 1782.

2. John Laurens (1754–82), a lieutenant-colonel in the rebel army, was killed at Combahee Ferry—almost the last life to be given in the rebel cause—on 27 Aug. 1782. (Wallace, p. 491.)

America. After many doubts and fears during the course of this war, I now see with unspeakable satisfaction this object secured, new constitutions of Government favourable to liberty civil and religious established in America, and a refuge there provided for the friends of truth and humanity. This is the consummation of the present contest which has been all along the object of my anxious wishes; and, I hope, I may now rejoyce with you on having lived to it. I am sensible, however, that it is not yet certain how the present negotiations will terminate. God forbid that thro' the pride of this country there should be a continuation of the war. Could my wishes have had any influence, our new ministers upon the first change would have immediately acknowledged the independence of America, and on this ground open'd a negotiation for a *general* peace and made such concessions as would most probably have brought it about before this time. I have allways deliver'd my sentiments freely to Lord Shelburne on these subjects. We have differ'd much in our opinions about them, but our friendship has continued. I am sorry to observe so much distrust prevailing with respect to him, and I hope he will prove it to be groundless by restoring to this country the blessings of peace and using the power he now possesses to establish oeconomy in our finances and to produce such a reformation in our Parliament as shall make it a *real* representation instead of such a mockery and nusance as it is at present.

I learnt with much pain some time ago from Dr Hamilton that you were ill of the gout and stone, but I have been lately informed that you are recover'd. May your life be preserved and crowned with every enjoyment that can make the remainder of it happy. I am getting fast after you into the evening of life. Soon the night will shut in upon us; but I trust, we shall see light again and be raised up to enjoy the happiness of brighter days in better regions. This, I don't doubt will be the lot of all the virtuous and worthy. I have lost within a few months about half a score of my acquaintances and friends. Such is the consequence of advancing far in the journey of life. One fellow-traveller drops after another till at last we are left to travel alone. I thank God my wife is continued to me; and she desires me to present her best respects to you. We are often talking of you at the little society of whigs at the London=Coffee= house. We are proud of still numbering you among our members; and I now begin to flatter myself with the hope, that the time may not be far distant when the return of peace may bring you among us once more.

In a little time I shall probably write to you again in order to introduce to your notice a Gentleman,[3] one of our club chosen since you left us, who is going to leave this kingdom and to settle for life with his fortune in America. Thither probably, when this contest is over, will many be flocking from all Europe.

Dr Priestley is warmly engaged in his litterary and philosophical pursuits. He has lately Discover'd that the *Phlogiston* of the Chymists is the same with

---

3. Mr Redford.

inflammable air; but of this and his other discoveries he will himself probably give you an account. There is in the press a new work of his about which he had taken great pains and from which I expect much instruction entitled *A history of the corruptions of Christianity*.[4] I am just now writing about loans, the finances and the public debts; but without the hope of doing much good. I have been for these two years employ'd in preparing a new edition of my Treatise on Annuities, Assurances of Lives, population &c. As this work has been well received and this is the 4th Edition of it I have been anxious about making it as complete as possible.[5] I have enlarged it to two volumes and one half of it will be new. Some time or other this winter I hope to be able to desire your acceptance of a copy.

I received some months ago a very kind letter from you which indeed made me very happy.[6] I hope you will continue to favour me with your correspondence. We may now, as you have observed, write more freely to one another. With the most affectionate regard, I am, my Dear Friend,

ever yours

Rich*d* Price

The inclosed letter from Miss Georgiana Shipley was sent me several weeks ago from *Chilbolton* (where the Bishop's family now is) to be delivered to the Gentleman mentioned in this letter, and which I then tho't would have been going soon for *Paris*. But this gentleman (Mr Retford) delaying his journey the latter has been kept by me, and is now sent by Mr Laurens. A match is agreed upon between Miss Shipley (the eldest single sister) and Mr Jones,[7] once the close and intimate friend of Mr Paradise but now unhappily separated by a quarrel.[8] Miss Georgiana also I find is engaged. The seal of her letter was broken by accident, but it has never been open'd.

---

4. *An History of the Corruptions of Christianity*, 2 vols. (Birmingham, 1782).

5. The fourth edition of *Observations on Reversionary Payments* appeared in 1783.

6. See Benjamin Franklin to R.P., 13 June 1782.

7. Anna Maria Shipley, the eldest daughter of Jonathan Shipley, married William Jones (who had been knighted on 20 Mar.) on 8 Apr. See Cannon, II, 606.

8. William Jones accompanied John Paradise to Nantes in August 1782, intending to embark with him for America. But when he heard of the change of ministry in London he wished to return to England immediately, and he advised Paradise that if he should not have returned to Nantes within three weeks to continue his journey to America without him. This advice Paradise refused to accept, and there ensued a violent quarrel between them which was never repaired. See Cannon, I, 362–63.

To Henry Laurens

Newington Green Nov: 19*th* 1782

Dr Price presents his best respects to Mr Laurens,[1]and wishing him and his son[2] a good journey, he requests the favour of him to deliver the inclosed letter[3] to Dr Franklin. Mr Laurens can scarcely conceive how kindly he took the visit he made him on Saturday. May Mr Laurens be blest with every support under trouble and every valuable enjoyment that can make his life most happy.

ORIGINAL: Viscountess Eccles.   TEXT: Original, with the kind permission of Viscountess Eccles.

1. Henry Laurens had been released from the Tower of London on 31 Dec. 1781 (see R.P. to [John Temple], 5 Oct. 1780). On 11 May 1782 he left London for Amsterdam and remained on the continent, mostly in Southern France, until October when he returned to London. On 12 Nov. while he was at Bath he received the Act of Congress which ordered him to join the Peace Commissioners in Paris, and he arrived there only two days before the signing of the preliminary articles on 30 Nov. See Wallace, p. 402.

2. Henry Laurens, Jr. (1763–1821), was educated at the Revd Richard Clarke's school at Islington, at Geneva and at Westminster School. He returned with his father to America in 1784 and was elected to the Legislature of South Carolina in the following year.

3. See R.P. to Benjamin Franklin, 18 Nov. 1782.

To the Earl of Shelburne

Nov: 20th 1782

My Lord,

I now transmit to your Lordship a second scheme[1] for raising money by the next loan. I leave it to speak for itself, and shall be very happy should the attention I have bestowed on this subject do any good. I have added to it some observations on the redemption of the public debts, and on Lord Mahon's[2]

ORIGINAL: Bowood.   TEXT: Original, with the kind permission of the Marquis of Lansdowne.

1. In this scheme entitled, "A second proposal for raising money by a loan for the service of 1783 with an account of a plan redeeming the public debts and some observations on a measure proposed by Lord Mahon", Price proposed that £410 millions should be raised by offering the proprietors of the 3%s £200 of a stock bearing 4% interest for £100 of 3% stock and £85 in cash. (MS Bowood.)

2. Charles Stanhope (1753–1816), second son of Philip, second Earl Stanhope, became Lord Mahon and heir to the peerage on the death of his elder brother in 1763. He married Lady Hester Pitt, sister of William Pitt on 19 Dec. 1774. He was MP for Chipping Wycombe from 1780 until 1786 when he became the third Earl Stanhope. Author of *Observations on Mr Pitt's plan for the reduction of the National Debt* (1786).

proposal for that purpose.[3] I shall send a copy of the whole to Mr Pitt, as soon as I can get it ready. I find it very difficult to put off Mr *Herrenschwand*. He has, I find, sent a paper to your Lordship in answer to a comparison which I stated of his scheme with another scheme by which 121 millions more debt would be paid off at a less expence in the same time.[4] He has sent me a copy of this paper; and, in compliance with his desire, I have answered it. I once intended to send your Lordship a copy of my answer; but I do not think it worth while to trouble your Lordship with it. The principal assertions at the beginning of Mr H[er-renschwan]d's paper are not true. Most of the observations that follow are just, but far less applicable to his scheme than to other schemes. I have since received another paper from him. In one of his first papers he had called upon me by regard to your Lordship and to the kingdom to declare whether the scheme he had deliver'd to your Lordship was not the most perfect possible. He now seems to own that it is imperfect for he tells me that it is the least perfect of the three plans which he has prepared and that it was intended to be introductory to them. Of one of these plans he has sent me a general account, at the same time in a manner *insisting* on a personal interview with me; but indeed, I am so tired of him, and so perfectly satisfy'd about his plans, that I must be peremptory in refusing to go on disputing with him. Mr Motteaux is an amiable man; and I am sorry not to comply with all his wishes in this instance.

Mr Smith[5] has given your Lordship an account of the new taxes he would recommend. The principal are a stamp duty on all wills, a tax, on all successions to personal estates; a tax upon Bonds proportioned to the sum for which the bonds are given; a tax upon licences for marrying and an addition to the tax upon Bills. He proposed likewise that ordnance debentures should be put into a fixed course of redemption so that the holders of them might be assured of the times of payment. This would sink the discount greatly and produce a considerable saving; but it would be still better to pay allways either with ready money or with bills which should never be outstanding above a limitted and short term. This, were it practicable, would have the happiest effect, for Navy and ordnance bills at present bear down public credit sadly, and oblige government to pay exorbitantly for all that it purchases.

Mr Smith further proposed that Government should apply to the public service all such stocks and Dividends at the Bank and South=Sea=House as have been unclaimed for a course of years. It is uncertain what sum these amount to, but an account of them might be soon procured. The unclaimed

3. Mahon proposed a conversion scheme in which £600 in 5% stock should be offered for £1,000 in 3% stock. Price thought that the premiums required to induce the creditors to convert would be too high. (See n.1. above.)

4. See "Comparison showing the inefficiency of Mr Herrenschwand's scheme for buying off the National Debt." (MS Bowood.)

5. See R.P. to Shelburne, 25 Oct. 1782.

stock at the South=Sea=House is, I am told, half a million; and the use made
of this interest of it is to increase the Dividend on South=Sea=Stock from 3 to
3½ per *cent*. I will add to Mr Smith's proposal that a considerable saving might
be made by incorporating the South=Sea=House with the Bank. As the
South=Sea company is not now a trading company, I know of no important
purpose that is answer'd by keeping it up; and the clerks and officers employ'd
there have very little to do.

To all the taxes proposed by Mr Smith and those I mentioned when I had
the honour of seeing your Lordship I will add the following. A tax of half a
guinea each on female servants. A tax of 2s:8d per 1000 on bricks for buildings;
and a tax upon all horses, particularly on hunting and race and saddle horses.
The last tax seems to have the concurrent voice of most that I converse with.
Some other taxes are mentioned in the letter which I have inclosed and which I
transmit to your Lordship because I think it contains some information which
deserves to be attended to. The disposition, mentioned in the second page and
at the close of the 3d, which prevails among the lower people to rise and to
plunder is a very serious fact. It is an evil that must encrease with the taxes,
and that shews they cannot be carried much farther without either producing
general anarchy or the horrid necessity of governing by the sword. The writer
of this letter is unknown to me. I have cut off the upper part of the first leaf
merely because it contains compliments.

All the taxes I have named, will not, I suppose, furnish half the fund
necessary for the next loan; and it will be necessary to have recourse to an
increase of some of the *old* taxes. There are no taxes which affect the poor by so
little and which are so proportioned to rank and property as those upon
windows, houses, coaches and male servants. These doubled would produce
near £700,000 *per Ann*. A clamour would follow, but there is no possibility now
of avoiding this.

I have been looking into Lord Stair's[6] pamphlet[7] on the public accounts and
find them sadly mis-stated in several particulars. Since I began this letter I
have consider'd Mr H[errenschwan]d's *second* plan. The reply I have sent him
is short, and therefore I have inclosed a copy of it. Your Lordship will learn
from it the opinion I entertain of him. Mr Motteaux I greatly respect. He
supports Mr [Herrenschwan]d, I suppose, chiefly from compassion for a man
who has reckon'd upon making his fortune by his schemes. I am sorry that I
am under the necessity of either standing in his way or violating my judgment.

6. John Dalrymple (1720–89), became the fifth Earl Stair on 27 July 1768.

7. Either *Facts and the Consequences, submitted to the Consideration of the Public at large; but more
particularly to that of the Finance Minister, and of those who are or mean to become Creditors of the State*
(London, 1782), or *The State of the Public Debts*. The imprint of the latter bears the date 1783, but a
copy was available at an earlier date as the views put forward in it were criticized by Denis
O'Bryen in a postscript which he added to his *A Defence of the Right Honourable the Earl of Shelburne
...* (London, 1782).

Happening to know the writer, I have been lately much offended with an abusive printed letter address'd to your Lordship. But I am taking up too much of your time. Hoping that the service I have attempted in the papers I have sent your Lordship will be favourably received whether the proposals they contain are approved or not, and wishing ardently that your Lordship may be made the happy instrument of much good to this kingdom, I am, your Lordship's most obedient

and Humble servant
Rich: Price

Mr Joseph Parker has lately addressed a memorial to the Treasury respecting some property of his that was illegally seized at St Eustatius. I have known Mr Parker from his infancy, and allways reckon'd him an honest tradesman. He tells me that the Treasury has lately made compensation for property of this kind; this has raised a hope in him that some attention will be paid to his case.

To the Earl of Shelburne

Newington Green Nov 24th 1782

My Lord,

Mr Pitt has, I doubt not, convey'd a letter and a second proposal and some other papers which I had folded up and was just going to send to your Lordship on wednesday last at the time his messenger came to me. I have since sent another copy of the proposal to him for his own and Lord Mahon's inspection.

Amidst the multiplicity of your Lordship's engagements, I don't know how to expect that you should spare time enough for reading all these papers. But I could not make them shorter; and having been written partly from a desire to be of use to your Lordship and in compliance with your Lordship's wishes, they will, I hope, be received with your Lordship's usual candour and kindness. The second scheme I reckon the most eligible.[1] It is so much approv'd by one person (the *only* person to whom I have communicated it) that he has sent me the inclosed remarks upon it.[2] Your Lordship will find that these remarks are written by an able hand. But a more important business than even this occasions the present letter.

Yesterday an account was sent me from the Continent, that in the negotiations for peace it is required by our court that *Congress* should make compensa-

---

ORIGINAL: Bowood.   TEXT: Original, with the kind permission of the Marquis of Lansdowne.

1. See R.P. to Shelburne, 20 Nov. 1782.

2. In a paper entitled "Remarks on a plan for raising money for the service of 1782" Thomas Rogers suggested that a general notice of the scheme should be published immediately after its adoption, but that no time should be suffered to elapse between the promulgation of the precise terms of the loan and the date fixed for acceptance by subscribers. (MS Bowood).

tion to the Loyalists for their losses, and that this claim is likely to retard the peace, and even to be the means of breaking off the negotiation. I should think it very improper in me to take notice of this to your Lordship had I not been particularly desired to do it. If true, I suppose that no more is meant than to *try* to do the best that can be done for these unhappy men; and not to continue the war, which may be the same with sacrificing the Kingdom, on their account. Certain it is, that America may as easily be brought to unconditional submission, as to consent to take such enemies into its bosom and make compensation to them for their losses. The states to which they belong must determine concerning them. The jurisdiction of Congress does not extend to them. The acknowledgement of the independence of America is an acknowledgement that no injustice has been done them. They reckon'd upon sharing in confiscated estates, and they must not complain that the issues of war have disappointed them. *It is suspected*, that the artifice of France is at the bottom of this demand. France is afraid, that by making up matters too easily with America and conciliating it too much we shall have its weight on our side in the negotiations. Such a demand, therefore, favours the views of France.

I hope to be excused if, in laying these observations before your Lordship, I have gone beyond my proper province. I hope your Lordship believes that, however I may err, I can mean nothing but to promote your Lordship's honour and the interest of the Kingdom. I dare not break in upon you, and therefore content myself with writing letters; but I am afraid that even in this way I take up too much of your Lordship's time, and make myself too troublesome.

Will your Lordship look over the inclosed letter? I leave it to speak for itself. The writer of it is an able man, one of the Secretaries of the Royal Society, who was lately the possessor of a place which has been very properly abolished.[3]

I am, your Lordship's most obedient and Humble servant

Rich*d* Price

May I desire the favour of your Lordship to convey the inclosed papers of remarks, after you have done with them, to Mr Pitt? I mentioned the writer of it to him in my last letter, but I had not then received these remarks. I find I cannot send off this letter without adding to what I have said about the negotiations that I know that America is particularly jealous, and suspicious of the British Court at present and that this affords the strongest reason for being as fair and liberal as possible in negotiating with them in order to gain their confidence and to draw them off from France.

---

3. When Price wrote this letter the Principal Secretary of the Royal Society was Paul Henry Maty; the other Secretary was Joseph Planta; the Foreign Secretary, Charles Hutton, and the Assistant Secretary, John Robertson. I have not been able to discover whether any of these relinquished a place or indeed whether they had places to relinquish, although earlier in his career Planta had been appointed to teach Italian to Queen Charlotte. See *Gent. Mag.*, XCVII (1827), 564–65.

To the Earl of Shelburne

Nov. 28th 1782

My Lord,

In compliance with your Lordship's desire I have been thinking of the subject about which we conversed yesterday; and I would propose that it should be intimated that the *public debts ought not to be considered as irredeemable, there being still, notwithstanding their late great increase, reason to hope that such regulations may be establish'd and such savings made and future loans so conducted as to furnish the means of putting them into such a fixed course of redemption as will gradually bring them within the limits of safety.*[1] But indeed I am ill qualify'd for suggestions of this kind; and your Lordship is best able to find such a mode of expression in this instance as will be properest and best adapted to your Lordship's views. That now proposed seems sufficiently general. Should the mention of loans be thought too particular, it may be left out. It seems, however, of some consequence because nothing can be more unfavourable to a plan of redemption than the old modes of borrowing. The schemes I have sent to Mr Pitt and your Lordship are not liable to this objection. The first is founded on a quick redemption of the sum borrow'd. And one of the chief recommendations of the second scheme is, that it will prepare the way for and expedite any plan of redemption that may be established.

I am, My Lord, with great regard

Your Lordship's most Obedient and Humble servant
Richd Price

ORIGINAL: Bowood. TEXT: Original, with the kind permission of the Marquis of Lansdowne.

1. In his biography of Price, William Morgan writes: "In the King's Speech, which was delivered at the opening of the session in December 1782, that part of it which expresses a wish 'that such regulations may be established, such savings made, and future loans so constructed as to promote the means of their gradual redemption by a fixed course of payment,' was suggested, and I believe inserted in the very words of Dr. Price." (*Memoirs*, p. 98.) The relevant passage from the King's Speech on the Opening of the Parliamentary Session on 5 Dec. 1782, which, although it does not follow Price recommendation exactly, does express his views on the importance of redeeming the National Debt, reads, "I must recommend to you an immediate attention to the great objects of the public receipts and expenditure: and above all, to the state of the public debt. Notwithstanding the great increase of it during the war, it is to be hoped, that such regulations may still be established—such savings made—and future loans so conducted, as to promote the means of its gradual redemption, by a fixed course of payment." (*Parl. Hist.*, XXIII, 209.)

To Christopher Wyvill[1]

Newington Green, Dec. 12, 1782.

Rev. and Dear Sir,

I cannot make myself easy without sending you these lines to thank you for the note with which you have honoured me, and for the communication which accompanied it of the Letter to the Westminster Committee. I wish also to lay before you my sentiments on the subject of that Letter. I think it indeed a most proper Letter, and I approve entirely of all the points of Reformation mentioned in it; but at the same time I cannot help being sorry for the intimation in it, that, in order to gain unanimity, the Yorkshire Committee is ready to sacrifice its wishes with respect to the abolition of some of the most corrupt Boroughs.[2] This I reckon the most important of all the points of Reformation, there being no abuse so flagrant as that a few beggars, subject to the Treasury, Admiralty, &c. should possess the power of chusing the majority of that Assembly which makes our laws, and disposes of our lives and fortunes. The addition of a hundred Knights to the Counties, without the removal of this abuse, will, in my opinion, do us little good. This is the time for struggling, when other Counties are happily emancipating themselves, and when our Ministers themselves are favourable to the views of the People, and have pledged themselves to support them. Such another opportunity for struggling successfully may never offer itself; and if we struggle, it ought to be for something worth the having. Your County is giving a noble example. Much may be expected from its weight and influence. May Heaven grant success to the present endeavours of the honest and enlightened part of the Nation, to procure for it a *real* Representation, instead of that mockery which now bears that name. Till this can be procured, we deceive ourselves when we think ourselves free; the first requisite to Constitutional Liberty being a fair and

---

PRINTED: Christopher Wyvill, *Political papers*, 6 vols. (York, 1794–1802), IV, 221–22. TEXT: *Political papers*.

1. Christopher Wyvill (1740–1822) was a wealthy landowner who lived at Burton Constable, North Riding. In 1779 he became Secretary of the Yorkshire Association and a prominent leader in the campaign for economic and parliamentary reform. The history of this movement is recorded together with a voluminous correspondence in *Political papers*. Wyvill also wrote *A Defence of Dr. Price and the Reformers of England* (London, 1792).

2. On 1 Nov. 1782, the Yorkshire Association agreed to include in their programme for parliamentary reform: the abolition of fifty 'obnoxious' boroughs, adding the seats thus released to the representation of the counties and the metropolis, the repeal of the Septennial Act, the extension of the franchise to copyholders and the reform of the representation in Scotland. They were, however, reluctant to press for the abolition of the rotten boroughs, and Wyvill, in a circular letter to the other counties, expressed their willingness to sacrifice this item in the interests of unanimity. See Wyvill, *Political papers*, II, 43–71.

equal Representation. Your exertions, Sir, in this cause, must be long remembered. Your merit is above any praise that can be bestowed upon it. Accept the gratitude, the ardent respect, and best wishes of

Sir,

Your most obedient and humble servant,

Rich. Price.

To the Earl of Shelburne

Newington Green, Dec. 14th, 1782.

Dr Price presents his respectful compliments to Lord Shelburne, and thanks him for the permission he has given to lay before him the enclosed case of three Natives of America now in Norwich Gaol. A very particular and long account of these has been sent him from Norwich composed by the surgeon who attends the prison; but he cannot think of troubling Lord Shelburne with it. He feels himself so moved with compassion for these three men that he cannot help earnestly requesting Lord Shelburne's attention to their cases. He is told, that the readiest and almost the only method of relieving them is by obtaining the King's pardon for them, in consequence of which they might be sent to Forton Prison to await there till they could be exchanged as American prisoners. Dr Price presents his best wishes to Lady Shelburne. He feels her present state of anxiety about her little son,[1] and hopes it will be soon happily removed. Mrs. Price also wishes to express her concern.

PRINTED: *T.U.H.S.*, IX (1947–50), No. 1, 35. TEXT: *T.U.H.S.*.

1. Henry Petty (after 1818, Petty-Fitzmaurice), (1780–1863), became the third Marquis of Lansdowne in 1809. *The Complete Peerage* (London, 1929), VII, 439–40.

To the Earl of Shelburne

Newington=Green, Dec. 30th 1782

My Lord,

Your Lordship will receive with this a copy of the papers relating to the new Birmingham Canal, which I have been desired to deliver to you. Mr Russel,[1] a

---

ORIGINAL: Bowood. TEXT: Original, with the kind permission of the Marquis of Lansdowne.

1. Probably William Russell (1740–1818), a merchant who was engaged in the export trade from Birmingham and Sheffield to Russia, Spain, and the United States. He was a friend and patron of Joseph Priestley, and his house at Showell Green was burnt down during the Birmingham Riots of 1791.

most active and respectable gentleman in Warwickshire who gave me these papers, wishes your Lordship would honor him so far as to admit him to a conversation on the subject of this Navigation some time *after* the recess and *before* the second reading of the Bill for establishing this Navigation now in the House of Commons.

In talking on saturday evening last about the loan with Mr Streatfield, a money'd man in this neighbourhood who is intimate with Mr Harman[2] and one of the persons amongst whom Mr Harman always divides his shares of the public loans, he observed without being led to it by any thing I had said, that he thought it a pity a loan could not be contrived that should give the holders of the old stocks a preference. I mention this to shew that a scheme of this kind would probably meet with the approbation of all important persons and even of some of the fairer part of the money'd people themselves. What Mr Streatfield said led me to tell him, that the preference he wished for was the foundation of a a scheme now under consideration, and to ask him whether he thought his friend Mr Harman was a proper person to be consulted about such a scheme. In his reply he express'd a great opinion of Mr Harman, but at the same time intimated a doubt whether he could be trusted in giving an opinion of a scheme that would deprive him of such gain and influence as he had hitherto derived from loans. He added that Mr Harman should, if I pleased, meet me at his house; but this I had rather avoid.

I mentioned to Mr Pitt, Mr Hussey[3] as a person very proper to be consulted; and I have since thought of Mr Jackson[4] of whose knowledge on this as well as other subjects I have a great opinion.

Yesterday, a banker in the City (but not Mr Rogers) came to me to tell me that he wished a method could be thought of to prevent sollicitations and interest making for shares in loans and complaints of partiality in the distribution of them. It fell in his way, he said, to see a great deal of the evil of them. They lessen'd industry and hurt trade. Multitudes of people sollicited shares who could not make one payment, and all asked for much more than they could take in order to secure some. I answer'd that there was a scheme in

2. John Harman, a partner in Gurnell, Hoare, Harman & Co., was the principal agent for Dutch and other foreign investors in the city, *Parl. Hist.*, XXVI, 24; Norris, p. 230.

3. William Hussey (1725–1813), a merchant. MP for St Germans, 1767–68; Hindon, 1768–74; and Salisbury, 1774–1813. He strongly disapproved of the American War and opposed North's administration. In the House he concentrated upon financial questions and was universally respected as an expert on the subject. North complimented him upon his financial abilities. See Namier and Brooke, I, 663–64; Norris, p. 128.

4. Richard Jackson (?1721–87), Dr Johnson's "the all knowing" MP for Weymouth and Melcombe Regis, 1762–68; and New Romney, 1768–84. He was Counsel to the Board of Trade from 1770 to 1782 and Lord of the Treasury in Shelburne's administration from July 1782 to April 1783. He was considered an expert not only in law, but also in economics and finance, in science and in agriculture. He won acclaim more as a scholar and a polymath than as a politician. Agent for Connecticut (1760–70), Pennsylvania (1763–70), and Massachusetts (1765–70). Namier and Brooke, II, 669–72; Norris, p. 43n.

contemplation which should it be adopted, would answer all his views and prevent the evils he mentioned. He suggested a method which had occurred to himself of doing this, and which I think will deserve consideration, and be highly proper to be adopted should it be found necessary to have recourse to the old modes of Borrowing. But this is a calamity which, I hope, will not happen.

Should the Treasury decide for the new scheme, some general notice of it might be published immediately in the way proposed by Mr Rogers. The stock=holders will want as long a preparation as can well be given them; and as little time as possible should be allowed the money=jobbers to practise their arts after opening the terms.

Be pleased to deliver my best respects to Mr Pitt. Wishing your Lordship and him well thro' this business and all the weighty affairs in which you are now engag'd, I am, My Lord, with sincere affection,

Your Lordship's most obedient and Humble servant
Rich*d* Price

To Sir Joseph Banks[1]

Newington=Green Jan*y* 1*st* 1783

Dr Price presents his respectful compliments to Sir Joseph Banks, and is sorry he cannot conveniently attend the meeting at his house this morning. He has observed with concern the late disputes in the Royal Society;[2] and wishes success to any measure that may be adopted for preserving the peace of the Society.

ORIGINAL: MS M.3804, Archive Department, Library Services, London Borough of Hackney. TEXT: Original, with the kind permission of the Archive Department, Library Services, London Borough of Hackney.

1. See Vol. I, 123.

2. This dispute began in 1782. Complaints were made against Dr Charles Hutton, Professor of Mathematics at Woolwich and Assistant Secretary in charge of foreign correspondence, for failing to attend to his duties punctually. A year later in Nov. 1783 the Council decided that all secretaries should reside in London, whereupon Hutton resigned. The question was later debated in the Society and Hutton received the support of Samuel Horsley, and P.H. Maty, Secretary to the Society. An attempt to censure the President, Sir Joseph Banks, failed, as did the move to rescind the rule concerning residence in London. Price supported Banks during the controversy. See *Banks Letters*, ed. Warren R. Dawson (London, 1958), p. 51. For further details of these disputes see H.C. Cameron, *Sir Joseph Banks* (Sydney, 1952), pp. 129–34; A. Kippis, *Observations on the Late Contests in the Royal Society* (London, 1783); [Anon], *An Authentic Narrative of the Dissensions in the Royal Society* (London, 1784).

To Benjamin Rush[1]

Dear Sir,

I return you many thanks for the letter which I received from you a few weeks ago. Your favourable opinion I shall always think of with pleasure and gratitude.

The account in your letter of the establish'd and quiet state of the governments in America, and of the disposition which prevails there to exercise equity and moderation with respect to the Loyalists, has given me great satisfaction. Many have been led here to entertain very different Ideas of your state. One point, however, remains still unsettled; and it is a point of the last importance; I mean, the federal union. The credit, the strength and even the existence of the united states seem to me to depend on the proper settlement of this point. It is obvious, that the greatest wisdom is required to find out such a plan as shall give due energy to the decisions of the delegation that forms the union without encroaching too much on the liberty and independence of the confederated states.[2] But I am touching a subject to which I am not equal. May Heaven grant to the united states the best direction.

I am glad to find that a college is to be erected in the back parts of Pensylvania on so liberal a plan as you describe.[3] This must be a situation in which such a seminary of learning is likely to be particularly useful, and I wish I could inform you that it is practicable to set on foot with success a subscription in this country for the purpose of assisting in establishing and endowing it. But I am afraid this cannot be done. It is too early a period of the peace for it. Friendship is not yet sufficiently restored between the two countries. The Dissenters among whom chiefly my interest lies are hardly able to keep up their own interest, and cannot look much abroad. I lament much that these and some other reasons make me incapable of giving you the encouragement you wish for in this instance. I have received other applications of the same kind from America, and been obliged to return the same answer. I should be glad to give the aid of my name and contribution; but this could do but little.

ORIGINAL: Rush MSS. LXI, The Historical Society of Pennsylvania, Library Co. of Philadelphia. TEXT: Original, with the kind permission of The Historical Society of Pennsylvania.

1. Benjamin Rush (1745–1813), physician, humanitarian, and signatory of the Declaration of Independence. Educated at Edinburgh and at St Thomas's Hospital, London. In 1783 he became a member of the staff of the Pennsylvania Hospital, and was actively concerned in the founding of Dickinson College. In 1803 he became President of the Pennsylvania Society for Promoting the Abolition of Slavery.

2. Price developed this theme in *Observations on the Importance of the American Revolution*. See Peach, pp. 187–89.

3. i.e. Dickinson College.

We are at present much overburden'd here, the taxes deficient, and our finances in a deplorable state. America, I hope, will learn to take care of itself. Thither many of us will probably be flying. I have convey'd to you with this letter, a set of Advertisements which have been printed on purpose to be distributed in America. You will know how much the cause of civil and religious liberty has been indebted to Bishop Hoadly.[4] Will you be so good as to take the trouble of presenting some of these Advertisements to the Academy and College at Philadelphia and of distributing the rest in whatever manner you think best. One of my friends interests himself for the widow of Dr Hoadly the Chancellor,[5] and she would be benefitted could she dispose of the remaining copies of this work. One set I shall send over by the first opportunity, and direct it to you to be presented from me to *Dickenson* College.[6]

I have also sent you a plan for observing meteors drawn up by Dr Maskelyne our Astronomer Royal.[7] Will you be so good as to present it to Dr Ewing;[8] and to inform him that Dr Maskelyne is very anxious about collecting all the observations on meteors which it is possible for him to procure in hopes of being able to ascertain their nature and causes. I have promised to circulate for him in America copies of this plan, and also of some observations of his from 1775 to 1782. I expect a parcel to be sent me very soon, some of which I shall transmit to Philadelphia. Dr Maskelyne wishes for a list of all the Universities, Colleges and Philosophical Societies in the united states; Could you supply me with such a list?

I have inclosed a parcel for Dr Styles.[9] It is too large to be sent from Philadelphia by the post. Perhaps it may not be difficult to convey it in some other way; by ship, or by some person going to Connecticut. I hope you will pardon me for giving you such a trouble. I was not willing to lose the opportunity which now offers itself of getting this parcel convey'd to Dr Styles.

4. Benjamin Hoadly (1676–1761), successively Bishop of Bangor (1715), Hereford (1721), Salisbury (1723), and Winchester (1734). In Price's view, Hoadly ranked with Locke, Sidney and Milton as a writer on moral and political subjects (see R.P. to Joseph Willard, 14 Mar. 1784). Hoadly was a trenchant opponent of Divine Right and a staunch defender of the view that political authority is founded in the consent of the governed. See, particularly, his famous sermon on Romans xiii, preached on 29 Sept. 1705, "The Measures of Submission to the Civil Magistrate Consider'd", *Sermons* (London, 1754), 63ff. See also *The Original and Institution of Civil Government Discuss'd* (London, 1710) and *A preservative against the principles and practices of the non-jurors both in church and state* (London, 1716). Hoadly also wrote in favour of the repeal of the Test and Corporation Acts. See *The common rights of subjects defended and the nature of the sacramental test consider'd* (London, 1719).

5. John Hoadly (1711–76), the youngest son of Benjamin Hoadly (see n.4. above), became Chancellor of the diocese of Winchester in 1735. His edition of his father's works in three volumes appeared in 1773.

6. See R.P. to Benjamin Rush, 14 Oct. 1784. Price also presented a set of Hoadly's works to Harvard. See R.P. to A. Eliot, 8 Mar. 1784.

7. Nevil Maskelyne, *A plan for observing the meteors called fire-balls* (London, 1783).

8. John Ewing, see Vol. I, 235.

9. See Vol. I, 149.

I am much pleased with the account you give in your letter of Mr Vaughn[10] and Mr Redford. When you happen to see either of them, deliver to them my kind remembrances. Mr Vaughn has been always one of my best friends; and I have great reason to love him and Mrs Vaughn and the whole family. I have a very good opinion of Mr Redford. America must profit by such acquisitions. With much respect I am, Dear Sir,

your very obedient and humble servant

Rich*d* Price

Should it be difficult to convey in the course of a few weeks the parcel directed to Dr Styles, I shall be obliged to you for opening it and only conveying to him by the post the letter which you will find inclosed in it.

---

10. John Vaughan.

To the Earl of Shelburne

Newington=Green Jan*y* 6*th* 1783

My Lord,

In my last letter I mentioned a proposal,[1] for preventing interest making for shares in loans and complaints of partiality in the distribution of them, made by a Banker in the City, which appeared to me proper to be adopted if it should be found necessary to return to the old modes of borrowing. But upon reconsidering that proposal, we are now both of us convinced, that it might produce some very dangerous consequences; and therefore does not deserve to be further thought of.

All that I hear convinces me more and more that the scheme[2] under consideration would meet the sentiments and wishes of the public. It seems, as far as I can learn, the general voice that a loan which should give the preference to the old stock=holders is desirable and would be honourable to administration. Should, therefore, this scheme *fail* in the execution, administration would gain credit, and consequently strength by *attempting* it; especially, when it appeared that it had been chosen not only on account of its equitableness, but as an important operation of finance for facilitating future loans and expediting a plan of redemption. But the only person to whom I have communicated it, thinks the success of it certain, and indeed there can be no reasons for doubting about its success provided liberal terms are offer'd; and in my opinion there are scarcely any terms which will be too liberal.

ORIGINAL: Bowood.   TEXT: Original, with the kind permission of the Marquis of Lansdowne.
1. See R.P. to Shelburne, 30 Dec. 1782.
2. See R.P. to Shelburne, 20 Nov. 1782.

The second Earl of Shelburne and first Marquis of Lansdowne (1737–1805).
Portrait dated 1764; after Reynolds. Reproduced by kind permission of the
National Portrait Gallery, London.

The first payment should not exceed 2 or 3 *per cent*, but it might be considerably increased by offering a handsome discount or some other encouragement to such as should pay 10 *per cent* or more. And if, notwithstanding this, enough should not be brought in at the first payment to supply the immediate necessities of government, I do not see why a million might not be borrowed of the Bank on a vote of credit or the growing produce of the sinking fund, or by an increase of Exchequer bills.

Should there be a Peace all will be sufficiently easy; and in this case, while your Lordship and your friends continue in office, I shall cease to despair of the public debts and the deliverance of the Kingdom. I cannot help adding that, in consequence of the King's Speech and the late measures, I think I see a diffidence which prevailed beginning to subside; and that I am full of hopes, that by peace and Oeconomy, by putting the debts of the kingdom into a certain course of payment and thus saving it from a dreadful convulsion; and above all, by reforming a wretched representation, restoring the securities of public liberty and destroying corruption, your Lordship will gradually gain the hearts of the nation; and become one of the first and best ministers this country ever saw. It is surprising that more of our ministers have not, for their own sakes, pointed their ambition to such objects, and chosen this path to glory.

> With great respect I am your Lordship's
> most obedient and humble servant
> Rich*d* Price

I wish to say a few words to your Lordship about Lord Fitzmaurice's going to Oxford; and I shall call with this view on wednesday morning.

Would not Mr Martin[3] be a proper person to be consulted about the scheme for the next loan? I am not acquainted with him; but the high character he bears as an upright man has prejudiced me much in his favour, and as a Banker he must be well acquainted with money matters.

---

3. James Martin (1738–1810), of the family banking house of Martin. He was MP for Tewkesbury from 1776 to 1807.

To the Earl of Shelburne

> Newington=Green Jan*y* 10*th* 1783

My Lord,

The perusal of the papers which I now return to your Lordship fully convinces me that great savings may be made by putting Navy and victualling

---

ORIGINAL: Bowood.   TEXT: Original, with the kind permission of the Marquis of Lansdowne.

Bills on a new footing. Either of the plans proposed in them would, as far as I can judge, answer this end; but the ready money plan, were it equally practicable, would be the best; for I am afraid, that by putting Navy Bills on the same footing with *India* bonds or *Exchequer Bills* (which is what the *printed* dissertation proposes) they would interfere too much with the other paper of this kind, and, by depretiating it, cause all such paper to fall (should the war continue) to a greater discount than is supposed in these proposals. It seems certain, however, that were no other alteration made than fixing regular and stated times for paying Navy Bills in the course of about a year and a half the present discount would be much lower'd, and a considerable saving produced—as to Ordnance debentures I cannot help thinking it a surprising instance of the inattention of our former ministers that they never attempted any thing in this way, but chose to go on paying a third or a quarter more than the value for Ordnance stores rather than alter the mode of payment.

The inclosed letter I received soon after the first change of ministry; and I then sent an account of the chief particulars in it to the Duke of Richmond, because desired to do so by the writer, who is a very respectable tradesman in the City. I now put the whole letter into your Lordship's hands notwithstanding the compliments to me at the beginning and end of it, to which indeed, I am by no means entitled, and which I know your Lordship will excuse.

I am glad your Lordship is possess'd of Mr Mitchel's Dissertation on the Navy debt.[1] The proposal he makes seems for the reason I have mention'd less eligible than the proposal in these papers, he has sent me a statement of the national debt during Lord North's administration, but it contains nothing of particular consequence. With great regard I am, My Lord,

Your Lordship's most
obedient and humble servant
Richd Price

---

1. Possibly Thomas Mitchell (1735–90), marine-painter and navy official, who was at one time employed as as assistant shipbuilder at Chatham and in the Navy Office. He later became Assistant Surveyor of the Navy. (*D.N.B.*)

To the Earl of Shelburne

Newington=Green Jany 20th 1783

My Lord,

Some scheme of a loan must now soon be resolved on. I shall, therefore, request the favour of your Lordship's and Mr Pitt's attention to the following observations.[1]

ORIGINAL: Bowood.   TEXT: Original, with the kind permission of the Marquis of Lansdowne.
1. For details of the two schemes to which Price refers in this letter see R.P. to Shelburne, 7 Nov. 1782 and 20 Nov. 1782.

If the 3 per cents are taken at 68 and the 4 *per cents* at 84 £100 will be the exact sum which ought to be paid for the conversion of £100 *three per cent* stock into £200 *four per cent* stock. Should, therefore, the loan be procured by such a conversion, the interest paid by government would be just 5 *per cent*. The new capital would be exactly equal to the sum borrowed; and supposing the sum *ten millions*, an old capital in the 3 *per cents* of ten millions would be at the same time converted into a 4 *per cent* capital. There cannot be much doubt but that the sum wanted for this year may with ease, should the stocks not fall below their present price, be obtained on these terms, leaving the newly created 4 per *cents* redeemable at pleasure. But if ordered not to be redeemable before the redemption has been completed of the old 4 *per cents* (a circumstance perfectly indifferent to the public) the loan may be obtained at a lower interest.

Mr Pitt, when I had the pleasure of seeing him at Shelburne=House, seemed doubtful whether he should not prefer borrowing by creating a new 5 *per cent* stock irredeemable for 21 years. I may venture to pronounce that the money lenders, supposing the 3 *per cents* not higher than they are now or 69, would not take such a stock at par; and that, consequently, it would be necessary to give them a premium consisting either of an additional capital or of a long or short annuity; and this would be falling again into the hands of the Jobbers, and returning to the old modes of borrowing. It would also oblige Government to delay paying off a stock bearing high interest for 21 years; which, tho' a matter of indifference when there exists stock bearing an interest equally high, is a disadvantage when the contrary is the case. But the main observation I would make is, that such a scheme would want all the advantages belonging to the other scheme and enumerated in the Proposal I had the honour of presenting to your Lordship, and Mr Pitt. In particular. Instead of having any tendency to raise the funds, it must depress them, as all loans have hitherto done. It is not equally subservient to a general plan of redemption because it leaves all the old stocks as they are. It is not so honourable to administration by excluding all possibility of partiality in the distribution of the loan. It does not confine the loan, as the other scheme does, to persons known at the time of subscribing to be possesst of property equal to the sums subscribed, and who pledge that property as a security for their payment. Nor has it that particular kind of equitableness which there is in confining the advantages of the loan to those who have been sufferers by the depretiation of the funds.

It may be thought that the selection of a number of money'd men and setting up the loan to Auction among them would prevent a charge of partiality. But even in this case there might be combinations among the money'd men, and ministers would be charged with partiality in the choice of these bidders. The Idea of putting up the loan to *all* bidders cannot, I suppose, be entertained; and an open subscription, except on the plan I have proposed, would throw the loan open to all sorts of indigent and interested men.

Ministers, indeed, supposing the scheme for which I am pleading adopted, might be charged with giving private hints to favourites in order to induce them to entitle themselves to the advantages of the loan by purchasing 3 per cent stock, before public notice was given of the intended preferences. But this would be charging ministers with a partiality the effect of which must be to strengthen public credit by raising the funds, and to enable the public to borrow on better terms; and this is a kind of partiality which could not be very severely censured. But probably few would think of such a charge. During the whole time between the notice and opening the terms that is, for some weeks, the advantages of the loan would appear to be open equally to all who chose to qualify themselves before the opening of the terms. Of what use then could any hints be, which could be given before the publication of the notice? Should it, however, be thought necessary, all suspicions of partiality might be render'd impossible by limitting the subscription to such persons as should appear by the Books at the Bank and South=Sea=house to have been proprietors of stock for some time given before the subscription was open'd. Should this time be even six or seven years, the subscription, tho' clogged, would probably be fill'd, and the advantages of the loan would be limited to such of the oldest stockholders as had paid from 86 to 112 for what is now worth only 69. The rise of the funds which this scheme has a tendency to produce, would indeed be lost by such a regulation, but this loss would be balanced by the advantages.

The first scheme I thought of was that on which I have made these remarks; and I went so far as to write a sketch of it with only this difference that I made the new 5 *per cent* stock irredeemable, not for 21 years but for the whole time, whether more or less, which would be taken up in redeeming the present 4 per cent Capital (that is, £26,750,000) which time, supposing a million *per Ann* applied to this purpose, is 18 years. But I threw away the sketch from a conviction of the preferableness of the two schemes which I presented to your Lordship.

I am afraid I am becoming too officious. I can rely on your Lordship's candour. I feel, indeed, a little anxious on this occasion for the more I consider the scheme I wish to recommend and the more I hear of the sentiments of others, the more I am persuaded of its utility and the credit it would give to administration. But I refer all to your decision and Mr Pitt's. My expectations are, perhaps, too high.

Should the establishment of a general plan of redemption be resolved on, I shall be glad to be allowed to give my Ideas of the best method of proceeding in order to produce as quick and effectual a redemption as possible. It is but little I can do to assist your Lordship; and if in any thing, it is in a business of this kind.

Your Lordship is receiving lists for the loan. A friend of Mr Harman's has been with me to enquire whether there was any impropriety in this. My reply was, that I did not know what scheme would be adopted, and that I did not see that it could be improper. Mr Harman gives out that he has been sent for by your Lordship; and it is suspected that he is too forward. He lost the advantage he expected from being one of the Jobbers for the loan of last year; and he is, I suppose, willing to take more care this year. A Bankrupt who was in the Gazette lately, told me yesterday that he had been offer'd the assistance of £100,000 in the next loan; and should it be a loan on the old plan he will probably get it.

I am cruelly detaining your Lordship by this long letter; but I cannot conclude without once more congratulating you on the Peace. My heart is now in a great measure at ease; and my resolution is to trouble myself as little for the future about Politics as possible. I reckon it enough that I have lived to see two great events which I have been long wishing for; I mean, the salvation of my country by a Peace, and a revolution in favour of the liberty of the world by the settlement with America. There remains still two events of the last consequence; and it is in the power of your Lordship and your friends to accomplish them both. I mean; *the reduction of the public debts*, and the *reformation of the representation*. Without the one, a convulsion must still come; and without the other, we cannot be called a free country. Mr Pitt does not know how much I admire him for his exertions in favour of the last of these objects. There is now more reason than ever for such exertions; for if every thing is not done to diminish the public burdens and to make the people easy and happy they will quit the country and fly to America. A disposition to this prevails, and some are now going.

I have been long in the habit of thus preaching to your Lordship; and you are so good, that I need not justify myself by claiming the privilege of a person who is getting into the evening of life and is honoured with your friendship, and who can have nothing in view but the good of his country and of mankind.

With great respect I am your Lordship's
most obedient and humble servant
Rich*d* Price

Will your Lordship be so good as to communicate this letter to Mr Pitt? I put into his hands some time ago a proposal of a tax, upon Undertakers and the pomp of funerals. The author is Mr Cotterell, a clergyman with whom I am well acquainted, and from whom I have just received a letter in which are these words—"I wish to know whether the objections to the Turnpike tax are insurmountable. I was much interested in its success, for it was model'd on a plan I gave in to the Treasury; but many clauses in my plan were omitted which would have made the tax more unexceptionable. I was the more disappointed at its being rejected, because I had hoped to ground on it a more effectual mode of collecting the Post=horse tax, which ought to be more productive than it is."

The Gentlemen at *Yarmouth* have just informed me, that they find Sir John Rous recommends a person to the vacant place in the Customs at *Southwood*, and that for this reason, they chuse to withdraw their petition, Sir John Rous's interest having no connexion with that corrupt interest which is so oppressive at Yarmouth.

I had writ this letter before I received the remarks on my plan.[2] I wish the author[3] of these remarks had been so good as to peruse the plan with more attention; for indeed he has mistaken it greatly. May I beg that there may be no determination to reject it before monday next when I hope to return the remarks with my reply and some further Observations?[4]

---

2. "Mr Baring's observations of Dr Price's scheme of finance for 1783" (MS Bowood). Baring's main criticism of Price's scheme was that Price was assuming that "the public will be able to sell their loan in the month of February for what will be its value in October or November .... The proprietor of the 3%s will not sell, nor change his stock without profit ... and any advance upon the 3%s is prejudicial to the publick as well as any decline upon the 4%s."

3. Francis Baring (1740–1810). Founder of the financial house of Baring Brothers & Co., Director of the East India Company, 1779–82. On 11 Oct. 1782 Shelburne appointed him Commissioner for supplying Troops in West Indies and North Americ. See Baker, pp. 135–60.

4. See R.P. to Shelburne, 4 Feb. 1783.

To the Earl of Shelburne

Newington=Green Jan*y* 22*d* 1783

My Lord,

The inclosed papers were brought to me by a foreigner who told me his name was *Christopher Chrysel*, and to whom I am an utter stranger. He assures the Treasury in them, that he is possess'd of a secret by which he can prevent the gold and silver coin from being melted down without detection for manufactures and exportation. It has seldom happen'd that the men who think they have discover'd secrets of this kind have not deceived themselves. This possibly is the case in the present instance; but such a secret supposing it discoverable, would be of such unspeakable importance to the public, that I cannot think it improper to attend to this man. I have, therefore, by his desire, taken the liberty to put his proposal into your Lordship's hands; and I have promised to inform him whether any attention is likely to be paid to it. Lord Mahon has consider'd this subject; and perhaps he would like to examine this man, and to try his proposal.

Mr Maltby,[1] I find, has received an order from the Treasury. Mrs Price and

---

ORIGINAL: Bowood. TEXT: Original, with the kind permission of the Marquis of Lansdowne.

1. Possibly William Maltby whose mother was a cousin to Price's wife, Sarah. The Maltby family were members of Price's congregation at Hackney. In the spring of 1788 they ran into financial difficulties, Price in his journal referring to Mr Maltby being 'broken'. William Maltby features in Price's will, receiving a legacy on his own account and being appointed to receive moneys in trust for other members of his family. See "Journal", pp. 385, 401.

I think ourselves particularly oblig'd to your Lordship for remembering him. I believe he is an honest man; and hope that employing him will be found an advantage to the public as well as to him.

It is with much reluctance that, in consequence of an application from Yarmouth, I [ ] your Lordship that there is a vacancy at Southwold of a riding officer's place in the Customs; and that the Gentlemen at Yarmouth who applied to your Lordship on a former occasion, have determined to petition for the appointment of one George Cross to that office. Probably your Lordship has received the petition. They are, I find, still anxious to obtain some reason for hoping that your Lordship will shew them some favour in opposition to the influence which Lord North's party have long had and continue to boast of having at Yarmouth.

Your Lordship may remember that I mentioned to you a gentleman from Warwickshire (Mr Russel) who is employ'd to attend a Bill for establishing a new Canal at Birmingham, and for completing the inland communication by water between the rivers Mersey, Trent, Severn and Thames.[2] He requests a short audience from your Lordship; and I will take the liberty to call on friday morning to ask whether your Lordship chuses to see him. Should your Lordship be too much engaged, an introduction of him to Mr Pitt would, I believe, satisfy him. This is a very popular Bill in Staffordshire, Warwickshire, Lancashire &c. It will be warmly supported by the Dukes of Bridgwater[3] and Marlborough,[4] and by many of the principal Gentlemen in those Counties.

Relying on your Lordship's usual indulgence, I am, My Lord,

Your very obedient and humble servant

Rich*d* Price

---

2. In 1783 an Act (23 Geo. III c. xxxiii) was passed "to render more effectual" previous Acts passed in George III's reign for making a navigable canal from the Trent to the Mersey. In the same year another Act (23 George III c. xcii) was passed to permit the construction of a canal from Birmingham to Coventry. See Charles Hadfield, *The Canals of the West Midlands* (Newton Abbott, 1966), pp. 34, 71.

3. Francis Egerton (1736–1803), third and last Duke of Bridgwater, who devoted his life to the construction of canals, including the canal from Worsley to Manchester which was completed in 1761, and the canal from Longford Bridge to Runcorn, linking Liverpool and Manchester, which was completed in 1772.

4. George Spencer (1739–1817), fourth Duke of Marlborough. He succeeded to the peerage in 1758, and from Apr. 1763 to July 1765 was Lord Privy Seal in the Grenville ministry.

To the Earl of Shelburne

Newington=Green Feb: 4*th* 1783

Dr Price presents his respectful compliments to Lord Shelburne, and returns the remarks of the proposed plan with his replies writ on the same paper.[1]

He has added two papers, one containing a further explanation of the scheme,[2] and the other Mr Roger's observations on the remarks.[3] Dr Price has still one paper more to communicate, in which he shall state the particular importance of this scheme consider'd as an operation of finance for facilitating future redemptions and loans;[4] and it seems to him that it is only by such a scheme the intimation given in the King's Speech can be properly made good, "that future loans should be so conducted as to promote the means of redeeming the public debts".[5] He is sensible, however, that Lord Shelburne and Mr Pitt will have occasion for some courage should they resolve to carry such a scheme into execution; for the Bankers, contractors, Jews, and others among whom the profits of loans have been usually distributed, begin *already* to be alarmed, and to clamour against all new schemes that may exclude them.

Dr Price wishes Mr Pitt would honour these papers with his perusal.

ORIGINAL: Bowood. TEXT: Original, with the kind permission of the Marquis of Lansdowne.
  1. Probably, "Notes on [Dr Price's] Scheme of Finance with Dr Price's Replies Thereto". The first set of notes were written by Francis Baring. (MS Bowood.)
  2. Probably "Comparison of Three Different Modes of a Scheme for Borrowing Ten Millions by Converting Part of the 3% Capital into a 4% Capital." (MS Bowood.)
  3. Probably "Mr Rogers' Observations on Mr Baring's Remarks." (MS Bowood.)
  4. "Observations on the Importance of a Proposal for Borrowing Money for the Service of 1783 Consider'd as a Measure Intended to Facilitate Future Redemptions and Loans." (MS Bowood.)
  5. *Parl. Hist*, XXIII, 209. The text reads "and future loans so conducted, as to promote the means of its gradual redemption, by a fixed course of payment."

To Francis Baring

Feb: 14th 1783

Sir,

I have sent you some observations[1] on the paper of remarks which I received last monday from Lord S[helburne]. These observations, except those which

ORIGINAL: A copy at Bowood in Price's hand of the letter he sent to Baring. TEXT: Original, with the kind permission of the Marquis of Lansdowne.
  1. "Observations on the Importance of a Proposal for Borrowing Money for the Service of 1783 Consider'd as a Measure Intended to Facilitate Redemptions and Loans." (MS Bowood.)

begin at the bottom of the 5th page, were written before I had the pleasure of conversing with you on wednesday. I shall send them in a day or two to Lord Sh[elburne] who together with Mr Pitt must judge ultimately in this business. It is indeed a business of great importance, and I wish there was a more perfect agreement between us. I have reason to suspect in myself a parental partiality; and I should be more influenced by this suspicion was not the only person who besides yourself has been consulted about it and whom I believe also to be a good judge more sanguine than I am with respect to both the practicability and the importance of the plan. *Your proposal* that the money for the present year should be borrowed, in the old way, by creating a 4 per cent stock not redeemable till the present 4 per cents have been redeemed, in order to prepare for a loan next year more sure of succeeding on my plan by establishing a stock which will then have found a value attended with one of the advantages proposed for that stock into which the 3 per cents are to be converted. *This proposal* I consider as one of the next best measures to the immediate adoption of the plan itself; and I shall like any thing which may be the means of introducing it. My objections are, that the public debts press so hard that the delay of a year in preparing for a plan of redemption is of too much consequence; and that there is indeed no occasion for any such delay there being *now* at market a 4 *per cent* stock which has found a value, and is, therefore, a sufficient guide. I am afraid also that the same reason will be given against adopting the plan next year which you give this year; namely, that the new 4 *per cent* stock then at market will not be a sufficient guide because the conversion into it of a 3 *per cent* stock will lessen the one and increase the other so much as to make the loan on such a plan impracticable, without incurring too great an expence. You will see at the end of the Observations I now send how I think on this subject.

I must add, that the Friend who has saved this country *by a peace* and from whose noble views and those of his friends alone I expect a second salvation of it by a redemption of the public debts if that is yet possible, may not be the minister of this country another year, and that therefore the opportunity which now offers itself of establishing a plan of redemption may be lost. Excuse the haste with which I have written this letter. Relying on your candour I am, Dear Sir

[No signature]

To the Earl of Shelburne

Newington=Green Feb*y* 15*th* 1783

My Lord,

I return with this one of the papers which your Lordship sent me on mon-day. When I first looked over it I tho't that it must have come from some person well acquainted indeed with the old modes of borrowing, but totally un:informed with respect to the plan called in it Dr Price's plan. I could not, therefore, but be surprised to find since, that it is Mr Baring's. Your Lordship may be assured that the statement of my plan which I have substituted in this paper is just; and if you will be so good as to shew it Mr Baring he will, I doubt not, acknowledge it to be so. I respect Mr Baring; and, therefore, am very sorry there is not a more perfect agreement between us. He owns the importance of the plan as a preparatory measure; but objects that it is not practicable without too much expence. On the contrary; I am convinced that it is practic-able without any extraordinary *present* expence worth regarding; and it is certain, that it may lay the foundation of great savings in future loans, and that in a plan of redemption if such a plan is to be establish'd, it will produce *a saving of more than a quarter of the whole present funded debt.*

Mr Baring also fears that it is a plan of too much magnitude for your Lordship to undertake in your present situation with prudence. It seems to me, on the contrary, that it will shew such enlarged views and such intentions of the most important service to the public as must recommend and strengthen your Lordship's administration.

The plan, however, cannot be too carefully examined before it is under-taken. I may be too partial to it. All I wish is, that it may have the justice d[on]e it of being examined by competent and disinterested j[ud]ges who will carry their views to future consequences.

[Th]inking it proper that you should be informed of all [tha]t passes between me and Mr Baring, I have inclosed a letter which I sent him yesterday in consequence of the conversation I had with him on wednesday. The obser-vations on his second paper of remarks refer'd to in this letter, I will send to your Lordship on monday or tuesday.[1] I am now copying them. May I hope for your Lordship's perusal of them? I know your thoughts must be deeply employ'd about a multitude of important objects. But this is likewise very important; and it is your judgment and Mr Pitt's, that must decide.

ORIGINAL: Bowood. TEXT: Original, with the kind permission of the Marquis of Lansdowne.
1. Price did not send these remarks to Shelburne, because before they were ready, Shelburne had fallen from power and Price did not think it worthwhile to trouble him further. See R.P. to Shelburne, 24 Feb. 1783.

Mr Hussey, Mr Jackson, and Mr Martin are respectable men conversant with figures and acquainted with subjects of this kind. Were the plan open'd to them and should they approve it they would be of great use in carrying it thro' the House of Commons. I lament extremely Mr Barre's incapacity of reading the papers on this subject. There is no one from whom I should expect a fairer and better judgment.

The present factious and shameful opposition will, I hope, be soon conquer'd. Hard it is to be opposed for saving a Kingdom. But such has been the fate of some of the best statesmen.

When I begun to write I intended a very short letter. I am sorry I have made it so long. Thinking it cruel to break in upon your Lordship, I chuse to satisfy myself with conveying my sentiments in this way.

With great regard, I am your Lordship's most obedient and humble servant,

Rich*d* Price

To the Earl of Shelburne

Newington=Green Feby 24th 1783

My Lord,

I have wished extremely to see your Lordship. I have called twice with this view, but finding you very busy, I did not chuse to come in.

The strange coalition of Lord North's party with the Rockingham party in order to condemn a Peace which has saved the kingdom, is one of the most scandalous events that ever happen'd. Indeed I could scarcely have thought it possible that any parties could have been so profligate. But every body sees that the peace is only a pretence, and the public, if I may judge from the sentiments of all I converse with, is on your Lordship's side; and should you be obliged to retire, you will do it with honour and credit; and I must add that your Lordship will have reason to be thankful. I am surprized that such stations should be so much desired. Your Lordship's successors will not be objects of envy; for I am much mistaken if they will not have very hard work to do about the finances. I hear many say, "Why is not the Parliament dissolved?" It seems indeed a pity this was not done some months ago. It is sad, that the man who has been one of the principal causes of the war and of the calamities of the kingdom, should still maintain so much importance in Parliament, in consequence of being surrounded there with a venal train introduced by himself.

ORIGINAL: Bowood. TEXT: Original, with the kind permission of the Marquis of Lansdowne.

I have not sent your Lordship the remarks on the plan for the loan, because I suppose it will not answer any end to think more of this subject. All my hopes of plans of redemption, Parliamentary reformation &c. will vanish with your Lordship. With all good wishes I have the honour to be your Lordship's most obedient

and humble servant
Rich*d* Price

Your Lordship will perhaps soon hear from Mr Smith,[1] a West India merchant I am well acquainted with. He has something to propose which he thinks of importance relating to the commerce between this Kingdom and France.

---

1. Possibly Benjamin Smith, a partner in Benjamin Smith, William Fitzhugh and Simon Halliday, who had held estates in the West Indies and was a member of the Society of West Indian Planters and Merchants. See Baker, pp. 30 and 229.

To Benjamin Franklin

10th March, 1783

My Dear Friend,

This letter will be deliver'd to you by Mr *Redford*, a gentleman for whom I have a great regard and who has my best wishes, He is going to settle for life in one of the thirteen united states; and he has already sent thither a part of his fortune. May I take the liberty to request your notice of him? Any assistance or information which you may be pleased to give him will be bestowed on a worthy man and a warm friend to universal liberty, who is well qualified to make an useful member of the united states. Indeed I can scarcely wish them better, than that they may be filled with men of his character, abilities and principles.

He has been in business about five years; but having in his education contracted habits which render him more disposed to litterary than mercantile pursuits, he does not intend to engage in commerce but to purchase an estate in order to turn it to the best account that the customs of the country will allow. He has been for some time a member of the Club of Whigs at the London= Coffee=House, who will be always proud of having had you for a member. The motives which have determined Mr Redford to settle with his property in

---

ORIGINAL: Yale University Library.   TEXT: Original, with the kind permission of Yale University Library.

America, are his zeal for liberty, his high opinion of the American governments, and his desire to share in the blessings and happiness of a rising country. I have given him a general testimonial which he will shew you. Would it be too much to beg that you would by a line at the bottom attest that it is my hand=writing?

Mr Redford is likely to be followed by many more emigrants from hence and from Ireland. He will inform you, particularly, of a body of people in Ireland who have resolved to remove to America, and commissioned Mr Noble, a major of the Irish armed volunteers to go before them in order to engage a tract of land for them. Mr Redford is to assist in transacting this business, and will think himself obliged to you for your advice.

Permit me to congratulate you on the late Peace, and on the Revolution in favour of liberty which has taken place by the establishment of the independence of America. I cannot express to you the satisfaction this has given me. I have wished to live to see this issue of the contest with America; and I am thankful that I have seen it. The world owes it partly to you; and may Heaven heap its blessings upon you, comfort you in the evening of life, and make you completely happy beyond the grave.

You probably well know what a detestable coalition of parties has lately taken place among us. Never surely was there an instance of such profligate conduct. Mr Fox, the pretended friend of the country, united to Lord North, the destroyer of the country—the *Rockingham* party, a body of men who would be thought zealous whigs, united to Tories and the friends of despotism to oppose and censure a peace which has saved the kingdom—I hope foreigners see this in its true light; as, merely, a struggle of ambitious and disappointed men to get into power. May the united states take care to guard against the danger and misery of such factions.

Relying on the indulgence and candour which I have always experienced from you, I am, with the greatest affection and respect,

Ever yours,
Richd Price

Many of your Friends are flattering themselves with the hope of seeing you in *England*. If not improper, deliver my respects to Mr Adams.

To Lord Shelburne

Chatham Square March 26*th* 1783

Dr Price presents his respects to Lord Shelburne, and returns him many thanks for the accounts he has sent him.

To the account of the totals of imports to and exports from the kingdom for the two last years which he is so good as to promise to send him, he wishes he would add an account of the deficiencies of the new taxes made good by the Sinking Fund for the quarter Oct 10th to Jany 5th last.

ORIGINAL: Bowood.   TEXT: Original, with the kind permission of the Marquis of Lansdowne.

To the Earl of Shelburne

Newington=Green Ap: 18th 1783

My Lord,

Not being able to attend the House of Commons on wednesday, I called yesterday on Mr Orde,[1] who received me with great civility; but I could expect no material information, the business of wednesday having been confined to the statement of the loan,[2] and nothing said about the ways and means and services and the state of the finances. The particulars of the loan your Lordship must be well acquainted with. It was sold yesterday at 7 *per cent* profit, and there is little reason to doubt but that a considerable share of it has been applied to the purpose of corruption. The terms are reckon'd very extravagant; and it is certain that offers were made which, had they been attended to, would have produced better terms. The money'd harpies had recourse to their usual practice of depressing the stocks for the purpose of gaining a cheap bargain, and they are now raising them again.

An additional capital of three millions, a long annuity worth more than a million and a half, and other advantages consisting of discount, lottery, advance of interest &c worth more than half a million, that is, above five millions

---

ORIGINAL: Bowood.   TEXT: Original with the kind permission of the Marquis of Lansdowne.

1. Thomas Orde, afterwards Orde-Powlett (1746–1807), MP for Aylesbury (1780–84) and for Harwich (1784–96). In July 1782 he was appointed Secretary to the Treasury in Shelburne's Ministry. He subsequently became the first Lord Bolton.

2. *Parl. Hist.*, XXIII, 771ff.

in all have been given to obtain twelve millions in money. Nothing can be more pernicious than such modes of borrowing. They are a declaration to the public that the debts are never to be paid, and have a tendency to keep down public credit. Had the loan been obtained without these exorbitant premiums and on a plan which appeared to be preparatory to the redemption of the public debts according to the intimation given in the King's Speech, it would, I doubt not have raised the stocks instead of sinking them. Mr Pitt, I am told, never shone more than he did on this occasion; and I see, with delight, the general disposition which prevails to applaud and admire him.

The general body of Dissenting ministers in London belonging to the three denominations took into consideration last tuesday at their annual meeting the propriety of carrying to the King an Address of thanks for the Peace. I was happy to see the unanimity which prevailed.

An order was given to the secretary to summon the body for the purpose of addressing as soon as an account came that the Definitive Treaty was signed. Many of us were for addressing immediately; but some, appearing to be influenced by the consideration that we had never on any former occasion addressed before the signing of the Definitive Treaty, it was thought best to yield to them and to wait in order hereafter to gain perfect unanimity. The address on Lord Bute's peace was gained with great difficulty, and not without much opposition and many debates. Nor, probably would it have been gained at all, had not Lord Bute influenced one of the leading ministers by committing to his disposal the whole Royal Bounty; a Pension to Dissenters which many of us dislike, and which I and several more have long resolved to have nothing to do with.[3]

Deliver my best respects to Lady Shelburne. Wishing her and your Lordship much pleasure in the country, I am with great regard

Your Lordship's most obedient and humble servant
Richd Price

Mrs Price sends her respectful compliments. I am grieved to hear of Lord Ashburton's ill state of health.[4]

---

3. John Stuart (1713–92), third Earl of Bute; First Lord of the Treasury, May 1762–Apr. 1763. Price wholeheartedly disapproved of the Regium Donum: "So deeply impressed was Mr Price with this sentiment, that being once applied to for his vote by the late Sir Edmund Thomas, when canvassing for the county of Glamorgan, and being offered that worthy baronet's interest to procure him the disposal of this money among his brethren, he immediately replied, that the best service Sir Edmund could render to him or his brethren would be, to advise the King's ministers to discontinue a donation which could only be regarded by every independent dissenter as the price of his liberty." *Memoirs*, 36–37.

4. Lord Ashburton (see Vol. I, 146) became blind in July 1783 and died on 18 Aug. 1783.

To Joseph Willard

Newington-Green, May 15th 1783.

Dear Sir,

I take the liberty to convey to you the two volumes[1] which accompany this; and I request the favour of you to present them to the American Society of Arts and Sciences as a testimony of my respect and best wishes. The Bearer is Mr Mullet, a merchant of the best character who has always been distinguished by his zeal for the principles of Liberty and the cause of America; and any notice which you may be pleased to take to him will, I am persuaded, be bestowed on a worthy man and gratefully received, I have set my name to a recommendation of him, which, probably, he will show you.

I congratulate you heartily on the termination of a cruel and detestable war, and the establishment of the Independence of America. The contest has issued in that very event which as a friend to mankind, I have been long ardently wishing for.

When you see Mr Foster or Dr Chauncy deliver my respectful compliments to them. I hope Mr Foster has had a prosperous voyage from this country to his family and friends at Boston. I am. Sir, with great regard,

Your most obedient and humble servant
RICH'D PRICE

PRINTED: *M.H.S.P.* (1909–10), 611–12. TEXT: *M.H.S.P.*
1. *Observations on Reversionary Payments*, 4th ed. See Joseph Willard to R.P., 31 Oct. 1783.

To Benjamin Franklin

Newington=Green May 19th 1783

Dear Sir,

This letter will be deliver'd to you by Mr Slaney, a young Gentleman of fortune who has been for some time on his travels and is ambitious of the honour of being introduced to you. I am not personally acquainted with him; but the account given me of him by a friend of his and mine assures me, that he is a Gentleman of the best principles and character. Any notice which you may be pleased to take of him will, I believe, make him very happy. Before this will be deliver'd to you the new Edition of my Treatise on Annuities, population, public credit &c.[1] will probably have reached you. Encouraged by the favourable reception which this work has met with I have in this edition enlarged it to

ORIGINAL: American Philosophical Society. TEXT: Original, with the kind permission of the American Philosophical Society.
1. *Observations on Reversionary Payments*, 4th ed.

two volumes, and taken great pains to make it as complete as possible. I reflect with pleasure that the part of it which is addressed to you will be the means of preserving some remembrance of our acquaintance and friendship. You will easily recollect the fact mentioned in the note p. 284, Vol. lst.[2] I have thot there could be no impropriety in introducing it into this Edition.

Wishing you all possible happiness,
I am most affectionately
Yours
Rich*d* Price

---

2. In the first draft of his paper "Observations on the Expectations of Lives", communicated to the Royal Society in the form of a letter to Benjamin Franklin and subsequently published in *Phil. Trans.* and in *Observations on Reversionary Payments*, Price referred to the American colonists as "Formerly an increasing number of *Friends*, but now likely to be converted, by an unjust and fatal policy, into an increasing number of ENEMIES." When the paper was read to the Royal Society the phrase "unjust and fatal policy" was omitted, but, nonetheless, Price writes, the passage gave offence. It was not included in the first three editions of *Observations on Reversionary Payments*.

To the Earl of Shelburne

Newington=Green May 28th 1783

My Lord,

The kindness of your letter which I received last Sunday impresses me much. The work[1] which your Lord=ship does me the honour to accept so favourably has indeed been the fruit of much attention and labour; but the reason I have to hope it has been of some use to the public rewards me sufficiently. It is now much improved; and it is a particular satisfaction to me that it is inscribed to your Lordship. To almost all that I converse with, your Lordship has appeared greater in going out of power than in coming into it; and the nation will for ever have reason to bless you for the Peace. I order'd the pamphlet on the public debts and finances[2] to be sent to Shelburne=House; and your Lordship has probably received it before this time. I have endeavoured to do justice to some of your Lordship's views; and, I hope, I have said nothing in it that can be justly thought wrong. In two or three places I have express'd pretty strongly my detestation of the Coalition, of the condemnation of the Peace, and of Lord North, who indeed I consider as one of the

---

ORIGINAL: Bowood.   TEXT: Original, with the kind permission of the Marquis of Lansdowne.
1. *Observations on Reversionary Payments*, 4th ed.
2. *The State of the Public Debts* (London, 1783).

worst enemies this country ever saw.[3] Many of his former Friends, as well as of Mr Fox's Friends, now give him up. Dr Johnson in particular in speaking of him lately to Dr Adams, the head of Pembroke College now in town from *Oxford*, said of him that all the paradoxes which can be united to form a bad minister would not form so bad a minister as Lord North. Your Lordship may possibly remember that you once express'd a wish that Dr Adams would take notice of Lord Fitzmaurice when at Oxford. I have mentioned this to him, and he would be glad to shew Lord Fitzmaurice all the regard in his power. He is indeed a man of the best character and principles. Perhaps Lord Fitzmaurice might not think it too much to call upon him some time or other. This would give him great pleasure.

The refusal of the Bank to advance money on the loan has produced much discontent, but it seems to be a necessary measure. An unfavourable course of exchange and the practice of drawing and re-drawing between this country and foreign countrys was likely to create too great a demand on the Bank. Had it not been for this refusal the Bank would probably have had almost the whole loan to pay, and the subscribers would have been at liberty to play with their heavy stock and to practise arts in order to sell it to the best advantage and then to get specie for exportation. This is the account I have heard of this matter, but your Lordship probably is much better informed about it. I suspect that many foreigners having bought our stocks when at the lowest are now drawing out after making all the profit they can expect to make.

I cannot conclude without expressing the great pleasure which your Lordship's private and domestic happiness gives me. In Lady Shelburne you have, I believe, the best means of such happiness. May it long continue, and your Lordship remain ever free from every embarrassment and connexion that may improperly affect your public conduct and make you less a blessing to the Kingdom.

My best respects wait on Lady Shelburne.

Mrs Price thinks herself much obliged to you for remembering her and sends also her best compliments. She has lately been very ill; and I have been exceedingly anxious about her; but she is now better. I am sorry your Lordship has not been quite well. I hope soon to have the pleasure of seeing you at Shelburne House.

With great regard and attachment I am, my Lord,

ever yours

Rich*d* Price

---

3. Op. cit., pp. 22, 23, and 33. Price attacked Lord North's financial policies on several grounds: because he persisted in the practice of raising Government loans on low-interest stocks issued at a large discount, thus inflating the capital of the debt unnecessarily; because he refused to make the Sinking Fund inalienable; because he held that redemption of the National Debt was impracticable; and because he held that the burden of the debt reduced to that of paying annuities—"the public debt is to be considered only as an annuity and [that] . . . it does not signify what the capital is."

I am sorry I am not more able to attend some of the debates in Parliament. I wish, particularly, I could have been in the House of Commons last monday. Dr Adams was there; and tells me, that he was charmed with Mr Pitt and that he discover'd an evident superiority to Mr Fox and Lord North. Mr Powell, it seems, has made away with himself.[4] What a sad end.

---

4. On 26 May John Powell committed suicide. At one time he had been a steward to Mr Stephen Fox, later Lord Holland, under whose influence he was appointed clerk, and later cashier, in the Pay Office. By the perquisites of office he became very wealthy. In Mar. 1783 Isaac Barré dismissed him together with Charles Bembridge on an alleged conspiracy. It is said that after his subsequent examination by the Lords of the Treasury he fell into a general state of insanity. (See Carl B. Cone, *Burke and the Nature of Politics*, 2 vols. (University of Kentucky Press, 1964), I, 92–94.

Extract from a letter to [a Member of Parliament]

[4 June 1783]

The plan proposed in your paper has been thought of by several other members of parliament; but I am afraid it will not be practicable to any great extent. Temporary annuities must be continually decreasing in value. They have no capitals which can be conveyed without loss to posterity. Hence it is that they have never been held in high estimation among the public creditors; and that the long annuity is now seven *per cent* below its true value, reckoning interest as it is in the 3 *per cents*; and were there much more of it, the price of it would probably be much lower. I will, however, reckon with you that 30 millions of 4 per cents and 140 millions of 3 *per cents* may be converted into an annuity for 77 years, by adding a *sixth* to the interest of these *stocks*; that is, by a surplus in the revenue of £900,000 per ann. Supposing this done, the nation would be obliged to bear, for 77 years to come, its present load of debt with all the additions to it which can become necessary during that time. Is there any reason to think this possible?

An appropriation of £900,000 *per ann* would, according to your proposal, discharge a capital of 170 millions in 77 years; but such an appropriation in a *sinking fund rendered unalienable*, and applied first to the discharge of 30 millions bearing a 4 *per cent* and afterwards to the discharge of 3 *per cents* at par would redeem, *in the same number of years*, 321 millions; and it would redeem 170 millions in 18 years and a half *less* time. Is it not then to be lamented that there should be any difficulty in establishing such a fund? I am firmly of opinion, that if any thing can still save the kingdom, it is this must do it; and, therefore, I

PRINTED: *The State of the Public Debts and Finances at Signing the Preliminary Articles of Peace in January, 1783*, 2nd ed. (London, 1783). TEXT: *The State of the Public Debts*, p. 36.

cannot help ardently wishing that you, Sir, and the rest of the able and virtuous part of the House of Commons, would unite your endeavours to *restore* this fund, and to get such regulations established as may give it a sacredness like that of the ark of God among the Jews, which could not be touched without death. If this cannot be done, it would be best to strike the name of *Sinking Fund* out of our accounts; for, by covering deficiencies and tempting to profusion, it is, in its present state, more an evil than a benefit.

To Per Wilhelm Wargentin

Newington=Green near London June 9th 1783

Sir,

I have great reason to blame myself for omitting so long to make my grateful acknowledgements to you for the kind communications which you made to me above a year ago of the Observations in *Sweden* on human mortality. I have defer'd this from time to time because I thought I might do it more properly and acceptably when I could desire your acceptance of the new Edition of my Book on Reversionary payments, and shew you how useful to me your communications have been.[1] It is, indeed, to these communications my work in the present edition of it owes its chief improvement; and I cannot sufficiently thank you for the very important assistance you have given me. The attention I have bestowed on this work has been more than can be well imagined; and I am very glad that it is now finished. I shall take the first opportunity I can get to convey it to you. In the meantime I have thought it best to send you these lines by the mail. You will find that I have frequently in the course of this work expressed the sense I have of your merit, and of my obligations to you, particularly in the Preface Vol. 1. P. 31. and in Vol. II. P. 7, 8, &c.[2]

With every possible good wish and great esteem and gratitude, I am, Sir,

Your very obedient and humble servant

Rich*d* Price

ORIGINAL: Kungl. Vetenskapsakademiens Bibliotek, Stockholm. PRINTED: N.V.E. Nordenmark, *P.W. Wargentin* (Uppsala, 1939), p. 263. TEXT: Original, with the kind permission of the Vetenskapsakademiens Bibliotek, Stockholm.

1. See R.P. to Per Wilhelm Wargentin, 24 Dec. 1781.

2. Of his debt to Wargentin, Price wrote, "By these [i.e. the Swedish] Tables I have been enabled to state minutely the different rates of mortality at all ages among males and females; and to form tables of the values of single and joint lives for *each* sex, as well as for both sexes collectively; in consequence of which, I have been farther enabled to determine the increase of the values of annuities payable during survivorship, occasioned by the longer duration of life among females, and thus to furnish a direction of some importance to the various societies in this kingdom and abroad for providing annuities for widows." (*Observations on Reversionary Payments*, 4th ed., pp. xxx–xxxi.)

To Benjamin Franklin

June 12th 1783

Dr Price presents his best respects to Dr Franklin and desires his acceptance of one of these Pamphlets.[1] The other one he desires Dr Franklin would be so good as to present to Mr Laurens if at Paris. If not, he wishes it may be presented to Mr Adams.

ORIGINAL: American Philosophical Society.   TEXT: Original, with the kind permission of the American Philosophical Society.

1. Probably *The State of the Public Debts*.

To Benjamin Rush

Newington=Green June 26th 1783

Sir,

I feel myself very happy in the approbation of my attempts to serve the cause of liberty which you express in the letter with which you have favour'd me; and which has been deliver'd to me by Mr John Vaughn. From a regard to the general rights of mankind and a conviction that all dominion of one country over another is usurpation and tyranny, I have allways defended, as far as I have been able, the cause of America and opposed the late wicked war; and in doing this, I have gone thro' much abuse and some danger in this country. The struggle has been glorious on the part of America; and it has now issued just as I wished it to issue; in the emancipation of the American states and the establishment of their independence. It is not possible for me to express to you the satisfaction this has given me. I think it one of the most important revolutions that has ever taken place in the world. It makes a new opening in human affairs which may prove an introduction to times of more light and liberty and virtue than have been yet known. This must be the consequence, if the united states can avoid the infection of European vices, and establish forms of government and a plan of political union that shall be perfectly favourable to universal liberty, and prevent future wars among themselves. Should this happen, they will without doubt be the refuge of mankind, and a great part of the world will endeavour to participate in their happiness. I wish I was capable of advising and assisting them. Were I to attempt this what I should recommend,

---

ORIGINAL: Library Co. of Philadelphia.   TEXT: Original, with the kind permission of the Library Co. of Philadelphia.

with particular earnestness, would be, a total separation of religion from state policy, and allowing an open field for improvement by a free discussion of all speculative points, and an *equal* protection, not only of all *christians*, but of all honest men of all opinions and religions. I see, with the greatest pleasure, that the new forms of government are in this respect liable to but few objections.

From what I have said you must conclude that I cannot but be deeply interested in all that is now passing in America; and that, therefore, it will be highly agreeable to me to be informed of any transactions there. Any information of this kind will be gratefully received; but I cannot promise much in return. There is more in this country to be avoided than imitated by America.

This letter is to be convey'd to you by Mr Vaughn. I have long had a particular respect for him and for good Mrs Vaughn and the rest of the family. May they be ever prosperous and happy.

With many thanks to you for your letter and the best wishes, I am Sir,

your very obedient, and humble servant
Rich*d* Price

To John Vaughan

Newington=Green June 26th 1783.

Dr Price presents his kind compliments and best wishes to Mr John Vaughan, and returns him many thanks for the information and instruction convey'd to him by the letter which he received from him just before he left London in order to sail for America. He requests the favour of Mr Vaughn to deliver the inclosed letter to Dr Rush, and the inclosed pamphlet to Mr Arthur Lee, who, being a member of Congress, may probably be now at Philadelphia. He also begs the favour of Mr Vaughn to convey to Dr Honeyman in Virginia the letter directed to him. Dr Honeyman's Brother died lately in Northumberland, and the letter comes from the widow. Several persons from Mr Wells's congregation[1] near Bromsgrove in Worcestershire are just going to sail for America in order to make enquiries there preparatory to Mr Wells's removal to America,

---

ORIGINAL: Richard Price Misc. Papers, Rare Books and Manuscripts Division, New York Public Library, Astor, Lenox and Tilden Foundations. TEXT: Original.

1. William Wells, was a Minister at the Independent Meeting House at Bromsgrove from 1770–1793. See Lionel Munn, *Bromsgrove Congregational Church Tercentenary 1672–1972* (1972), p. 11. The records of the Meeting House refer to a Mr Thomas Carpenter as a Trustee of the Meeting House from 1729 to 1793. If these were the Mr Wells and the Mr Thomas Carpenter to whom Price refers it is clear that the project to emigrate to America did not bear fruition, at least not at the time indicated in the correspondence. I am indebted to Miss Margaret Sanders, Mr Lionel Munn and the Revd A. McLellan for their help in trying to identify these persons.

and also the removal of several of his neighbours. The name of one of these persons is Mr Tho's Carpenter, and should he and the friends who are with him come to Philadelphia to make enquiries there, they will probably find out Mr Vaughn; and any assistance or information which Mr Vaughn may be so good as to give them will be well bestowed and gratefully received. Mr Wells is a dissenting minister of very good character.

To Francis Maseres

Newington Green July 14th 1783

Dear Sir,

I cannot make myself easy without sending you a few lines just to return you my thanks for your book on the principles of the Doctrine of Annuities.[1] It is a valuable and useful work writ with perfect clearness, and capable of being understood by any person who will read it with any degree of attention. I wish parti[cu]larly that what you say about the national debt may be attended to. I have refer'd to your book in the last edition of my Treatise on Reversionary payments Vol: 2nd P. 194,[2] and also in the pamphlet on the public debts p. 34.[3] I order'd Mr Cadell to send you both these publications, and I hope you have received them. The notice which you have taken of me and Mr Morgan[4] in your book is very handsome, and we are much obliged to you for it. Your candour is indeed conspicuous in all your writings; and this is a quality in which I wish earnestly to imitate you. With sincere respect I am

your very obedient and humble servant

Richd Price

ORIGINAL: The late Mr G.V.M. Heap. ADDRESSED: To/Mr Baron Maseres/ King's bench Walk/ No. 2 Inner Temple. TEXT: Original, with the kind permission of the late G.V.M. Heap.

1. *The Principles of the Doctrine of Life-Annuities; Explained in a Familiar Manner so as to be Intelligible to Persons not Acquainted with the Doctrine of Chances; and accompanied with a Variety of New Tables of the Value of such Annuities at Several Different Rates of Interest both for Single Lives and for Two Joint Lives, Accurately Computed from Observations.* (London, 1783).

2. *Observations on Reversionary Payments,* 4th ed.

3. *The State of the Public Debts.*

4. William Morgan, author of *The Doctrine of Annuities and Assurances on Lives and Survivorships Stated and Explained.*

To Lieut.-Colonel Sharman[1]

Brighthelmstone, Aug. 7, 1783

Sir,

I think myself greatly honoured by the letter addressed to me, in the name of the Committee of which you are Chairman. It is indeed with a satisfaction not to be expressed, I find the people of Ireland, after rescuing their trade and their legislature from the oppression of a sister kingdom, are now undertaking to rescue themselves from an *internal* oppression, no less inconsistent with liberty.[1] The occasion is great, and the undertaking important and arduous in the highest degree. Should they be blest with success, they will have completed their own happiness, and exhibited an example which will for ever shine in the annals of mankind. The subjoined paper [A] will shew that I have been for some time wishing they would carry their views to this object. It was shewn to Mr Gratton[2] above a year ago, and written when the Duke of Richmond, the Earl of Shelburne, Lord Camden,[3] Mr Pitt, and other friends to a Parliamentary Reform, were in power. We are now governed by an odious Coalition, formed between Whigs and the Conductors of the late war, to gratify ambition and party rage by censuring the peace. These united parties are, in general, hostile to Reformation; and this will make it more difficult for the people of Ireland to succeed in their views; but *nothing can be difficult to a people determined to recover their rights*—IF UNANIMOUS AND FIRM. The

---

PRINTED: *Proceedings Relative to the Ulster Assembly of Volunteer Delegates on the Subject of a More Equal Representation of the People in the Parliament of Ireland in 1783* (Belfast, 1783), pp. 26–32; *A Collection of the Letters ... Addressed to the Volunteers of Ireland, on the Subject of a Parliamentary Reform, etc.* (London, 1783), pp. 80–83; *Dublin Evening Post*, 25 Sept. 1783. TEXT: *A Collection...*

1. After Ireland's success in gaining virtual legislative and judicial independence, the Irish Volunteers assembled at Lisburne in July 1783 decided to press for parliamentary reform. A committee was formed under the chairmanship of Lieut.-Colonel Sharman who wrote to several of the leading English and Irish reformers for advice. He wrote to Henry Grattan, Lord Charlemont, William Pitt, John Jebb, Christopher Wyvill, John Cartwright, the Earl of Effingham, the Earl of Abingdon, the Duke of Richmond, and Price. The replies he received from Wyvill, Richmond, Jebb, Effingham, Cartwright and Price were published in *Proceedings relative to the Ulster Assembly of Volunteer Delegates on the Subject of a More Equal Representation of the People in the Parliament of Ireland in 1783.* The replies he received from Cartwright, Effingham, Jebb, Wyvill and Price were also published in *A Collection of Letters which have been Addressed to the Volunteers of Ireland on the Subject of a Parliamentary Reform* from which the text of the letter reprinted here is taken. Price's ideas on parliamentary reform were relatively moderate, as a comparison of his contribution with those by Cartwright, Jebb and Richmond will show. He was particularly concerned to secure a reform of the representation, a more equitable distribution of seats, and a wider, but not a universal, franchise.

2. Henry Grattan (1746–1820), who entered the Irish Parliament in Dec. 1775, was the prime mover in securing legislative independence for Ireland.

3. See Vol. I, 162.

motive commonly urged to check such exertions, "not to disturb what is quiet," would prevent all improvements, and perpetuate darkness and slavery amongst mankind. It would, in particular, had it influenced in America, have prevented the Revolution in favour of the rights of mankind, which has lately taken place there; and had it influenced Ireland, it would have prevented that emancipation of which has been lately so happily effected. The blessings of legitimate government, and a free Constitution, are inestimable. Too much cannot be sacrificed to acquire them; and no country has acquired them whence the body of the people, equally and fairly represented, have not the chief share in the powers of Government.

I can by no means pretend to that degree of information and knowledge, which is necessary to enable me to give any proper answer to the queries contained in your letter; and the shortness of the time between this and the 20th of August, together with the dissipated state I am now in at Brighthelmstone, will not allow me to be very full and explicit. The Committee will therefore, I hope, accept the following general observations, as the best reply to their queries that I can at present give:

The principles of civil liberty require, that every independent agent in a state (that is, every one who can be supposed to have a will and judgement of his own) should have a vote in the choice of his Governors.[4] But it has been seldom practicable to extend the right of voting so far.[5] In America, where new forms of government are established more liberal than any the world has yet seen, this right is limited to persons who pay taxes and possess property. Perhaps it may not be prudent in Ireland to go even this length. In these cases, to avoid the danger of losing all by aiming at too much, the attempts of enlightened men should be governed by a regard to what is most practicable, considering present circumstances, and the attachment which always prevails in a country to old establishments. In England I have wished, that the friends of reformation[6] had confined their views at present to the extension of the right of voting to Copyholders, and Leaseholders; and the substitution of a hundred knights for counties in the room of a hundred members for boroughs. This, though in theory unspeakably too little, would have been a very important reform; and less than this, I have not thought much worth contending for. The people in Ireland are more alive, and therefore, probably much more may be

---

4. Cf. *Observations on the Nature of Civil Liberty*, Peach, pp. 69–72; and *Additional Observations*, Peach, p. 140.

5. Price did not hold the view that political rights can be deduced simply and directly from the principle of self–government. Other considerations, he held, are relevant, "Liberty, though the most essential requisite in government, is not the only one. Wisdom, union, dispatch, secrecy and vigour are likewise requisite; and that is the best form of government which best unites all these qualities; or which, to an equal and perfect Liberty, adds the greatest wisdom in deliberating and resolving, and the greatest union, force and expedition in executing." *Additional Observations*, Peach, p. 139.

6. Price was a founder member of the Society for Constitutional Information.

attempted there with success. But how much more I am not qualified to say. Suppose the right of voting was extended to all who possess property of a certain value, and every county divided into six districts, each of which should chuse one Representative leaving the remaining representatives to be chosen by the largest towns and boroughs. Would this be too great an object? Is it too much to be undertaken without destroying unanimity?

The duration of Parliaments seems a point of less consequence. If chosen by the People at large, they will be short; for it is impossible that a People should not see that the long possession of power will corrupt, and that their security against the abuse of power depends on keeping their Representatives in a constant state of dependence and responsibility.

If, on the contrary, Parliaments are not chosen by the people, shortening their duration will be no remedy. They will not in this account be less usurpations and mockeries.

Annual Parliaments seem to me preferable to Parliaments of any longer duration; not only because they keep the Representative Body more subject to the controul of its constituents, but also because being chosen more frequently they will be chosen more of course, and with less tumult and riot.

There seems to be no reason for changing the number of the Representative Body in Ireland.

I am so much an enemy to persecution that I cannot help wishing the right of voting, could be extended to Papists who possess property in common with Protestants. It is unjust to deprive any man of his Rights on account of his religion, unless self-defence makes it absolutely necessary.[7]

The danger from Papists is perhaps more produced by the Penal Laws against them, than by their religion. These detach them from the rest of the community, give them a separate interest, and *make* them enemies. Why should not a Papist be attached to the liberties of his country as well as a Protestant, if he is allowed to share in them? In truth, a country which allows him no rights, he cannot reckon *his* country. It is nothing to him whether it is enslaved or free; nor can he care what becomes of it.

If there is any remedy for the evil which occasions the objection against increasing the number of Members for counties, it is that extension of the right of voting and division of counties into districts which I have mentioned.

The proprietors of the enslaved boroughs do not seem, in reason, entitled to a compensation, because they hold them by usurpation and a kind of robbery. It seems, however, necessary, that a compensation should be allowed and it would, I suppose be allowed in England were the rotten boroughs disfran-

---

7. Cf. D.O. Thomas, "Proposed Protest concerning Dissenters: Richard Price and the Earl of Chatham", *T.U.H.S.*, XVI, No. 2 (1976), 49–62. "The maxims of sound policy, as well as the principles of Christianity, require civil governors to protect all good subjects; and to extend Toleration to every mode of faith and worship, that is not inconsistent with the safety of the State."

chised. The necessity of abolishing such boroughs, I think, very apparent. There cannot be worse nuisances in a State.[8]

I am sensible, Sir, of the great imperfection of these remarks, and must rely on the candour of the Committee. Indeed they have done me too much honour by supposing me capable of advising them.

From the Duke of Richmond, Mr Pitt, Etc., they may receive advise that will be more worth their attention. But there is no one whose heart and wishes are more with them. May Heaven grant them success! and may the example of Ireland influence this country and shame it to imitation.

With all possible respect,

I am, sir,
Your most obedient and humble servant,
Richard Price

P.S. Ireland is peculiarly situated in two respects. A great majority of the inhabitants are Papists; and a distribution of property, more unequal than in England or America, subjects them more to aristocratic tyranny. I have hinted, as a remedy for the former inconvenience, the admission of Papists to equal rights; but there may be stronger objections to this than I am aware of.

Trade and liberty, will, it is to be hoped, in time, diffuse more in Ireland, and produce a less unequal distribution of it.

[A: Price's appendix]

To the associated VOLUNTEERS OF IRELAND

A native of England, but a citizen of the world,[9] and a warm friend to universal liberty, congratulates them with great satisfaction, on their success in obtaining, without bloodshed, that precious blessing for which torrents of blood have been shed in America; and, rejoicing in their emancipation, he wishes to propose to them the following queries.

1st   Having seized the favourable opportunity which the war with America has offered them, should they not be anxious about improving it to the utmost, from a conviction that such another opportunity may never offer itself.

2dly   Having succeeded in gaining *external* liberty, should it not be their next concern to gain *internal* liberty? And while they want the latter, can they possess any just security for the former?

3dly   Is not a free and equal representation essential to the *internal* liberty of a kingdom?

---

8. Cf. R.P. to Christopher Wyvill, 12 Dec. 1782.
9. Cf. *A Discourse on the Love of our Country*, 2nd ed., pp. 10 and 44.

4thly   Is Ireland possessed of such a representation? Or is not, on the contrary, a vast majority of its House of Commons chosen, not by the people, (but as in England) by a few Grandees and Beggars?[10]

5thly   By establishing an equal representation, may not the people of Ireland do their sister kingdom a most important service, by provoking its emulation, and rendering it ashamed of its own corrupt and mock representation?

6thly   Have they not reason to expect, from the liberality of the new Ministers, and the endeavours which some of them are now using to gain an equal representation of England, that they will rejoice to see this work undertaken in Ireland, and give it their encouragement and support?

Lastly,   Is it not therefore almost certain, that the Volunteers and Patriots of Ireland will easily succeed in this understanding, if they set themselves to it with that glorious zeal which they have hitherto discovered, and by which they have exhibited to the world an example of public spirit and virtue scarcely ever before known, and which must render them the admiration of future ages?

July, 1782

---

10. Cf. *Observations on the Nature of Civil Liberty*, Peach, p. 71n., "In *Great Britain*, consisting of near six millions of inhabitants, 5723 persons, most of them the lowest of the people, elect one half of the House of Commons; and 364 votes chuse a ninth part." Price refers to James Burgh, *Political Disquisitions*, I, bk. 2, ch. 4. Cf. also *A Discourse on the Love of our Country*, p. 42n. "A representation chosen principally by the Treasury, and a few thousands of the dregs of the people, who are generally paid for their votes".

From Benjamin Franklin

Passy, near Paris, Sept. 16 1783

My dear Friend,

Having this opportunity by Mr Bingham,[1] who has the Honour of being known to you, I seize it to thank you for your excellent Book,[2] and other Favours, and to let you know that I continue well, except a little Gout, which perhaps is not more a Disease than a Remedy. Mr Petrie inform'd me of your being also well with Mrs Price lately at Brighthelmstone, which gave me great Pleasure: Please to present my affectionate Respects to that good Lady.

ORIGINAL: Library of Congress.   PRINTED: *Franklin*, Bigelow, X, 188.   TEXT: Original.

1. William Bingham (1752–1804), banker. A founder and director of the Pennsylvania Bank which was incorporated as the bank of North America in 1781. He served in the Continental Congress (1786–89), the Assembly of Pennsylvania (1790–95), and the United States Senate (1795–1801).

2. Either the fourth edition of *Observations on Reversionary Payments* or *The State of the Public Debts*, the first and second editions of which were published in 1783.

All the Conversation here at present turns upon the Balloons fill'd with light inflammable Air, and the means of managing them so to give Men the Advantage of Flying.[3] One is to be let off on Friday next at Versailles, which it is said will be able to carry up a 1000 pounds weight, I know not whether inclusive or exclusive of its own.[4] I have sent an account of the former to Sir Joseph Banks, our President, and shall be glad to hear if the Experiment is repeated with Success in England.[5] Please to forward to him the enclosed Print.

Inflammable Air puts me in mind of a little jocular Paper I wrote some Years since in ridicule of a Prize Question given out by a certain Academy on this side the Water, and I enclose it for your Amusement.[6] On second Thoughts, as it is a mathematical Question, and perhaps I think it more trifling than it really is, and you are a Mathematician, I am afraid I have judg'd wrong in sending it to you. Our Friend, Dr Priestley, however, who is *apt* to give himself *Airs*,* and has a kind of Right to every thing his Friends *produce* upon that Subject, may perhaps like to see it, and you can send it to him without reading it.

We have at length sign'd our Preliminary Articles as definitive;[7] all the Additions we have been so long discussing, being referr'd to a future Treaty of Commerce. I have now a little leisure, and long to see and be merry with the Club,[8] but I doubt I cannot undertake the Journey before Spring. Adieu, and believe me ever, my dear Friend,

Yours most affectionately
B. Franklin

They make small Balloons now of the same materials with what is called Gold-beaters Leaf. Inclos'd I send one which being fill'd with inflammable Air, by my Grandson,[9] went up last Night, to the Ceiling in my Chamber, and

* [Franklin's note] 'i.e. fix'd, deflogisticated, &c, &c'.

---

3 On 27 Aug. Paris had witnessed its first balloon ascent, conducted under the direction of J.-A.-C. Charles from the Champ-de-Mars. It was a repetition of an experiment undertaken by the Montgolfier brothers at Annonay near Lyons in June. Over 50,000 were present to witness the spectacle. See Van Doren, *Benjamin Franklin*, (New York, 1957), p. 700.

4. At Versailles on 19 Sept. Joseph Montgolfier sent up a balloon containing a sheep, a cock, and a duck.

5. Franklin wrote to Sir Joseph Banks from Passy on 30 Aug. 1783 describing the balloon ascent of 27 Aug. (see n.3 above), *The Writings of Benjamin Franklin*, ed. A.H. Smyth, IX, 80.

6. Franklin's bagatelle entitled *Letter to the Academy at Brussels* is also referred to as *Essay on Perfumes*. Price acknowledged receipt of it in his letter to Franklin dated 6 Apr. 1784.

7. The preliminary articles of peace between Britain and America were signed at Hotel de York in Paris on 3 Sept. 1783.

8. The Honest Whigs.

9. William Temple Franklin (1760–1823), Benjamin Franklin's grandson, was the illegitimate son of William Franklin (1731–1813). He acted as secretary to his grandfather during the latter's stay in Paris. He edited Benjamin Franklin's papers.

Remained rolling about there for some time. Please to give it also to Sir Joseph Banks. If a Man should go up with one of the large ones, might there not be some mechanical Contrivance to compress the Globe at pleasure, and thereby incline it to descend, and let it expand when he inclines to rise again?

To Lord Monboddo

Newington Green Sept 25*th* 1783

My Lord,

I think myself much obliged to your Lordship for the letter which I received from you in July last, and for your favourable acceptance of my book upon Annuities, population, etc.[1] It is a great relief to me that the labour this work has cost me is now over. I have nothing to add to what I have offer'd on the population of the kingdom. The observations in your Lordship's letter on this subject are certainly very just. On another subject I have had the misfortune not to be able to think with your Lordship. I am very glad to find that on this we are agree'd. The Act of the Legislature in 1744[2] which your Lordship takes notice of, by which, in order to raise money, the prohibition of spirituous liquors was taken off, was indeed very pernicious. The consequence was that the lower people destroy'd themselves so fast by drinking Gin as to oblige our governors in 1751 to restore the prohibition. The grand business of government among us has been for many years raising money and increasing the Revenue by all possible means. The value of every thing has been estimated by its effect in this way. The value of America in particular was thus estimated; and an attempt made to tax it. But never did a measure defeat its own end so miserably. By attempting to draw a pepper-corn to the revenue from America

---

ORIGINAL: The National Library of Scotland.   PRINTED: Knight, pp. 257–58 (incomplete). TEXT: Original, with the kind permission of the National Library of Scotland.

1. *Observations on Reversionary Payments*, 4th ed.

2. In 1736 Parliament attempted to stem the evils arising from an excessive consumption of gin. An Act (9 Geo. II, c. xxiii) was passed which was designed to discourage if not stop the retailing of spirits. A duty of 20*s*. a gallon was laid on all spirits, and retailers were required to take out annual licences costing £50. This Act, however, led to an extensive illicit traffic, and in 1743 it was repealed. It is this Act—the Act of 1743—that Price seems to have in mind: the virtual prohibition of the sale of spirits was given up, but an attempt was made to control the trade by confining the sale of spirits to those who had alehouse licences, and by increasing the price of spirits (16 Geo. II, c. viii). An Act of 1747 (20 Geo. II, c. xxxix) allowed distillers, who had been prevented by the Act of 1743 from selling liquor, to retail spirits under a £5 licence. But this measure brought back all the old evils, and a further attempt was made to control the trade in 1751 (24 Geo. II, c. xl). The duty on spirits was raised again, and distillers, grocers and chandlers were forbidden to retail. See M.D. George, *London Life on the Eighteenth Century* (London, 1966), pp. 47–50.

we have lost one of the main sources of our opulence and added to a debt before intolerable 120 millions. Thanks be to Lord North for this. The inclosed pamphlet[3] may give your Lordship an idea of our state in this respect. The first edition of it was publish'd in May last, but I hope it is not now too late to desire your acceptance of it as a farther testimony of gratitude for your Volumes on Antient Metaphysics, from which, tho' I do not always agree with you, I have derived pleasure and instruction. Dr Priestley is likely to be engaged in a warm controversy. What he has said in his late History of the Corruptions of Christianity[4] concerning the opinion of the primitive church with respect to the Pre-existence of Christ has been opposed with zeal, and among others by Dr Horsley who has just published a pamphlet on this subject.[5] Dr Priestley will soon reply; but I do not expect that the dispute will be as amicable a one as that between him and me on the subjects of materialism and necessity.[6]

Finding a relaxation from study and a change of scene and air to be sometimes necessary, I have been for some time at Brighthelmston trying the effect of sea-air and sea-bathing on my health and spirits. I have lately returned, and find myself a good deal recruited. I mention this, because it is the reason why the favour of your letter has not been sooner noticed.

May your Lordship's life and health be long preserved. With much gratitude for your attention and great regard

I am, my Lord,

Your Lordship's most obedient and humble servant

Rich*d* Price

3. *The State of the Public Debts* (London, 1783).

4. *An History of the Corruptions of Christianity*, 2 vols. (Birmingham, 1782).

5. This controversy between Samuel Horsley and Joseph Priestley began with a sermon which Horsley, as Archdeacon of St Albans, preached to his clergy on 22 May 1783. In it he attacked the account which Priestley had given in *An History of the Corruptions of Christianity* of the development of opinions on the nature of the personality of Christ. This sermon and Horsley's further contributions to the ensuing controversy were published in Samuel Horsley, *Tracts in Controversy with Dr Priestley* (London, 1789).

6. *A Free Discussion of the Doctrines of Materialism, and Philosophical Necessity* (London, 1778).

An extract from a letter to Ezra Stiles

29 September [1783]

I hope Yale College, over which you preside will accept my warmest thanks for this testimony of their approbation. I should be one of the happiest mankind, could I think that the account given of me so handsomely, in the diploma, did not go beyond any merit that I can justly claim. The circumstance,

PRINTED: Abiel Holmes, *The Life of Ezra Stiles* (Boston, 1798), pp. 287–88. TEXT: Abiel Holmes, *The Life of Ezra Stiles*.

mentioned in your letter, that the honour[1] done me by the College, was granted me at the same time with GENERAL WASHINGTON, has made a greater impression upon me, than can be easily conceived. It is a circumstance that makes the honour distinguishing, beyond all that my ambition could reach to. General Washington's name must always shine among the first, in the annals of the world.

It will go down to all future generations, universally applauded and admired. Mine, perhaps, may follow; but it will be but a little way, and at a vast distance.

---

1. On 24 Apr. 1781, Yale conferred the degree of LL D on George Washington and Richard Price. On 18 Mar. Ezra Stiles, President of Yale, entered in his diary: "Writing Dr Price's Diploma" and on 3 May 1783 he wrote, "Took leave of Mr Tutor Fitch, by whom I send the Diploma of a Doctorate in Laws to The Reverend Richard Price, D.D. of London." *The Literary Diary of Ezra Stiles, D.D., LL.D.*, ed. F.R. Dexter (New York, 1901), III, 63 and 70.

To Joseph Willard

Newington-Green, near London,
Oct: 6th, 1783.

Dear Sir,

I think myself much obliged to you for the letter with which you favoured me some time ago informing me that I had been unanimously chosen a member of the American Academy of arts and sciences. I reckon this a great honour, and I beg you would deliver to the members of the Academy my best acknowledgements. The approbation of me which it implies cannot but give me particular satisfaction, because it gives me reason to hope that my attempts to serve the cause of truth and liberty have been favourably received and may therefore be of some use. May the American Academy prosper, and become as distinguished by its improvements in the arts and sciences as the united states are by the blessings of civil and religious liberty. Several months ago I committed to the care of Mr Mullet, a Bristol merchant, and directed to you, the new Edition (enlarg'd to two volumes) of my Treatise on Life-Annuities, reversionary payments, population, public credit, etc.[1] I hope it has been safely convey'd and received, and that the American Academy will accept it, as a small testimony of my respect and good wishes. I am very glad that it happens to be in my power to answer your enquiries about the new planet,[2] and to give you and the Academy the following account of it:

The elements of the orbit as determined by several of the best Astronomers and Mathematicians are

---

PRINTED: *M.H.S.P.*(1909–10), 614–16. TEXT: *M.H.S.P.* (1909–10).

1. *Observations on Reversionary Payments*, 4th ed.

2. The planet Uranus which had been discovered by William Herschel on 13 Mar. 1781.

Place of the Node...	2S	11d	49'	30"
Inclination of the Orbit...			43'	35"
Place of the Perihelion...		172°	13'	17"
Time of the Perihelion passage		Sept. 7th, 1779		
Excentricity of the Orbit		.82034		
Half of the greater Axis...		19.07904 (the earth's 1)		
Revolution...		83.3364 Sydereal years		

Mr Herschel's observations make the *apparent* Diameter not to be less than 4" nor much greater. Hence its *real* Diameter is found to be that of the earth as 4.454 to 1. It appears, therefore, to be of a considerable size; and, except Saturn and Jupiter, by far the largest of the planets. The best method of finding it will be, by some fixed instrument to take the place of the most considerable small telescopic stars in the neighbourhood of the 44th. *Geminorum* of Flamstead's catalogue,[3] and to repeat the same a few days after, when it will be discover'd that one of them is no longer in its former place; and thus its motion will point it out. For unless a very perfect instrument of a power not less than 200 or 250 be used to view it; there will be great difficulty in distinguishing it from a star of between the 6th and 7th magnitude; and yet, after it is once pointed out, a telescope of less power may confirm the planetary appearance. This account has been given me by Mr Herschel himself, who by discovering this planet, has made his name as durable as the Solar System. He has, from a compliment to the King who has taken him under his patronage, christen'd it Georgium Sidus; but it will more probably bear his own name. He is a Hessian, and came over here in a Hessian regiment, and for some years directed the musick at Bath. The Telescopes with which he observes are the *Newtonian* reflecting Telescopes made by himself, some of which magnify the Diameters of objects above 6000 times. A peculiar ability which he has of observing with these high powers, together with his constant attention to the heavens, has enabled him to make many more discoveries among the stars. But of these you have an account in the last numbers of the Philosophical Transactions;[4] and, therefore, I need not take any more notice of them. Be so good as to deliver my respectful compliments to Mr James Winthrop[5] and to communicate to him this account. It contains a full answer to a letter which I

---

3. John Flamsteed (1646–1719), the first Astronomer Royal. His *Historia Coelestis Britannica* was published in three folio volumes in 1725; the third volume contained the "British Catalogue" in which Flamsteed listed 2,935 stars observed at Greenwich.

4. See "A Letter from William Herschel, F.R.S." *Phil. Trans.*, LXXIII (1783), 1–3; William Herschel, "On the Diameter and Magnitude of the Georgium Sidus", *Phil. Trans.*, LXIII (1783), 4–14.

5. James Winthrop (1752–1821), son of John Winthrop, Professor of Mathematics and Natural Philosophy at Harvard. James graduated at Harvard in 1769, and was appointed Librarian to the College in 1772. He was one of the first members of the American Academy of Arts and Sciences and a founder of the Massachusetts Historical Society. (*D.A.B.*)

have just receiv'd from him by Mr Gorham[6] containing an enquiry about the new planet. I sensibly feel the expressions of kindness and civility in his letters, which gave me the more pleasure because it came from the son of the excellent Dr Winthrop, who was one of my correspondents for whom I had a high respect and whose memory I revere.

I have not time at present to answer Mr Winthrop's letter; and the same is true of the letters which Mr Gorham bro't me from Dr Chauncy and Mr Temple, to whom, when they come in your way, I shall be obliged to you for presenting my respects. I writ to both of them not long ago.

I have convey'd your letters to Dr Priestley and Mr Brand-Hollis.[7] I can only add, Dear Sir, that I am, with great regard,

Your most obedient and humble servant

Rich: Price

---

6. Nathaniel Gorham (1738–96), merchant and land speculator. He sat in the Colonial Legislature of Massachusetts (1771–75), in the Provincial Congress (1774–75), on the Board of War (1778–81) and in the State Constitutional Convention (1779–80). He attended the Continental Congress as a delegate for Massachusetts in 1782–83 and in 1785–87, and presided over the Federal Constitutional Convention for three months in 1787 (Boatner, pp. 440–41).

7. Thomas Brand-Hollis (c.1719–1804). Thomas Brand was educated at Glasgow University where he studied under Francis Hutcheson. Elected FRS in 1756 and FSA in 1757. He was an intimate friend of Thomas Hollis who bequeathed to him a large part of his fortune. Brand took his benefactor's name after his death in 1774. In that year he was elected MP for Hindon, but the election was contested. Brand-Hollis lost his seat and was prosecuted at Salisbury in 1776 for attempting to bribe electors. Being found guilty he was fined a thousand marks and imprisoned for six months. He was a prominent Dissenter and a member of Theophilus Lindsey's congregation in Essex Street. He played a leading part in the affairs of the Society for Constitutional Information and was a patron of New College, Hackney. See John Disney, *Memoirs of Thomas Brand-Hollis, Esq.* (London, 1808).

To Henry Marchant[1]

Newington=Green Oct 6th 1783

Dear Sir,

Accept my best thanks for the letter with which you have favoured me. I remember with pleasure the acquaintance I commenced with you when you were in London, and our subsequent correspondence.[2] The war which has interrupted this correspondence has indeed, as you say, been unnatural and cruel; and I participate with you heartily in your joy on the conclusion of it and

---

ORIGINAL: The Rhode Island Historical Society.   TEXT: Original, with the kind permission of The Rhode Island Historical Society.

1. See Vol. I, 149.

2. Marchant visited England from Aug. 1771 to July 1772.

the revolution in which it has terminated. A more important revolution scarcely ever took place among mankind. A more striking instance can scarcely be conceived of the wisdom of Divine Providence in drawing good out of evil and employing the wickedness of man to effect the best ends. America has made a noble stand against tyranny, and exhibited a bright example to the world. The influence of this example has already done much good. It has emancipated one *European* country,[3] and is likely soon to emancipate more. God grant that the united states may wisely improve the liberty they have earned, and take care to avoid the danger they are now in of fighting with one another and sinking into anarchy. This is the greatest danger that now threatens them; and should they not be able to guard against it, an event which might have proved a blessing to them and to the world may prove a curse. One of the fairest experiments in human affairs will fail, and the friends of liberty will be discouraged. You may, therefore, imagine that I have heard with distress of the dissensions among them, their prejudices against one another, and the reluctance of some of them in giving energy to the decisions of the delegation which forms their union, and in providing funds for maintaining their credit and redeeming their debts.

You have done me, Sir, great honour by joyning in the invitation which was sent me by Congress.[4] This invitation I shall always look upon as one of the principal honours of my life. That favourable opinion of me which it imply'd I highly value. It makes me amends for the abuse which my attempts to serve the cause of general liberty have brought upon me in this country, and some danger to which I have been exposed by them.

That part of your letter which relates to the state of the Congregation at Newport to which you belong, gives me much concern. I beg you would be so good as to deliver my respectful compliments to Mr Ellery[5] and the other members of the Committee, and inform them that it is by no means in my power to promote such a collection for the assistance of the congregation as they request, and that in the *present circumstances of things and at this early period of the peace* there is no reason to think that it can be attempted with any success. But were success possible, it is only a particular application to individuals among the Dissenters by a person sent over for this purpose that can make it so. I should, however, be very apprehensive that were such an agent sent, he would be sadly disappointed. The truth is, that the Dissenting interest in London is declining, and that it is more than our charitable people can do to support the necessities of our own poor congregations and ministers, whose difficulties have been lately much increased by a load of new taxes. We cannot,

---

3. Ireland? See R.P. to Lieut.-Col. Sharman, 7 Aug. 1783.
4. See Benjamin Franklin, Arthur Lee, and John Adams to R.P., 7 Dec. 1778.
5. Possibly William Ellery (1727–90), lawyer. Member of Congress (1776–86), Commissioner of the Continental Loan Office for Rhode Island 1786–90. Grandfather of William Ellery Channing.

therefore, look much abroad. America, I hope, will be able to take care of itself. Dr Gibbons[6] concurs with me in these sentiments, and desires me to *add* to my own *his* respects to you and the rest of the Committee. Mr Joseph Jennings[7] has been dead some time. I must not omit to add that there is no such deputation in London representing the body of Dissenters as that to which the petition is address'd. There is one chosen by the Dissenters in London for taking care of the civil rights of the Dissenters;[8] but as it never extends its views to charity, the petition cannot with any propriety be presented to it. There are several charitable boards and trusts but they are all confined to particular objects from which they cannot deviate. I am grieved, Dear Sir, to give you and the other gentlemen of the Committee such an answer as this to your application. I feel for the distresses of the congregation; and I should receive the greatest pleasure from being instrumental in helping it were this in my power.

Mrs Price is obliged to you for remembering her in your letter. She returns her respects to you. At present she is in a very sad state of health and I am much distrest about her. A supprest gout brought upon her last week some paralytic symptoms which are very threatening. I am myself in tolerable health; and should be very happy could I see her better. But I refer myself and her to that perfect wisdom and goodness by which all events are directed.

Under a grateful sense of your attention and civility and with sincere respect and the best wishes

I am, Sir, your very obedient and humble servant

Rich*d* Price

---

6. Thomas Gibbons (1720–85), Dissenting Minister. He had been a pupil at Moorfields Academy where Price was educated. In 1753 he became Minister at Haberdasher's Hall, and from 1754 was a tutor at Mile End Academy.

7. Joseph Jennings, the son of David Jennings (1691–1762) who succeeded John Eames at Moorfields Academy in 1744. Joseph Jennings married a daughter of Daniel Neal, the historian.

8. The Committee of the Protestant Dissenting Deputies.

To Ezra Stiles

Newington=Green Oct 23*d* 1783

Dr Price presents his very respectful compliments to Dr Styles, and hopes he has received the letter[1] which he sent to him by Dr Beardsley.[2] He now takes the opportunity of Mr Fitch's[3] return to America to send him the following account of the new Planet which he has lately received from Mr *Herschel* the discoverer.

[Here Price repeats the passage "The elements of the orbit ... planetary appearance" which he had earlier included in his letter to Joseph Willard, 6 Oct. 1783]

Mr Herschel has made several other discoveries among the stars; but of these a particular account is given in the last Numbers of the Philosophical Transactions. He has in particular, added greatly to the number of stars which appear *single* to the naked eye but thro' a good Telescope appear *double* or *triple*. He has also found reason for concluding that the Solear System has a proper motion in absolute space. He makes his own Telescopes which are not the common *Gregorian* reflecting Telescopes, but the *Newtonian*, some of which he makes to magnify the Diameter above 6000 times.

[No signature]

ORIGINAL: Yale University Library. TEXT: Original, with the kind permission of Yale University Library. A note in Stiles's hand added to the letter reads: "1784 Observations of the Comet at Yale College. Jan*y* 20.*th* At VI in the Evening a Comet was discovered in the S.W. It sat 22' before VIII, apparent time by a Clock regulated the previous noon, W.33.S."

1. In his diary for 11 Dec. 1783, Ezra Stiles noted "I received a letter from Dr Price of London dated Sept. 29th ult. acknowledge the Receipt of the Diploma I sent him creating him a Doctor of Laws." *The Literary Diary of Ezra Stiles* (New York, 1901), III, 101.

2. Ebenezer Beardsley (1756–91), "an eminent physician of New Haven ... an ingenious Man." *The Literary Diary of Ezra Stiles*, III, 415.

3. Ebenezer Fitch, a tutor at Yale who left for Europe in April 1783. He took with him the diploma of a Doctorate in Laws to present to Price. When Fitch returned to America he brought this letter which Stiles received on 8 Jan. 1784. On 14 Sept. 1786 Fitch was elected Senior Tutor at Yale, and on 21 Jan. 1791 he accepted the call to become Preceptor of the Academy at Williamstown. See *The literary diary of Ezra Stiles*, III, 62, 70, 104, 239, 410.

From Joseph Willard

University in Cambridge,
Commonwealth of Massachusetts,
October 31, 1783.

Rev'd and dear Sir,

I received your favor, together with your two volumes upon annuities and reversionary payments,[1] for the American Academy, by Mr Mullet. As soon as ever the Academy meets, I shall present them; and I am sure the Members will feel themselves extremely obliged by so valuable a present; and particularly, as immediately coming from the Author, for whom they have the high regard and esteem, as everyone must, who is a friend to true worth and to the liberties of mankind. These volumes have come very opportunely for me, as I am one of a Committee for forming a plan, for a fund to make provision for Minister's widows.[2]

Mr Mullet has been at Cambridge, and has seen the public rooms in the College. He appears to be a worthy man, and I hope he will succeed in the business he is upon, agreeably to his wishes.

I thank you, Sir, for your congratulations upon the acknowledgement of the independence of the United States of America. I trust it will be happy for the liberties of mankind. I hope the citizens will highly prize and wisely improve the privileges they enjoy above the generality of mankind.

I think the passage of the Poet may be properly applied to them, "O fortunatos nimium si sua bona norint."[3] May they always be sensible of their felicity, and do nothing to forfeit it!

I hope the oppressed friends of liberty, of other lands, will ever find this country a happy asylum; and that the rights of mankind will always be in the highest security among us.

The Bearer of this is Jonathan Jackson Esqr.,[4] an inhabitant of Newbury= Port, who has for a considerable number of years, been a distinguished merchant in that large trading town, but, who has been far from confining his

---

ORIGINAL: Harvard University Library.   TEXT: Original, with the kind permission of the Harvard University Library.

1. *Observations on Reversionary Payments*, 4th ed. See R.P. to Joseph Willard, 15 May 1783 and 6 Oct. 1783.

2. In 1785 the General Court of Massachusetts incorporated a society known as The Massachusetts Congregational Charitable Society for the provision of annuities for the widows and orphans of Congregational Ministers and University Presidents and Professors. See R.P. to Joseph Willard, 18 Mar. 1786.

3. *Georgics*, ii, 458 [Ah blest beyond all bliss did they but know their happiness.].

4. Jonathan Jackson (1743–1810), merchant. He graduated from Harvard in 1761 and was Treasurer of Massachusetts from 1802 to 1806. *M.H.S.P.* (1903), 327.

knowledge and enquiries to commerce. He had a regular education in this University; and you will find him a Gentleman of excellent abilities and improvements. He is a true Patriot; has exerted himself to serve his country, and through the whole of our late contest, has preserved a character remarkable for uniformity and integrity. He has been employed in our General Assembly, in seasons of great difficulty, and has also had a seat in the Congress of the United States. He is very desirous of an acquaintance with you, Sir, of whom he entertains the highest esteem; and I have presumed upon the liberty of introducing him to you, and doubt not you will be pleased by an intercourse with him, while in London.

Accompanying this letter is one for the Astronomer Royal,[5] which I should be obliged to you to deliver him. Please, Sir, in your next, to let me know the age of that Gentleman.

Dr Chauncy is well. Mr Foster will soon sail for England.

With the sincerest wishes for your health and happiness,

I subscribe, Rev'd Sir
Your very humble and obedient servant
Joseph Willard

Novr 12, 1783. This day the American Academy of Arts and Sciences met. I communicated your letter and presented your present. As their Corresponding Secretary, I am directed, Sir, to transmit to you the vote of thanks, which you will find enclosed.

J. Willard

5. Nevil Maskelyne.

From Jonathan Trumbull, the Elder

Lebanon 1st December 1783

Sir,

The veneration with which your Character, as an Assertor of the rights of humanity, and of American Liberty, has inspired my Mind, must apologize for me, in this Address to you.

My Son,[1] who has experienced your goodness, and whose singular situation when in England Two Years ago, you will doubtless recollect, will have the

ORIGINAL: An unsigned draft, The Connecticut Historical Society. TEXT: Original, with the kind permission of The Connecticut Historical Society. Trumbull composed this draft on 20 Nov., but altered the date later to 1 Dec. 1783.
1. John Trumbull, see R.P. to [John Temple], 18 Sept. 1780.

pleasure to deliver this, and to convey to you from me, the Testimonies of regard and respect with which I have charged him. That cruel Jealousy, which heretofore was the cause of so much misfortune and disappointment to him, has now I hope, ceased forever between your Country and ours; and flattering himself that he shall at this Time, meet a more cordial reception than before, he ventures himself on a second attempt, at the improvement of his Pencil. A Knowledge of your former kindness emboldens me to commend him to your further goodness and protection, as a friend to Literature and the Arts.

That superintending Providence which influences the Affairs of Men, has severed that intimate Tie, which once, so happily for both, connected the people of this Country, with those of your Island, under one common Sovereign; and has given to these U States an independent Rank among the Nations of the Earth. Shall this event produce a total Disunion between us? I think not—forbid it Policy! forbid it Wisdom! Altho the relation of fellow subject is dissolved, other Bonds will unite us. Similarity of Manners, Character and disposition, national Consanguinity, mutual Interests and Wants, supported and interchanged by Commerce, must yet connect us. Resentments however and a sense of Injuries must have Time to subside; and the most conciliating Policy must be applied to heal the Wounds which have been too liberally given. Among the particular modes to be adopted for this purpose, Reparation for manifest Injuries, may perhaps be tho't to be one.

If so, the Case of Mr Jn° Temple is a singular one—his Character as a Crown Officer previous to the War, his Conduct during the Contest, with the constant Tenor of his Information to the then Ministry, are too well known to need a particular detail; Information and advice, which had it been properly attended to, might have prevented the separation which is now experienced. But the Die is 'cast'. The great event is accomplished, and a Retrospect is of little consequence, but as it may lead us to a correction of future Error. Should Mr Temple, who I am informed means to be a Solicitor, meet with that Compensation, which he expects, it may prove a singular Means of Conciliation. His Friends in This Country, Rank among the most wealthy and respectable—and as such, will command their proportionate Influence and Weight in the Scale of reconciliation. I presume not to dictate on your Side the Water—a Hint may be excusable.

As Matter of Literary Curiosity, the inclosed pamphlet may not be an unacceptable present to you

> With much esteem and regard
> I have the Honor to be &c.
> [No signature]

To the Earl of Shelburne

Newington=Green Dec: 30th 1783

My Lord,

I have received with much pleasure your Lordship's letter, and think myself greatly obliged to you for it and for your kind enquiry about Mrs Price. I have been ever since the middle of last summer in great anxiety about her. In November last she was in imminent danger, attended by Dr Hulme,[1] Mr Watken and other medical friends; but she is now better again, and, tho' far from perfectly restored and incapable of writing or reading, or doing much of any kind of business, she can go about the house and is tolerably comfortable and chearful. She desires me to express to your Lordship the grateful sense she has of your goodness in thinking of her and enquiring about her.

I am very happy that I only hear of the commotions in the political world. They cause me to enjoy more my own private and tranquil situation. But it gives me concern to learn that this is a happiness which your Lordship is likewise enjoying. I have wished indeed much that you had been lately in London to add the weight of your exertions in opposing the India=Bill and resisting one of the most daring attempts that was ever made by a party to establish itself in power by corruption in opposition to King and country. I have also wished to see your Lordship's name in the new arrangement of ministry; not at all on your own account for there is the hardest work to be done, but on the public account. Your Lordship, I know, has great views; and there never was a time when vigour and wisdom at the helm were more necessary to carry such views into execution. It will give me pleasure to find that the new ministry can stand its ground; but it is so young a ministry that I know not how to expect this.

What would tend most to strengthen it would be the immediate revival of the funds, now in the most deplorable state and what alone can effect this is entering immediately upon measures which shall convince the public that the establishment of a plan of redemption is seriously meant. I have been lately looking into the eleventh Report of the Commissioners for stating the public accounts.[2] I am glad to find that at the conclusion they strongly recommend

---

ORIGINAL: Bowood. TEXT: Original, with the kind permission of the Marquis of Lansdowne.

   1. Possibly Nathaniel Hulme (1732–1807), who was born in Yorkshire, educated at Edinburgh, where he took the degree of MD in 1765, admitted a Licentiate of the College of Physicians on 28 Mar. 1774, and appointed physician to the Charterhouse in the same month. See W. Munk, *The Roll of the Royal College of Physicians of London*, 2nd ed. (London, 1878), II, 298. I am indebted to Mr Robin Price of The Wellcome Institute for the History of Medicine for this information. In his will Price bequeathed £10 to D. Hulm ("Journal", p. 402).

   2. "The eleventh report of the commissioners for examining, taking and stating the public

the establishment of a sinking fund invariably apply'd, as the only means of discharging the public debt. Their account of the funded debt agrees with that I have given, after adding to the capital as they have given it (211 millions) a valuation of the temporary annuities which they have omitted. The difference between their account and mine of the unfunded debt I shall account for in a new edition of my pamphlet on the state of the finances.[3]

Will your Lordship excuse me for mentioning to you the following affair? Having this occasion to write to your Lordship I know not how to omit it.

Mr Sturt[4] introduced Mr Scott[5] at Bridport at the last general election. Mr Sturt now intends to introduce one of his sons[6] at Bridport, and pretends to leave Mr Scott to stand on his own interest. Mr Scott, knowing the Corporation to be adverse to the coalition and friendly to the Peace and to your Lordship's administration professes his concurrence with them in this; but did they think him not sincere, or suspect any collusion between him and Mr Sturt in order to enable the latter to introduce two members instead of one, they would withdraw their support from him and probably transfer it to a friend of mine, a Gentleman of considerable fortune in Dorsetshire[7] with whom, in

accounts", *H.C.J.*, XXXIX, 771ff. Price was gratified to see that the Commissioners recommended many of the measures that he had been advocating for many years. They held that the widest publicity should be given to the state of the public finances, that the people should be informed of the size and nature of the National Debt, that a surplus of revenue over expenditure should be created, that the Sinking Fund should be revived and its produce invariably applied to the redemption of debt, and that further delay would only bring nearer the prospect of catastrophe and ruin.

3. Two editions of *The State of the Public Debts* were published in 1783, but as far as is known Price did not publish a further edition in 1784. He did however publicize his disagreements with the Commissioners in *A Postscript to a Pamphlet, by Dr Price, on the State of the Public Debt and Finances*, which was published on 22 Mar. 1784. Price argued that the Commissioners had underestimated the total of the funded and the unfunded debt. Whereas they had given it as £238 million, Price put it at £280 million. Price estimated that extra taxation to the value of £823,642 per annum would be required to balance revenue and expenditure, and that a further million per annum should be raised to finance Sinking Fund operations. The question whether there was a deficiency in the revenue was a matter of public controversy. John Dalrymple, Earl of Stair, was more pessimistic than Price and thought that there was an annual deficiency of £3 million. See John (Dalrymple) Earl of Stair, *The State of the Public Debts, etc.* (London, 1783), pp. 5, 6, 14–16, 21. Sir John Sinclair, on the other hand, was much more optimistic than either Price or Stair. He thought that with the cessation of hostilities there would be an annual surplus of £2,262,526. *Hints, addressed to the Public Calculated to Dispel the Gloomy Ideas which have been lately entertained of our State of Finances* (London, 1783), p. 57.

4. Humphry Sturt (?1725–86), MP for Dorset, 1754–84. He voted against Shelburne's peace preliminaries.

5. Thomas Scott (1723–1816) represented Bridport from 1780 to 1790. Although returned for Bridport on the Sturt family interest, he voted for Shelburne on the peace preliminaries and for parliamentary reform in May 1783. He was therefore sincere in claiming to agree with the members of the Corporation at Bridport on these issues.

6. Charles Sturt (1763–1812), MP for Bridport, 1784–1802. Both Charles Sturt and Thomas Scott were returned for Bridport in 1784.

7. Probably William Morton Pitt (1754–1836), MP for Poole, 1780–90, and Dorset, 1790–1826. He contested the Bridport election unsuccessfully in 1784 and the interest which Price showed in his candidature was to no avail.

respect of ability, Mr Scot is not to be compared. By this Gentleman (not Mr Brand-Hollis) I am requested to mention to your Lord=ship the following enquiries.

Whether Mr Scot did not apply to your Lordship when minister for a place in the Custom=house at Bridport, and whether your obliging the corporation with it was not one cause of Mr Sturt's and Mr Scott's being inimical to your administration?

Whether your Lordship looks upon Mr Scot to be sincerely what he professes to the corporation, a zealous friend to your Lordship and adverse to Mr Fox and his party? And also, whether your Lordship thinks Mr Sturt and Mr Scot to be, as they pretend, unconnected with one another.

I would not give your Lordship the trouble of writing on this subject. I hope I shall soon have the pleasure of seeing you in town; and it will be time enough then for me to be informed of your sentiments about it.

The associated Volunteers in Ireland, as your Lordship may probably well know, are much exasperated against the Parliament there for rejecting their plan of reform.[8] They are procuring an application by petition (or rather requisition) from all the Counties, Cities and towns; and should this likewise fail there will be great danger of a convulsion.

Lady Shelburne will, I hope, accept of mine and Mrs Price's best respects. With all good wishes I am, my Lord,

Your Lordship's most obedient and humble servant
Richd Price

Should Lord Fitzmaurice be at Bowwood or Colonel Barre, I beg my respects may be deliver'd to them.

---

8. In November 1782, a Convention of the Volunteers of Ireland under the leadership of Flood prepared a comprehensive plan of parliamentary reform. This plan restricted the franchise, except for those owning freehold or leasehold property of £20 a year, to those who had resided in the constituency for six out of the preceding twelve months; abolished rotten boroughs, prevented those who held pensions under pleasure from sitting in Parliament; required those who were awarded pensions for life or a place under the Crown to submit themselves for re-election; and limited the duration of Parliaments to three years. These resolutions were introduced into the Irish House of Commons on 29 Nov. 1782 in the form of a Reform Bill, but the motion to receive the bill was defeated by 157 votes to 77. (Lecky, VI, 337–45.)

From [An unidentified correspondent]

Edinburgh, Jan. 10 1784

I AM very desirous of having a Society established in Edinburgh, for the widows of Contributors there, and every where else in this part of the kingdom,

---

PRINTED: <i>Plan for Annuities to Widows with two Letters relative thereto</i> (Edinburgh, 1784), I am much indebted to Mr John Stephens for making copies of this letter and Price's reply to it available to me.

who may incline to contribute, agreeable to the plan laid down by you in your last edition[1] of *Observations on Reversionary Payments*, &c. vol I. pages 97, 98, and 99, for those under 40 years of age; and to include, in the same scheme, your plan, page 100, for those who are 40, and above that age, giving those under 40 an option to contribute in either way, and giving the whole an option to contribute for larger annuities. In short, I wish to adopt precisely the whole particulars mentioned in these four pages, with the addition only of making each Contributor pay at entry, one Guinea towards the expence of management, and obtaining a charter to entitle the Contributors to act as a legal society by Directors, &c. But this I will only attempt, upon receiving your sanction, that the payments are adequate for the inhabitants of this place, and the country, including other towns whose inhabitants may contribute, and taking into consideration the different values of males and females at the same age.

I KNOW you are impressed with a belief of the inhabitants of Edinburgh being very bad lives.[2] In a former letter I endeavoured to explain that this was, in part, owing to want of proper information of the real state of the inhabitants. Whatever may be the situation of the lower class, I am of opinion, that respecting those who would become Contributors, they will be found to be equal in value, with the hypothesis of an equal decrement[3] of life to 86;[4] and if such were to be aided by Contributors in the country, I would have little doubt, upon the whole, of their being equal to, if not better than the Northampton table.

UNTIL I tried the calculations, I had some doubt of the great effect given to the small annuities; but, after doing so, I was entirely satisfied. The hypothesis for all ages under 40, requires a small additional payment, to what is required for an annuity to Widows by the Northampton table. I therefore thought it safe to calculate upon the hypothesis, by which the four guineas for 5l. 10l. and 20l. may be tried in a few minutes, by deducing the value of all the annuities which can come upon the fund, at the end of the first seven years, from the amount of the contributions at that period. As, by the result, I make the fund at 4 *per cent*,

---

1. i.e. the 4th ed. (1783).

2. On the basis of data collected for the years 1739 to 1758 Price concluded that the expectation of life in Edinburgh was lower than it was in Breslau, Northampton and Norwich. In general it was similar to that in London, except that it was lower in Edinburgh for those past the age of 30. The relatively low expectation of life in these cities was due, Price thought, to the pernicious effects of life in cities, to uncleanliness and overcrowding. See *O.R.P.*, 1st ed. (1771), 209–11. This account was repeated in all the later editions of the work without alteration.

3. Printed text reads 'discernment' for 'decrement'; amendment inserted in MS on printed text.

4. i.e. De Moivre's hypothesis which supposes an equal decrement of life. See Price's references in his notes to his letter to Franklin of 3 April 1769, *Corr.*, vol. I, 59–60. Although, when he wrote this letter to Franklin he thought that De Moivre's hypothesis was an excellent one, he later came to the view that the accumulation of data on the expectation of life had shown it to be misleading. See *O.R.P* 4th ed. I, 314–18.

more than sufficient, I beg leave, in a few words, to state the method I took, in case I have committed an error.

SUPPOSED 51 Contributors aged 35, and of equal ages with their wives, by which, neglecting the small chance of a husband and his wife dying in the same year, two marriages would be dissolved and one widow left annually; at the end of 7 years, one widow would not be entitled to any annuity, two of them to 5l. each and the other four to 10l. each.—At the end of 7 years, the Contributors will have made eight payments; and, subtracting the values of the different annuities from the fund, there will remain a capital of about 1250l. producing, at 4 *per cent.* 50l. *per annum.*

This, added to the contribution(s) of 214l. makes 264l. *per annum*, a sum more than sufficient for payment of the value of an annuity of 20l. at the age of 43, being only 253l.

In this view, the fund appears to be more than sufficient; as no widow, under 43, will be entitled to 20l. annuity; and most of them will be much older, and consequently of less value. Besides there would be always fourteen Contributors out of every fifty-one, whose widows would be entitled only to 5l. or 10l. annuity; and instances will happen of the husband's dying in the first year, whose widow, on that account, would be no burden upon the fund.

By continuing the plan in your last edition, and adding thereto the other plan, page 100, for husbands of any age, I presume you think such payments sufficient for any set of persons whose lives are equally good with the hypothesis; even taking into consideration, that the lives of women are better than the lives of men.

I join with you in thinking those plans are the most equitable, and most encouraging of any that can well be devised; and when contrasted with other schemes for equal annuities from the beginning, will appear to the Public in such a view as may induce many to become Contributors; as altho', by equal annuities, in the event of a husband's dying in a few years, his widow will receive a very undue advantage; yet it is natural for people in health to estimate their lives above their value; and these would prefer a scheme, which adds to the annuity, in proportion to the length of joint lives, for which, at the same time, less money appears to be payable.

SUPPOSE 40 the age of husband and wife, 30l. the annuity; and supposing the joint lives to continue so as to make twenty payments, and computing at 4 *per cent.*

I. By the first part of the proposed plan, for sixteen guineas in hand, and four annually equal to 152l. a contributor would entitle his widow to an annuity of 30l. worth 263l.

II. The second part, for 15l. in hand, and 5l. annually, equal to 182l. would entitle a widow to the same annuity.

For an annuity of 30l. certain, a contribution of 10l. 6s. *per annum* must be paid by a husband during marriage, which at the end of twenty years is equal to 306l.

SUPPOSE the husband and wife to live so as to make twenty-five payments,
THE first, for a sum equal to 219l. would entitle his widow to an annuity of
30l. equal to 224l.

The second, for a sum equal to 247l. would entitle his widow to an annuity of
35l. equal to 262l.

WHEREAS a married man, contributing for an annuity of 30l. to his
widow, would at that time have paid equal to 429l. which, at the end of
twenty-five years, is only worth 224l.

If such a scheme should take place, the medium of annuities, for every four
guineas in the one plan, and 5l. in the other, must be calculated, in order to
ascertain the amount of the capital necessary to be raised for their payment.

It would assist the fund to make the annuity to commence only at the first
term of Whitsunday or Martinmas, which first should happen, after the expir-
ation of twelve months from the death of the husband; and to continue thereafter yearly, at that term, so long as the widow should survive it; that is, that it
shall cease and determine at the term of payment immediately preceding her
death.

[No signature]

[To an unidentified correspondent]

Newington Green,
Jan. 29, 1784.

I HAVE received with pleasure, your letter of the 10th of this month; and I
heartily wish you success in establishing, at Edinburgh, the plan mentioned in
it, for providing for Widows and Orphans. The observations you make in this
plan, are all perfectly just; and I have no doubt of its sufficiency to support
itself, notwithstanding the lower values of lives at Edinburgh than in the
country, and the excess of the values of the lives of females above the lives of
males. The subscribers to such a plan will, as you observe, consist of persons in
the higher station, at Edinburgh; who, being better accommodated, and living
generally in more airy situations, must be less likely to be short-lived than the
general mass of the town inhabitants. For this reason, the values of their lives
may probably be safely taken to be equal to the values of lives according to the
hypothesis; or, if they should not, the difference will be compensated by the
greater value of lives of country Contributors. The excess of the values of the
lives of females deserves more regards; but the contributions in the plan being

---

PRINTED: *Plan for Annuities to Widows with two Letters relative thereto* (Edinburgh, 1784).

given rather higher than they ought to be given, according to the hypothesis, I do not think that any danger will result from hence, especially when I consider, that the money contributed may be improved at a higher interest than four *per cent*. The only alteration I would propose is, requiring from a Contributor, when the difference of age between him and his wife exceeds ten years, (his own age being forty or less) a present payment of *two guineas* for every year of excess; and when his age at admission exceeds forty, and when, therefore, the second scheme (p. 99&c.) must be chosen, *three guineas* for every year of excess supposing it above ten years, allowing no excess above twenty years. I take it for granted, that care will be taken, to guard against the fraudulent intrusion of bad lives; for though the danger from hence is much less on this plan than any other, yet there will still be some danger. The calculations suppose that a whole year's annuity is to be paid to a Widow at the end of half a year, from the death of her husband. If, therefore, the first yearly payment is not to be made till the Whitsunday or Martinmas, after the lapse of a year from the death, as you propose, a great advantage will be gained; but I do not think it will be much wanted.

It would be difficult, if not impossible, to ascertain the median of annuities payable to Widows, in order to discover the capital necessary to be raised. Most probably it will be always varying, in consequence of the different ages at which contributors will enter, and the different options[1] they will take at different periods. A comparison of the rate of mortality among the Contributors, with the rate of mortality in Mr de Moivere's hypothesis will be sufficient at all times to enable you to determine the state of the scheme. If the former is less than the latter (or nearly equal to it) the scheme must succeed, and the capital must rise to a sufficient sum. If, on the contrary, the former should prove permanently greatest the scheme will want to be amended and strengthened. You are so well acquainted with this subject, that you might soon, by making a number of calculations in particular cases on Mr de Moivere's hypothesis, at four *per cent*, find how far the schemes I have proposed are likely to answer. I did this before I proposed them, but I am far from having time to go over the work again.

I am. &c.

RICH. PRICE.

---

1. Printed text reads 'orphans' for 'options', corrected in MS on Edinburgh copy.

To Andrew Eliot[1]

8 March 1784

Dr Price presents his compliments to Mr Eliot, and begs to be informed by him when he is to sail for Boston. He wishes to convey thither two letters,[2] and a set of Bishop Hoadly's works consisting of three volumes in folio which he intends to offer as a present to the University at Cambridge;[3] and, if not inconvenient for Mr Eliot, he will be glad to consign them to his care. He intended to have called upon Mr Eliot long before this time; but has been prevented by a wound in his leg from a fall which has confined him for some time, and still confines him to his house. Dr Price requests the favour of an answer by the bearer.

Monday morning

ORIGINAL: Harvard College Library. Addressed: To/Mr Eliot/Thavies Inn/No 3/ Holbourn. TEXT: Original, with the kind permission of Harvard College Library.

1. See Vol. I, 53.
2. See R.P. to Joseph Willard, 14 Mar. 1784.
3. See R.P. to Benjamin Rush, 1 Jan. 1783.

To Joseph Willard

Newington-Green, near London
M'ch. 14th, 1784

Dear Sir,

I take the opportunity of Mr Eliot's return to Boston to send by him a set of Bishop Hoadly's works, which I hope, the University at Cambridge will accept as a small offering to testify my respect and good wishes.[1] His name as a Divine stands very high; but among the writers on civil and religious liberty it stands next to the names of Sidney and Lock and Milton.

In a former letter I gave you an account of all that has been determined here

---

PRINTED: *M.H.S.P.* (1909–10), 616–17. TEXT: *M.H.S.P.*

1. See R.P. to Benjamin Rush, 1 Jan. 1783, and R.P. to A. Eliot, 8 Mar. 1784. The editors of *M.H.S.P.* (1909–10) note, p. 616:

"At a meeting of the President and Fellows of Harvard College, June 24, 1784:

Voted, that the thanks of this board be given to the Rev. Doctor Richard Price, of London, for his valuable present, to this University, of a new and elegant Edition, in three volumes Folio, of the Works of the late celebrated Doctor Benjamin Hoadly, Bishop of Winchester, a warm Assertor of Liberty & Friend to the rights of mankind; . . . And that the President be desired to improve the first opportunity to transmit a copy of this vote to Doctor Price.

concerning the new planet.[2] This discovery, together with the American Revolution and the progress made in France in the power of flying by the Aerostatic machines,[3] render the present time a new *epoch* in the affairs of mankind.

The Royal Society have this winter disposed of two prize medals, one to Mr Hutchings for discovering the congelation of Mercury when the Thermometer falls to 40 degrees below nought;[4] and the other to Mr Goodrick (a Gentleman in Yorkshire) for discovering a variation in the light of the star Algol, which it goes thro' every three days, its light in this time gradually diminishing till from a star of the first magnitude it becomes a star of the 4th or 5th magnitude, and afterwards recovering itself again.[5] Since the disposal of these medals there has been read to the Royal Society two ingenious papers, one by the honourable Mr Cavendish[6] containing some new facts concerning inflammable and dephlogisticated air,[7] and the other by Dr Blagden[8] on the meteors of last year, and the nature and causes of meteors in general.[9] But the greatest part of our time this winter has been spent in a manner very unsuitable to the design of our institution; I mean, in violent altercations and disputes occasioned by complaints of misconduct in Sir Joseph Banks our President and attempts to oblige him to resign. These attempts have not succeeded, and at present he seems to be confirmed in the chair and the Society is returned to its usual business.[10]

I have been for some time confined by a wound in my leg from a fall. This confinement, together with the very low and sad state of my wife's health, has press'd upon my spirits. But I have great reason to be thankful; for indeed my life has hitherto been a happy life, and my heart is full of gratitude to the giver of it. When you see Mr Winthrop deliver to him my kind respects. I cannot forget the kind civility of the letter he writ to me. The enquiry in it about the new planet I answer'd in my last letter to you.[11] Wishing you, Dear Sir, all possible happiness I am, with great respect, Your obliged and very obedient servant

Richard Price

---

2. See R.P. to Joseph Willard, 6 Oct. 1783.

3. The editors of *M.H.S.P.* (1909–10) note, p. 616: "See *The nation*, December 30, 1909, 648."

4. Thomas Hutchins, "On the point of mercurial congelation," *Phil. Trans.*, LXXIII (1783), 303ff.

5. John Goodricke, "A series of observations on, and a discovery of, the period of variation of light of the bright star in the head of Medusa, called ALGOL," *Phil. Trans.* LXXIII (1783), 474ff.

6. Henry Cavendish, see Vol. I, 103.

7. "Experimentation on Air", *Phil. Trans.*, LXXIV (1784), 119ff.

8. Sir Charles Blagden (1748–1820), FRS, army medical officer. He was elected Secretary to the Royal Society in May 1784.

9. "An Account of some Fiery Meteors, and Observations," *Phil. Trans.*, LXXIV (1784), 201ff.

10. See R.P. to Sir Joseph Banks, 1 Jan 1783. On the failure to remove Banks from office, Paul Henry Maty resigned his secretaryship and was succeeded by Sir Charles Blagden.

11. See n. 2 above.

I hope you have received the new edition of my Treatise on Annuities[12] which I sent by Mr Barrett, and which I request the favour of the American Academy of Arts and Sciences to accept.

12. *Observations on Reversionary Payments*, 4th ed.

To Benjamin Franklin

Newington=Green Ap 6th 1784

My Dear Friend,

I have been long intending to write to you, and I feel ashamed that I have not done it sooner. Your letter[1] which was brought me by Mr Bingham gave me great pleasure. It inclosed a case for an air Balloon and a print which in conformity to your desire, I deliver'd to the President of the Royal Society. Soon after Mr Bingham's arrival Mr Daggs brought me your paper on a Mathematical prize Question, proposed by the Royal Academy of B[russels]. I convey'd this to Dr Priestley, and we have been entertained with the pleasantry of it and the ridicule it contains.

The discovery of air Balloons seems to make the present time a new Epoch; and the last year will, I suppose, be always distinguish'd as the year in which mankind begun to fly in France. Nothing has yet been done here in this way of any consequence. In the Royal Society a great part of the winter has been employ'd in a manner very unworthy of Philosophers. An opposition has been formed to the President. Motions for censuring him have been repeatedly made at our weekly meetings, and supported by Dr Horseley,[2] the Astronomer Royal, Mr Maseres, Mr Maty,[3] &c. &c and these motions have produced long and warm debates. Lately there has been a suspension of these debates, but there is now some danger that they may be revived again, for Mr Maty has just resigned his place of Secretary in resentment.

In your letter you have intimated that you then entertained some thoughts of visiting London in the Spring. This is very much wished for by your friends here; and, particularly, by the Club at the London=Coffee=House which you have so often made happy by your company. Dr Priestley intends coming

ORIGINAL: American Philosophical Society. PRINTED: *Franklin*: Bigelow, X, 301. TEXT: Original, with the kind permission of the American Philosophical Society.
1. See Benjamin Franklin to R.P., 16 Sept. 1783.
2. Samuel Horsley.
3. Paul Henry Maty (1745–87), son of Matthew Maty (1718–76). In 1776 he was appointed Assistant Librarian at the British Museum, and in 1782, Under-Librarian. He was Foreign Secretary to the Royal Society from 1776 to 1784.

to London from Birmingham in about a fortnight, but could he reckon upon the pleasure of meeting you in London at anytime he would contrive to come up at that time. He has, I find, been chosen a member of the Royal Academy of Sciences at Paris.[4] This is indeed a singular honour, and it must give him particular pleasure.

I can scarcely tell you with what emotions of concern I have heard that you have for some time been suffering under symptoms of the stone. What a sad calamity it is to be visited in the last stage of life by so dreadful a distemper? Dreadful I know it to be from experience. I have, however, been so happy as to discharge the stone; and my only present trouble is the sad state of health into which my wife is fallen. About a month ago she was struck a third time with paralytic symptoms. She is extremely debilitated and I live in a constant state of painful apprehension about her. She hopes you will accept her best respects.

Political affairs in this country are at present in great confusion. The King, after dismissing from his service the leaders of the late odious coalition, and appointing ministers in their room to the great joy of the kingdom, has at last found it necessary, in order to maintain the new ministers in power and to carry on the public business, to dissolve the Parliament. We are, therefore, now in the midst of the heat and commotion of a general election; and such is the influence of government on elections and also the present temper of the people, that probably the new ministers will have a great majority in their favour in the new Parliament.

The more wise and virtuous part of the nation are struggling hard to gain a Parliamentary reform; and think, with great reason, that while the Representation continues such a mockery as it is, no change of ministers can do us much good. But an equal representation is a blessing which probably we shall never obtain till a convulsion comes which will dissolve all governments and give an opportunity for erecting a new frame.

In America there is, I hope, an opening for a better state of human affairs. Indeed I look upon the Revolution there as one of the most important events in the History of the world. Wishing, for the sake of mankind that the united states may improve properly the advantage of their situation, I have been lately employing myself in writing *sentiments of caution and advice* which I mean to convey to them as a last offering of my good=will.[5] I know I am by no means qualified for such a work; nor can I expect that any advice I can give will carry much weight with it, or be much worth their acceptance. I cannot however satisfy my own mind without offering it, such as it [is]. I always think of your friendship with particular satisfaction, and consider it as one of the honours and blessings of my life. You have attained an eminence of credit and useful-

---

4. Joseph Priestley was elected an *associé étranger* of the Paris Academy of Sciences on 26 Feb. 1784. (Gibbs, p. 152.)

5. These sentiments matured to form *Observations on the Importance of the American Revolution.*

ness in the world to which few can aspire. That it may be continued as long as the course of nature will allow, and that you may enjoy every comfort that can make you most happy is, Dear Sir, the sincere wish of yours most affectionately

Rich*d* Price

Should Mr Jay[6] or Mr Adams be at Paris, be so good as to deliver my respectful remembrances to them. You probably well remember Mr Paradise, a friend of Sir William Jones and a very worthy man, who has considerable property in Virginia and to whom you have been kind. He has lately been in great trouble. The folly, ill temper and extravagance of his wife produced for some weeks a separation between him and her and made him one of the most unhappy men I ever saw. But they are come together again.

---

6. John Jay (1745–1829), lawyer, diplomat, statesman. President of Congress, 1778; Minister to Spain, 1779; Secretary of Foreign Affairs, 1784–90; Chief Justice of the United States, 1789; Governor of New York State, 1795–1800.

To the Earl of Shelburne

Newington=Green May 8th 1784

My Lord

I am quite ashamed that I have been so long without acknowledging the obligation I am under to your Lordship for the kind letter with which you favoured me soon after leaving London. This omission has been occasioned partly by my consciousness that I had nothing of consequence to communicate, and partly by a very bad cold and cough which have hung badly for the last three weeks upon my strength and spirits. This mild and fine weather will, I hope, relieve me.

I am extremely sorry your Lordship should have been put to any trouble about the paper I mentioned to you; and I beg you would think no more of it. It is of no consequence, all the particulars in it being capable of being collected easily from other papers which I have by me. I have been often greatly obliged to your Lordship for allowing me the perusal of many papers which have been of much use to me.

I am glad your Lordship is happy in your present private situation. It is the situation most favourable to tranquility and self-enjoyment; but yet my regard for the public does not permit me and many others to wish your Lordship may continue in it. There is much very important business to be done; and I do not know how to believe that Mr Pitt will be able to get thro' it without the aid of

---

Original: Bowood. Text: Original, with the kind permission of the Marquis of Lansdowne.

more experienced persons. I think I see a tendency in the tide of popularity to turn against him. He will be thought too ambitious, if he continues to hold both the posts he now enjoys.[1] True wisdom would engage him to keep himself a little back. It will, probably, be difficult to manage Ireland; and many begin to augur ill concerning Mr Pitt's administration from *what* has lately passed there. Our affairs with the American states seems also in a bad train. If I am rightly informed, there is a greater probability of a commercial war than a commercial treaty with them; and the majority of the Council are under the influence of the most miserable mis=information with respect to them.

Your Lordship must be much better informed than I am about Mr Pitt's intentions with respect to our finances. Indeed I know nothing of them. I have communicated my Ideas to the public and I leave them to be regarded or neglected just as events may turn out. I have always valued the tranquility of a low and un:incumber'd station; and the stage of life I am now in makes this more than ever valuable to me. I have now for many years been honoured by your Lordship's friendship and experienced your Lordship's candour. I should be very unworthy of them did I not feel the warmest gratitude for them.

My best respects wait on Lady Shelburne. I wish also to be kindly remember'd to Colonel Barre should he be with you. With the greatest regard I am, my Lord,

Your Lordship's most obedient and humble servant
Rich*d* Price

Mrs Price sends her best respects. She continues much the same that she has been for some time.

---

1. Pitt was both First Lord of the Treasury and Chancellor of the Exchequer.

To William Pitt

Monday morning June 7th 1784

Dr Price presents his very respectful compliments to Mr Pitt, and takes the liberty to convey to him the inclosed letter. It comes from a banker in the City of great credit and knowledge, and seems to contain several important observations. The scheme proposed in it for obtaining the next loan[1] is much the

---

ORIGINAL: PRO 30/8/169 (inclosing a letter from a banker in the City containing a scheme for the next loan). TEXT: Original, with the kind permission of the Public Record Office.

1. The author of the scheme advocated a plan in which a loan could be raised and Navy Bills funded at the same time. It was hoped to raise £6 millions. Holders of Navy Bills should be offered £266.13s.4d. in the 4 per cents for £100 Cash and a £100 Navy Bill. Price thought that the terms should be £200 in the 4 per cents for £50 cash and a £100 Navy Bill.

same with that which Dr Price has in a former paper represented as the most advantageous; and he imagines that, for the reason assigned in the second page of his letter,[2] it would be certainly successful. Perhaps, however, it would be improved and simplify'd by offering (as Dr P[rice] has proposed) to the holders of Navy bills for *half* the amount of their bills in money *twice* their amount in a 4 *per cent* stock with such advantages annex'd as he has mention'd.

2. That the holders of Navy Bills, especially those who had held them for more than three years, would welcome an opportunity to use Navy Bills in the purchase of stock.

To Benjamin Franklin

Newington=Green July 12*th* 1784

Dear Sir,

I request your acceptance of the pamphlet[1] which accompanies this letter. It is intended entirely for America, and you are one of the first persons to whom it has been communicated. Most of the few copies which I have printed will be convey'd to America; and I hope the united states will forgive my presumption in supposing myself qualified to advise them. Indeed I almost feel myself ashamed of what I have done, but the consciousness which I have that it is well intended, and that my address to them is the effusion of a heart that wishes to serve the best interests of society, helps to reconcile me to myself in this instance, and it will, I hope, engage the candour of others.

The letter from M. Turgot[2] which you will receive with this stands at present in the Press, and will stand there till I shall be made acquainted with your opinion concerning the propriety of making it public by conveying it to the united states with my own pamphlet. The reason of my doubts about this is the charge of secrecy with which it concludes and which you will find written in the margin. In compliance with this charge I have hitherto kept this letter private, but lately I have considered that probably it was only some apprehension of personal inconvenience that led him to give this charge, and that consequently the obligation to comply with it ceased with his life. Dreading, however, every thing that might be reckon'd a breach of confidence, my scruples are continually returning upon me; and I feel them the more, when I think that possibly he may have left a family which may suffer in *France* when it

ORIGINAL: American Philosophical Society. PRINTED: *Franklin*: Bigelow, X, 360. TEXT: Original, with the kind permission of the American Philosophical Society.
1. *Observations on the Importance of the American Revolution.* See R.P. to Benjamin Franklin, 6 Apr. 1784.
2. See A. Turgot to R.P., 22 Mar. 1778.

appears there that he was so much a friend to liberty as this letter will shew him to be. In this state of mind I cannot make myself easy in any other way than by determining to request the favour of your judgment and to abide by it.

Should you think that no ill consequences can result from publishing this letter to any family that M. *Turgot* may have left, and that his death has free'd me from any obligation to keep it secret, I will order it to be printed off and send it to America with my pamphlet. Should you think the contrary, it shall be suppressed and I shall depend on your being so good as to destroy the copy now sent you. You will add much to the obligation I am under to you for all your friendship by giving me a few lines on this subject as soon as may be convenient to you. Should you think it improper to write by the post, a letter or any parcel you may wish to convey to London, may be sent by Miss Wilkes[3] who is on a visit with the *Dutchess de la Valliere* at Paris, and will return the 2nd of August.

I writ to you by the post about three months ago,[4] and hope you received my letter. I have heard lately with pleasure that you are pretty well. May your health and life and usefulness be continued as the course of nature will admit. Are we never to have the satisfaction of seeing you again in London? I have lately been at Birmingham to visit Dr Priestley. He is very happy there and going on successfully with his experiments.

Mrs Price desires to be respectfully remember'd to you. She is in a very weak and low state, but not worse than she has been for sometime. We are thinking of spending the next month at Brighthelmston. Wishing you every blessing, I am, my Dear Friend, with the greatest regard

ever Yours
Richd Price

Perhaps some passages may occur to you in M. *Turgot's* letter which might be best omitted, should you approve of publishing it. I have marked one in p. 91 and another p. 102.

---

3. Mary 'Polly' Wilkes (1750–1802), the daughter of John Wilkes. When Wilkes was Lord Mayor of London, Mary was his Lady Mayoress, a position in which she enjoyed considerable success. See W.T. Treloar, *Wilkes and the City* (London, 1917), p. 140. Price sent this letter to Miss Wilkes by Lord Fitzmaurice, Shelburne's elder son. She was to deliver it to Franklin together with the two pamphlets which accompanied it. See R.P. to Benjamin Franklin, 21 July 1784.

4. R.P. to Benjamin Franklin, 6 Apr. 1784.

To Benjamin Franklin

Newington=Green July 21*st* 1784

Dear Sir,

The bearer of this, Mr Lewis, is an honest tradesman, and an attendant at the Meeting=House in Newington=Green. I cannot resist his desire that I would give him a line to introduce him to you. He has always been a warm favourer of the American cause, thinks of you with veneration, and wishes just to see you. Any notice, therefore, that you may think fit to take of him will give him particular pleasure. He goes abroad with no other views than those of amusement and pleasure.

I sent a letter to you by Lord Fitzmaurice,[1] Lord Shelburne's eldest son, who set out last week for Paris in order to pay a visit to the Abbe M[ ].[2]

This letter accompany'd with two pamphlets made a part of a parcel directed to Miss Wilkes at the Duchess de la Valliere's; and Miss Wilkes was to convey to you. I am now hoping for the favour of your opinion on the subject mentioned in that letter. I have lately been informed that Mr Turgot left no family, and this removes one of the reasons of my scruples.

With great respect and affection, I am, Dear Sir, ever yours,

Rich*d* Price

ORIGINAL: American Philosophical Society. TEXT; Original, with the kind permission of the American Philosophical Society.

1. See R.P. to Benjamin Franklin, 12 July 1784.

2. Abbé André Morellet (1727–1819), an economist, was an associate and a close friend of Turgot. He translated Beccaria's *Dei Delitti e delle Pene* into French (1766) and was elected to the Académie Francaise in 1785. Shelburne first met him on his visit to France in 1771. Morellet visited Bowood in the following year and again in 1773 (*Mémoires de l'Abbé Morellet*, 2 vols., Paris, 1821). Shelburne acknowledged that he owed to him the liberalization of his ideas on economics and politics, and was instrumental in obtaining a pension of 4,000 francs a year for him in 1783. After the treaty negotiations Vergennes expressed a wish to show by any means in his power his appreciation of Shelburne's conduct. Shelburne replied that since it was to Morellet that he owed his liberal ideas on commercial matters and his sense of the relations that should exist between England and France, a favour shown to Morellet would be a favour shown to him. Morellet reciprocated Shelburne's high regard. On 9 July 1785, he wrote, "Vous m'y apprenez la nouvelle du monde la plus interessante, en me disant que vos principes sur la liberté du commerce et de la communication des nations se répandent et s'accréditent parmi vos négociants et vos manufacturiers et jusque dans votre capitale, où l'esprit de monopole a été, je crois, plus dominant qu'en aucun autre lieu de l'Europe. Il m'est bien clair que ce progrès dans les lumières de votre nation est dû a vous-memes. M. Smith, et quelquefois le Doyen Tucker chez vous, les ont bien saisies, ces vérités, mais ils n'ont fait que les mettre dans les livres et vous les avez mises dans le monde." *Lettres de l'Abbé Morellet*, ed. Fitzmaurice (Paris, 1898), p. 209.

Samuel Mather[1]

Newington=Green July 22d 1784

Dear Sir,

Accept my best thanks for the pleasure you have given me by the kind letter which I received from you some time ago. Such testimonies of regard from good men in America cannot but be very agreeable to me. They are a compensation which I think very valuable for the part I took in favour of the united states during the late war, and the danger to which it exposed me. The Revolution in which this has terminated I think one of the most important events that has ever happen'd; and I have found myself incapable of satisfying my own judgment on this occasion without addressing some sentiments of caution and advice to the united states. Some printed copies of the pamphlet containing this Address will be soon sent over to America;[2] and I shall desire your acceptance of one of them in return for the pamphlets which you have been so good as to send me. I admire the seriousness and piety with which these pamphlets are written; and I hope that which you call your dying Legacy will be attended to and do good. The war has left the finances of this country in the most embarrass'd state; and I am afraid it will not be possible to save us from a convulsion. Mr Pitt is now drinking the dregs of Lord North's cup, and has very hard work to do. There seems to be no probability of any settlement between us and America with respect to commerce. I am strongly for having it as free and open as it was before the war; but the prejudices in this country against a relaxation of the Navigation Act will not suffer this.

I wish you, Sir, the best supports and comforts in the evening of life; and with much respect I am

Your obliged and very humble servant
Rich*d* Price

ORIGINAL: American Antiquarian Society.   TEXT: Original, with the kind permission of the American Antiquarian Society.

1. Samuel Mather (1706–85), Congregational minister. MA (Glasgow), 1731; DD (Aberdeen), 1762; DD (Harvard), 1773. He was the son and biographer of Cotton Mather. The pamphlets he sent to Price might have included *All Men will not be Saved for Ever* (Boston, 1782); and *The Dying Legacy of an Aged Minister of the Everlasting Gospel* (1783).

2. *Observations on the Importance of the American Revolution.*

To Joseph Willard

Newington-Green, July 23d, 1784

Dear Sir,

I am glad to embrace the opportunity offer'd me by Mr Gorham's return to send you a few lines. I think myself much obliged to you for your letter by Mr Jackson, and for introducing me to his acquaintance.[1] He is, I find, likely to stay with us some time longer, and I hope to be favoured with more of his company. I have sent by Mr Eliot a set of Bishop Hoadley's works for Harvard College; and I have by mistake informed you that the two volumes of my Treatise on Reversionary payments which he has also been so good as to convey, were intended for the *American Academy*; but having before by Mr Mullet desired their acceptance of these volumes, I wish those bro't by Mr Eliot may be presented with Hoadley's works to *Harvard* College. The vote of thanks which you have transmitted to me from your Academy is more than this present deserved. It was intended as a testimony of respect, and I am made happy by the favourable manner in which the Academy is so good as to receive it.[2]

I am often looking to your country as the part of the world where liberty, science and virtue are likely to flourish to a degree which has been yet unknown. I am however much mortify'd by accounts which have been sent me of the state of manners in some of the United States. There is, I am informed, among them an avarice, a rage for foreign fineries, an excess of jealousy, etc., etc., which are likely to do them the greatest injury, and to disappoint the hopes of the friends of liberty. I have lately employ'd myself in addressing to them some sentiments of caution and advice with which my own mind is greatly impress'd. The pamphlet containing this Address[3] is now almost printed and I shall send the copies to America in a few weeks. The acceptance of a parcel of them by my friends of Boston will be particularly requested. I know I am not qualify'd to advise the united States. The goodness, however, of my intentions, and the warm part I have all along taken in favour of their cause will, I hope, procure for me a candid hearing.

I have writ to Mr Professor Williams,[4] by Mr Eliot. Deliver to him if you please my respectful compliments, and also to Mr Winthrop. I am sorry Mr Gorham has not been more encouraged in his collection here. He has met with

---

PRINTED: *M.H.S.P.* (1909–10), 618–19. TEXT: *M.H.S.P.*

1. See Joseph Willard to R.P., 31 Oct. 1783.

2. Ibid.

3. *Observations on the Importance of the American Revolution.*

4. Samuel Williams (1743–1817) was Hollis Professor of Mathematics and Natural Philosophy at Harvard from 1780 until 1788. (Allibone.)

many difficulties and embarrassments. Indeed I never expected he would be very successful. I wish I could have been of more service to him.

I know of no Philosophical intelligence worth communicating to you at present. Wishing you, sir, every valuable blessing I am with great respect, Your most obedient and humble servant

RICHARD PRICE.

From Benjamin Franklin

Passy, Aug 2, 1784.

My Dear Friend,

I received your favour of the 12th past[1] with the Pamphlet of Advice to the Americans, for which I thank you much; it is excellent in itself and will do us a great deal of Good. I communicated immediately to Mr Dupont[2] the Letter of Mr Turgot, thinking him the properest Person to consult on the Subject, as he has the Care of the Papers left by that great Man. He sent me thereupon the Note enclos'd dated July 26, and this Day brought me the Proof corrected, which I enclose; and gave me his Opinion that the whole Letter may well be printed even with the manuscript part at the End, you only adding a Note to the purpose of what he has written. He only desires two small Omissions, which are mark'd and the Place of the words omitted to be fill'd with Points or Stars to show that something is omitted. It will be well to send him if you please a few copies, and I wish to have two or three myself.

M. Dupont waits while I write, so that I cannot enlarge. I receiv'd the former letter[3] you mention and purpose writing to you soon. My best Respects to Mrs Price, and believe me ever with sincere and great esteem, Dear Sir, Your most obedient humble servant

B. Franklin

ORIGINAL: Mr R.O.M. Williams. TEXT: Original, with the kind permission of Mr R.O.M. Williams.

1. R.P. to Benjamin Franklin, 12 July 1784.

2. Pierre-Samuel Dupont de Nemours (1739–1817), economist, physiocrat, and biographer of Turgot. His *Mémoires sur la Vie et les Ouvrages de Turgot* was published in Paris in 1782.

3. R.P. to Benjamin Franklin, 6 Apr. 1784.

From Benjamin Franklin

Passy, August 16, 1784

Dear Friend,

I some time since answered[1] your kind letter of July 12,[2] returning the proof of Mr Turgot's Letter, with the Permission of his Friends to print it. I hope it came safe to hand.

I had before received yours of April 6 which gave me great Pleasure, as it acquainted me with your Welfare, and that of Dr Priestly.

The Commencement here of the Art of Flying will, as you observe be a new Epoch. The Construction and Manner of Filling the Balloons improves daily. Some of the Artists have lately gone to England. It will be well for your Philosophers to obtain from them what they know, or you will be behind-hand, which in mechanic Operations is unusual for Englishmen.

I hope the Disagreements in our Royal Society are compos'd. Quarrels often disgrace both sides: And Disputes even on small Matters often produce Quarrels for want of knowing how to differ decently; an Art which 'tis said scarce any body possesses but yourself and Dr Priestly.

I had indeed Thoughts of visiting England once more, and of enjoying the great Pleasure of seeing again my Friends there; but my Malady, otherwise tolerable, is I find irritated by Motion in a Carriage, and I fear the Consequences of such a Journey; yet I am not quite resolved against it. I often think of the agreable Evenings I used to pass with that excellent Collection of good Men, the Club at the London, and wish to be again among them. Perhaps I may pop in some Thursday Evening when they least expect me. You may well believe it very pleasing to me to have Dr Priestly associated with me among the Foreign Members of the Academy of Sciences. I had mention'd him upon every Vacancy that has happen'd since my Residence here, and the place has never been bestow'd more worthily.

When you wrote the letter I am now answering, your Nation was involv'd in the confusion of your new Election. When I think of your present crazy Constitution, and its Diseases, I imagine the enormous Emoluments of Place to be among the greatest, and while they exist I doubt whether even the Reform of your Representation will cure the Evils constantly arising from your perpetual Factions. As it seems to be a settled Point at present that the Minister must govern the Parliament, who are to do everything he would have done; and he is

---

ORIGINAL: The Historical Society of Pennsylvania. PRINTED: *Franklin*: Bigelow, X, 406. TEXT: Original, with the kind permission of The Historical Society of Pennsylvania.

1. See Benjamin Franklin to R.P., 2 Aug. 1784.
2. See R.P. to Benjamin Franklin, 6 Apr. 1784.

to bribe them to do this, and the People are to furnish the Money to pay these bribes, such a Parliament appears to me a very expensive Machine for Government, and I apprehend the People will find out in time that they may as well be governed, and that it will be much cheaper to be governed, by the Minister alone, no Parliament being preferable to the present.

Your newspapers are full of fictitious accounts of Distractions in America. We know nothing of them. Mr Jefferson, just arriv'd here, after a Journey through all the States from Virginia to Boston, assures me that all is quiet, a general Tranquillity reigns, and the People well satisfy'd with their present Forms of Government, a few insignificant Persons only excepted. These Accounts are I suppose intended as consolatory, And to discourage Emigrations. I think with you, that our Revolution is an important Event for the Advantage of Mankind in general. It is to be hoped that the Lights we enjoy, which the ancient Governments in their first Establishment could not have, may preserve us from their Errors. In this the Advise of wise Friends may do us much Good, and I am sure that which you have been so kind as to offer us, will be of great Service.

Mr Jay is gone to America; but Mr Adams is just arrived here, and I shall acquaint him with your Remembrance of him.

Poor Paradise, whom you mention, I respect and pity: But there is no helping him. He seems calculated by nature for Unhappiness, and will be equally miserable whether with or without his Wife, having no Firmness of Mind. I doubt his Property in Virginia may suffer by his Irresolution.

Many thanks for your kind wishes respecting my Health and Happiness, which, I return fourfold, being ever with the highest Esteem, my dear Friend, yours most affectionately

B. Franklin

P.S. I wrote you a few lines by your Friend Mr Lewis, as he might meet with you at Brighthelmstone. The Bearer is my Grandson and Secretary, a worthy good Young Man. I beg leave to recommend him to your Civilities and if convenient I wish he may be introduced one Evening to our Club. He stays but a short time in London.

My respects and best Wishes attend good Mrs Price.

From Benjamin Franklin

Passy, Sept. 7. 1784

Dear Friend,

The Bearer, Count Mirabeau,[1] who much respects your Character, has desired a Line of Introduction to you. He is the Son to the Marquis de Mirabeau,[2] Author of L'Ami des Hommes; is himself an excellent Writer, and has prepared for the Press a small Piece, much admired by the best Judges here, on the subject of Hereditary Nobility, which he proposes to get printed in England. I recommend him to your Civilities and Counsels, and am with sincerest Esteem and Respect, my ever dear Friend,

Yours most affectionately
B. Franklin

ORIGINAL: American Philosophical Society. TEXT: Original, with the kind permission of the American Philosophical Society.

1. Honoré-Gabriel Riquetti, Comte de Mirabeau (1749–91), came to London in 1784 to arrange for the publication of his treatise on the nobility. He incorporated in this publication a translation of Price's *Observations on the Importance of the American Revolution* and a copy of Turgot's letter to Price dated 22 Mar. 1778. This work was published under the title *Considérations sur l'Ordre de Cincinnatus, ou Imitation d'un Pamphlet Anglo-Américain* (London, 1784).

2. Victor Riquetti, Marquis de Mirabeau (1715–89), economist. His chief work, to which Franklin refers, *L'ami des Hommes, ou Traité de la Population*, was published at Avignon in 1756.

From Benjamin Franklin

Passy, Sept. 13. 1784.

Dear Friend,

You have a kind of Right to receive from me every thing that appears [here] on the Subject of Finance. I therefore send you herewith the late Edict for establishing a new Sinking Fund,[1] which seems to give great Satisfaction to the Public Creditors here. No one is better if so well qualified as your self to make a

---

ORIGINAL: Glasgow University Library, MS Gen. 510/14. ADDRESSED: Cover has in Price's hand: Letter fm Dr F[   ]n Sept: 1784 conveying the Edict of the King of France Aetat. 78 TEXT: Original, with the kind permission of the Librarian of Glasgow University Library.

1. This edict had been published in France in Aug. 1784. See Marcel Marion, *Histoire Financière de la France depuis 1715* (Paris, 1927–31), I, 364. For Price's reply see his letter to Franklin, 21 Oct. 1784. See also Shelburne to R.P., 7 Oct. 1784.

sound Judgment of it, and at some leisure Moment I could wish you would drop me a few lines of your Opinion. I wrote to you lately by my Grandson. I hope you continue well, being ever, my dear Friend,

Yours most affectionately

B. Franklin

To William Temple Franklin

Newington=Green Sept: 25*th* 1784

Dr Price presents his respects to Mr Franklin, and takes the liberty to remind him of his promise to drink tea and spend the evening with him and some friends of his next thursday at Mr Morgan's at the Equitable Assurance office near Black=Fryars=Bridge.

Mr Franklin would confer an additional obligation on Dr Price by asking the favour of Mr *Mirabeau* to accompany him, should he have any opportunities of seeing him.

ORIGINAL. American Philosophical Society. TEXT: Original, with the kind permission of the American Philosophical Society.

To Thomas Cadell

[Aug./Sept. 1784][1]

Dr Price presents his kind compliments to Mr Cadell. He is fully sensible that it will be proper to publish a translation of Mr Turgot's letter and, therefore, he will be oblig'd to Mr Cadell for procuring a good translation of it.

ORIGINAL. Liverpool City Libraries: Hornby Library. TEXT: Original, with the kind permission of the Liverpool City Libraries: Hornby Library.

1. Through Benjamin Franklin Price received permission from Dupont de Nemours, Turgot's literary executor, to publish Turgot's letter to R.P. of 22 Mar. 1778 (See Benjamin Franklin to R.P., 2 Aug. 1784). It is unlikely that Price would have troubled himself about procuring a translation until this permission had been received. Sometime before 8 Oct. Mirabeau had undertaken to translate Turgot's letter as on that day Price wrote to Jonathan Trumbull, "I wish'd to convey with Turgot's letter, a translation of it into English; but this will soon be done by the Count de Mirabeau." Since this note to Cadell does not mention Mirabeau, it is likely that it was written some time after Price received permission to publish Turgot's letter and sometime before he wrote to Trumbull.

From the Earl of Shelburne

Bowood Park 7*th* Octob*r* 1784

My dear Friend,

I take the earliest opportunity of acquainting you, that I hope I have found in the Anabaptist Preacher at Calne a person capable of forwarding the Schemes I had regarding the Poor.[1] He is a Man of an excellent private Character of a serious disposition, and has a manner of preaching and lecturing which takes I find with many of different Sects, who have been to hear him, without bordering even upon methodism. It will be a great comfort to me, if he answers the purpose. The difficulty of finding a Teacher shews the want there is of Teaching, and I can never reconcile myself to living in the midst of so great a number of my Fellow Creatures, who are to my own knowledge more neglected in point of Education and Religion than they would be under any Government in Europe, except it may be Russia. I have thoughts of adopting the Chatechism you sent me of Dr Watts,[2] but I wish it still shorten'd and simplified—I should be very glad that at any leisure time you could look it over with this view—My Idea is to inculcate the ordinary Duties of a Country Life under the hope of Reward and Fear of Punishment in the plainest and most direct Language possible. I will take the liberty of sending you the other particulars of our Plan, as soon as we shall be able to compleat it.

I take it for granted that you have seen the Edict just now publish'd in France adopting your Principles into their Finance, as far as comes within the power of their Government, without overturning the principles of it.[3] If you have not, I can send it to you. I likewise see they have establish'd Free Ports, and are likewise taking several other very important steps which mark their Foresight activity and Wisdom—It's very mortifying at the same time to see our time spent with Faction, and the Impression which our Misfortunes made

---

ORIGINAL: Bodleian.   PRINTED: *M.H.S.P.* (1903), 321.   TEXT: Original, with the kind permission of the Bodleian Library.

1. For details of the way in which Shelburne proposed to help the poor, see Fitzmaurice, II, 306n.

2. Isaac Watts (1674–1748), the celebrated hymn writer was educated at the grammar school at Southampton and at the Academy, Stoke Newington, under Thomas Rowe. In 1679 he became assistant pastor to Isaac Chauncy at Mark Lane, succeeding to the pastorate in 1702. The congregation moved to Pinner's Hall in 1704, and to Bury Street, St Mary Axe, in 1708. Samuel Price, Richard Price's uncle, became assistant to him in 1703, and co-pastor in 1713. Watts was not robust in health and a large portion of his duties at Bury Street fell to Samuel Price. From 1712 to the end of his life Watts lived in the household of Sir Thomas and Lady Abney, either at Theobalds or at Stoke Newington. His published works include *Horae Lyricae* (1706), *Hymns* (1707), *The Psalms of David* (1719), *The Christian Doctrine of the Trinity* (1722), *Logick* (1725), *Catechisms* (1730), and *The Improvement of the Mind* (1741).

3. See Benjamin Franklin to R.P., 13 Sept. 1784.

upon us turn'd to no account. I know no more of what is passing in London than I do of what is doing at Constantinople, but I hope Government is forming some vigorous Plan of Finance and regulations of Trade, which may bring back some of our Wealth, excite a fresh Spirit of Industry, and check the disposition universally gaining ground to dissipation and Corruption. I am in daily expectation of seeing the Abbe Morellet[4] here, who takes the opportunity of Lord Fitzmaurice's return to make us another Visit. It would give Lady Shelburne and me great pleasure if you could spend some days with him here, but I have too much respect and regard for Mrs Price to think of proposing it. I beg to be kindly remember'd to her.

> I am with sincere Regard
> your affectionate and
> obliged humble servant
> Shelburne

4. Morellet was at Bowood from Oct. to Dec. 1783. See *Mémoires de l'Abbé Morellet*, 2 vols. (Paris, 1821), I, 274.

To the Earl of Shelburne

[Oct. 1784]

My Lord,

I have received with particular pleasure your Lordship's letter.[1] I had been in hopes of hearing of a person qualify'd to answer your Lordship's excellent views among the poor at Caln; but I am glad that I have no occasion for farther enquiry, and that you have found one so proper as the person you mention. It is a great recommendation of him that he is zealous without being a methodist, and that he has for some time lived on the spot and can have no views to preferment. The general state of the poor is indeed melancholy. Their education is almost totally neglected. They grow up ignorant and irreligious, and therefore unprincipled and vicious. The attempt to remedy in some degree this evil at Caln is worthy of your Lordship; and I heartily wish you success in it. I have looked over Dr Watts's first Catechism, and think, as your Lordship does that it is not short and simple enough. I shall attempt to compose one that shall be less liable to this objection and better adapted to your Lordship's Ideas as soon as I can get a little more leisure.

Mrs Price has lately been attacked a fourth time with the palsy, and reduced

ORIGINAL: Bowood. TEXT: Original, with the kind permission of the Marquis of Lansdowne.
1. See Shelburne to R.P., 7 Oct. 1784.

to a state of depression and helplessness that can scarcely be described. For some time she could hardly either speak or swallow or turn in bed, and I lived under the dismal apprehension of losing a companion, partner and friend to whom for 27 years the happiness of my life has been in great measure owing. She is now revived a little, and I entertain the hope that she will be again in some degree restored. Such is the order of nature. It is I doubt not right. My judgment acquiesces, but I find it difficult to reconcile my spirits to it.

I have sent your Lordship the pamphlet which I mentioned to you. It will need your candour. You will probably think that I have carried my notions of liberty too far. What I have said, particularly on church establishments would give offence were the pamphlet to be publish'd here, but I have no thoughts of doing this.[2] It is intended only for the American states, and my mind is much impress'd with a conviction of the importance of the advice I have given them. They are beginning a new plan. The senseless cry against innovation (so hostile here to the correction of abuses and to improvement) cannot influence them. They have the experience of past ages to guide them. They stand upon free and open ground. Their situation, therefore, is favourable, and I have been anxious about contributing the little in my power towards leading them to make the most of it for the advantage of the world. I have printed only a few copies of this tract all of which I am sending to America, where possibly it may be reprinted. I have likewise some reason to expect that it will be translated into French by an able hand at Paris.

I beg the favour of your Lordship to send me the French Edict mention'd in your letter. I have not seen it, nor did I know that any plan of finance on my principles had been formed by the French government before I saw the intimation of it given a few days ago in the News=papers.[3] The *French* are indeed getting the start of us fast, while we are wasting our time, as your Lordship says, with faction. Our funds are in a state of depression which I could scarcely have thought possible in a time of peace. No measures have been yet adopted for preserving us from the calamities with which they threaten us. I hear of nothing that Mr Pitt is doing for this purpose. On the contrary; by the attempt to discharge Navy bills at *a discount well-meant but extremely injudicious*, he has

---

2. *Observations on the Importance of the American Revolution*. In this pamphlet Price attacked state established religions, "Civil establishments of formularies of faith and worship are inconsistent with the rights of private judgment. They engender strife. They turn religion into a trade. They shoar up error. They produce hypocrisy and prevarication. They lay an undue byass on the human mind in its enquiries, and obstruct the progress of truth." (1784 ed., p. 31; see Peach, p. 195). In *The Evidence for a Future Period of Improvement* Price maintained that the most that should be allowed to the magistrate in any circumstances is the power to create, "an equal support of religion in general, by requiring a contribution for that purpose, payable by every citizen, but with liberty to apply it to the support of that worship he likes best." (Appendix, containing footnote to p. 19.)

3. When he wrote this, Price had not, it seems, received Franklin's letter of 13 Sept. 1784. See R.P. to Franklin, 21 Oct. 1784.

wounded public credit much, particularly abroad, and it is certain that nothing can recover it, but a plan of redemption in which the public shall have some faith. Could I obtain my wishes with respect to America such measures of conciliation would be adopted and such a reciprocity in trade would be establish'd as might end in a family compact, and render America more an advantage to us than ever. But this is not the policy that is likely to take place. A commercial war with America is prefer'd to a family compact, and all foresight and wise regulations seem to be left to France.

I shall be obliged to your Lordship for presenting to the Abbe Morellet the pamphlet directed to him. I should have desired Dr Franklin to present it to him at Paris had I not been informed that your Lordship expects him at *Bowood*. My respectful compliments wait on him and on Lord Fitzmaurice. I think myself oblig'd and honoured by Lady Shelburne's and your Lordship's invitation of me to meet them at *Bowood*. But it is not possible for me to think of leaving Mrs Price in her present state. As you say nothing of your health I conclude that it is not worse than it was. That it may be perfectly restor'd and long continued to make your life comfortable and honourable and useful to the world is the sincere wish of

your Lordship's most obedient and
humble servant
Rich*d* Price

My best respects wait on Lady Shelburne. Mrs Price also sends her best respects. Thanks for the hare and two excellent pine apples.

To Ezra Stiles

Newington=Green Oct 8*th* 1784

Dr Price presents his best respects to Dr Styles, and requests his acceptance of these pamphlets.

He had begun a letter in answer to several with which he has been lately favoured by Dr Styles; but not having been able, thro a variety of causes, to finish it before the sailing of the ship that conveys this to Boston, he is obliged to reserve it for the next ship that sails for America which, he is informed, will be soon.[1]

One of the pamphlets that accompanies this note he wishes may be presented to Mr *Fitch* and another to Dr *Beardsley* as a testimony of his respectful remembrance of them.

ORIGINAL: Yale University Library. TEXT: Original, with the kind permission of Yale University Library.

1. See R.P. to Ezra Stiles, 15 Oct. 1784.

To Jonathan Trumbull, the Elder

Newington=Green near London
Oct 8th 1784

Sir,

I return you my best thanks for the letter with which you have honoured me and which has been deliver'd to me by your son; and also for the present of your farewell Address to the general Assembly of Connecticutt[1] and Dr Styles's election sermon.[2] I have since received the latter from Dr Styles himself, and I have derived from it instruction and pleasure. Your Address, likewise, I have read repeatedly with emotions which are not easily to be express'd. It is, indeed, in my opinion excellent, and gives the best advice to the state of which you have been so long and so usefully and happily the governor. As a small expression of gratitude for the notice you have been so good as to take of me I request your acceptance of the tract[3] which you will receive with this letter. Should you honour it with a perusal you will find that with respect to the enlargement of the powers of Congress and some other points there is an entire agreement between your sentiments and mine. I am happy when I reflect on this agreement but I cannot flatter myself so far as to hope that you will think me right with respect to *all* the points which I have discussed in this pamphlet. I must therefore rely on your candour. I have writ from my feelings and best judgment. I have meant, like you in your Address, to give advice to the united states which I think of the utmost importance; but at the same time I am almost ashamed when I think of my presumption in supposing myself qualify'd for such an office. One part, however, of this pamphlet needs no Apology. Mr *Turgot's* letter, must be acceptable to the united states; and my consciousness of the service I do them by conveying this letter to them, relieves me under my apprehensions of the faults that may be found in the other parts of this pamphlet. I wish'd to convey, with Mr *Turgot's* letter, a translation of it into English; but this will be soon done by the *Count de Mirabeau* in a tract which he is now printing in London on Hereditary honours and Nobility, and which will probably deserve the particular attention of America.

ORIGINAL: The Connecticut Historical Society. TEXT: Original, with the kind permission of The Connecticut Historical Society.

1. *An Address of his Excellency Governor Trumbull, to the General Assembly and the Freemen of the State of Connecticut, declining any Further Election to Public Office* (New London, 1783).

2. *The United States elevated to Glory and Honour. A Sermon preached before his Excellency Jonathan Trumbull ... and the Honourable the General Assembly of the State of Connecticut ... at the Anniversary Election, May 8th, 1783.*

3. *Observations on the Importance of the American Revolution.*

The establishment of the independence of the united states gives a new direction to the affairs of the world; and will, I hope, prove the greatest blessing to it. This country, in particular, might be the greatest gainer by it, were it wise enough to reform its representation, and to study by all measures of conciliation, and, particularly, by consenting to a perfect reciprocity in all the intercourses of commerce, to bring about a family compact with the united states. In this way we might derive greater advantages from them than we ever derived from any dominion over them. I have given my opinion strongly to this purpose to our present minister; but I cannot hope that it will be much regarded.

I have communicated the account in your letter of Mr Temple to Mr Pitt. What the issue will be I know not. I love and respect Mr Temple, and wish his information and advice may be attended to. But an infatuation with respect to America still prevails among us. You, Sir, have enjoy'd a distinguished happiness. If my Ideas of the state of Connecticut are right, it has long been in the very best condition of human society. This I have intimated in Pag [57][4] of my pamphlet. You have spent your life in doing good to this state. You have been for many years its first magistrate, honoured and beloved; and now you have seen it carry'd thro' a most dangerous struggle and its liberty completely established. I congratulate you on your happiness. There are now waiting for you the yet greater honours of a better world; honours to which none in this world can be compared, but which few of the governors of it ever think, like you, of securing.

With the greatest respect I am, Sir, your obliged
and most obedient and humble servant
Rich*d* Price

---

4. Price did not complete this reference in his letter. On p. 57 (of the 1784 ed.) of the *Observations on the Importance of the American Revolution* he writes, "The happiest state of man is the middle state between the *savage* and the *refined*, or between the wild and the luxurious state. Such is the state of society in CONNECTICUT, and some others of the *American* provinces." (Peach, p. 208.)

To Benjamin Rush

Newington=Green Oct 14th 1784

Dear Sir

You will receive with this a few copies of a pamphlet[1] which I have just printed. Two of them I wish you to be so good as to present from me to the

---

ORIGINAL: The Library Company of Philadelphia.   TEXT: Original, with the kind permission of the Library Company of Philadelphia.

1. *Observations on the Importance of the American Revolution.*

Governor of your state[2], the excellent author of the farmer's letters for whom I have long entertained a warm esteem.[3] I wish also that two copies may be presented to Dr Ewing with my respectful compliments. The remaining copies I leave to your disposal. This tract being intended as a last testimony of my good will to the American states, I have no thoughts of publishing it in this country, and therefore I have printed only such a small number as may be sufficient to enable me to make it known in America by sending it to my friends there leaving it to be reprinted by them should they think it likely to be of any use and that the sale will answer the expence. I have desired my friends at Boston to present a few copies to Congress, with a Note to acquaint Congress that a Translation into English of *Mr Turgot*'s letter printed at the end of my pamphlet will soon be convey'd to America by the *Count de Mirabeau* in a tract, *on hereditary honours and Nobility*[4] which will probably deserve much of the attention of the united states.

I have been afraid of giving you too much trouble, and therefore I have sent a parcel of copies to Mr Vaughn, and requested the favour of him to convey them to the persons in the different states, to whom they are directed.

I think with some pain and anxiety of what I am doing in this instance. I am afraid that some parts of the advice I have given will not be generally liked; but my own mind is deeply impress'd with the conviction of its importance; and my consciousness of having nothing in view but the best interest of the united states (and thro' them of the world) leads me to hope that I shall be an object of candour; and that, if thro' partial views or misinformation, I have fallen into any mistakes I shall be excused. I want no apology for Mr Turgot's letter. The reflexion on the service I may do the united states by conveying this letter to them relieves me under my apprehensions of the faults that may be found in the other parts of this tract.

I return you, Dear Sir, many thanks for your letter by Captain Truston and for your introduction of Dr Rodgers[5] to me. All information of what passes among the united states is very interesting to me. I am sorry for the unsettled state of the *Pensilvania* government. It is in this respect, I am told, singular, all the other governments being quiet and tolerably well settled. It becomes not

---

2. John Dickinson (1732–1808), became President of the Supreme Executive Council of Delaware in 1781 and holder of the same office in Pennsylvania in the period 1782–85. (Boatner, p. 331; Bailyn, pp. 660–67.)

3. *Letters from a Farmer in Pennsylvania to the Inhabitants of the British Colonies* (Philadelphia, 1768). See Vol. I, 90.

4. *Considérations sur l'Ordre de Cincinnatus.* See Benjamin Franklin to R.P., 7 Sept. 1784.

5. Dr John R. B. Rodgers, "an eminent physician of New York, and for a number of years, one of the medical professors of Columbia College." He was the son of The Revd John Rogers, DD, (1727–1811) also of New York. The father, according to his biographer Samuel Miller, had corresponded with Price, but none of these letters, apparently, have survived. The son was introduced to Price when he visited London in 1784. See Samuel Miller, *Memoirs of the Rev. John Rodgers, D.D.* (New York, 1813), pp. 94n and 211.

me to say anything of the disputes which have arisen among you. I wish they may be soon terminated in a manner that shall be most favourable to the happiness of the state and the general interest of liberty and justice.

By the conveyance which brings this letter I have sent you Hoadly's works for Dickenson College.[6] I wish I could do it a more substantial service. It bears a good name, and I hope it will prosper.

Having many letters to write, and being at present in a state of much anxiety on account of my wife who has been lately reduced by the palsy to a degree of helplessness and depression which is very alarming and distressing, I can only add, that with the best wishes and great regard, I am

Your oblig'd and very obedient and humble servant
Richd Price

6. Dickinson College. For details of Price's gift see R.P. to Benjamin Rush, 1 Jan. 1783.

To Ezra Stiles

Newington=Green Oct 15th 1784

Dear Sir,

I sent you about a fortnight ago by a ship for Boston a parcel of pamphlets consigned to the care of Mr Willard the President of Cambridge University. I also requested Mr Willard's care of another parcel for his Excellency Governor Trumbull.[1] Both these parcels have, I hope, been received, and will be accepted as a testimony of my affection and respect. I request your candour with respect to any points in which your opinions may be different from mine. I have writ from my feeling and conviction. I am indeed much impress'd with a belief of the importance of the Advice I have given to the united states. They are beginning a new plan. The senseless cry against *innovation* (so hostile here to improvement and a correction of abuses) cannot influence them. They stand on free and open ground. Their situation, therefore, is peculiarly favourable; and I have been anxious about contributing the little in my power towards engaging them to make the most of it for their own good and the improvement of the world.

Mr Turgot's letter will undoubtedly be acceptable; and this will, I hope, procure for me some indulgence with respect to other parts of the pamphlets. I ought to have accompany'd the letter with an English translation, and I think

ORIGINAL: Yale University Library.   TEXT: Original, with the kind permission of Yale University Library.

1. See R.P. to Ezra Stiles, and R.P. to Jonathan Trumbull the Elder, both dated 8 Oct. 1784.

with pain of the disappointment that will be occasioned by this omission. But I have informed the President of Congress that a translation will soon be sent over by the *Count de Mirabeau*, an excellent writer, who is now in London, was acquainted with Mr Turgot, and intends to convey to America a tract[2] on the subject which I have touched in P. 71st of my pamphlet;[3] I mean, *hereditary honours and Nobility*.

Not intending to publish in this country I have distributed the small number of copies which I have printed in America leaving it to be reprinted there should my friends there think the sale may answer the expence, and that it may be of any use.

I think myself much oblig'd to you for taking candidly the information I sent you that in the present circumstances of this kingdom, and particularly of the Dissenters, no collection could be attempted among us for the relief of the congregation at Newport with any hopes of much success. Indeed, the time has come when the Dissenters in England have more reason to look to America, than America has to look to them. I hope, for the sake of mankind, that the united American states will prosper, not by extending dominion or the splendour of trade and luxury; but by such simple and virtuous manner as I suppose take place in *Connecticut* (according to the account I have given of it in P. [68–69] of my pamphlet)[4] and by the establishment of such a plan of civil, intellectual and religious liberty as shall invite the wise and good to them and render them an example to the world.

I have not at present time to give you any particular account of the transactions in science here; nor do I know of anything very important that could be communicated to you. You may I believe be assur'd that the account of the elements of the new planet which I sent you from Mr *Herschel* are nearly right;[5] but the observations of a few years more are necessary to settle them with perfect precision.

Mr *Herschel* has given the King's name to the new planet in order to express his gratitude to him for his patronage; but it will most probably be always best known by his own name. He is proceeding very diligently with his observations. He has discover'd a Volcano in the moon, and several new Nebulae among the stars; but I am not able to give you any particular account of these discoveries.[6] This is vacation time with our Royal Society. We are to begin our

2. *Considérations sur l'Ordre de Cincinnatus.*

3. Price's pagination here is the same as that found in the 1785 (London) edition of *Observations on the Importance of the American Revolution*; see Peach, p. 209, "It is ... with peculiar satisfaction that I have found in the Articles of Confederation an order that no titles of nobility shall be ever granted by the United States."

4. See 1785 edition of *Observations on the Importance of the American Revolution*, Peach, p. 208, and R.P. to Jonathan Trumbull the Elder, 8 Oct. 1784, n.4.

5. See R.P. to Ezra Stiles, 23 Oct. 1783.

6. "On several occasions Herschel was convinced that he could see entire volcanoes on the Moon; once in 1783, when the appearance of a red, luminous spot on a dark portion of the lunar

usual meetings in November, and during the course of the winter Mr Herschel may perhaps give us more account of his observations. There seems reason to believe that our Solar System is a part of an unspeakably larger system which itself is one of a number of other systems so distant as to appear to one another under the form of a *Nebulae*.[7] How vast is the Universe? It is certain that all we can *imagine* falls infinitely short of its real magnificence and grandeur? How pleasing is the reflexion that it is the seat of boundless and ever-increasing happiness and under the care and guidance of perfect wisdom and goodness? How transporting the hope that we are to exist for ever to survey and examine its wonders and to grow in knowledge and virtue?

I am oblig'd to you for sending me your observations on the comet that appeared last winter. I have convey'd them to our Astronomer Royal. I also return you my best thanks for your very agreeable Election Sermon. I have read it with avidity and been much entertained and instructed by it.[8] His Excellency the Governor of your state had before done me the honour to send me a copy of it. I rejoyce to find that we are agree'd in our ideas of the importance of the American Revolution. Deliver my kind respects to Mr Fitch and Dr Beardsley. I am sorry I have not seen the two Gentlemen by whom you sent your last letters—I mean Mr Townshend and Mr Leavenworth. I happen'd not to be at home when they called; and having left no directions I know not where to find them in order to pay my respects to them.

We have lately begun to fly here. Hitherto we have been behindhand in this instance. But an order begins now to prevail which perhaps will cause us to get the start of France.

With all good wishes and great regard, I am, Dear Sir,

ever yours

Rich*d* Price

Dr Priestley has just discovered a method of filling the largest air Balloon with the lightest inflammable air in a very short time and at a very little expence; which removes one of the great impediments to the improvement of the art of flying.[9]

---

surface was confirmed by friends viewing it through his instrument, and again four years later when he made his observations the subject of a short report to the Royal Society." Angus Armitage, *William Herschel* (London, 1962), p. 51. Herschel's paper "Account of three volcanos on the moon" was published in *Phil. Trans.*, LXXVII (1787), 229. For Herschel on galaxies see "Account of some observations tending to investigate the construction of the heavens", *Phil. Trans.*, LXXIV (1784), 437ff.

7. Sir William Herschel, "On the construction of the heavens", *Phil. Trans.*, LXXV (1785), 213ff.

8. See R.P. to Jonathan Trumbull, the Elder, 8 Oct. 1784, n.2.

9. At this time Priestley was interested in finding out economical ways of producing inflammable air or hydrogen and of utilizing it commercially in filling air-balloons for aeronautical purposes. In September 1784 he demonstrated his apparatus to Faujas de St Fond, who visited him at Birmingham, and explained how tubes of a greater calibre could be used for filling aerostatic balloons. See Gibbs, 153, and Joseph Priestley, "Experiments and Observations relating to air and water", *Phil. Trans.*, LXXV (1785), part 1, 279–309.

From William Hazlitt

Boston, 19 Octr 1784.

Dear Sir,

I have wished to write to you almost every week, since my first arrival in this country,[1] but was restrained by this consideration, that I had nothing satisfactory to communicate, respecting myself. The same reason, might still induce me to throw away my paper. But, I can no longer deny myself the satisfaction of addressing you.

I can convey to you no intelligence, concerning the civil and political state of this country, which has not already reached you from other hands.

I learn, that you express a wish, in your letter to Mr Clark[2], that the subject of Dr Chauncy's book[3] had never been started at Boston, apprehensive of its unpromising influence upon the morals of the people. But, I believe it will have an effect, contrary to what you imagine. There is another doctrine circulating in this country, and received with great avidity by many persons, which the Doctor's book will have a tendency to overthrow. The doctrine, I mean, is published in different places, and with greater success than could be supposed, by one Murray,[4] a man of some popular talents, and a disciple of

---

ORIGINAL: American Philosophical Society. PRINTED: *M.H.S.P.* (1903), 322ff. TEXT: Original, with the kind permission of the American Philosophical Society. Price wrote on the MS in shorthand: From Mr *Hazlett*, Oct. 19 1784 at Boston giving an account of his situation, the state of things in *Massachusetts* and desiring me to recommend to Dr *Chauncy*. The last done but the letter not answered March 1785.

1. See R.P. to Shelburne, 1 June 1782. Hazlitt went to America in 1783 and stayed in Philadelphia for fifteen months. (*D.N.B.*)

2. John Clarke (1755–98), a colleague and friend of Charles Chauncy. He graduated at Harvard in 1774 and was ordained minister at the First Church in Boston in 1778.

3. *The Mystery hid from Ages and Generations, made manifest by the Gospel-Revelation: or, the Salvation of All Men the Grand Thing aimed at in the Scheme of God, as opened in the New Testament Writings, and entrusted with Jesus Christ to bring into effect* (London, 1784). A second edition of this work was published in 1787. Price had earlier entered into controversy with Chauncy on the question whether or not the whole of mankind are destined to be saved. At least in his early career Price was apprehensive lest the doctrine of universal salvation should prove to be morally debilitating. Hazlitt implies that the doctrine preached by James Relly and John Murray would be found to be even more deleterious.

4. John Murray (1741–1815), founder of Universalism in America. In London in 1759 Murray came under the influence of James Relly, the Evangelical preacher, and was converted to his faith in universal redemption. After a critical period in his life when he lost his wife and his child and became heavily involved in debt, he emigrated to America where he began to preach Universalism. In Jan. 1779 he became Minister of the Independent Church of Christ at Gloucester; in 1793 he was installed pastor of a Universalist Society at Boston. The central doctrine of Murray's creed, considered heretical by the Calvinists, was that "every individual shall in due time be separated from sin, and rendered fit to associate with the denizens of heaven." See *Letters and sketches of sermons*, 3 vols. (Boston, 1812–13), I, 144, cited in *D.A.B.*

Reiely's[5] of London. This reference will fully acquaint you what this doctrine is.

In twenty, or thirty years, there will probably be here as much freedom of thinking upon religious subjects, as there is at present amongst the Dissenters in England. Dr Mayhew[6], with the noble spirit of a man, conscious of the dignity and importance of truth, led the way to this. The late war, which helped to dissolve the attachment of the people to their old systems, afforded some others an opportunity of pursuing it. The majority of the Boston ministers, and a great number of those who are dispersed through the country, are already Arians, but are yet generally afraid to avow their sentiments. I am very acceptable as a preacher in this part of America, and have some dark prospect of a settlement. Dr Chauncy, and many others, treat me with great civility and friendship. Your favourable mention of me to the Doctor, in your next letter, would do me an essential service. I am afraid that that busy bigot Dr Gordon endeavours to injure me.

You have been told, I presume, by others, that I lived a considerable time at Philadelphia, and how I succeeded there, and that I was seized with a fever in Maryland, last year, which rendered me useless, whilst I was groaning under a great expence, almost six months.

If you have any enquiries to make concerning America in general, or any part of it in particular, I will endeavour to give you all the satisfaction in my power.

In the mean time, I wish greatly to know the complexion of the times, and the whole state of things amongst you.

When you have the leisure to favour me with a line, be pleased to direct to me the care of the Revd Mr Lathrop, Boston.[7]

Wishing you all happiness that can be possibly enjoyed, in this world, and that better world, which is approaching, I am, dear Doctor, with the utmost esteem and affection, your often obliged and very humble servant

W. Hazlitt

---

5. James Relly (1722–78) was born at Jeffreston in Pembrokeshire. Early in his career he came under the influence of George Whitefield and preached in the vicinity of Narberth. Later he broke with Whitefield on doctrinal grounds, the latter maintaining that the Universalist doctrine which Relly defended was antinomian. For a short while (1750–53), together with his brother John, he joined John Harris "of S. Kennox" to form an independent sect. Later he moved to London and preached, in succession, at Coachmakers' Hall, Bartholomew Close, and Crosby Square. During his ministry in London he profoundly influenced John Murray, who later became the founder of Universalism in America. (*D.N.B.* and *D.W.B.*)

6. Jonathan Mayhew (1720–66), Pastor of West Church, Boston. He graduated from Harvard in 1744 and was called to the pastorate in which he served for the remainder of his life in 1747. He preached a rational Christianity based upon the scriptures, rejected Trinitarianism, attacked Episcopalianism, and defended free will, the rights of individual judgement and puritanism.

7. John Lathrop (1740–1816), Minister of the Second Church at Boston.

To Benjamin Franklin

Newington=Green Oct 21 1784

My Dear Friend,

I received a few days ago your letter by Mr Hartley,[1] and think myself much obliged to you for it, and for conveying to me the King of France's Edict for establishing a new Sinking Fund. I received soon afterwards another Copy of the same Edict from Lord Shelburne.[2] My curiosity has been much gratify'd by it; but at the same time I have been mortify'd to find that our rivals are getting so much the start of us. I admire the language and spirit and wisdom of this Edict. Nothing but a faithful execution of the plan establish'd by it can be necessary to extricate *France* from the embarrassments of its debts. This plan is the same with that which I have been long writing about and recommending in this country to no purpose. It is strange that nations should hitherto have thought so little (particularly since *funding* has been practised) of employing the powers of compound interest to liquidate debts and to make themselves rich and powerful. But we see continually that the same want of foresight, extravagance and infatuation prevail in governments which prevail among individuals.

I am not sufficiently acquainted with the nature of the public debts of France to understand properly the particulars in the second Table annex'd to this Edict, but the general purport of it is obvious.

I see that by the arrangements proposed and the operations of the Sinking Fund if not interrupted a revenue of six millions sterling *per Ann* will be liberated in 25 years, above the two millions and a half of which will be liberated in 13 Years. This kingdom would be in less danger were any thing like this practicable here; but the nature of our debts (consisting almost entirely of perpetual annuities) does not admit of it. I have promised to draw up a table, during the next session of Parliament, similar to the first in the French Edict, and marking as that does, distinctly for every year the progress of a Sinking fund in order to shew its powers, and I have some reason to expect that there will be a struggle in our Parliament to get such a fund establish'd,

---

ORIGINAL: American Philosophical Society. TEXT: Original, with the kind permission of the American Philosophical Society.

  1. Probably David Hartley, the younger. See R.P. to David Hartley, the younger, 30 May 1780. He was an intimate friend of Franklin and sympathetic to the American rebels as appears in his *Letters on the American War* (1778–9). Partly on account of his relationship with Franklin he was appointed a plenipotentiary to conduct the peace negotiations in Paris. His attempts to conclude a trade agreement failed, but on 3 Sept. 1783, he and Franklin drew up and signed the Peace Treaty between Great Britain and the United States of North America.

  2. See Shelburne to R.P., 7 Oct. 1784.

and consigned to the care of Commissioners in order to render diversions of it less practicable.[3]

I have inclosed a little pamphlet publish'd in April last[4] because I am doubtful whether it has been sent you before.

We have at last begun to fly here. Such an ardour prevails that probably we shall soon in this instance leave France behind us. Dr Priestley, in a letter which I have just received from him tells me that he is eager in pursuing his Experiments and that he has discover'd a method of filling the largest Balloons with the lightest inflammable air in a very short time and at a very small expense. I sent you a pretty long letter with a parcel of my pamphlets on the American Revolution about a fortnight ago. This letter will be convey'd by a countryman of yours, Mr Jonathan Jackson who has been in London some time and in whose acquaintance I have been happy. I have sent a considerable number, of these pamphlets to America where I hope they will be favourably received as a well meant tho' weak attempt to serve the best interests of civil society.

Mrs Price, I thank God, continues better. She desires to be respectfu[lly] remember'd to you. With the highest regard I am

ever yours
Rich*d* Price

I have not seen Mr Franklin[5] lately, but I have the prospect of dining in his company in a few days. He was so good as to take the care of the parcel I sent you.

---

3. Price prepared the relevant tables in the winter of 1784–85 for some time before the end of April they had been delivered to Pitt. (See R.P. to John Wilkes, 28 Apr. 1785.)

4. Probably a reference to Price's *Postscript to a pamphlet by Dr Price on the state of the public debts and finances* (London, 1784).

5. William Temple Franklin (see B. Franklin to R.P., 16 Aug. 1784).

From Jonathan Shipley

Chilbolton Oct 21st [1784][1]

Dear Sir,

I am much obliged to you for Mr Turgot's excellent Letter[2] and more for your own kind remembrance of me. I am glad to find you have not yet done with Politicks which I look upon as the noblest and most valuable part of our Duty, even of our Christian Duty. I agree with Turgot in almost every one of his propositions and wish they were as practicable as they are true. That they are not practicable is owing to the degenerate state to which mankind are reduc'd by the corrupt principles and wicked Administration of allmost all modern Governments. The natural Tendency of almost every ministerial measure We have seen has been to discourage publick Integrity and to make men in general worse than they would otherwise have been. I do not exclude our Church Government in its present state from its share in the censure. Judge then how little likely I am to disapprove, and I cannot possibly be offended with, any thing you are likely to say against Establishments.

Had I sufficient influence, our thirty nine Articles would be reduced to very few indeed. It is absurd to limit the Doctrines of Religion and Duty to any number of Propositions. The knowledge of Religion like that of any other

---

ORIGINAL: Yale University Library.   TEXT: Original with the kind permission of Yale University Library.

1. This letter was probably written either in 1784 or in 1785. It is unlikely that it was written earlier because Price's *Observations on the Importance of the American Revolution* in which he first published Turgot's letter to Price of 22 Mar. 1778—the letter for a copy of which Shipley was thanking Price—first appeared in 1784. Moreover the comments made by Price on Church Establishments to which Shipley refers may well have been those included in the *Observations* (Peach, pp. 194–200). It is, however, possible that Price sent a printed copy of Turgot's letter independently of his pamphlet, as we know that a printed version lay in the press waiting for Price to obtain permission to publish from Turgot's literary executor; but if this was the case it is highly unlikely that he would have sent Shipley a copy before he obtained permission to publish, a permission that was not obtained before August 1784. The letter could not have been written later than Oct. 1785, for Mrs Price to whose illness Shipley refers died on 20 Sept. 1786. Of the two years 1784 and 1785, the former is the more probable for the following reasons. First, Shipley, as a member of the "Honest Whigs", would have been an early recipient of Price's pamphlet. Secondly, it is likely that Shipley's references to the "new system of administering justice by transferring the rights of the jury to the judge" is to the celebrated case of *Rex* v. *Shipley* in which the Bishop's son, William Davies Shipley, was a defendant, and in which Justice Buller, when the case was heard at Shrewsbury on 6 Aug. 1784, directed the jury to find only as to whether the item had been published and to leave the question as to whether the words constituted a libel to the Court (see W.S. Holdsworth, *A history of English law* (London, 1938), X, 672ff., and Howell, *State trials*, XXI, 970–1041). Thirdly, if Georgiana Shipley was at Chilbolton when the letter was written, as the postscript suggests, the year would have been 1784, as by 21 Mar. 1785, she had eloped with Francis Hare-Naylor and settled at Aix-la-Chapelle (see R.P. to Benjamin Franklin, 21 Mar. 1785).

2. R.P. to A. Turgot, 22 Mar. 1778.

Science, is in a progressive state, and it will probably continue to improve as long as the present constitution of nature exists. Yet some good has arisen from Establishments: they have encourag'd a learned Education and diffus'd knowledge more generally. It was owing to that superiority of Education that in real improvement our Church for some time took the lead of Yours. But I think religious Establishments are only a secondary Consideration. Let our Government be founded on principles of Equity and the common good which is all the civil Liberty I want, and such a Government will soon learn from Experience and Reflection to regulate its religious as well as its civil Institutions in the wisest manner. Yet I apprehend that some publick Establishments, at least in our corrupt and ignorant days to explain and teach the principles of Duty and to form a body of Men qualified to instruct the rest, are useful and even necessary. Perhaps in America, where the common People have property and have been much better educated than ours, where Superstition and Enthusiasm of every kind have been formerly planted and being left to themselves have totally wither'd and perish'd: there perhaps it might be safe to trust the regulation of religion to the common sense and experience of Men without the interference of Government. Mr Turgot I fear is in the right in censuring our Countrymen for neglecting the Study of Morals and Politicks and I think that the new system of administring Justice by transferring the rights of the Jury to the judge is a Proof of it.[3] A Doctrine founded on the poorest subtleties and the most impudent Nonsense could never have been imposed without resistance, but on a servile and ignorant People.

I feel sincerely for your domestick Affliction and the dangerous Illness of Mrs Price. Her Complaint I fear will not admit of a Cure: but is often attended with long Intervals of Ease and tolerable health. Wishing you and her all the blessings which this short and precarious state of Existence affords

I am, Dear Sir

Your faithful and affectionate

humble Servant

J St Asaph

Mrs Shipley[4] and her Daughters[5] are tolerably well, poor Georgiana excepted and desire their compliments

---

3. See n. 1 above and R.P. to Shelburne, 27 Nov. 1784.

4. Anna Maria Shipley, née Mordaunt (1716–1803) was a niece of the third Earl of Peterborough. She married Jonathan Shipley in 1743.

5. Anna Maria and Jonathan Shipley had five daughters: Anna Maria (see R.P. to Benjamin Franklin, 18 Nov. 1782); Emily (1752–1800), who married William Charles Sloper; Elizabeth (1754–96); Georgiana (see R.P. to Benjamin Franklin, 18 Nov. 1782); and Catherine Louisa, "Kitty", (1760–1840). Cannon, I, 65.

From Lord Monboddo

Monboddo October 23d 1784

Dear Sir,

I had the favour of your Letter by which I am glad to learn that you had the patience to read thro' my last volume. This is what I believe many have not done; but have thrown away the Book, as vilifying the Age in which they live, and by consequence themselves; for we must all partake more or less of the degeneracy of our age. Vanity is a quality very predominant among us; and in my opinion makes a very considerable part of our happiness. No Man of common understanding can be really satisfied with the State of our Public affairs, whatever he may pretend to be. There are but few, I am affraid, who have much reason to be pleased with their families or friends, or the State of their private affairs—what then remains to us but to be pleased with ourselves. Whoever therefore would rob us of that pleasure, however, delusive it may be we may say of him, what the man in Horace says of his friends who cured him of an agreeable Madness;

"Pol me occidistis, amicei, non servastis," ait, "cui sic extorta voluptas et demptus per vim mentis gratissimus error."[1]

There is one effect of the vanity of this age, which has often surprised me. Men who have never studied the antient Philosophy, and perhaps do not understand even the Language in which it is written, pronounce decisively that we moderns excel the Antients in Philosophy as well as in other Sciences. Now allowing them to understand perfectly the modern Philosophy, I should think that it required a wonderful deal of Genius and Natural parts to be able to compare together two things one of which we only understand; and to decide with certainty upon the preference of the one to the other. And yet I doubt those among us, who prefer the Moderns so much to the Antients, and speak of the wonderfull improvements we have made in Arts, Sciences and Philosophy are Men of that kind; for I have never found or heard of any Man who was a Scholar and learned in Antient Philosophy and Science who did not think that every thing we pretend to have discovered in Logic, Morals, or Metaphysics, was not contemptible compared with the Antient Discoveries, excepting only the Astronomy of Sir Isaac Newton, which is truely a Science

---

ORIGINAL: Bodleian.   TEXT: Original, with the kind permission of the Bodleian Library. The MS bears a note in Price's hand: Letter from Lord Monboddo/dated oct. 23d 1785 [?]/ not answered [in shorthand]/ Feb: 22d 85

1. "Indeed you have killed me, not saved me, my friends," he said, "from whom [referring to himself] pleasure has thus been torn away and a most pleasant error of the mind has been forcibly removed." *Epistles*, the Loeb edn. II, 2, 138–40. (The Loeb edn. reads "amici" and has a comma after "Pol". I am indebted to Dr D. A. Rees for this reference and translation.

and a great Science, which the English Nation may boast they have discovered; for as to the facts of Natural History, which we have added to the Antient Stock of knowledge, no body who knows what Philosophy or Science is, will say that they are either one or tother, tho' they be the Materials out of which Philosophy and Science may be made; but that is what is not yet done. As to the liberal Arts; I think Modern vanity has not yet gone so far, as to prefer our Painting, Statuary or A[r]chitecture to the Antients. As to Music, I have heard it indeed maintained that the Antients knew nothing of Music in parts, which we are now assured the Barbarians of the South Sea practice; and there is not a Company of Russian Peasants met together to make merry, who do not sing Songs in parts. The reason of this so absurd Vanity is that we have none of the musical performances of the Antients, that have come down to us, as their works of Statuary and Architecture have done, thro' we are well assured that they cultivated Music more then either of those two Arts; and made a Political use of it, to which we moderns have not so much as dreamed that it could be applied: and it is for this reason likewise that our Music is so mean and trifling an Art compared with the Antient Music according to the account we have of it.

As to the Principles of Philosophy upon which Sir Isaac Newton's astronomy is founded, as you continue of the same opinion, you may perhaps have discovered what some mathematicians in Edinburgh are in search of but have not found out, viz. A Demonstration that the Circular or Elliptical Motion cannot be simple, as Aristotle supposes it to be,[2] but must necessarily be Compounded. This will at once put down all my Philosophy upon the Subject, and will establish Projection and Gravitation beyond the possibility of Doubt, but till that be done, allow me to tell you that you cannot believe in the projection and gravitation of the Celestial Bodies, and at the same time believe in God or even in *Nature*, at least the *Nature of Aristotle*, in which as there is nothing wanting, he says that neither is there any thing superfluous.[3]

But perhaps you are not learned in Lines and Figures, which is my case; and therefore I am obliged to take in that matter the word of Aristotle and Doctor Horsley, tho' at the same time I think I know enough of Mathematics to be able to understand any Demonstration that may be given of a proposition so simple. I will therefore go on to another thing, which I know you have studied and that is the primitive State of man, as described in our Sacred Books, and the long lives of the antediluvian Patriarchs. As to the first, I think it is impossible to maintain that the account which Moses gives us of the Garden of Eden, and the life of our first parents there is not Allegorical; for my own part I

---

2. *De Caelo*, Bk. I, ch. 2.

3. "God and nature create nothing in vain," *De Caelo*, Bk. I, ch. 4, 271a, 33; cf. *De Caelo*, Bk. II, ch. 11, 291b, 13–14; "Nature does nothing superfluously or in vain," *De Generationes Animalium*, Bk. II, ch. 6, 744a, 36–37.

could as well believe that *Christian* and *Faith*, and the other personages in the Pilgrims Progress were real personages, as that there was a real Tree of Knowledge of Good and Evil, or of Life. The very names in my opinion, as well as those in the Pilgrims Progress makes the Allegory evident, which in my opinion is this, that there was a time, when Men lived under the direction of superior powers, and were conducted by them as much as Flocks and herds now are by Shepherds; but that in process of time they grew vain and arrogant, to which we are sure human nature has a great propensity, and believing that they themselves could distinguish good from Evil;, they withdrew themselves from under the government of superior wisdom, and lived according to their own opinion; which is what Moses calls the fall and is most certainly the Source of all human misery. This Explanation of the Mythology of Moses perfectly agrees with what Plato tells us, that there was a time when the Gods governed Men as a Shepherd does his Flock,[4] which I am persuadedPlato learned in Egypt,[5] for the Egyptian traditions as recorded in their Sacred Books tell the same story, that men in Antient times in their Country were governed by Gods, that is Beings of superior Intelligence. Now I should be very glad to know what you think of this meaning I give to Moses's Allegory, or whether you think it an Allegory at all, but believe it to be literally true.

As to the other point concerning the long lives of the Antediluvian Patriarchs, whatever any of us may believe concerning the Creation of the World, or the primitive state of Men, as recorded by Moses, I think it is impossible that any Man of good understanding and a judge of the truth of History, can doubt that the account given by Moses of the Progenitors of the Jewish nation is true History, and the most exact Chronological account of the first ages of a nation that is anywhere to be found, and in this respect preferable to any History that we have of the beginning of any other Nation, that it not openly gives us the Chronology of the Nation, but in doing so informs us of a most Curious fact, viz. the length of Lives of Men in the State of nature or in the first ages of Society, which is the *desideratum* in the History of our Species as much as in the History of wild Animals. Now if you agree with me, which I am persuaded you will, that the History of the long lives of those Ancestors of the Jewish Nation is true History, I should next desire to know whether you believe that it was by a Miracle that they all lived so long, and likewise that their Bodies were so much bigger and stronger than ours, as we must suppose the Bodies of Men to be, who lived 800 or 900 years; or whether it happened in the ordinary Course of Nature, and from the Causes which I suppose, Viz. living in a more natural way, following the most healthfull of all Vocations, and inhabiting a Country and Climate as favourable to Longevity as I believe

---

4. *Statesman*, 271; cf. *Critias*, 109.
5. For a discussion of Plato's links with Egypt and a possible visit there, see W.K.C. Guthrie, *A History of Greek Philosophy*, vol. IV (Cambridge, 1975), p. 15.

any in the world. And, secondly, whether you do not think that supposing the Longevity of those Patriarchs might be accounted for from Natural Causes, the Deluge, which according to Moses was Universal, but according to the Greek Traditions was only partial, overflowing only the Country of Chaldea and Babylonia and joining the Euxine Sea to the Mediaterranian, might not have produced so great as Alteration in the Lives of Men, tho' not immediately, but by degrees, as Moses informs us. Of this enough.

Among other advantages we have over the Antients, I am told your friend Dr Priestley is of opinion that we are improved and are dayly improving in Morals as well as in Arts and Sciences.[6] What your opinion in that matter is, I do not know, but I should be glad to know Dr Priestley's opinion upon two points very important in the Political System, the Numbers of People and the produce of Corn to maintain them. As to the first of these, I think I know your Sentiments. But as to the other I should be glad to know what you and your friend Dr Priestley think. As I am a farmer, I have studied the art of raising Corn a good deal, and have made my Observations upon it, wherever I have been both in England and Scotland, as well as upon the numbers of the people; and I was long in doubt whether the people or the Corn they feed upon would fail the soonest. But I am now come to this determination, that in England tho' I know the produce of the Corn is there diminished, yet the people will sooner fail than bread for them to eat; but in Scotland where our agriculture is not so good as yours, I hold the Contrary will happen; and that if we go on as we are doing, our Lands will be so sterile in not many generations, as not to be able to maintain the few people that will then remain. The decrease of the produce of Corn in Scotland within these last 50 or 60 years, can be proved to be prodigious by authentic Records, such as the Custom-house Books, wherein the quantities then exported are set down; whereas now there is none exported, but a great deal imported. Now I think it is a great pity that among the many Sciences we have improved the Political Science is not one, and particularly that part of it which regards Population, and the producing food for the people. For you will agree with me that it would be a thousand Pities if a people, so excellent as we suppose ourselves, should die out; and this too by the most cruel of all deaths, by Starving.

This Letter has drawn out to a great length, and I am affraid will weary you; but I really desire information from you, which I hope will make you excuse the length of this Letter

I ever am with great regard and esteem
Your faithfull humble servant
Jas. Burnett

---

6. See *An Essay on the First Principles of Government*, 1st ed., p. 3, "While our faculties of perception and action remain in the same vigour, our progress towards perfection must be continually accelerated; and that nothing but a future existence, in advantageous circumstances, is requisite to advance a mere man above everything we can now conceive of excellence and perfection."

To [a Member of the Great Yarmouth Church[1]]

Newington Green Nov. 15. 1784.

Dear Sir,

I have received your letter with much pleasure; and you would have heard from me sooner in answer to it had I been informed by Mr Morgan (my nephew at Norwich)[2] that the purpose for which you honoured me with it was answered by the recommendation of Mr Hawkes[3] to your congregation. I am acquainted with Mr Hawkes, the father,[4] and feel a high respect for him; but I have not the pleasure of knowing the son, who, I doubt not, is worthy and able, and a proper object of the recommendation that has been given him. Before I received this information from my Nephew I had thought over all my acquaintance among the dissenting ministers and consulted Dr Kippis and Dr Rees and some other friends in order to be able with more satisfaction to comply with the request in your letter.

I am very glad that now I have no occasion for any further enquiry; and I wish your congregation settled in a minister who may by his good character, ability, and usefulness, be the means of promoting the credit of the Dissenters at Yarmouth and of maintaining that political consequence which they have so happily acquired.

Mr Beaufoy[5] spent part of last friday with me. The whig electors of Yarmouth are indeed very happy in both their Representatives.[6] Mr Beaufoy possesses the best principles, and is likely to make a distinguished figure. He has particularly at heart a reform of the representation of the Kingdom, which at present is little better than a mockery. I have reason also to know that Mr

---

PRINTED: *T.U.H.S.*, VI, No. 2 (Oct. 1936), 163–66. TEXT: *T.U.H.S.*

1. The editors of *T.U.H.S.* note that although the identity of the recipient of the letter is unknown he must have been a member of the Great Yarmouth Church. John Whiteside was the minister there from 1761 until 1784, and from 1772 until 1784 he was assisted by John Matthew Beynon who succeeded him in 1784.

2. George Cadogan Morgan.

3. The editors of *T.U.H.S.* note: William Hawkes (1759–1820) minister at Failsworth, 1781–85; at Bolton (assistant) 1785–89; and at Upper Brook St, Manchester, 1789–1820.

4. The editors of *T.U.H.S.* note: William Hawkes, minister at Birmingham New Meeting, 1754–80.

5. Henry Beaufoy (1750–95). MP for Minehead (1783–84) and Great Yarmouth (1784–95). In Parliament he was a frequent speaker on a wide range of topics, particularly those concerning commerce and finance. In 1787 and 1789 he moved the repeal of the Test and Corporation Acts, and on 3 Mar. 1790 he seconded Fox's motion for their repeal. Secretary to the Board of Control (India Office), 1791–93.

6. The other Whig representative elected on 3 April 1784 was Sir John Jervis, who was to represent Great Yarmouth until 1790 when he became the member for Chipping Wycombe. He took part in the naval action of Ushant under Keppel and was knighted after the capture of the Pégasse in 1782. He became Earl St Vincent in 1797 (Namier and Brooke, I, 682).

Pitt is zealous on this point. In the next session of Parliament he is to make another motion for this purpose. But it is a service in which no minister can hope to succeed without the concurrence and aid of the people. I ardently wish Mr Pitt as much as possible of this aid; and, particularly, from that body of men who have hitherto always distinguished themselves in the cause of liberty; I mean, the Dissenters.

Perhaps, when the Parliament meets, such of them as have influence in the great towns of the kingdom will think of setting forward addresses and petitions with this view. Should this happen, the Dissenters at Yarmouth will, I dare say, be among the foremost. Indeed, should the people continue as torpid with respect to this essential object as they seem to be at present, they cannot expect the services of a virtuous minister, nor will they deserve them. Sometimes it has happened that a people have been saved without their own consent, and against their wills; but such precedents are dangerous, a people having always the only right of judging and determining in what their own salvation consists. If they are to become so corrupt and abject as to prefer a *nominal* to a *real* representation, and consequently slavery to liberty, they are fit only for slavery, and in that condition they must remain.

Deliver my best respects to Mr Hurry and all my other friends at Yarmouth. Wishing you and your family every possible blessing, I am, Dear Sir, with great regards

Your very obedient and humble servant
Richard Price

To the Earl of Shelburne

Nov. 27th 1784

My Lord,

In consequence of a wish express'd by your Lordship in the letter with which I was some time ago favoured I have looked over carefully Dr Watts's Catechisms,[1] and cannot help agreeing with your Lordship in being dissatisfy'd with them. The first Catechism is not short and simple enough, and has expressions in it not well adapted to the conceptions of a child and which have a tendency to give very improper Ideas of the Deity. The second Catechism is still more liable to these objections, and at the same time full of a very absurd system of Divinity. I have looked over some other Catechisms, but found none that entirely meets my Ideas. I have therefore composed that

ORIGINAL: Bowood. TEXT: Original, with the kind permission of the Marquis of Lansdowne.
1. See Isaac Watts, *The First Sett of Catechisms and Prayers: or the Religion of Little Children under Seven or Eight Years of Age* (London, 1730); *The Second Sett of Catechisms and Prayers* (London, 1730).

which I now send, but I have not been able to satisfy myself. Such as it is I submit it to your Lordship's inspection. The first part is perhaps enough to be taught children under six years of age; and the second part might be more properly taught children above that age. But indeed this is new work to me, and I should not have thought of undertaking it had not your Lordship led me to it. I received a letter last week from the Bishop of St Asaph which affected me much. His favourite daughter, Miss Georgiana, the delight (as he says) and the pride of his heart has just left his house and married one Mr Hare a spendthrift and a rake who cannot shew his head for debt and is obliged to quit the country.[2] He has also been much troubled by the prosecution of his son[3] which he calls a *ministerial* persecution of him, but surely without reason. The doctrine about libels given out by the judges ought not in my opinion to be submitted to. It subverts the foundation of civil liberty by transferring the rights of Juries to the judges and making them (the creatures of the crown and constant expectants from it) licensers of the Press. I hope, therefore, it will be taken up in Parliament and reprobated. Mr Fox, I am told intends to do this. What I saw of his immoral and indecent conduct at Brighthelmston convinces me that this cannot be expected from his virtue; but it will make a fine handle for opposition and for recovering popularity. The papers have lately talked much of negotiations with your Lordship. Some of the people in the Alley, I understand, think that there would be a great change for the better in the stocks were your Lordship to come into power. They expect that then something would be done towards establishing a plan of redemption and reviving public credit which has lately been in a languishing and almost expiring state. I hear that the discontents at Manchester, occasioned by the Cotton and fustian tax, run very high. It is so improperly and absurdly laid, they say, that it must ruin the manufacture. Some of the manufacturers are now in town. They have been with Mr Pitt, and complain that he will not attend to them.[4]

I beg my respectful compliments may be deliver'd to the Abbe Morellet, and also to Count Mirabeau[5] if at Bowood. Mrs Price sends her best respects to Lady Shelburne and your Lordship. She continues better; but is still in a very

---

2. See R.P. to Benjamin Franklin, 10 May 1778.

3. William Davies Shipley (1745–1826) became Vicar of Ysceifiog in 1770, Vicar of Wrexham in 1771, Rector of Llangwm in 1772, Chancellor of St Asaph in 1773 and Dean of St Asaph in 1774. His publication of Sir William Jones's *The Principles of Government, in a Dialogue between a Scholar and a Peasant* led to his being charged with seditious libel (see Jonathan Shipley to R.P., 21 Oct. [1784]).

4. In his budget for 1784 Pitt levied an additional excise duty on printed and stained linens and calicoes. These duties proved to be very unpopular with the cotton manufacturers and those on calicoes were repealed in 1785. The taxes on printed goods were, however, retained. See *Parl. Hist.*, XXIV, 1028 and XXV, 478ff; and William Kennedy, *English Taxation, 1640–1799* (London, 1913), pp. 158ff.

5. See Fitzmaurice, II, 308–10.

weak and depress'd state. Wishing your Lordship and lady Shelburne every valuable enjoyment, I am, with great respect,

Your very obedient and humble servant

Rich*d* Price

I have inclosed Dr Priestley's short catechism.[6] It is the best I have read; and perhaps you may like it better than mine.

---

6. Joseph Priestley, *A Catechism for Children and Young Persons* (London, 1767). Price's catechism does not appear to have been published, and no copy of it has been traced.

To Henry Beaufoy

Newington=Green Dec 22*d* 1784

Dear Sir,

I have examined with much attention the account which I now return of your Brother's[1] experiments. I cannot pretend to be a proper judge of the subject of them; but it appears to me that they are ingenious and curious as well as new,[2] and will make a valuable communication to the Royal Society.[2] I am convinced that the resistance which solids meet with in moving thro' water depends on such a number of circumstances the effect of which cannot be determined except by experiments, that all deductions by calculations from Theory must be very fallacious. Your Brother's experiments afford a proof of this, and contain an information which must be of use in naval architecture.

The principal remark which has occurred to me in considering these experiments is the following.

In the last paragraph but one it is said that if a solid moves with a velocity less than that with which the water presses to the opening behind it occasioned by its motion, its velocity will be diminished. This diminution of its velocity implies an increase of the resistance, and yet in the subsequent paragraph it is said that when the contrary happens, that is, when the velocity of the solid is greater than the velocity with which the water presses to fill the opening, the resistance is likewise in this case increased. I should think that both these

---

ORIGINAL: The National Library of Wales. TEXT: Original, with the kind permission of the National Library of Wales.

1. Mark Beaufoy (1764–1827), astronomer, physicist. He began experiments on the resistance of water to moving bodies when he was fifteen. It was mainly by his exertions that the Society for the Improvement of Naval Architecture was established in 1791. He was the first Englishman to climb Mont Blanc. Colonel of the Tower Hamlets Militia in 1797. Elected FRS in 1815. (*D.N.B.*)

2. It does not appear that Beaufoy's paper was published in *Phil. Trans.*

assertions cannot be true. The latter seems undoubtedly so. A similar fact takes place in the motion of bodies thro' the air, for when a cannon ball moves with so great a velocity as to leave a vacuum behind it, the resistance becomes so great as to render useless an increase, beyond a certain degree of the charge of powder. This, if I remember right, Mr Robins discover'd.

I could, therefore, almost imagine that your Brother in the former assertion used the word *velocity* when he meant *resistance*; and this would make it correspond to my Ideas, for I cannot help thinking that the moving solid must be pushed forward when the velocity of the fluid behind it is greater than its own velocity. I will add that this is an effect which perhaps will take place when, in consequence of the length of the way which the water *before* has to pass in order to get *behind*, it cannot at all (or more imperfectly) counteract the pressure of the water *behind*. I am disposed to imagine that this is a consideration which may help to account for the curious fact discovered by your Brother, that a solid meets with less resistance in consequence of being lengthen'd by a cylinder in the middle of it. I cannot help remarking further that perhaps double cones, double wedges, double pyramids and cylinders rounded at one end are more resisted than single cones, wedges and pyramids and cylinders flat at both ends, because the water behind cannot act with the same force that it would exert had it a flat surface to act against.

But all that I have now said may be too crude, and I am afraid your Brother will find it to be so. The experiments will, I hope, be soon communicated.

I have sent you the account of the Navy debt as I received it about a fortnight ago. I have taken no copy of it and therefore shall be obliged to you for returning it when you have done with it. My respectful compliments wait on Mrs Beaufoy.[3] Wishing you and her all happiness,

I am Dear sir, with great respect,
Your obliged and humble servant
Rich*d* Price

When you see Dr D'Ivernois[4] deliver to him my best thanks for the present of his History of the revolutions of Geneva. I am beginning to read it, and believe I shall find myself much interested by it. Since writing the above I have copy'd the account of the Navy debt, and therefore it need not be returned.

---

3. Elizabeth Beaufoy, née Jenks, daughter of William Jenks of Shifnal, Salop.

4. Sir Francis D'Ivernois (1757–1842), writer. His *Tableau Historique et Politique des Révolutions de Geneve dans le Dix-Huitième Siècle* was published in Geneva in 1782; an English translation by J. Farell was published in London in 1784 under the title *An Historical and Political View of the Constitution and Revolutions of Geneva in the Eighteenth Century.*

From Samuel Vaughan

Philadelphia 4th January 1785

My dear Sir,

The admiration entertained in common with the liberal minded for your character and active endeavours for promoting the public weal, together with my sincere affection, arising from personal knowledge of your disinterested motives, ability and activity in the public cause, and that at an important crisis, have often and repeatedly prompted the wish of keeping up our friendly intercourse by correspondence, now obstructed by absence, but when I reflected on your constant engagements in your pastoral charge, your political and philosophical pursuits, with your extensive connections, I was unwilling to break in upon your more important time, more especially as from long confinement with the gout and other avocations, I had not the means of information worth your notice; yet as a testimony of my sincere regard, I having lately made a tour to the N.E., I shall venture to hazzard such observations as have occurred to me. Those made on the tour (the necessarily too rapid) I have sent to my son Benjamin, to which (if worth perusal) I refer you.

On my first arrival in a country just emerging from a state of civil war confusion and temporary bancruptcy, I was most sensibly struck with the remarkable chearfulness, ease and tranquility of the inhabitants, in active business, without the vestige of those consequences generally attending devastation and civil war wherein the most oppulent American families were reduced to pennury and want while some of the most inferior rank, by privateering and other less honorable means, have been raised to oppulence; yet, set aside the remains of ruined houses, every thing appears tranquil and happy. Hence may be concluded the Americans are not destitute of philosophy or submission to providential dispensations; at the same time, it must also be confessed that altho the very *severe* services and sufferings of the Army in the field had fitted and prepared them for returning to their more *easy* occupations of domestick life, (insomuch that great numbers raised to consequence and command have condescended to the most humble walks in life so that both in town and country, houses of entertainment are generally kept by Captains and Majors and Colonels, while others are building Log-houses and opening ground in woods, hitherto the habitations of wild beasts;) yet, from habits contracted in the field and especially with their gay volatile allies in Camp and cities, they have aroused a general relaxation of that moral simplicity of manners that prevailed before the war, with a prepensity in the towns to shew, expence and dissipation [   ] that living in Cities is become more expensive than in London (?), and

---

ORIGINAL: Library of Congress. TEXT: Original.

which must cause many bankruptcies in Trade which is greatly overdone and many living on the proceeds of objects procured on credit, and this has been highly promoted and encouraged by the unseasonable enormous credit, injudiciously by the Merchants and Manufacturers in England, who must be severe sufferers, as the produce of the Continent will not for years be sufficient to pay for the Importations since the peace (as for the public Debt there are ample resources); this has and must cause the exportation of Bullion, and eventually destroy Credit and bring people in general to their sober senses, to their usual level, and at length a reformation, devoutly to be wished, but this must be a work of time, which will also be requisite for the regulating and establishing wholesome Laws and a good police in the several states. Mean time this of all others is certainly the best country for farmers, labourers and tradesmen to settle in, as land is [procured?] on easy terms, provisions in the Country cheap and plenty, labour universally high, and children (the expensive at home) constitute the wealth of families here, by their early usefulness. This country however is by no means calculated for men of fortune, out of business, to take up their abode for *present* emoluments, [   ] they have future views and objects; but on the whole from the immense extent of country, variety of soil, with the innumerable Rivers, calculated for producing and conveying to each other every necessary of life, (if not of luxury) within themselves, the advantages of foreign trade, toleration, with civil liberty, and security of property, there can be little doubt that that it will become the general Asylum of all the liberal minded in every part of Europe, who prefer those advantages to the restrictions incumbrances and despotism of the old world; nor is it likely to be less favourable to the Arts science and general knowledge, as the Americans are acute and inquisitive, with a great share of persevering emulation. The Seminaries of Learning in this place, Boston, and New York, are respectable, and annually turn out many youth of considerable ability for the learned professions; and those only might be sufficient for the Continent; but it is feared the zeal for other Colleges, and new ones intended up the country, may lessen the respectability of the old Institutions and shortly dwindle into common schools; but it may be expected the large extensive field in the new world for the extension of natural knowledge, philosophy, and general knowledge will not only stimulate the natives but invite many of the first ability to prefer the tour of North America (as yet almost unexplored) to that of Europe, where little new is to be expected, I wish I could be equally sanguine in my expectation of rational Religion being cultivated and promoted; at present the English, Irish, and Germans, are of narrow calvinistical principles, the Dissenting Ministers mostly Scotch; but as the people here are observant and think for themselves, there is reason to hope, a concern of the last importance cannot long escape their notice, attention and investigation, which will readily lead them to understanding and knowledge of the truth. Having no Unitarian place of worship here, I officiate regularly as high priest in my own family, which is the greatest, if not the only objection I have to the Country. Mr Hazlet[1] gave evening lectures last winter, and preached occasionally, was well attended and much liked, and had he taken the advice of his friends, he might have had a good School, and there was a prospect of procuring him a professorship of History and Geography, in which case it was thought he might have raised a congregation; but tho happy in his private study, he was thoughtless, unaccomodating, and changable with respect to the world; he is now in Boston, where I hear he might have had a settlement in a congregation of Unitarians, but for like causes and imprudence. He often preaches occasionally and has a guinea for the [   ]; I feel for him, but much more for his family.

How long will your Administration remain under their fatal delusion? vain will be their endeavours to exclude American vessels from the West India trade, as Canada and Nova Scotia cannot furnish the necessary supplies as wanted, more especially for the Leeward Islands; nor can ships from England by circuituous voyages carry them; therefore for American enterprise and the Islands wants, that trade must be carried on clandestinely, or to free ports, at an exorbitant expence to the purchaser; besides America may retaliate. When I reflect on the continuance of such measures, your unnatural parties, your intolerable burthens, the loss of power and energy of the few representatives of the people, while the form only remains of that excellent constitution that has stood the test of Ages (and which deludes and culls the comonalty of the people who only can bring about a reformation to the original principles of Government) I am dejected and deeply deplore the beloved Country and people I have left that justified in bringing my family to the New World, where the principles of Government are not only original, but firmly stand; and are cal[   ] the permanant security of the rights of mankind [   ]. I have not time to [write?] the family by this convey[   ]. You may acquaint my sons that the family are all well; they all have you in frequent remembrance and most heartily join with me in affectionate regard and esteem for yours, Doctor Priestley's and Mr Lindsey's[2] families; and I request your giving my best respects to and wishes for our friends of the Club at the London Coffee House,[3] many of whom I often wish to see in America, but happiness was not intended to be the portion of Mankind in this world, yet have I a lively hope and confidence in meeting with you and other beloved friends in that world, where improvement and enjoyment will be united through the endless stages of eternity; in the mean time believe me to be with sincerity and truth,

My dear Sir,
Your ever affectionate
Sam*l* Vaughan

1. William Hazlitt.
2. Theophilus Lindsey, see Vol. I, 147.
3. The Honest Whigs.

P.S. I have not been able to procure a convenient residence for my family; nor I am I yet determined in which state I shall pitch my tent. I shall now defer any determination, until the arrival of my son, shortly expected.

To Christopher Wyvill

Newington-Green, Jan 6th, 1785

Dear Sir,

I have received with particular pleasure your Letter, and return you my best thanks for it. I rejoice to find that Mr Pitt is so much in earnest and reforming

---

PRINTED: Christopher Wyvill, *Political Papers*, (York, n.d.), IV, 445–47. TEXT: Christopher Wyvill, *Political Papers*. Wyvill appends the following note:

"This, and the preceding Letter, by Dr Price [see R.P. to Christopher Wyvill, 12 Dec. 1782] are the only Letters of his which have been preserved, or, as he believes, were received by the Editor. The candid Reader, who has considered them with attention, will probably agree with him in the opinion, that they are written with a spirit of moderation and affection for the Constitution, on its genuine principles, which is far remote from any resemblance to the fierce revolutionary spirit imputed by Mr Burke to Dr Price. If plans of Revolution had been floating in his mind *at this time*, it is highly probable, that some mark of dislike to the Constitution, some indication of a mind which contemplated more extensive changes in our form of Government, some phrase expressing that atrocity of temper which could encounter, and even promote the convulsions of a Revolution, without fear or scruple, would have escaped him. This might have been expected, especially in this second letter, which was written by Dr Price when his mind must have been elevated with hope, from Mr Pitt's recent declaration of support. But nothing like it is observable; and therefore it is reasonable to conclude, that, at this time, the views of Dr Price were confined to improve and perpetuate the Constitution. How far Dr Price may have approved Republican institutions in countries which are in circumstances more or less different from those in which Britain is placed, the Editor is unable to determine. He could offer nothing but his own conjecture, or what others may have conjectured, perhaps on no better grounds. But let it be admitted, for argument, that Dr Price approved the Republican Government of America; that he even thought superior happiness was attainable in a society so constituted, than under a Monarchal Government like that of Britain. Yet, in perfect consistence with this supposition, he may have been adverse, in speculation and in practice, to any Republican innovation here. He may have thought our limited Monarchy better adapted to a rich, luxurious, and extensive country like this, in which, though property be widely diffused, it is yet divided, in not a few instances, with great inequality: he may have thought that a moderate Reform was all that could be hoped, from pacific exertions; and greater changes were impracticable, without plunging the country into calamities too horrid to be compensated by any form of Government whatever. Such may have been the light in which the question was considered, *at this time*, by the mild and venerable Price; and his Correspondence, here published, confirms the supposition.

But if this were his settled way of thinking in 1785, how great is the improbability that he had changed his sentiments in 1790, and turned his endeavours to effect a Revolution here, after recent experience had taught him how little disposed the Nation was, when lulled by Peace, to support even that moderate scheme of reform which the Minister himself had brought forward.

It is true that the more recent Revolution in France had re-animated the hopes of our moderate reformers, and Dr Price has expressed with them his exultation at the rising spirit of Liberty in England, and the fall of Despotism in France. It may be true that some enthusiastic men had then

the Representation of the Kingdom.[1] No object surely can be more important to a People who wish to preserve Liberty. I had before received this information from a friend of Mr Pitt's; and, in consequence of it, had writ to some friends in the country, in order to put them upon procuring support for him by Petitions.[2] London and Westminster will, I doubt not, be ardent in the business; and I am glad to learn from you, that Yorkshire is likely to resume its zeal. This makes me hope something will be done; for I cannot feel any

---

formed extravagant hopes, or even criminal designs of a Revolution here. But, on such grounds, it would be highly uncandid to rank Dr Price with these rash Innovators. His advanced age, his political experience, his cool and calculating head, his moderation during the struggle for Reform, his temper, his habits, his virtues, all forbid the suspicion. Against the combined force of these considerations, what would it have availed Mr Burke, in less heated times, that Dr Price had publicly expressed a wish that the Parliament of Britain might become a National Assembly?[3] instead of that mockery of Representation, which in this Letter he condemns. In more equitable times a glowing word would have been easily excused; a concise sententious phrase, innocent in one sense, deeply criminal in another, would have been construed in the obvious and inoffensive sense; and the long-established character of a good man would have been unimpaired by the malignant cavils of his Accuser. Or what blame, what suspicion could have been fixed on Dr Price, in any times but those of extreme infatuation, for having maintained that the British Government stands on the ground of *Public Consent*, and that a Government standing on that ground must be liable to modification or change by the same authority to which it owed its existence. These are the doctrines of the most sincere defenders of our Constitution from the age of Locke to that of Price. In such wishes and opinions there is neither Treason nor Sedition; and that he publicly uttered them, furnishes not the shade of a pretence to charge this excellent Man with revolutionary designs. In times uncommonly jealous, the misrepresentations of his eloquent, but most passionate Adversary, did succeed, and in such times only they would have succeeded to render Dr Price an object of public distrust. His feeling mind was too much hurt by the unmerited insults of his Opponent, and the injustice of the Public, and his grey hairs were soon brought with sorrow to the grave. He died the victim of Calumny and Political Intolerance; but Posterity will do him justice."

[For a further defence of Price by the same author see Christopher Wyvill, *A Defence of Dr Price and the Reformers of England* (London, 1792). For an assessment of the republican and democratic elements in Price's thought, see my 'Neither Republican nor Democrat,' *The Price–Priestley Newsletter*, No. 1 (1977), 49–60; and for a different interpretation see Jack Fruchtman, Jr., *The Apocalyptic Politics of Richard Price and Joseph Priestley; a Study in Late Eighteenth Century English Republican Millenialism* (Philadelphia, 1983).]

1. In Dec. 1784, Pitt's interest in Parliamentary Reform revived and Christopher Wyvill was invited to organize an extra-Parliamentary campaign to promote it. Pitt was resolved, as Wyvill put it in a letter to James Wilkinson dated 9 Dec. 1784, to "put forth his whole power and credit, *as a man* and *as a minister*, honestly and boldly to carry on a plan of reform," (Christopher Wyvill, *Political Papers*, IV, 19). Pitt's proposals were modest: the main feature was a plan which provided for the elimination of 'rotten boroughs' by voluntary disfranchisement, the electors in all cases being handsomely compensated. The seats thus released were to be distributed among the counties and the towns and cities. In addition there was to be an extension of the franchise to include forty-shilling copyholders and some leaseholders, and provision was to be made for the improved conduct of elections. But the project failed. Leave to bring in the Bill was refused on 18 April, 1785.

2. R.P. to [a Member of the Great Yarmouth Church], 15 Nov. 1784.

3. On 4 Nov. 1790, when he presided at a meeting of the Revolution Society, Price proposed a toast, "The Parliament of Britain, may it become a National Assembly." See Appendix to *Preface and Additions to the Discourse on the Love of our Country* (London, 1790).

diffidence with respect to the sincerity of Mr Pitt's zeal in this instance, not-withstanding two objections which I hear often urged against him, and which indeed I cannot answer; I mean the characters of *some* of his associates, who are known to be determined enemies to Reformation, and his not promoting a reformation in *Ireland*, where the body of the people are more alive, and more unanimous than they are here.

It seems to me strange, that no Minister has yet taken the path Mr Pitt seems determined to take, from political views only. Certain it is, that the King would be much greater at the head of an independent, honest, and real Rep-resentation of the Kingdom, than he is at the head of the present Mockery of a Representation, which is so capable, as he found lately, of being turned against him; and a Minister who could exert himself to the utmost in gaining such a Representation for the Kingdom, would be idolized; and, if turned out, would be brought back again, and in time, if it appeared that he persisted in his efforts, and maintained his integrity, would become omnipotent, as Mr Pitt's father once was.

I beg your acceptance of the Pamphlet which will be conveyed to you with this Letter.[4] I have printed but a few copies of it, and they have been almost all sent to America. It is the fruit of warm conviction; but I am afraid some strong sentiments in it will need your candour.

Under a sense of your distinguished character and merit, and with great respect I am, Sir,

Your most obedient and humble servant
Rich. Price

P.S. I find your Letter has been published in the papers; but I am entirely ignorant how it got there, for that which I had the pleasure of receiving has never been out of my own hands, except for about half an hour to be perused by one of my neighbours.

---

4. *Observations on the Importance of the American Revolution.*

From John Wheelock[1]

Dartmouth College 25th January 1785

Dear Sir,

I deferred writing till this time to give you the satisfaction of knowing that your donation arrived yesterday in safety, of which some time since an account was received in your obliging letter of July 25th. The Trustees desire that their most sincere thanks may be accepted. The books will be preserved in the library as a monument of virtue, patriotism, and a system of political oeconomy. What a contradiction of scenes, my dear Sir, does the theatre of human life display! what guides in philosophy and jurisprudence, but how few followers! Eminent lessons of civil policy are acknowledged by all, while in republics most are attached (and ostensibly too) to the interest of themselves or their party. In regard to the last these States have three happy barriers. Equality of property, especially in the north, prevents the idea of undue influence; being without a redundancy of wealth the people have no leasure for partial combinations, while the spirit of industry and gain triumphs over the spirit of faction.

I am sorry that the indisposition of your Lady continues. May nature in the hand of God afford a better remedy than the art of physic. The pains of our friends excite commiseration, and sometimes an anxiety, which even rouses the stoic from his apathy, and much more moves the heart of a true humane philosopher.

The College is in a prosperous way; and I cannot but hope, that, under a divine providence, the wishes of the good respecting it will be greatly answered.

I am much obliged, Sir, by your kind attention to Mr Rowland's plan. It is needless to say how much we should have valued the strictures and emendations of so great a judge. History is subjected to that uncertainty, which proceeds from ignorance, inattention, or prejudice—large sources of error. And, the farther we trace back the annals, the greater is the doubt. But I will

---

ORIGINAL: American Philosophical Society.   PRINTED: *M.H.S.P.* (1903), 324.   TEXT: Original, with the kind permission of the American Philosophical Society.

1. John Wheelock (1754–1817), became the second President of Dartmouth College in 1779 upon the death of his father Eleazar Wheelock, the founder and first President of the College. In 1783 he visited France and Holland in an attempt to raise funds for the College. John and his brother James arrived in London on or about 1 July 1783 and left for America on 3 Oct. 1783. They were shipwrecked off Cape Cod on the morning of 2 Jan. 1784 and lost all their possessions including the collections they had made for the College, about five thousand pounds. See Frederick Chase, *A History of Dartmouth College and the Town of Hanover*, ed. John K. Lord (Cambridge, Mass., 1891), pp. 571–73.

desist, before my pen misguides me too far, by only beging that you would accept of the highest regard and esteem for yourself and your works of a very respectful friend. I am, Sir,

Your most obliged
obedient and humble servant
Jn Wheelock

From Benjamin Franklin

Passy, Feb. 1, 1785.

My dear Friend,

I received duly your kind Letter of Oct. 21, and another[1] before with some of your excellent Pamphlets of Advice to the United States. My last Letters from America inform me that every thing goes on well there; that the new elected Congress is met, and consists of very respectable Characters with excellent dispositions; and the People in general very happy under their new Governments. The last Year has been a prosperous one for the Country; the Crops plentiful and sold at high Prices for Exportation, while all important Goods, from the great Plenty, sold low. This is the happy Consequence of our Commerce being open to all the World, and no longer a Monopoly to Britain. Your Papers are full of our Divisions and Distresses, which have no Existence but in the Imaginations and Wishes of English Newswriters and their Employers.

I sent you sometime since a little Piece intitled, *Testament de M. Fortuné Ricard*, which exemplifies strongly and pleasantly your Doctrine of the immense Powers of compound Interest.[2] I hope you received it. If not I will send you another. I send herewith a new Work of Mr Necker's on the Finances of France.[3] You will find good Things in it, particularly his Chapter on War. I imagine Abbé Morellet may have sent a Copy to Lord Lansdowne.[4] If not, please to communicate it. I think I sent you formerly his *Conte rendu*.[5] This Work makes more Talk here than that tho' that made abundance. I will not say that the Writer thinks higher of himself and his Abilities than they deserve, but I wish for his own sake that he had kept such Sentiments more out of sight.

With unalterable Esteem and Respect, I am ever,
my dear Friend, Yours most affectionately,
B. Franklin.

ORIGINAL: Yale University Library. PRINTED: *M.H.S.P.* (1903), 325. TEXT: Original, with the kind permission of Yale University Library.

1. See R.P. to Benjamin Franklin, 21 July 1784.
2. The author of this piece was Charles Joseph Mathon de la Cour. Price included a translation of it in an appendix to the 1785 edition of *Observations on the Importance of the American Revolution*.
3. J. Necker, *De l'Administration des Finances de la France* (Paris, 1784).
4. Shelburne became the first Marquis of Lansdowne in Dec. 1784.
5. J. Necker, *Compte Rendu, présente au Rois au mois de Janvier, 1781* (Paris, 1781).

From Thomas Jefferson

Paris Feb 1st, 1785.

Sir,

The copy of your Observations on the American Revolution which you were so kind as to direct to me came duly to hand, and I should sooner have acknowledged the receipt of it but that I awaited a private coveiance for my letter, having experienced much delay and uncertainty in the posts between this place and London.

I have read it with very great pleasure, as have done many others to whom I have communicated it. The spirit which it breathes is as affectionate as the observations themselves are wise and just. I have no doubt it will be reprinted in America and produce much good there. The want of power in the federal head was early perceived and foreseen to be the flaw in our constitution which might endanger its destruction. I have the pleasure to inform you that when I left America in July the people were becoming universally sensible of this, and a spirit to enlarge the powers of Congress was becoming general. Letters and other information recently received show that this has continued to increase, and that they are likely to remedy this evil effectually. The happiness of governments like ours, wherein the people are truly the mainspring, is that they are never to be despaired of. When an evil becomes so glaring as to strike them generally they arouse themselves, and it is redressed. He only is then the popular man and can get into office who shews the best dispositions to reform the evil. This truth was so obvious on several occasions during the late war, and this character in our governments saved us. Calamity was our best physician. Since the peace it was observed that some nations of Europe, counting on the weakness of Congress and the little probability of a union in measure among the States, were proposing to grasp at unequal advantages in our commerce. The people are become sensible of this, and you may be assured that this evil will be immediately redressed, and redressed radically. I doubt still whether in this moment they will enlarge those powers in Congress which are necessary to keep the peace among the States. I think it possible that this may be suffered to lie till some two States commit hostilities on each other, but in that moment the hand of the union will be lifted up and interposed, and the people will themselves demand a general concession to Congress of means to prevent similar mischeifs. Our motto is truly "nil disperandum". The apprehension you express of danger from the want of powers in Congress,[1] led me to

---

PRINTED: *Jefferson*: Boyd, VII, 630–31.

1. In *Observations on the Importance of the American Revolution* Price maintained, "Without all doubt the powers of Congress must be enlarged. In particular, a power must be given it to collect, on certain emergencies, the force of the confederacy, and to employ it in carrying its decisions into execution." See Peach, p. 187.

note to you this character in our governments, which, since the retreat behind
the Delaware, and the capture of Charlestown, has kept my mind in perfect
quiet as to the ultimate fate of our union; and that I am sure, from the spirit
which breathes thro your book, that whatever promises permanence to that
will be a comfort to your mind. I have the honour to be, with very sincere
esteem and respect, Sir,

Your obedient and most humble servant,
Th. Jefferson

From Henry Laurens

Charleston 1st Feby 1785

Dear Sir,

At the end of a pleasant Voyage which had commenced at Falmouth the 22d
June I landed at New York the 3d August last—finding a perfect vacation in
the Government of the United States, Congress in recess by adjournment, and
the Committee of the States self dissolved, being on my part exceedingly
desirous of meeting Congress and of obtaining an honourable discharge from
my late Mission, I determined to wait at Trenton for the new Session expected
on the first Tuesday in November. That and many more days passed without a
meeting, when being in a state of uncertainty when or whether nine States
would convene, the depth of Winter looking me in the face, accounts for my
Attornies of the deplorable Situation of my private Affairs, demanding my
immediate presence, with other considerations, I took the Advice and consent
of the Delegates of three States on the spot, and availing myself of their
Opinions entered upon my Journey homewards the 24th November—Bad
Roads and bad Weather were both my opponents. With able horses and
diligent travelling, I did not reach this habitation until the 14th Ultimo. I
found the house unfurnished, repairs unfinished and in very bad condition,
My Son[1] and myself have been hard at Work to make in it a comfortable
provision for my Daughters[2] whom We expect sometime in this or the next
month, this Business has kept us both closely engaged, but I am descending
from public to my own petit concerns. I know Sir, you will grieve, for the
delinquencies above mentioned, don't be too anxious all will come right in due

---

ORIGINAL: The Pierpont Morgan Library. TEXT: Original, with the kind permission of the
Director of the Pierpont Morgan Library.

1. Henry Laurens, Jr. See R.P. to Henry Laurens, 19 Nov. 1782.
2. Martha and Mary Eleanor, see H. Laurens to R.P., 31 Aug. 1782.

time, but as Common Sense replied to me when I was at Trenton and half lamenting at the prospect of our affairs, "We are not yet quite wrong enough." One of these days when leisure permits I will, I can't say with pleasure, the work may give me pain, transmit as much as I am acquainted with of the State of our politics, at present every moment of my time is pledged, with difficulty I have redeemed the few which this hasty performance will occupy.

The 24th Ultimo I had the honor of receiving your very obliging Letter of the 22nd October with a packet containing six Copies of your, "Observations on the Importance of the American Revolution". The general Assembly of this State being then recently convened I distributed five of them, Viz. one to the Governor,[3] One to the Senate, One to the Speaker of the House of Representatives,[4] One to Mr Gervais member of Senate,[5] the fifth to Mr Izard of the other house.[6] I had reserved the 6th for my own reading in the Country, where I intend to go tomorrow for some ten days or a fortnight. What are the Ideas of No. 1. 2. and 4. I can only conjecture from their silence, those of No. 3 & 5. will appear in the inclosed Copy of a Letter from the Speaker to which I have subjoined copy of my Answer. My worthy friend will perceive I persevere in the old plain stile, I shall leave Comments to himself.

I have since perused your particular observations on the Negro trade and slavery which in my view stands all well till we come to, "I rejoice that on this occasion I can recommend to them the Example of my own Country." If I did not know Dr Price to be a Man of Candor and Sincerity, I should suppose this intended as a bitter Sarcasm. Britain is the fountain from whence We have been supplied with Slaves upwards of a century. Britain passed Acts of Parliament for encouraging and establishing the Slave Trade, even for monopolizing it in her own Provinces. The Inhabitants of those Provinces might purchase but not enjoy the benefits arising from a direct trade to Africa. A British Law was specially enacted for making Slaves in the Provinces, Chattels, liable to be seized and sold for payments of Debts, with a long train of &c. Nor is it quite a decided fact that the moment a negro sets his foot on British Ground, he becomes a free Man, Lord Mansfield[7] left this a moot point in his Judgment in

---

3. Benjamin Guerard (1740–88), a lawyer, was Governor of South Carolina from Feb, 1783 to Feb. 1785. His successor was William Moultrie (1730–1805) who held the office until 1787. See John W. Raimo, *Biographical Directory of American Colonial and Revolutionary Governors 1607–1789* (Mechler Books, 1980).

4. John Faucheraud Grimké (1752–1819), was Speaker of the South Carolina House of Representatives in 1785 and 1786.

5. John Lewis Gervais (1741?–1798), a planter merchant. Born in Hanover he emigrated to America in 1764 and entered into partnership with Henry Laurens, Member of House of Representatives (1775–78) and Senate (1779–86) of South Carolina. See *Biographical Directory of the South Carolina House of Representatives* (Columbia, S.C., 1981), III, 256–58.

6. Ralph Izard (1741–1804) represented South Carolina in Congress in 1782. Subsequently he served in the South Carolina House of Representatives and became a member of the US Senate upon the adoption of the Federal Constitution by South Carolina in May 1788.

7. William Murray, lst Earl of Mansfield. See Vol. I, 162.

the cause, Stewart vs. Somerset,[8] tis true indeed by the Quirks and Chicanery of the Attendants of British Courts even Negroes purchased of Englishmen under the sanction of Acts of Parliament, are in effect freed, whenever they arrive within the verge of Parliamentary Jurisdiction. Shame and Disgrace to Britain in one case or the other or in both. Admitting however Sir that in this particular you have erred the Error will not vitiate your principle—the inhumanity, cruelty, Wickedness and Devilishness, which you impute to the Traffic applies in the first instance and more directly to your "own Country". Was not Parliament lately petitioned to prohibit the Slave trade, did they shew the least regard to the Petition. In replying to the Speaker I had almost said, "Neither Moses and the Prophets, nor one rising from the dead" will make Dr Price's doctrine palatable in this Country, but when the poor Slaves shall struggle for themselves, peradventure We may be converted.[9] Slavery in the United States, so far as Virginia Southward is either totally abolished or dwindling. North Carolina, South Carolina and Georgia, reason in the language of Mr Speaker, the time however for general Emancipation will come, I foresee it as clearly as in the year 1776 I foresaw and predicted that Great Britain would lose her Colonies by attempts to enslave the Inhabitants. 13th April.

'Tis uncertain what I had intended to say in conclusion of this when I was interrupted the lst February, from that time to the present moment a variety of business and some sickness have prevented my resuming it, perhaps to intimate the mode of treatment to those Negroes who are called mine, of this at present I shall speak very generally; they are as happy and as contented as

---

8. Somersett's Case (1771–72), 20 *State Trials*, 1, is traditionally regarded as having established that English law will not recognize the institution of slavery, so that a slave brought to England becomes at once a free man. See Sir William Holdsworth, *A History of English Law*, XI, 247. On the interpretation of Mansfield's judgment see E. Fiddes, "Lord Mansfield and the Somersett Case," *Law Quarterly Review*, l (1950), 499–511. Fiddes notes the conflict of interests: between the slave's right to freedom and the slave-owner's right to have his property protected, and argues that "the legal position that he [Mansfield] established was not that a slave in setting foot in England became free, but that he could not be forcibly removed from England to the rigours of American slavery." Holdsworth notes, "It may be true that Lord Mansfield's decision was, not that the slave was free but that the master could not forcibly remove him from England . . . but his decision involved the consequence which Blackstone had previously drawn (*Comm.* i. 424) that 'the law will protect him in the enjoyment of his person and his property,' so that in effect he was free as Blackstone said (ibid., 425); the fact that he might be obliged to serve his master was no proof that he was not free, for that was an obligation to which an apprentice was subject."

9. In his reply to Grimké, dated 31 Jan. 1785, Laurens wrote: "As an apology for presenting a Book, the contents of which I was ignorant of, Permit me Sir, to say, I had received a previous intimation of the work from a judicious friend in London, who in general terms highly applauded it, this circumstance in addition to the celebrated Character of the author and his known friendship to the United States induced me to distribute the Copies immediately upon Receipt, but had I been fully apprized of the parts, thought to be exceptionable, a suppression would have involved a greater crime, setting up my judgement of the merits as a standard." See MS Henry Laurens, *Personal–Miscellaneous Papers*, Rare Books and Manuscripts Division, New York Public Library.

labouring people can be, and some of them to whom I proffered absolute freedom wisely rejected it. On my part I am endeavouring to prevent their ever being absolutely Slaves, time is required for maturing my plan. Your perceive Sir a whole Country is opposed to me, it is necessary to proceed with discretion, to some of them I already allow Wages, to the whole every reasonable indulgence. I have not yet replied to your Letter so fully as I ought, your goodness will indulge me till I have a little more leisure, meantime lamenting the melancholy case of poor Mrs Price, and wishing all that is fit and proper for her in this Life. And recollecting how much these States are indebted to you for the Peace they enjoy, and how much myself as an Individual, I subscribe with great Affection, Esteem and Respect,

Dear Sir, Your sincere friend and much obliged humble Servant.

Henry Laurens

From the President and Fellows of Harvard College

March 3. 1785

Voted, that the thanks of this Corporation be presented to the Reverend Doctor Richard Price of London, a Patron of humanity, a benevolent Assertor of the civil and religious liberties of mankind, and a warm Friend to the United States of America, for his highly acceptable present, to this University, of a collection of his learned and valuable Works: And that the Doctor be informed, that this Body think themselves under great obligations to him for the particular attention he has manifested to the University.

Copy
Attest
Joseph Willard, President

ORIGINAL: Massachusetts Historical Society.   TEXT: Original with the kind permission of the Massachusetts Historical Society.

From Benjamin Franklin

Passy, Mar. 18. 1785.

My Dear Friend,

My nephew, Mr Williams,[1] will have the honour of delivering you this Line. It is to request from you a List of a few good Books, to the Value of about Twenty-five Pounds, such as are the most proper to inculcate principles of sound Religion and just Government. A new Town in the State of Massachusetts, having done me the honour of naming itself after me, and proposing to build a Steeple to their Meeting House if I would give them a Bell, I have advis'd the sparing themselves the Expence of a Steeple for the present, and that they would accept of Books instead of a bell, Sense being preferable to Sound. These are therefore intended as the Commencement of a little parochial Library,[2] for the Use of a Society of intelligent respectable Farmers, such as our Country People generally consist of. Besides your own Works I would only mention, on the recommendation of my Sister, Stennett's Discourses on personal Religion,[3] which may be one Book of the Number, if you know and approve it.

With the highest Esteem and Respect, I am ever, my dear Friend,

Yours, most affectionately

B Franklin

ORIGINAL: American Philosophical Society. PRINTED: *Franklin*: Bigelow, XI, 20. TEXT: Original, with the kind permission of the American Philosophical Society.

1. Franklin's grand-nephew, Jonathan Williams (1750–1815), was a grandson of Anne, Franklin's sister. He joined Franklin in London in 1770, accompanied him to France in 1776 and became agent to the Commissioners of Congress at Nantes. He returned with Franklin to America in 1785.

2. For further details of the parochial library, see R.P. to Benjamin Franklin, 3 June 1785.

3. Samuel Stennett, DD (1728–95). He became assistant to his father at Little Wild Street in 1748 and Pastor in 1758. John Howard was, at one time, a member of his congregation. His *Discourses on Personal Religion* was published in 1769.

To Benjamin Franklin

Newington=Green M*ch* 21*st* 1785

My Dear Friend,

Your letters always make me happy. That which Dr Bancroft brought me has given me great pleasure.[1] I rejoyce to find that the united states are not in

---

ORIGINAL: American Philosophical Society. TEXT: Original, with the kind permission of the American Philosophical Society.

1. See Benjamin Franklin to R.P., 1 Feb. 1785.

that confusion and distress which we are led to believe here. For the sake of the world I wish them all possible prosperity.

I cannot sufficiently thank you for the present you have sent me of Mr *Neckar's* book on the administration of the Finances of *France*. It contains a great deal of important information, and gratifies highly my curiosity. I wish the sentiments in the Chapter on war could be impress'd on the hearts of all the potentates in the world. We are just now alarmed here by the news that a war must take place on the Continent. I have hitherto been disposed to admire the Emperor; but I now execrate his conduct. Perhaps, however, this is a false alarm; and he will take more time for consideration before he suffers his ambition to involve Europe in blood.

The danger of a pirated Edition has obliged me to publish in this country my Tract on the American revolution. The instructive and striking pleasantry in the Testament of M. *Fortune Ricard*, which you have been so good as to send me by Mr *Jackson*, has determined me to make a translation of it an Appendix to this publication. This, I hope, you will not disapprove. It conveys sentiments which I have endeavoured to inculcate in a way that is more likely to make an impression and to be remembered than any serious reasonings. I have left out a line or two in a few places; and I have added a few short notes and remarks, particularly, those at the beginning of the Tables. One of the passages which I have omitted seemed of a nature rather too light for such a publication as mine; and the other passages I either did not understand, or they alluded to customs in France which I could not explain. I have sent you four copies; one of which I wish to be presented to Mr Franklin, your Grandson, one to Mr Jefferson, and one to Mr Adams with my best respects. I should have desired the Abbe *Morellet* to accept of a copy; but I am afraid of making this parcel too burdensome, and he has already done me the honour of accepting the first edition. When you see him be so good as to deliver to him my very respectful remembrances.

Your favourite and mine and the favourite of all that conversed with her; I mean Miss Georgiana Shipley, is now Mrs Hare, and resides at Aix la Chapelle, Mr Hare having been obliged to quit this country for debt. You probably know what inexpressible trouble this has given to the excellent Bishop and his family.

We talk of little here at present besides the propositions for establishing a perfect reciprocity on trade between this kingdom and *Ireland*. These propositions have produced a violent clamour, and there is some danger that the ministry will be overthrown by them. It is obvious, that this gives little room for hoping that a liberal plan will be adopted with respect to the commerce of America.

Mrs Price desires me to put you in mind of her by presenting to you her best respects. She is miserably shatter'd by the Palsy, but retains perfectly her senses and recollection. I live in a constant state of apprehension and anxiety about her. I hope your sad malady does not grow worse. May a life so distinguished and useful be continued as happy as possible. With invariable regard and affection I am ever yours.

Rich*d* Price

Will you be so good as to convey the inclosed letter to Mr Jefferson.[2]

---

2. See R.P. to Thomas Jefferson, 21 Mar. 1785.

To Thomas Jefferson

Newington=Green M*ch* 21*t* 1785

Dear Sir,

I received with peculiar pleasure the favour of your letter by Dr Bancroft, and I return you my best thanks for it.[1] Your favourable reception of the pamphlet which I desired Dr Franklin to present to you cannot but make me happy; and I am willing to infer from it that this effusion of my zeal will not be ill received in America. The eyes of the friends of liberty and humanity are now fixed on that country. The united states have an open field before them, and advantages for establishing a plan favourable to the improvement of the world which no people ever had in an equal degree. Amidst the accounts of distress and confusion among them which we are often receiving in London, the information which you and Dr Franklin have communicated to me comforts and encourages me, and determines me to maintain my hopes with respect to them.

Such an enlargement of the powers of Congress as shall, without hazarding too much public liberty, make it capable of preserving peace and of properly conducting and maintaining the union, is an essential point; and the right settlement of it requires the greatest wisdom. You have gratify'd me much by acquainting me that a sense of this is becoming general in America, and by pointing out to me that character of the confederated governments which is likely to preserve and improve them. The character, however, of popular governments depending on the character of the people; if the people deviate from simplicity of manners into luxury, the love of shew, and extravagance the governments must become corrupt and tyrannical. Such a deviation has, I am afraid, taken place along the sea coast of America and in some of the principal towns, and nothing can be more threatening. It is promoted by a rage for

---

ORIGINAL: Library of Congress.   PRINTED: *Jefferson*: Boyd. VIII, 52ff.   TEXT: Original.
1. See Thomas Jefferson to R.P., 1 Feb. 1785.

foreign trade; and there is danger, if some calamity does not give a salutary check, that it will spread among the body of the people till the infection becomes general and the *new* governments are render'd images of our *European* governments.

There is, I fancy, no probability that *Britain* can be brought to consent to that reciprocity in trade which the united states expect. This is sad policy in *Britain*; but it may turn out to be best for *America*; and should the issue be our exclusion from the American ports, *we* may be ruined; but I do not see that *America* would suffer in its true interest. The fixed conviction, however, among us is that such an exclusion cannot take place, and that we are able to supply America on so much better terms than any other country that, do what we will, we must have its trade. But, Dear Sir, I ask your pardon for detaining you by entering on a subject of which probably I am not a competent judge. I meant by these lines, when I begun them, only to make my grateful acknowledgements to you for the kind notice you have taken of me by your letter; a notice the agreeableness of which is much increased by the high opinion I have been led to entertain of your character and merit. With great respect and every good wish, I am, Sir, your most obedient and humble servant,

Richd Price

I have desired Dr Franklin to convey to you a copy of an edition of my *Observations* &c. which has been just published here. You will find that I have made considerable additions by inserting a translation of Mr Turgot's letter and also a translation of a French tract convey'd to me by Dr Franklin.[2] The Observations are the very same except two or three corrections of no particular consequence; and an additional note in the section on the dangers to which the American states are exposed.

---

2. See Benjamin Franklin to R.P., 1 Feb. 1785, and R.P. to Benjamin Franklin, 21 Mar. 1785.

To William Gordon [Extract]

Newington, March 23, 1785.

I had occasion to apply to Mr Pitt in a case when there [were] rather stronger reasons for expecting compensation than in Cap. Dashwood's case, but I found there was no possibility of success. I am sensible that the United States are a very heterogeneous mass, and that there is danger that events may

---

PRINTED: Extract from MS quoted in Sotheby's Sale catalogue, 23 Nov. 1900, Lot 59. TEXT. Sotheby's Sale Catalogue.

not turn out as happy there as the friends of liberty and humanity in Europe earnestly wish. It is a great satisfaction to my mind that I have, according to the best of my judgment, endeavoured to contribute to this. The issue I leave to providence, hoping, it is working in America for the general good. The United States will indeed be inexcusable if they should not abolish the Negro Slavery. Strengthening the Federal Union by enlarging the powers of Congress I think also an essential point.

To [William] Adams

Newington=Green M*ch* 25*th* 1785

Dear Sir,

Some parts of the pamphlet[1] which I now convey to you will need your candour; but there are few on whose candour I can rely with more confidence, or of whose good sense and liberality I have so high an opinion. I, therefore, put it into your hands without much apprehension; believing that you will not condemn me should you think that I have in any instance carried my Ideas too far. I am conscious of intending, according to the best of my judgment, to contribute the little in my power towards the improvement and happiness of civil society. The united states of *America* are on free and open ground. The cry against innovation, so hostile in this country to reformation and improvement, cannot there influence. No people ever enjoy'd a better opportunity for establishing a plan favourable to an amendment in human affairs. These considerations together with the reason I had to hope that I should be attended to by them, led me to convey to them in Autumn last this pamphlet. It has been now reprinted and published here, because there was danger of its being pirated. Deliver my best respects to Mrs Adams and Miss Adams. May I not expect the pleasure of seeing you in town soon? Mrs Price has been a long time in a state of health that has filled me with anxiety. At the beginning of this winter she was struck a fourth time with the Palsy.

May your valuable life be continued as happy as possible. I always think with pleasure and gratitude of your friendship; and am, Dear Sir, with great respect and affection, your very obedient and humble servant

Rich*d* Price

ORIGINAL: Massachusetts Historical Society. TEXT; Original, with the kind permission of the Massachusetts Historical Society.

1. *Observations on the Importance of the American Revolution.*

To George Washington

[March, 1785][1]

To *George Washington* Esq., lately Commander in chief of the American Armies, but now retired to enjoy the happiness of private life after delivering his country and establishing a Revolution which may prove a blessing to the world, this pamphlet is presented by the Author as a small testimony of the highest respect.

While employ'd in writing this pamphlet the author has been animated more than he can well express by General Washington's excellent circular letter to the united states.[2]

ORIGINAL: Princeton University Library.   TEXT: Original, with the kind permission of Princeton University Library.

1. It is not known when this note was written. Price sent a parcel of the 1784 edition of *Observations on the Importance of the American Revolution* to R.H. Lee for distribution to members of Congress. See R.H. Lee to John Adams, 1 Aug. 1785, *Letters of Members of the Continental Congress*, ed. Burnett (Washington, 1921–26), VIII, 174. On 10 Jan. 1785, Lee sent a copy to Washington, who on 5 Feb. 1785 wrote to Benjamin Vaughan asking him to convey his thanks to "Doctr. Price, for the honble mention he has made of the American General in his excellent observations on the importance of the American revolution addressed 'To the free and United States of America', which I have seen and read with much pleasure." See John C. Fitzpatrick (ed.), *The Writings of George Washington from the Original Manuscript Sources, 1745–99*, 39 vols. (Washington, 1931–44), XXVIII, 62–63; cited by Cone, p. 114. It is conceivable that Price sent this note with the pamphlets he sent to Lee, but a later date is more probable. It was in Nov. 1785 that Washington wrote to Price to thank him for a copy of his pamphlet. At that time he may well have been acknowledging the receipt of a copy of the 1785 edition that appeared in London in March. When it was published Price sent copies of it to Franklin, Jefferson and Adams, and he may well have sent one to Washington as well, accompanied by the note published above. .

2. Washington's circular letter to the Governors of the States, dated 8 June, 1783. See *The Writings of George Washington*, ed. W.C. Ford, 14 vols. (New York, 1889–93), X, 254–65.

From John Adams

Auteuil near Paris, April 8th, 1785.

Sir,

Sometime since I received from Dr Franklin a Copy of the first Edition of your Observations on the Importance of the American Revolution, and lately

---

ORIGINAL: The Adams Papers, Massachusetts Historical Society.   TEXT: Original, with the kind permission of the Trustees of the Adams Papers.

a Copy of the Second.¹ I am much obliged to you Sir for your kind attention to me, and for these Valuable Presents.

I think it may be said in Praise of the Citizens of the U.S. that they are sincere Enquirers after Truth in matters of Government and Commerce, that there are among them as many in Proportion of this Liberal Character, as any other Country possesses. They cannot therefore but be oblig'd to you, and any other writers capable of throwing light upon these objects, who will take the Pains to give them advice.

I am happy to find myself perfectly agreed with you that we should begin by setting Conscience free. When all Men of all Religions consistent with Morals and Property shall enjoy equal Liberty, Property, or rather security of Property, and an equal Chance for Honours and Power, and when Government shall be considered as having in it nothing more misterious or divine than other Arts or Sciences, we may expect that Improvement will be made in the human Character and the State of Society.

But at what an immense distance is that Period. Notwithstanding all that has been written from Sidney and Locke down to Dr P and Abbe de Mably,² all Europe still believes Sovereignty to be a divine Right, except a few Men of letters. Even in Holland, their Sovereignty, which resides in more than four Thousand Persons, is all divine.

But I did not intend to enter into details. If you will permit, I shall be glad to communicate with you [ ] these things.

[No signature]

---

1. See R.P. to Benjamin Franklin, 21 Mar. 1785.

2. Abbé Gabriel Bonnot de Mablay (1709–85), author of several works on morals and politics, including *Le Droit Public de Europe* (1748), *Entretiens de Phocion sur la Rapport de la Morale avec la Politique* (1763), *De la législation* (1776), and *Principes de la Morale* (1784). In the year in which Price's *Observations on the Importance of the American Revolution* appeared Mablay published *Observations sur le Gouvernement et les Lois des Etats-Unis d'Amérique* both in Amsterdam and in Paris. An English translation was published in London. The following year, 1785, another edition *avec des Remarques d'un Républicain* was published in Dublin. Dublin also saw in the same year the publication of an English translation of this edition.

From John Clarke

Boston 11th April 1785

Reverend and honoured Sir,

Your late publication[1] is a noble testimony of that affection, which you always professed for these American States. We are all sensible of the honour you have done us; and we gratefully acknowledge our obligation. Dr Chauncy is delighted with the work. He thanks you most sincerely for the generous concern you have discovered for his country. And he hopes, his country will have wisdom to adopt the measures you have recommended. They certainly must approve themselves to the understanding of every patriot, and the sober reason of every Christian.

My venerable colleague[2] would write to you by this opportunity did not his years and infirmity prevent. But they must be his excuse. The labour of writing has now become intolerable. He has therefore directed me to assure you of his most affectionate regards, and particularly to thank you for the work already mentioned. By my pen he will answer any letters which you may send him in future and I shall think it an honour to have it so employed.

Nothing unusual either in the civil or religious world has occurred this winter. The treatise on Universal Salvation[3] is universally esteemed a monument of the author's ingenuity. Some are afraid to read it. In others it has produced conviction. While a third class have been excited by it to review the principles of their education, and to compare them with the Oracles of truth.

You, Sir, have greatly encouraged liberal inquiry. Your chapter upon that subject can not be sufficiently admired.[4] I think it has already liberated some minds. May it be candidly read by all: and may you have the exalted happiness of seeing rational Christianity flourish by your labour.

ORIGINAL: American Philosophical Society, with shorthand notes, and draft in shorthand of R.P.'s reply to Clarke.   TEXT: Original, with the kind permission of the American Philosophical Society. Price's shorthand notes on the MS. read: From Mr Clark dated Ap[ril] 1785, acquainting me with the reception of my pamphlet. Not answered in August 1785. To say when it is answered that I could not serve Captain Dash[wood]; that I mentioned his case to the President of the Council[5] but found there was no room for hope. Answered by Mr Drake, May [?] 1786.

1. *Observations on the Importance of the American Revolution.*
2. Charles Chauncy.
3. *The Mystery hid from the Ages and Generations.* See William Hazlitt to R.P., 19 Oct. 1784.
4. See Peach, pp. 190–94.
5. Lord Camden (see Vol I, 162) who succeeded Earl Gower as Lord President of the Council in Nov. 1784.

This letter is accompanied by one to Mr Hugh Farmer.[6] You know his place of residence, be pleased to convey it to him. In so doing you will greatly oblige both Dr Chauncy and [myself.]

[Letter is incomplete]

---

6. See Vol. I, 142.

To an unidentified correspondent

Newington Green, Apl 12 1785

Dear Sir,

I am obliged to you for these papers and for the letter to Mr Rippon.[1] There are some parts of them with which I am much pleased; but what is intimated in them concerning an attempt to oblige the Baptists to contribute towards supporting a religious worship from which they dissent gives me much concern. Nothing can be more inconsistent with religious liberty; and it is also contrary to the declaration of rights which forms the foundation of the Massachusetts constitution.[2] I shall be in London on Thursday and shall call at Mr Dilley's[3] about 2 o'clock; and should you happen to be there I shall be glad to meet you

With all good wishes, I am,

Yours

Rich*d* Price

ORIGINAL: B.L. Add. MSS 25388 F. 324 (Copy). PRINTED: *The Baptist Annual Register (1790–1793)*, pp. 387–88. TEXT: Original, with the kind permission of the British Library. The MS has the following endorsement in Rippon's hand, "Copy of a letter from Dr Price. J.R." Another endorsement in another hand reads "Dr Price's letter. Apr. 12 1785." I am indebted to Mr John Stephens for drawing my attention to this MS.

1. John Rippon (1751–1836), Baptist divine. He became pastor of the Baptist Church in Carter Lane, Tooley Street on 1 Aug. 1773, and served in the ministry until his death, a period of 63 years. In 1792 he received the degree of DD at the Baptist College, Providence, Rhode Island. From 1790 until 1802 he edited *The Baptist Annual Register*.

2. The Constitution of Massachusetts was particularly admired by Dissenters in Britain, partly because it embodied the principle that "every denomination of Christians demeaning themselves peaceably and as good subjects of the commonwealth, shall be equally under the protection of the law; and no subordination of any one sect or denomination to another shall ever be established by law", and partly because it stipulated that all taxes raised for the support of religion should be used to support the religious denomination of the person paying the tax. See Bonwick, pp. 145–46, 200–203, and 208; Peach, pp. 199–200; and Joseph Priestley, *Lectures on History and General Policy* (Dublin, 1788), p. 382.

3. Charles Dilly (1739–1807) and his brother Edward (1732–79) were partners in a highly successful firm of publishers and booksellers. They were both Dissenters and published, as *D.N.B.* records, "much in the divinity of that school." On the death of his brother in 1779, Charles continued the business alone. He became Master of the Stationers' Company in 1803. The brothers became famous for the literary dinner-parties held at their house in the Poultry. It was there that Johnson had his celebrated meeting with John Wilkes (see *Boswell's life of Johnson*, ed. Birkbeck Hill and L. F. Powell (Oxford, 1934), III, 64–79).

To John Wilkes

Newington=Green Ap: 28th 1785

Dr Price presents his respectful compliments to Mr Wilkes. He has recollected that he told Mr Wilkes that he would send him the inclosed paper; and he is sorry that it has not been sent sooner. The Tables with the explanations and remarks have been for some time in Mr Pitt's hands; but Dr Price does not know how far the plan they contain will or will not be adopted.

ORIGINAL: The British Library, Add. MSS 30872 f. 266.   TEXT: Original, with the kind permission of the British Library Board.

From Jonathan Trumbull, the Elder[1]

Lebanon 29th April 1785

Sir,

I have received and return you my best thanks for your most agreable Letter of the 8th October last with the Tract you did me the Honor to send with it.[2] My farewell Address to our General Assembly was done with sincere intentions to promote the public good, and it gave satisfaction to the mind to meet with the Approbation of good Men, and that you especially entirely agree with my Sentiments.

Your Tract I have distributed to such as will I trust make a good use of it; it hath been printed in our Newspapers, and also reprinted at Hartford, and will undoubtedly prove very Serviceable. I repeatedly perused it with pleasure, instruction and profit. Your Observations and Advice I think of the Utmost Importance, and needs no Apology. M. Turgot's letter is very excellent, much to that good Minister's honor and to be highly regarded.

As the Establishment of the independence of these united States gives a new

ORIGINAL: The Connecticut Historical Society.   TEXT: Original, with the kind permission of The Connecticut Historical Society. The outside of the letter has: Copies/ 30th April 1785/ To/ Dr Price and Colonel John Trumbull/ sent Colonel Jonathan Trumbull/ To Boston/ at Mr West's Newman Street Oxford Road/ London.

1. In a draft of a letter to his son on the same day, the MS of which is also in the of Connecticut Historical Society, Jonathan Trumbull writes: The Enclosed to Dr Price you will deliver to him. I am much pleased with His Observations. The pamphlets he sent me are disposed among Friends.

2. See R.P. to Jonathan Trumbull, the Elder, 8 Oct. 1784, with which Price enclosed a copy of *Observations on the Importance of the American Revolution*.

direction to the Civil Affairs of the World, so Dr Seabury's³ plan,⁴ whereof my Son acquainted me in one of his Letters, and I conclude you are informed, may make a new Era in the History of Religion, to advance that liberality and Wisdom, which will promote the happiness of Mankind.

In my retirement, I heartily wish for the Literary correspondence of Friends, among which I have the happiness to reckon you one highly esteemed

by Sir

Your much Oblidged and most Obedient humble Servant

Jon*th* Trumbull

---

3. Samuel Seabury (1729–96), Bishop of Connecticut and Rhode Island. He graduated from Yale in 1744, and until the outbreak of the War of American Independence he served the Episcopalians at Huntington, New Brunswick, Jamaica (Long Island), and Westchester. On a visit to England in 1752 he was ordained priest. He was Loyalist in his sympathies and in 1776 had to take refuge on Manhattan Island where he served as a chaplain to the British forces. In June 1783 as Bishop-elect of Connecticut he went to England to seek consecration, which, being refused by the English Archbishops, he received at the hands of the Scottish Episcopalians at Aberdeen in Nov. 1784. In 1789 he became the first Presiding Bishop of the Protestant Episcopal Church in America, and in 1790 he was declared Bishop of Rhode Island. When Trumbull wrote this letter Seabury was returning to America as Bishop of Connecticut. Seabury believed that he had been refused consecration by the English Primates because of the influence on Pitt of the Dissenters, "particularly the Reverend Dr Richard Price"; his reasons were not well grounded for Price was not averse to "Spiritual Bishops" as the warm welcome he extended at a later date to the consecration of Samuel Provoost and William White testifies. See Bruce E. Steiner, *Samuel Seabury 1729–1796. A Study in the High Church Tradition* (Ohio University Press, 1971), p. 207. For Price's opinion of Seabury see his letter to Ezra Stiles, 5 Dec. 1785.

4. Trumbull is probably referring to Seabury's proposals for the creation of an American Episcopate which he drafted in 1777. See "Proposals for establishing the Church of England in America" in Samuel Seabury Papers, General Theological Seminary, New York, cited by Steiner, p. 182. Seabury was anxious that the functions of the Bishop should be conceived largely in spiritual and ecclesiastical terms. The powers to be given to them were to be the minimum necessary to secure an effective diocesan administration. The only coercive authority over laymen would be the right to cite them as witnesses in cases involving delinquent clergymen. Bishops were, however, to be members of the councils of the colonies included in their dioceses. (Steiner, ibid.) Doubtless, it was the emphasis placed upon the spiritual and ecclesiastical functions of the Bishops that enabled Trumbull to recommend Seabury's plan in such warm terms to Price.

To the Marquis of Lansdowne

Newington=Green May 6*th* 1785

My Lord,

I should have writ to your Lordship sooner, had I not been disappointed in my expectations with respect to the Clergyman who I thought would have

---

ORIGINAL: Bowood. TEXT: Original, with the kind permission of the Marquis of Lansdowne.

answer'd your views at Calne. He is Brother to the partner in trade of one of my friends in the City and curate in a Parish in Yorkshire, disposed to Methodism and an acceptable preacher among the common people, but I have lately found that he does not chuse to quit his present situation. There are two more zealous Clergymen of the same cast about whom I am enquiring; but I enquire to some disadvantage, because I cannot give a distinct answer to some questions that are asked, particularly, the question what the encouragement is likely to be in point of income.

Your Lordship's absence was much lamented last tuesday at the Dispensary dinner.[1] The company was considerably larger than usual.

I can say little that is not better known to your Lordship about public affairs. Mr Pitt in my opinion judges very wrong in delaying as he does the establishment of a plan of redemption. Nothing is so necessary. Merely the laying out of a plan and marking its progress in an Act of Parliament would have a great effect, and had this been done last year, and at the same time one or two new taxes laid under the denomination of *Redemption* taxes to be inviolably apply'd, the public would by this time have begun to acquire a conviction that its debts were in the way to be reduced, a disposition to favour strong measures for perfecting the plan would have taken place, and the stocks would probably have been in a very different state. But instead of this, Mr Pitt has chosen to wait for such an increase of the productiveness of the *present* taxes as shall bring in a sufficient surplus; and on the poorest and most precarious grounds he has endeavoured to lead the public to expect that such an event will happen in another year. Thus he loses an opportunity of gaining for himself the greatest honour; and two years of peace have been wasted. There is such a conviction in the Alley that your Lordship would go upon different measures, that every rumour of your coming into power has a tendency to raise the funds.[2]

Mr Watken the surgeon tells me that he is in possession of a petition to the King, and that in order to give it more weight he wishes he could find the means of engaging your Lordship to present it. I have promised to mention this. Mr Watken says that it is a petition for the continuance of a stipend to which no objections are likely to be made.

Mrs Price sends her best respects to Lady Lansdown and your Lordship. She continues in her usual low and broken state. In hopes of seeing you soon in town I am, my Lord, with every good wish and invariable regard,

Your Lordship's most obedient and humble servant

Richd Price

---

1. The dispensary movement began in 1769. It was a charitable movement, its aim being to establish centres at which the poor might attend for free medicine and advice. See Dorothy George, *London Life in the Eighteenth Century*, (London, 1966), p. 62.

2. On 11 April Pitt had told the House of Commons that he hoped that in the coming year there would be a surplus on the revenue of a million pounds which could be devoted to the redemption of debt. *Parl. Hist.*, XXV, 420.

If Mr Barre is at Bowood deliver my respectful compliments to him. I was much obliged to him for the honour he did me in calling upon me before he left London.

To James Bowdoin

Newington=Green near London May 31*st* 1785

Sir,

I received with particular satisfaction your kind note and the copy printed at Boston of my pamphlet on the *American* Revolution.[1] Your attention to me in this instance does me great honour and deserves my best thanks. I commit to Providence this attempt to assist the united states in making such an improvement of their present situation as may render it a blessing to them and to the world. I may be mistaken in many points; but I am conscious of having no other intention than to promote, according to the best of my judgement, the best interests of society. There has been lately an edition of this pamphlet publish'd in London with a translation of Mr Turgot's letter and some other additions. I have sent a few copies of this edition to Boston by Mr Jackson, who, probably, will be arrived there long before this letter can reach you, which is to be convey'd in a packet directed to two Brothers of the name of *Lewis*, who have for some time resided at Boston and carried on the business of Linnen=drapers there. I am informed that these two young men are, on account of their coming immediately from Hallifax, suspected to be Tories and refugees. But no suspicion can be more unjust. There are few families with which I have been so long and so well acquainted. The father was a dissenting minister in this country of the best character and principles. He left six sons and a daughter who, I believe, are all of them virtuous and worthy and zealous friends to civil and religious liberty and American independence. The daughter has a large family and makes a valuable part of my congregation. I hope you will have the goodness to excuse me for mentioning these particulars. I mean nothing but to prevent two honest men from suffering by a groundless suspicion; and my principle intention in this letter is to convey to you my grateful acknowledgements of the notice you have taken of me, and to assure you that, with great respect and all good wishes, I am, Sir, your very obedient and humble servant

Rich*d* Price

ORIGINAL: Massachusetts Historical Society.   TEXT: Original, with the kind permission of the Massachusetts Historical Society.

1. This edition was published by Powars and Willis in 1784, see "Checklist", p. 99.

I have just seen Mrs Temple. I find that it is probable that you have now received the highest testimony of approbation that can be given by the voice of a free people.[2] Should this be the case, I hope you will pardon the impropriety in my manner of addressing you and accept my sincere congratulations.

2. Bowdoin was elected Governor of Massachusetts in May, 1785.

To the Marquis of Lansdowne

Newington=Green June 2d 1785

My Lord,

I return you many thanks for the letter with which I was honoured about a fortnight ago. I am ashamed of having given you the trouble of getting my tables transcribed. When I mentioned this I meant that your Lordship might keep my papers upon condition I could be saved the trouble of taking a copy of them. I shall, therefore, leave one of the copies which have been sent me at Lansdowne=House and hope you will be so good as to accept it.

I am concerned to find that your Lordship intends so long an absence from London as till next January. Mr Pitt, I think, might go on better with your Lordship's counsel and assistance. The tax on shopkeepers is an injudicious, partial and oppressive tax, and will make him unpopular.[1] It would have been better to have given it up immediately, for it will produce so much discontent that probably it will be necessary to give it up in the next or following year. I cannot conceive why this class of people, generally some of the poorest and already so much burden'd, should be selected from the rest of the kingdom to be the objects of taxation. The tax upon female servants is likewise exceptionable.[2] It subjects to the heaviest burdens those who have the largest families of children, and whom it has been the policy of the wisest states to entitle to exemptions. In short such a multiplicity of little, vexatious and teazing taxes is enough to make the kingdom mad. It is a pity they cannot be reduced to a few capital taxes.

I am by no means sufficiently informed to be able to judge of the Irish

ORIGINAL: Bowood.   TEXT: Original, with the kind permission of the Marquis of Lansdowne.
   1. The shop tax was introduced in 1786, and proved to be, as Price predicted, highly unpopular. It was withdrawn in April, 1789. See Binney, p. 72.
   2. In 1780 North had introduced a tax on male servants (exempting agriculture, manufacture or any pursuit from which the employer made a profit). In 1785 this tax was increased and extended to female servants. See Binney, pp. 68–69.

propositions,[3] but I find it difficult to reconcile myself to them. It appears now that had Mr Pitt done what he was going to do and what he was near doing, that is, passed these propositions in their first form, great inconveniencies would have arisen; and if he has not taken care to be assured that his amendments will pass in Ireland, he will be more embarrassed than ever. I like much the principles in Dean Tucker's pamphlet.[4] I am for demolishing all monopolies and for rendering trade as well as religion and government, free thro all the world. But it must be consider'd that this Kingdom is peculiarly circumstanced in consequence of the burden of debt which it has to sustain, a burden vast and unparallel'd. On this account it cannot now part with its monopolies. It is like a building on a false bottom which cannot be taken away and a better substituted without the utmost danger.

I have just read Mr *Craufurd*'s Essay on the resources for re-establishing the finances of Great Britain.[5] It is one of the strangest productions I ever read. If he is not crazy, he cannot be serious.

Your Lordship knows probably that Dr Franklin has obtained leave to withdraw and return to America, and that Mr Jefferson is appointed in his room. Mr Adams is arrived in London as minister plenipotentiary from Congress to our court with an appointment of £1700 *per Ann.*

Count Sarsfield[6] did me the honour to call upon me last week. He brought me a present from the Marquis de Condorcet[7] of a Quarto volume which he has just publish'd entitled an Essay on the application of Algebra to the prob-

---

3. On 7 Feb. 1785 Thomas Orde introduced ten resolutions in the Irish Commons for the regulation of Anglo-Irish affairs. They provided for the liberalization of trade between the two countries and the provision of an Irish contribution towards maintaining the naval forces of the Empire. These proposals aroused fierce opposition, especially in Britain, from those whose interests were safeguarded by protectionist policies. When Pitt's measures were debated in the House of Commons in May, the original ten resolutions had been transformed into sixteen propositions embodying many concessions to the Opposition. They passed the House of Commons at Westminster but failed in the Irish House. Pitt suffered a severe reverse, but whether his failure was attended by the embarrassments that Price expected is more questionable. According to John Ehrman, "When the Propositions failed, and the system of protection was left intact, Ireland's economy flourished for the best part of a decade." (*The Younger Pitt* (London, 1969), p. 213.)

4. Josiah Tucker, *Reflections on the Present Matters in Dispute between Great-Britain and Ireland* (Dublin, 1785).

5. *An Essay on the Actual Resources for Re-establishing the Finances of Great Britain* (London, 1785).

6. Guy-Claude, Comte de Sarsfield (1718–1789), a French officer and diplomat of Irish extraction (see Franklin: *Papers*, XIV, 205, and Richard E. Amacker, *Franklin's Wit and Folly: the Bagatelles* [New Brunswick, N.J., 1953], 175). According to the *Annual Register* (XXX [1789], 210), he was the great grandson of "the gallant General Sarsfield who so greatly distinguished himself at the battle of Limerick". John Adams considered him to be "one of the most learned and sensible French Noblemen" he had known (see *Jefferson*: Boyd, XVII, 437n.).

7. Marie Jean Antoine Nicolas Caritat, Marquis de Condorcet (1743–94), mathematician and philosopher. He was elected to the Perpetual Secretaryship of the Academy of Sciences in 1777, and to the Académie Francaise in 1785. His *Essai sur l'Application de l'Analyse aux Probabilités des Décisions prises à la Pluralités des Voix*—the work presented to Price—was published in 1785, but the work by which he is best known, *Esquisse d'un Tableau Historique des Progrès de l'Esprit Humain* was

ability of decisions by a plurality of voices. It seems a learned work full of analytical deductions.

Mrs Price is a little less depress'd than she has been. She sends her best respects. I cannot leave her for any time without giving her and myself too much pain and anxiety; and therefore I shall probably stay at home all the summer.

Your Lordship has seen in the News=papers that Alderman Atkinson[8] is dead. He has made a great noise and bustle, and rose from a mean station to wealth and honours. But what does it all now signify?

I am glad that your Lordship has determined to employ again the Baptist minister, and I heartily wish your excellent views in this instance may be answer'd.

I have just received a letter from Sir Francis Hutchinson in which he laments the ill policy of administration in abolishing franking between England and Ireland because it checks the free intercourse between the two kingdoms. But I am in danger of tiring your Lordship. My very respectful compliments wait on Lady Lansdown. With gratitude for all your attention to me and great respect, I am, my Lord, your Lordship's most

obedient and humble servant

Rich*d* Price

written towards the end of his life when he was hiding from his Jacobin persecutors. This work embodied the doctrine of the continuous and indefinite perfectibility of man, a doctrine of which he claimed Turgot, Price and Priestley were the "first and most brilliant apostles". See *Sketch for a Historical Picture of the Progress of the Human Mind*, trans. J. Barraclough (London, 1955), p. 142.

0. In 1775 the firm in which Richard Atkinson was the dominant partner, Mure, Son and Atkinson, received a contract to supply the armed forces in America with rum. This and subsequent contracts became the focus of bitter attacks in Parliament by members of the Opposition on the administration's relations with contractors. It was widely believed that exorbitant prices were being paid by the administrators for supplies, that merchants were making considerable fortunes, and that some of the officials at the Treasury were involved in corrupt practices. (See Baker, pp. 162–75.) He became an Alderman in 1784 (ibid., p. 218n.). At the time of his death his estate was evaluated at £300,000 (Namier and Brooke, II, 32). Atkinson's rum contracts were severely criticized by Horne Tooke and Price in *Facts* which was published anonymously in 1780.

To Benjamin Franklin

Newington=Green June 3d 1785

My Dear Friend,

An affair which interests my compassion a good deal obliges me to send you this letter by the post. A person of the name of *Bourne* in considerable business as a Broker absconded suddenly from London four years ago leaving behind him, to shift for themselves, a wife and *four small children*. During all this time he has not once sent any account of himself to his wife or any of his friends, nor probably would they have heard anything of him if Mr *Bingham* had not told me sometime ago that he had heard of such a person and seen him at Philadelphia. Mr Bingham now says that he saw him lately at Paris; and in compliance with the earnest desire of his wife, has writ to Mr *Craufurd* who pointed him out to him for farther information. With the same view, I take the liberty to write to you, and to request that, if any opportunity offers, you would have the goodness to acquaint him with the great distress of his wife and her wishes that he would take some notice of her and give her some account of himself. I will only add that she is an agreeable and worthy woman with whom he was happy, and that his conduct in this instance is reckoned very unaccountable. It is with pain I make thus free with you fearing I may put you to too much trouble; but I have in some measure been induced to it by the consideration that what I have said of Mr Bourne may prove a direction to you should he, as it is suspected he will make applications to you and resolve to return to America.

I writ to you and Mr Jefferson a few weeks ago, and sent you some copies of the edition lately published here of my pamphlet on the American Revolution.[1]

Mr Williams has given me much pleasure by calling upon me, and bringing me a letter from you. I have, according to your desire, furnish'd him with a list of such books on religion and government as I think some of the best, and added a present to the parish that is to bear your name, of such of my own publications as I think may not be unsuitable.[2] Should this be the commencement of parochial libraries in the states it will do great good.

Mr Williams tells me that you have obtained permission to resign, and that you are likely soon to return to America there to finish your life; a life which, without doubt, will be one of the most distinguished in future annals. Indeed I

ORIGINAL: American Philosophical Society. PRINTED: *Franklin*: Bigelow, XI, 53 (in part). TEXT: Original, with the kind permission of the American Philosophical Society.

1. See R.P. to Benjamin Franklin, 21 Mar. 1785.

2. The MS of the list which Price sent to Franklin does not seem to have survived. But there is extant *A Catalogue of those books in Franklin Library which belong to the Town* ... drawn up by Franklin himself, MS Yale University Library. I am indebted to Professor Leonard W. Labaree for drawing my attention to this document.

cannot wonder that, after being so long tossed on the sea of Politics, and seeing your country, partly under your guidance, carried thro' a hard contest, and a most important revolution established, you should wish to withdraw into rest and tranquillity.

May the best blessings of Heaven attend you, and the sad malady under which you are suffering be render'd as tolerable to you as possible. You are going to the New World. I must stay in this; but I trust there is a world beyond the grave where we shall be happier than ever. I shall be always following you with my good wishes, and remain, with unalterable respect and affection,

Yours
Richd Price

Deliver my respects to Mr Franklin, your Grandson, if at Paris. I wish also to be respectfully remember'd to Mr Jefferson, and the Abbe *Morellet*.
Mr Adams is arrived in London, but I have not yet seen him. The Bishop of St Asaph and his family are just gone to Twyford to stay till Christmas. Mrs Price, sadly broken by the palsy, sends you her respects and wishes.

To Benjamin Franklin

Newington=Green June 5th 1785

Dear Sir,

In a letter which I sent you by the post last thursday[1] I stated to you the sad distress of Mrs Bourne, the wife of Mr Bourne, a Broker in London who four years ago eloped from his family, and after having been in America is supposed now to be at Paris. The Bearer of this, Mr Brocksop, is the Brother in law of Mrs Bourne. From compassion to Mrs Bourne but very inconveniently to himself he has undertaken to go to Paris to enquire after, and if possible, to find out Mr Bourne. I know I can rely so far on your goodness as to request that you would give him any information or assistance that m[a]y happen to be in your power. Mr Bingham has been so kind as to give Mr Brocksop a letter of recommendation to Mr Craufurd. With every good wish, I am, my Dear Friend most affectionately

Yours
Richd Price

ORIGINAL: American Philosophical Society. TEXT: Original, with the kind permission of the American Philosophical Society. The MS bears a note, not in Price's hand: Mr Bp Lodges at the Hotel de York, Rue Jacob.
 1. See R.P. to Benjamin Franklin, 3 June 1785.

From Joseph Clarke[1]

Lying-in Hospital, Dublin
June 9, 1785

Sir,

In your very useful Treatise on Life Annuities, &c. you remark, that "it has been observed, that the Author of nature has provided, that more *males* should be born than females, on account of the particular waste of males, occasioned by wars and other causes. That perhaps it might have been observed, with more reason, that this provision had in view that particular weakness or delicacy in the constitution of males which makes them more subject to mortality; and which, consequently, renders it necessary that more of them should be produced, in order to preserve in the world a due proportion between the sexes."[a] And further, you elsewhere remark, that "the *facts* recited at the end of your fourth Essay *prove*, that there is a difference between the mortality of males and females; but that you must however observe, that it may be *doubted*, whether this difference, so unfavourable to males, be *natural*; and that there are facts which prove that you have reason for such a doubt."[b] After stating a number of very satisfactory facts of this kind you remark, that "the inference from them is very obvious; that they seem to shew sufficiently, that human life in males is more brittle than in females, only in consequence of adventitious causes, or of some particular debility which takes place in polished and luxurious societies, and especially in great *towns*."[2]

What those adventitious causes are, or how this particular debility is produced and operates, are questions which appear to me highly interesting and curious. I have therefore been at considerable pains to examine and arrange a very accurate and extensive registry in such a manner as I hope will throw some light on these questions. As it is to the accuracy of modern registers that we are originally indebted for our knowledge of the facts in question, I apprehend, it is from the same source only that we shall be enabled satisfactorily to explain them.

(a) [*Observations on Reversionary Payments*, 4th ed. (London, 1783)], Vol. I, p. 373.
(b) [Ibid.,] Vol. I, p. 247.

PRINTED: *Phil. Trans.*, LXXVI (1786), part 2, 349–56. TEXT: *Phil. Trans.*
The notes preceded by letters of the alphabet in lower case are from *Phil. Trans.* The material within square brackets has been added by the present editor.
  1. Joseph Clarke (1758–1834), physician. Educated at Glasgow and Edinburgh Universities, graduating in medicine from the latter in 1779. In 1781 he began his career at the Lying-in Hospital in Dublin, becoming Master of the hospital in 1786, a post which he held for seven years. He retired from practice in 1829. See Robert Collins, *A Short Sketch of the Life and Writings of the late Joseph Clarke* (London, 1849).
  2. *Observations on Reversionary Payments*, II, 248.

Of the registry inclosed, I beg leave to observe to you, Sir, that it has been kept from its commencement by a man of uncommon accuracy (one of the under-clerks of our House of Commons); and that as the poor women and their children are obliged to pass through his office, before leaving the Hospital, his situation is such that there is no likelihood of his being deceived. It exhibits to our view the occurrence of 28 years in above 20,000 instances: a number which I am inclined to think can hardly appear insufficient for establishing some general inferences and conclusions on a tolerably sure foundation. Although my reasoning on these matters should not appear very conclusive, or my calculations perfectly accurate, yet I flatter myself, that the facts will neither be unacceptable nor useless to you.

I believe it may be safely asserted, that anatomy has not hitherto detected any internal difference between the animal oeconomy of the male and the female, which can be supposed to account for their difference of mortality, more especially in early Infancy; and this (it deserves to be particularly re-marked) is the period during which the chances are much the greatest against male life. It is a matter of common observation that *males, caeteris paribus*, grow to a greater size than females, both *in utero* and every subsequent period of their growth. Consequently, they must meet with more difficulty, and endure more hardship and fatigue, in the hour of birth. Accordingly, practitioners in mid-wifery, taught by experience, know that, when any considerable difficulty occurs in the birth of a child (for example, in all the different kinds of preter-natal labours) they stand a much better chance of saving the life of a female than of a male. It is on this principle we can explain what our registry concurs with others in proving, *viz.* that near one-half more males than females are still-born. Naturalists are agreed, that the head of the human foetus is larger in proportion to its body than that of any other animal; and I believe it is certain, that no animal whatever brings forth its young with so much difficulty, pain, and danger, as a woman. Now as we know that the head contains one of the most important organs of the body to life, it is highly reasonable to suppose, that any additional injury which it sustains in delivery may produce very material effects on the whole system. These effects though often may not be always immediate. They may operate in weakening the male constitution so as to render it more apt to be affected by any exciting cause of disease soon after birth, and less able to struggle against it. It may be asked, how this will apply to the difference of mortality in great towns and country situations? The answer evidently is, that in great towns, rickets, scrophula, and other diseases affecting the bones, and producing consequent mal-conformation of the female sex, are more frequent than in healthy country situations.

There is another circumstance, Sir, which may have some influence in producing that particular *debility* which you mention. It is this: as the stamina of the male are naturally constituted to grow to a greater size, a greater supply of nourishment *in utero* will be necessary to his growth than to that of a female.

Defects in this particular, proceeding from delicacy of constitution or diseases of the mother, must of course be more injurious to the male sex. And although the male children may be so lucky as to escape abortion and the perils of delivery, it is probable, that they will be more apt to languish under disease, or die at some future period, from the application of noxious causes to an originally half-starved frame. To a person little accustomed to consider physiological subjects, this reasoning may appear somewhat obscure. It may, perhaps, be somewhat illustrated by considering that nourishment of the foetus *after* birth which nature has provided for. Suppose every mother in a great city obliged to suckle and nurse her own child, *without* the assistance of spoon-meat;[3] and every mother in the adjacent country to do the same. Of the former there would be not perhaps be one *good* nurse in *five*; and of the latter, perhaps, *not one* bad in *ten*. The difference of mortality that would ensue both to mothers and children thus situated, and the greater sufferings of the male than female sex, may be easily conceived, but not easily calculated. We see that, when a woman conceives twins, and has two foetuses *in utero* to nourish instead of one, it becomes peculiarly fatal both to her and her offspring. The chances are above four to one greater against her than against a woman bringing forth one child, and about two to one against her issue.[c]

Give me leave, Sir, to call your attention a little further to the facts relating to twins. They are singular and curious, at the same time that they serve to confirm some of the preceding reasoning. Near *one-half* more twins die, and near *one-third* more are still-born, than of single children. And why? It is not because they meet with greater difficulties in the birth. On the contrary, it is a known fact, that, being much less than other children, women bring them forth with more ease. Does it not then proceed from a scanty nutrition, by which they are oftener blighted *in utero* than single children; and, when born alive, have less strength to support life through the first stages of its existence.

It is farther worthy of observation, that though *double* the numbers of twins die and are still-born, compared to single children, yet the proportion of male twins lost to females is *less*. Only one-fifth more of the male sex die than of the female, and only one-third more is still-born. Whereas of single children, whose proportional mortality is one-half less, *one-fourth* more of the male sex die, and near double the number is still-born. To what then are we to attribute this lessened mortality in favour of male twins? Probably to their brain and nervous system suffering less during delivery, on account of their heads being much smaller than those of single children. Were I disposed to be prolix, I could offer many more plausible arguments on this subject; but to you, Sir, I am sure they would be unnecessary. There is only one circumstance remaining

(c) Compare the 7th and 14th, 6th and 13th inferences in the annexed extracts [published in *Phil. Trans.* LXXVI (1786), part 2, 363–64].

3. Soft or liquid food to be taken with a spoon, especially by infants or invalids (*O.E.D.*)

relative to the proportion of the sexes, which I cannot pass over in silence. We see evident wisdom in the creation of a greater number of males than females; but why the proportion they bear to each other differs in different countries and situations, and why there should be a seventeenth more males born of single children than twins, are questions which I leave to be decided by those philosophers who understand the theory of generation better than I do. Be this as it may, I am convinced that the majority in favour of the male sex is sooner destroyed than the generality of writers seem to be aware of. Did the limits of this letter permit, I think, I could prove from Dr SHORT's[4] own data,[d] that the majority of males is destroyed long before the common marriageable period; but I shall content myself with an observation or two on the registry before us. If one-half of the whole born in this hospital die before three years, which is the established computation for great cities; and if, on the loss of somewhat more than a *third* of this half, a majority of 1177 be reduced to 483 by a loss of 694, as appears from the registry, it is pretty evident, that by the death of the two remaining thirds, a majority will be left in favour of the female sex. It is obvious, that the statement with regard to twins corroborates this supposition; for of them, instead of a fifth, there is near one *half* dead and still-born, the consequence of which is, that we send out a majority of females. It may be objected, that their males do not bear so great a proportion to the females; and that, therefore, it is not to be expected they should keep up their majority so long. But there is only a seventeenth fewer males produced; whereas it has been already shewn, that there is a much greater proportion between the deaths of single and twin males against the former and in favour of the latter.

Such are the outlines, Sir, of my sentiments on this subject. I have assumed the liberty of addressing them to you without ceremony, as a well-wisher to every member of the republic of letters. I shall be happy, should your sentiments happen to coincide with mine, or if I can be of any farther service in promoting your very laudable inquiries.

I am, Sir, with great respect, etc.

Joseph Clarke

(d)   *New Observations, [Moral, Civil and Medical, in the City, Town, and Country Bills of Mortality* (London, 1780)], p. 72ff.

---

4. See Vol. I, 70.

From Thomas Jefferson

[*circa* 10 June, 1785]

Th: Jefferson begs Doctor Price's acceptance of a copy of these Notes.[1] the circumstances under which they were written, with the talents of the writer, will account for their errors and defects. the original was sent to Monsieur de Marbois[2] in December 1781, being asked for a copy by a friend who wished to possess some of the details they contain, he revised them in the subsequent winter. the vices however of their original composition were such as forbid material amendment. he now has a few copies printed with a design of offering them to some of his friends, and to some other estimable characters beyond that line. a copy is presented to Doctor Price as a testimony of the respect which the writer bears him. unwilling to expose them to the public eye, he asks the favor of Doctor Price to put them into the hands of no person on whose care and fidelity he cannot rely to guard them against publication.

PRINTED: A photograph of the original is reproduced in *Jefferson*: Boyd, VIII, opp. p. 246.

1. Thomas Jefferson's *Notes on Virginia* was first published anonymously in an edition of 200 copies in Paris in 1784.

2. Francois de Barbé-Marbois (1745–1837), diplomat. While he was French Consular-General at the American Congress, he married Elizabeth Moore, the daughter of William Moore, President of Pennsylvania. On behalf of France he negotiated the sale of Louisiana to the United States.

To George Washington

Newington Green June 11th 1785

Dr Price presents his best respects to General Washington, and hopes he does not take an improper liberty by acquainting him that he has known Mr Baynham,[1] the bearer of this for several years; and that he has reason to believe that he is a person of unexceptionable character, friendly to the independence of the united states of America, and an able Anatomist and Surgeon.

ORIGINAL: The Historical Society of Pennsylvania. TEXT: Original, with the kind permission of The Historical Society of Pennsylvania.

1. William Baynham (1749–1814), a son of Dr John Baynham of Carolina. He came to London when he was twenty to study at St Thomas's Hospital where from 1776 onwards he assisted Professor Else as an anatomist. Disappointed at not succeeding Else as Professor of Anatomy in 1781 he practised surgery in London and returned to America in 1785. He established a practice in Essex, Virginia. (*D.A.B.*)

To William Eden

Newington=Green June 15*th* 1785

Dear Sir,

I am much obliged to you for the letter with which you have favoured me. It gives me such pleasure by acquainting me with your favourable acceptance of the papers I sent you. I was encouraged to send them by the experience I have had of your attention and candour. Mr Pitt indeed seems to have been too hasty in the account he gave of the Revenue, and it was injudicious to raise the expectations of the public on such insufficient grounds. Our prospect is certainly discouraging, and nothing but strong measures and a government strong by the respect of the people can extricate us. While the public debt continues such a monstrous load as it is, war is invited and rival powers are tempted to insult us. But this, Sir, you know better than I can tell you. I am very glad that such accounts as you mention are to be laid before the House of Commons. May I request the favour of you to send me a copy of them after they have been presented and printed? It will gratify my curiosity much to be able to compare them with the accounts I have sent you.

Hoping to be excused the liberty I now take with you, I am, with great regard,

Your oblig'd and very obedient servant
Rich*d* Price

ORIGINAL: The British Library, Add. MSS 34,420, f. 29. TEXT. Original, with the kind permission of the British Library Board.

To Thomas Jefferson

Newington=Green July 2nd 1785

Dear Sir,

This letter will probably be deliver'd to you by *Dr D'ivernois*,[1] lately a citizen of Geneva, and the author of an interesting work lately publish'd and entitled *An Historical and Political view of the constitution and Revolutions of Geneva in the 18th century*. He wishes to be introduced to you; and I doubt not but the respectableness of his character and abilities and the active part he has taken in defending the liberties of a republic once happy but now ruined, will recommend him to your notice and esteem. His habits and principles carry his views

ORIGINAL: Library of Congress. PRINTED: *Jefferson*: Boyd, VIII, 258–59. TEXT: Original.
1. Sir Francis d'Ivernois; see R.P. to Henry Beaufoy, 22 Dec, 1784.

to America; and should he remove thither he will make a very valuable addition to the number of virtuous and enlighten'd citizens in the united states.

Accept my best thanks for the account of Virginia[2] which you were so good as to send me by Mr Adams. This has been, indeed, a most acceptable present to me, and you may depend on my performing the condition upon which you have honoured me with it. I have read it with singular pleasure and a warm admiration of your sentiments and character. How happy would the united states be were all of them under the direction of such wisdom and liberality as yours? But this is not the case. I have lately been discouraged by an account which I have received from Mr Laurens in South-Carolina.[3]

Mr *Grimkey* the Speaker of the House of Representatives, and Mr *Izard* have agree'd in reprobating my pamphlet on the American Revolution because it recommends measures for preventing too great an inequality of property[4] and for gradually abolishing the Negro trade and slavery;[5] these being measures which (as the former says in a letter to Mr Laurens[6]) will never find encouragement in that state: and it appears that Mr *Grimkey* thought himself almost affronted by having the pamphlet presented to him by Mr Laurens. Should such a disposition prevail in the other united states, I shall have reason to fear that I have made myself ridiculous by speaking of the American Revolution in the manner I have done; it will appear that the people who have been struggling so earnestly to save *themselves* from slavery are very ready to enslave *others*; the friends of liberty and humanity in *Europe* will be mortify'd, and an event which had raised their hopes will prove only an introduction to a new scene of aristocratic tyranny and human debasement.

I am very happy in the acquaintance of Mr Adams and Colonel Smith.[7] I wish them success in their mission, but I have reason to fear that this country is still under a cloud with respect to America which threatens it with farther calamities. With the greatest respect I am, Sir, Your very obedient and humble servant

Rich: Price

Should Dr Franklin be still at Paris deliver to him my best remembrances.

---

2. See Thomas Jefferson to R.P., [*circa* 10 June, 1785].

3. See Henry Laurens to R.P., 1 Feb. 1785.

4. See *Observations on the Importance of the American Revolution*, "It is a trite observation that 'dominion is founded on property.' Most free states have manifested their sense of the truth of this observation by studying to find out means of preventing too great an inequality in the distribution of property." (Peach, p. 208).

5. "The negro trade cannot be censured in language too severe." (Peach, p. 213.)

6. See Henry Laurens to R.P., 1 Feb. 1785.

7. William Stephens Smith (1755–1816), an American diplomat, was appointed aide-de-campe to Washington in 1781. When John Adams came to London as Minister Plenipotentiary in 1785, Smith was made Secretary of Legation. On 12 June 1786 he married Abigail, John Adams's only daughter.

To Jonathan Trumbull, the Elder

Newington=Green near London
July 9th, 1785

Sir,

I was made happy not long ago by a visit from your son. He brought me a letter from you which could not be but very agreeable to me and for which I return you many thanks.¹ Your candid and favourable reception of my Observations on the American Revolution gives me great satisfaction, there being but few persons by whom I wish so much they may be approv'd. I commit this effort of my zeal to Providence and shall be easy whatever may be its fate, knowing that my intention has been to promote at a very important Crisis the improvement and happiness of civil Society according to the best of my judgment. The accounts I have received from some of the Southern states give me no encouragement. I find my tract has given offence there by advising the gradual abolition of the Negro slavery, and measures for preventing too great an inequality of property.²

You are now Sir, retired from public business and enjoying in tranquillity the happiness arising from reflecting on your services to your country and the prospect of a better state where virtue will meet with its full reward. Being now enter'd into my grand Clima[c]teric I begin also to wish much for retirement. Hitherto I have pass'd thro' life comfortably, and I have reason to be thankful to the benevolent giver of it; but having lately become more a public man than I am fit to be or ever thought of being, I feel myself much encumber'd. The partner of my life to whom I owe a great part of its happiness, being sadly broken by the palsy, is in a condition that is often filling me with painful apprehensions and depressing my spirits. All must soon be over. What alone is desirable is the testimony of a good conscience.

Mr Adams with Colonel Smith his secretary, arrived here lately as minister Plenipotentiary from Congress to our Court. I am happy in their acquaintance but fear they will not meet with the success they wish for. There is still an hostility among us against your country which gives me a great concern. Could I have had my wishes we should from the first moment of the Peace, instead of throwing you off as aliens and commencing a commercial war against you, have consider'd you still as one people with us, and pursued every measure that might have a tendency to conciliate and to produce in time a

---

ORIGINAL: Yale University Library.   TEXT: Original, with the kind permission of Yale University Library.

1. Jonathan Trumbull, the Elder to R.P., 29 April 1785.
2. See R.P. to Thomas Jefferson, 2 July 1785, nn. 4 and 5.

perfect family harmony and attachment between us. In this way, I am persuaded we might have derived greater advantages from you than ever.

But things may be best for you as they are.

I cannot, as far as your interest is concerned, be sorry for any checks your foreign trade receives.

I have no particular litterary news to communicate to you. Should any such intelligence occur to me I shall mention it in a letter to Dr Styles which I hope soon to write. At present I am oblig'd to conclude. With every good wish and the greatest respect I am, Sir,

Your most obedient and humble servant
Richd Price

P.S. I have sent this letter by Mr *Curtauld*, a young person of whom I have a very good opinion, and who has taken a resolution to turn his property into money and to carry it with him to America in order to buy land with it in some of the interior parts of one of the eastern states and to settle them as an industrious farmer. He will probably shew you a testimonial I have given him. The assistance he wants is to be directed to an agreeable spot where he may make a purchase of land cleared or half cleared and be advised by good neighbours.

To John Jay

Newington Green, nr. London
July 9th, 1785.

Dear Sir,

I hope you will excuse the liberty I take in introducing to you the bearer of this letter, Mr Curtauld. He and his Mother and sisters have for several years made a part of my congregation at Hackney, and his character is unexceptionable. He has converted his little property into money which he intends to employ in purchasing land in some of the interior parts of America with no other view than to occupy it himself and to become an industrious farmer. Any information or assistance which you may be so good as to give him will confer an obligation upon me as well as upon him. The United States must be in some danger from needy and worthless adventurers who will often be going over to them from Europe. There is, in the present instance, no danger of this kind, for Mr Curtauld's views are laudable, and he will, I am fully persuaded, make an

---

PRINTED: *Correspondence and Public Papers of John Jay* (New York, (1890–93), III, 158–59. TEXT: *Correspondence and Public Papers of John Jay.*

honest and useful member of the United States. I directed to you in autumn last copies of my pamphlet on the American Revolution.

This was an effort of my zeal to promote, according to the best of my judgement, the improvement and happiness of mankind in general and of the United States in particular. The recommendations in it of measures to abolish gradually the Negro-trade and Slavery and to prevent too great an inequality of property have I find offended some of the leading men in South Carolina; and I have been assured from thence that such measures will never be encouraged there.

Should a like disposition prevail in many of the other States, it will appear that the people who have struggled so bravely against being enslaved themselves are ready enough to enslave others: the event which has raised my hopes of seeing a better state of human affairs will prove only an introduction to a new scene of aristocratical tyranny and human debasement: and the friends of liberty and virtue in Europe will be sadly disappointed and mortified.

I rely, dear Sir, on your candour and goodness to excuse the liberty which I now take with you. I am afraid that the acquaintance which I had the happiness to commence with you when in London is not sufficient to warrant it. With every good wish and great respect for your character, I am,

Your most obedient and humble servant,
Richard Price.

To Benjamin Rush

Newington Green July 22d 1785

Dear Sir,

The letter which I have just received from you, together with the considerations address'd to the legislature of Pensilvania, have given me a good deal of pain by the account they have brought me.¹ Before I received them I knew nothing of the test law in Pensilvania,² and I am truly sorry that such a law is maintained there ┼ chiefly, it seems by the Presbyterians┤ contrary to every principle of justice and good policy. The reasonings upon this subject in the pamphlet you have sent me do the writer great honour and appear to me

---

ORIGINAL: Library Company of Philadelphia.   PRINTED: *Pennsylvania Gazette*, 14 Sept. 1785; see *Rush Letters*, I, 372n.   TEXT: Original, with the kind permission of the Library Company of Philadelphia. The passages within lined through square brackets are lined through in the MS.

1. *Considerations upon the Present Test-Law of Pennsylvania: addressed to the Legislature and Freemen of the State* (Philadelphia, 1784).

2. In his *Observations on the Importance of the American Revolution*, Price had, however, noted, "In Pennsylvania every member of the House of Representatives is required to declare that he "acknowledges the Scriptures of the Old and New Testament to be given by divine inspiration." (Peach, p. 200.)

scarcely capable of being resisted by unprejudiced and disinterested men. That is a miserable legislature which relies much on the use of tests; for in general they bind only honest men.[3] This test is express'd so strongly that real friends to the American cause and particularly Quakers might very well scruple taking it when first proposed; but to continue *now* the disfranchisement it occasioned, and thus to deprive two fifths of the inhabitants of the rights of citizens while any foreigner may entitle himself to these rights is an act of oppression which I should have hardly thought possible to take place in Pensylvania.

╀I doubt not however but the majority of those who refused this test were influenced by very improper motives; but this should now be forgotten, and the magnanimity of forgiveness should be exercised.╀ The credit of the united states would have been much higher had this been done, as far as it could be done without too much danger. Indeed, Sir, I have, since the publication of my Observations on the *American* Revolution, heard so much that I do not like; that I have been sometimes afraid of having made myself ridiculous by what I have said of the importance of this Revolution. One of my correspondents in America who has been all along zealously attached to the American cause assures me that nothing can be more utopian than the expectations I have formed; and he informed me of facts which, if true, have a considerable tendency to lower my hopes. From *South=Carolina* I learn, that my pamphlet will by no means suit that State, and that some of the leading men there are offended by the recommendation it contains of measures for abolishing the Negro Slavery[4] and preventing too great an inequality of property.[5] I will, however, still hope that the American Revolution will prove an introduction to a better state of human affairs; and that in time the united states will become those seats of liberty, peace and virtue which the enlighten'd and liberal part of Europe are ardently wishing to see them.

This letter will be convey'd to you by Dr Franklin. He is leaving for ever this part of the world. May God grant him a prosperous voyage.

His excellency Mr Adams, in whose acquaintance I am very happy, desires me to present his compliments to you. Your tract on spirituous liquors[6] I have

3. In the General Introduction to (1778) *Two Tracts on Civil Liberty*, Price summarized his objections to state interference in religious matters, "Religious tests and subscriptions in general and all establishments of particular systems of faith with civil emoluments annexed, do inconceivable mischief, by turning religion into a trade, by engendering strife and persecution, by forming hypocrites, by obstructing the progress of truth, and fettering and perverting the human mind, nor will the world ever grow much *wiser* or *better* or *happier* till, by the abolition of them, truth can gain fair play, and reason free scope for exertion." (Peach, p. 55n.)

4. *Observations on the Importance of the American Revolution*, Peach, p. 213.

5. Ibid., pp. 208–209.

6. *An Enquiry into the Effects of Spirituous Liquors upon the Human Body and their Influence upon the Happiness of Society* (Philadelphia, n.d.). On the difficulties of determining the date of publication, see *Rush Letters*, I, 272. An edition of this work was published in Edinburgh in 1791.

not yet read. A friend took it from me soon after I received it; but it will be sent back in a day or two, and I doubt not but I shall read it with pleasure. I thank you for it and also for sending me the *Pensilvania* Newspapers.

With great regard and every good wish I am, Dear Sir,

Your very obedient and humble servant
Rich*d* Price

To Benjamin Franklin

Newington Green July 22*nd* 1785

My Dear Friend,

I writ to you at Paris a few weeks ago,[1] and intended by it to take my leave of you before your departure from America. But I cannot make myself easy without using the opportunity given me by Mr Williams's return to you to repeat my wishes that you may be blest with a safe and prosperous voyage and a happy remainder of life. You will probably receive a visit from the Bishop of St Asaph at Cowes.[2] I wish I could partake with him in the pleasure he will receive. The inclosed letter is an answer to a letter which I received this week from Dr Rush at Philadelphia.[3] May I request the favour of you to get it convey'd to him?

I am ever most affectionately yours
Rich*d* Price

Mrs Price sends her best respects and wishes. She continues sadly broken by the Palsy.

ORIGINAL: Cornell University Library. TEXT: Original, with the kind permission of Cornell University Library.

1. See R.P. to Benjamin Franklin, 5 June 1785.
2. Jonathan Shipley, who was staying at Twyford at the time, travelled down to Southampton to see Franklin whose boat docked there from 25 to 27 July. He took Franklin a copy of Paley's *Sermons* as a parting gift. See Brown, p. 337.
3. See R.P. to Benjamin Rush, 22 July 1785.

To Ezra Stiles

Newington=Green Aug 2*d* 1785

Dear Sir,

I have lately received from Mr Hubbard a letter from you dated February 9th and a note dated February 13th for which I return you many thanks. I wish

ORIGINAL: Yale University Library. TEXT: Original with the kind permission of Yale University Library.

I could have more opportunities for shewing my attention and regard to Mr Hubbard, but his short stay, the season of the year and other causes deprived me in a great degree of this pleasure. You have been very kind in taking the trouble to distribute the copies I sent you of my pamphlet on the American Revolution.[1] I commit it to Providence being conscious of having *meant* by it to promote the best interests of civil society and to contribute the little in my power to lead the united states to a just improvement of a situation new among mankind and favourable in the highest degree. I cannot expect that your sentiments should agree with mine on all the points noticed in this pamphlet. The separation of civil policy from religion I lay great stress upon;[2] but I find that you are less zealous in this subject than I am. Civil magistrates should in my opinion be nursing fathers to the Church only by maintaining a fair and open field for discussion of religious doctrines, by equally protecting all religious sects so far as they offer no injury to one another, and by countenancing religious virtue by their practice, their example and the execution of laws for keeping the peace and preventing and punishing immoralities. They can go to no extreme in this way. It is thus only they can in the end best promote religion and serve the church of christ. They should not aim at supporting truth by any kind of civil sanctions till they are *sure* that they are in possession of it, and we can all agree where it lies. *Before* this happens their interposition will do mischief; and *after* it happens it will be needless. I have commended the conduct of Gallio; but he certainly failed in his duty by suffering *Sosthenes* to be beat if he could have prevented it.[3]

In a former letter which I hope you have received long before this time I acknowledged the favour you did me in sending me your Election Sermon.[4] I read it with eagerness, and I was much pleased with it. It displays much ability and I doubted about nothing of consequence in it except a few expressions which seemed to exhort civil magistrates to take religious truth and the church of Christ under their patronage. They have done so too much; and the consequences have been dreadful.

I am obliged to you for sending me Mr Strong's Lectures.[5] I shall take care to deliver the copy address'd to the Royal Society and also that to the

---

1. *Observations on the Importance of the American Revolution.*

2. Cf. R.P. to Benjamin Rush, 26 June 1783; R.P. to Thomas Jefferson, 3 Aug. 1789; and Richard Price, *The Evidence for a Future Period of Improvement in the State of Mankind*, p. 32 and note in appendix to p. 19.

3. Acts 18: 12–17. Price commends Gallio, the Proconsul of Achaia, for refusing to intervene in questions of "words, names, and of your law" but censures him for failing to prevent Sosthenes, the chief ruler of the Synagogue, being beaten by the Greeks. Cf. Peach, p. 191.

4. See R.P. to Jonathan Trumbull, the Elder, 8 Oct. 1784, and R.P. to Ezra Stiles, 15 Oct. 1784.

5. Nehemiah Strong (1729–1807) whose *Astronomy Improved; or, a New Theory of the Harmonious Regularity Observable in the Mechanism of the Planetary System* was published in New Haven in 1784. This book consists of three lectures read in the chapel of Yale College, the first being given on 17 Feb. 1781.

Astronomer Royal. Present my best respects to the Author. He appears to be well acquainted with Sir Isaac Newton's Theory of Gravitation and the nature of the curves described by the secondary planets in Absolute space; and he has thrown light on these subjects.

In one of your letters you express'd a doubt about the possibility of determining the elements of the orbit of the new planet from the observations hitherto made. It is true that it moves so slowly that the observations made since the last discovery of it are scarcely sufficient for this purpose; but there is reason to believe that it is the same star with one observed by *Mayer*[6] about 25 years ago and by *Flamstead*;[7] and it is on this supposition that the elements have been determined.

I am very apprehensive that there is no probability of a happy commercial settlement between this country and yours. On the contrary; everything seems to tend towards a commercial rupture. I am continually lamenting the infatuation of my country in this instance; but it may be best for the united states that their rage for foreign trade should be checked, and that they should be oblig'd to find all they want within themselves, and to be satisfy'd with the simplicity, health, plenty, vigour, virtue and happiness which they may derive from agriculture and internal colonization.

A copy of a new Edition of my pamphlet on the American Revolution accompanies these lines which I hope you will accept.

With the greatest respect I am, Dear Sir,

Your very Obedient and humble servant
Rich*d* Price

His Excellency Mr Adams, in whose friendship I am very happy, desires me to present his kind compliments to you.

---

6. Christian Mayer (1719–83), Jesuit theologian and astronomer. Appointed Professor of Mathematics and Physics at Heidelberg in 1752. *D.Sc.B.*, IX, 231–32.
7. John Flamsteed. See R.P. to Joseph Willard, 6 Oct. 1783.

To Noah Webster[1]

Newington=Green Aug 2*d* 1785

Dear Sir,

Accept my best thanks for sending me your Institutes of Grammar and your Sketches of American Policy. I rejoyce to find in the United States writers so

---

ORIGINAL: Noah Webster Papers, Rare Books and Manuscripts Division, New York Public Library, Astor, Lenox and Tilden Foundations. TEXT: Original, with the kind permission of New York Public Library.
1. Noah Webster (1758–1843), lexicographer, whose *American Dictionary of the English Language*

liberal and so wise who are pleased to honour me with their notice. Your institutes of Grammar must be useful and your Sketches of American Policy will contribute to spread those principles of Government and civil Liberty which I think of the utmost importance, and wish to take root and to flourish in the united states in order to render them examples and blessings to the world. As a small return for your present, I hope you will accept of a copy of an Edition published here of my Pamphlet on the American Revolution, and which will be convey'd to you by the bearer of this letter.

Wishing you, Sir, all that can encourage you in your endeavours to enlighten your country and that can make you happy

[Concluding words and signature torn away]

---

was published in 1828. The works which he presented to Price were *A Grammatical Institute of the English Language in Three Parts* (Hartford, Conn., 1783–85), and *Sketches of American Policy* (Hartford, Conn., 1785). In the latter Webster argued for a strong federal government, a position with which Price was in complete sympathy.

From Thomas Jefferson

Paris Aug. 7 1785.

Sir,

Your favor of July 2. came duly to hand.[1] the concern you therein express as to the effect of your pamphlet in America, induces me to trouble you with some observations on that subject. from my acquaintance with that country I think I am able to judge with some degree of certainty of the manner in which it will have been received. Southward of the Chesapeak it will find but few readers concurring with it in sentiments on the subject of slavery. from the mouth to the head of the Chesapeak, the bulk of the people will approve it in theory, and it will find a respectable minority ready to adopt it in practice, a minority which for weight and worth of character preponderates against the greater number, who have not the courage to divest their families of a property which however keeps their consciences inquiet. Northward of the Chesapeak you may find here and there an opponent to your doctrine as you may find here and there a robber and a murderer, but in no great number. in that part of America, there being but few slaves, they can easily disencumber themselves

---

ORIGINAL: American Philosophical Society. PRINTED: *Jefferson*: Boyd, VIII, 356–57. TEXT: Original, with the kind permission of the American Philosophical Society.

1. R.P. to Thomas Jefferson, 2 July 1785.

of them, and emancipation is put into such a train that in a few years there will be no slaves Northward of Maryland. in Maryland I do not find such a disposition to begin the redress of this enormity as in Virginia. this is the next state to which we may turn our eyes for the interesting spectacle of justice in conflict with avarice and oppression: a conflict wherein the sacred side is gaining daily recruits from the influx into office of young men grown and grown up. these have sucked in the principles of liberty as it were with their mother's milk, and it is to them I look with anxiety to turn the fate of this question. be not therefore discouraged. what you have written will do a great deal of good: and could you still trouble yourself with our welfare, no man is more able to give aid to the labouring side. the college of William and Mary in Williamsburg, since the remodelling of it's plan, is the place where are collected together all the young men of Virginia under preparation for public life. they are there under the direction (most of them) of a mr Wythe[2] one of the most virtuous of characters, and whose sentiments on the subject of slavery are unequivocal. I am satisfied if you could resolve to address an exhortation to those young men, with all that eloquence of which you are master, that it's influence on the future decision of this important question would be great, perhaps decisive. thus you see that, so far from thinking you would have cause to repent of what you have done, I wish you would do more, and wish it on assurance of it's effect. the information I have received from America of the reception of your pamphlet in the different states agrees with the expectations I had formed. our country is getting into a ferment against yours, or rather have caught it from yours. god knows how this will end: but assuredly in one extreme or the other. there can be no medium between those who have loved so much. I think the decision is in your power as yet, but will not be so long. I pray you to be assured of the sincerity of the esteem and respect with which I have the honour to be Sir

Your most obedient servant
Th: Jefferson

P.S. I thank you for making me acquainted with Monsr. D'Ivernois

---

2. George Wythe (1726–1806), a lawyer. In 1775 he represented Virginia in Congress and signed the Declaration of Independence. He undertook, with Edmund Pendleton, the revision of the laws of Virginia. In December 1779, Wythe became the first incumbent of a Professorship of Law and Police—the first chair of law in an American College—at the College of William and Mary.

From Jonathan Jackson

Boston 8th Aug*st* 1785

Dear Sir,

After a short passage in the month of May I had the pleasure to find my Family and Friends all well. My Chest and other baggage which I had ordered from Bristol to Cork did not reach there before I embarked, and coming without them I came without the last packets you entrusted to my Care for several of your friends here; this disappointment to them may be attended I hope with no great inconvenience to you. I mentioned to Doctor Chauncy and to President Willard that if I recollected right you had charged me with a packet to each of them, the direction of the others I have forgot. My Chest, etc., have not yet come from Cork but I expect them by the first vessel. When I left London I had to travel by land thro' a considerable part of England and Ireland, or I would have found a place in my Portmanteau for your packets. The late Edition of your Pamphlet which you did me the Honor to send me just before my departure, I handed to our new Governor, Mr Bowdoin, for his perusal and he lately returned it me with thanks, being much pleased with the Additions you have made to the last.[1] Our people in the late Choice of their Governor have discovered a Discernment which does them Credit; we have a good deal to expect from his prudence and his Integrity. The complection of our Affairs in general, of our Commerce in particular is gloomy enough. I wish to see less connection with your Country in the way of Traffic, in the Import-ation at least of unnecessary and useless Articles, and more Connection in friendly Intercourse and good Offices, provided your Administration becomes well managed and we can meet you upon equal terms and to mutual Benefit. The appointment by Congress of a Minister to your Court, I hope will soon be followed by a like appointment from you to us; such Measures will lead more than any other to restore Harmony and an Association of Interests between the two Countries, and which I am persuaded might be made highly beneficial to both. The appointment of Mr Adams which is here considered a very judicious one, I hope may soon lead to a liberal Treaty of Commerce, which

---

ORIGINAL: American Philosophical Society. PRINTED: *M.H.S.P.* (1903), 327ff. TEXT: Orig-inal, with the kind permission of the American Philosophical Society.

1. *Observations on the Importance of the American Revolution.* The most noteworthy additions that Price made in the second edition of this pamphlet were the advertisement and footnotes in which he commented on the development of scientific knowledge and the expectation that progress will eventually restore the paradisaical state; noted proposals for constitutional reform in Massa-chusetts; and drew attention to Thomas Day's *Fragment of an Original Letter on the Slavery of the Negroes.* (See Peach, pp. 179, 183, 206–7, 213). The second edition includes an appendix con-taining a translation of Mathon de la Cour's 'Testament de le fortuné Richard' and a set of tables, neither of which are reproduced by Peach.

may give to this Country greater Facility in paying the debts already contracted with yours'—tho' in some instances they were injudiciously contracted on
both sides, the like of which it is to be hoped will not soon again take place—
but such a Treaty will also tend to soften the minds of People here and remove
prejudices on both sides, which the sooner they are done away will the sooner
bring us to such good offices as to forget we have quarrelled, and that so
foolishly.

When our federal government will be reinforced and braced up so as better
to answer the purposes of its Institution it is impossible to tell; the Conviction
seems to be general that something is needed, but what from an ill founded
Jealousy, as I think, of delegating too much power to the supreme Head, and
from a supposition of contrary Interests in the different States, not so well
founded, if we are to make one Republic, and that a respectable one, nothing is
yet matured, and I fear it will be some time before anything effectual is done.
Necessity, however, must finally lead to it. A reform such as might be projected for a supreme Legislative, Judicial and Executive to manage the federal
Union, or rather I would say to manage our large family, dropping the distinction of separate Sovereignties, by which Reform an equal Representation
might now be introduced and always kept up, and such a Representation is
perhaps a *sine qua non* to the Continuance of Liberty under any Government—
this, and perhaps one more Reform in our manners or rather Fashions only,
that of confining ourselves to an Uniform Habit thro' out our Republic,
changed only as the Seasons change, we being subject thro' all our Climates in
some measure to both Extremes of Heat and Cold, these alone, it appears to
me, would secure to us Peace, Liberty and Happiness as far as Societies can
enjoy it together. The last mentioned Reform would cut off one half, if not
more, of the useless Fopperies we import from Europe, and for which we make
ourselves Slaves to that Country. It would not only abate the Attention of the
younger part of the Community at least to what are the greatest Trifles in
Nature, and which fixes in many of them trifling Habits all their Lives perhaps, but it would in time, if not immediately, lead to a Reform in Sentiments
and Manners very beneficial to our Forms of Government. But these Reveries
of the Closet and the Pillow can seldom be introduced into practice—this I
have been obliged to learn several years since and that one must only indulge
themselves in them among their Friends.

I wished to see your friend Mr I.H. Brown[2] before I left England, and called
for that purpose one of the last days I was in London, but was not fortunate
enough to meet him. I hope that he gave himself no uneasiness that I did not
meet Mr Pitt. I daresay it was no fault of Mr Brown's, and that the Minister's
Engagements were such then, what with Irish affairs and a Parliamentary
Reform, he had no time to attend to less Concerns, as he might think those

2. Isaac Hawkins Browne, see R.P. to Isaac Hawkins Browne, 30 Mar. 1780.

which related to America to be; for your Administration since the Earl of Shelburne quitted it have at least affected to hold us in an unimportant and diminutive Light, a strange reverse of what was held up to the Nation of our Importance when they were endeavouring to subjugate us. It might have been perhaps no disservice to me personally to have seen Mr Pitt or some of your Administration while I remained in England, provided a Communication and free Intercourse should ever again take place between our two Countries, and any Supplies should be needed from hence for your Fleets or Forces which may at any time be stationed in our Neighbourhood at Nova Scotia or Newfoundland, more especially if the same Administration should continue, as I think it would not have been difficult for me while in England, and might not now be, to give them full assurance that my partner, Mr Higginson, and myself had as many Facilities to serve them and would do it as faithfully as they might find any others here to do it. The gloomy appearance here of Commerce in general leads me to seek some such safe Business, if I could find it, to provide for a large and increasing family, it having been the Business I was bred to. In the mercantile Phrase our Firm is—Jackson and Higginson, at Boston. We are both well known to Mr Adams whom I have no doubt, if enquired of, would affirm to our Rep[ut]ations being fair. I made an Acquaintance last year with Mr S. Smith, Member of Parliament who lives in Bloomsbury Square,[3] and with whom I flatter myself that I left some favourable Impressions.

Should Affairs between us be coming round in the accomodating way and any public contracts or commissions for supplies should be sent this way, if you, my good Sir, when you may be in the Minister's Closet, which I suppose is sometimes the case, should see no impropriety in it, and could just drop our Names as fit persons here, it may essentially serve me, and I dare aver as a Man of Truth and Honor that no one here shall more faithfully do any Business of the kind mentioned if committed to us than Mr Higginson and myself, a reasonable Commission or allowance being made us for our Trouble.

My Expectations are not very sanguine that such Accomodations will come round as to lead to any opening of this kind, and still less but that other Seekers more importunate and greater favourites will get the Employ I have turned your attention to. You will therefore please to excuse my taking up your time upon a matter so little promising.

I should be much gratified, if your Correspondents are not already too numerous, to have your Communications now and then, as your Leisure will permit, upon such speculative subjects as you think may be usefull to our rising States, or any Movements in the political Line which are taking place, or like to, and which have a veiw to us. I am sensible this is asking almost too much of a man whose daily labours must be considerable in his own

---

3. Probably Samuel Smith, see R.P. to Shelburne, 7 Nov. 1782.

Profession and upon whom the Public has learnt to make so great Claims. If I request too much you must not hesitate to refuse me.

I wish that Heaven may continue your Health and Usefulness and restore that of Mrs Price's. Tho' personally unknown to her please to present my respects to her and to the Lady who presided at your Table when I had the pleasure of being there.

Your Friend Doctor Chauncy appears to be in good Health for an old gentleman past Eighty. He complains, however, of having arrived to his second dotage, and perhaps he is not mistaken, for he has been lately, since my return, paying his addresses to a Widow of forty, to whom he would have given his Hand had not she and her Friends been possessed of more Discretion. This communication is to excite you to a little Merriment.

I am, as I left England with warm Impressions of your favourable Attentions to me while there, with great respect and esteem,

my good Sir, your sincere friend and obliged servant

Jona Jackson

From John Wheelock

Dartmouth College August 13th 1785

Reverend and dear Sir,

I hope you have before this time received a letter which was dated and forwarded last January.[1] In that I had the honour to acknowledge the receipt of a very valuable benefaction in the gift of your works, and to desire that the thanks of the College might be acceptable to you for a favor so highly prized.

Your *Observations on the Importance of the American revolution* I have since had the pleasure to read with particular attention. I cannot tell you, Sir, how great the applause is, which its author receives throughout these States. The Constitution of this Commonwealth has but lately begun to operate. The President,[2] confined by a lingering disease, wrote a letter to the Assembly at their Session last February, inclosing the *Observations* etc. He informed the legislature that the remarks in the pamphlet were the best legacy, which he could leave them.

ORIGINAL: American Philosophical Society. PRINTED: *Memoirs*, p. 107 (extract only). TEXT: Original, with the kind permission of the American Philosophical Society. The MS contains a draft in shorthand of R.P.'s reply to Wheelock (undeciphered).

1. See John Wheelock to R.P., 25 Jan. 1785.

2. Meshech Weare (1713–86) was elected President of the State of New Hampshire in 1784. From 1776 to 1784 he had been President of the Executive Council and Chairman of the Committee of Safety. From 1776 to 1782 he had also been Chief Justice. He did not enjoy a long tenure as President, because failing health forced him to resign the office in 1785. (*D.A.B.*)

He prayed earnestly that the spirit of them might animate the manners and disposition of legislators and people to the latest age.[3]

The citizens of the States are now beginning to see their true interests and the rage of foreign commerce does certainly abate. It is, Sir, hard to tell how much we feel by our unfortunate measures in trade; but it is not too late for a cure. Our sufferings themselves will lead us to the best remedy. It must be a cogent motive which can induce a people to enter upon the new and untried labors of manufactory and mechanics—great disadvantages by a neglect will do it to best purpose.

I hope that your Lady has recovered. May you together very long enjoy health with the best of other blessings.

With the most sincere respect and esteem, I have the honor to subscribe myself, Dear Sir,

Your very obedient and affectionate servant
John Wheelock

---

3. Weare wrote to the General Court of New Hampshire in Feb. 1785, "Perhaps the United States were never in a more critical situation, or more depended on the measures that may be adopted, than at this time. Give me leave to recommend to your Perusal, Doctor Price's Observations on the importance of the American Revolution, tho' perhaps you may not fully agree with him in all his Sentiments, there are certainly many things in them, which deserve serious attention. It is my earnest wish, that such measures may be adopted as may issue in the prosperity of this and the United States." Quoted by Carl B. Cone, "Richard Price and the Constitution of the United States" in *American Historical Review*, LIII (July, 1948), 739, from "Revolution 1784–1786," Manuscript State Papers, X, 79.

To Mr Cotton[1]

Yarmouth, 26th August, 1785

Dear Sir,

I have received with particular satisfaction the letter you have sent me, by the desire and in the name of the Congregation at Hackney;[2] and I feel sincere gratitude for the candour with which you and the other subscribers and members accept my services. Nothing could make me happier than any service or labour by which I could advance their best interests, and could I believe that the Sermons I have lately preached to them would answer this end, and be the means of communicating juster sentiments of the gospel of Christ, and of promoting a liberality of temper among the different denomi-

---

PRINTED: Rutt, XX, 500. TEXT: Rutt.
1. See Vol.I, 86.
2. See Rutt, XX, 500.

nations of Christians, I should undoubtedly resolve to publish them. But I suspect the danger of plunging myself into controversy, which would give me trouble, and for which I am unfit. Some of my good Socinian friends would immediately attack me, and they are so full of zeal and so assured they are right, that I am afraid of encountering them. I have less apprehension from those in the opposite scheme, from *Calvinists* and *Churchmen*; but, probably, some of them would also attack me. I cannot, however, say, that I have no thoughts of publishing these Sermons.[3] The approbation with which my friends at Hackney have honoured them, and their request, cannot but influence me strongly; and they may probably, make a principal part of a volume of Sermons, the publication of which, some time or other, I have long had in view. I shall be obliged to you for communicating to the congregation these sentiments, delivering at the same time, my best respects and wishes,

I am &

Richard Price

---

3. In 1787, Price published his *Sermons on the Christian Doctrine as received by the Different Denominations of Christians. To which are added Sermons on the Security and Happiness of a Virtuous Course, on the Goodness of God and the Resurrection of Lazarus.* The volume was inscribed "To the Congregation of Protestant Dissenters Assembling at the Gravel-Pit Meeting House, in Hackney, these discourses published at their request are dedicated." In the advertisement to the first edition Price announced his determination not to enter into controversy over the account which he had given of Christian doctrine. In an Appendix to the second edition of the *Sermons*, also published in 1787, he did, however, include a series of notes which were prompted by some objections made to his interpretation of Christian doctrine by Joseph Priestley, who was a Socinian, and, as such, opposed to Price's Arianism. In introducing these notes Price re-affirmed his intention not to enter into controversy, being content merely to summarize the most important of Priestley's arguments so that "our readers may be better able to form their judgments on the points about which we differ."

From John Jay

New York, 27th September, 1785.

Dear Sir:

I have had the pleasure of receiving the letter of the 9th of July last which you wrote me by Mr Curtauld.[1] Your recommendation will be of great use to him and you may rely on my readiness to do him any friendly offices in my power.

I hope my letter, in answer to the one which enclosed a number of your political pamphlets, has reached you by this time. I do not recollect the date, but it went in one of the last vessels.

PRINTED: *The correspondence and public papers of John Jay*, III, 168. TEXT: Printed.

1. See R.P. to John Jay, 9 July 1785.

The cause of liberty, like most other good causes, will have its difficulties, and sometimes its persecutions, to struggle with. It has advanced more rapidly in this than in other countries, but all its objects are not yet attained; and I much doubt whether they ever will be, in this or any other terrestrial state. That men should pray and fight for their own freedom, and yet keep others in slavery is certainly acting a very inconsistent as well as an unjust and, perhaps, impious part; but the history of mankind is filled with instances of human improprieties. The wise and the good never form the majority of any large society, and it seldom happens that their measures are uniformly adopted, or that they can always prevent being overborne themselves by the strong and almost never-ceasing union of the wicked and the weak.

These circumstances tell us to be patient, and to moderate those sanguine expectations which warm and good hearts often mislead even wise heads to entertain on those subjects. All that the best men can do is, to persevere in doing their duty to their country, and leave the consequences to Him who made it their duty; being neither elated by success, however great, nor discouraged by disappointments however frequent and mortifying.

With sincere esteem and regard, I am, dear sir,

Your most obedient servant,

John Jay

From Benjamin Rush

Philadelphia, October 15, 1785

Dear Sir,

I took the liberty of publishing, with your name, your excellent letter[1] on the test law of Pennsylvania. It has already had a great effect on the minds of many people, and I doubt not will contribute more than anything to repeal that law. Dr Franklin, who has succeeded Mr Dickinson as our governor, has expressed his surprise at the continuance of such a law since the peace, and we hope will add the weight of his name to yours to remove such a stain from the American Revolution.

The Doctor enjoys in his eightieth year the full exercise of all faculties of his mind. While Spain boasts of her Ximenes,[2] France of her Fleury,[3] and Britain of her Mansfield, all of whom sustained the burden of government after they

---

PRINTED: *The American Museum*, I, 132–34 (Feb. 1787); *Rush Letters*, I, 371–7. TEXT: Printed.

  1. See R.P. to Benjamin Rush, 22 July 1785.
  2. Francisco Ximenes de Cisneros (1436–1517), Spanish cardinal and statesman.
  3. Hercule André de Fleury (1653–1743), French cardinal and statesman.

had passed the eightieth year of their lives, America claims a Franklin, inferior to none of them in activity of mind and clearness of perception on the great affairs of government. We expect, in consequence of his arrival, a revolution in favor of reason, justice and humanity in our country. He has already begun to point out abuses and to propose schemes that are full of wisdom and benevolence.

I was made very happy by observing that the dissenters of all denominations had united with the Quakers in England to petition Parliament to put a stop to the African trade. We perceive already the good effects of the abolition of Negro slavery in Pennsylvania. The slaves who have been emancipated among us are in general more industrious and orderly than the lowest class of white people. A school has been set on foot for their children by the Quakers in this city; and we have the pleasure of seeing them improve in religion and morals under their instructions, as well as in English literature.

Learning begins to spread in all directions through our country. Dickinson College grows daily in funds, pupils, and reputation. The two colleges in Maryland, founded by Doctor Smith,[4] bid fair for being useful to that state.[5] The spring which the human mind acquired by the Revolution has extended itself to religion. The Episcopal clergy and laity have held a convention in this city and agreed on such alterations in their discipline, worship, and articles as will render the Episcopal Church the most popular church in America. They have adopted a form of ecclesiastical government purely republican. A church judicatory is to consist of a bishop, three presbyters, and two or three laymen. They have reduced their thirty-nine articles to nineteen and have reserved from their creeds only the Apostles'. Their baptism, their marriage and burial services are likewise made more consonant to common sense as well as true Christianity. While these changes are going forward in the Episcopalian Church, the Presbyterians and Baptists are showing an equal spirit of innovation. A considerable body of them who had been educated in the strictest principles of Calvinism, and many of whom are people separated from their respective churches and are now forming an independent society under the direction of Mr Winchester,[6] an eloquent and popular Baptist preacher who has openly and avowedly preached the doctrine of final restitution. Tenets of the same kind are now spreading rapidly in New England. &c.

---

4. William Smith (1727–1803) became the first Provost of the College of Philadelphia in 1755. He founded Washington College at Chestertown in Maryland in 1782. In the following year he was elected Bishop of Maryland by the Episcopalians, but he was not consecrated by the English bishops when they were allowed by Act of Parliament to consecrate three American bishops. See Thomas Firth Jones, *A Pair of Lawn Sleeves* (Philadelphia, 1972), 154.

5. Washington College, Chestertown, Maryland, chartered in 1782 through the efforts of William Smith, and St John's College, chartered in 1784. Professor L.H. Butterfield notes that Smith had no part in the founding of St John's (*Rush Letters*, I, 372).

6. Elhanan Winchester (1751–97), an itinerant preacher and one of the principal founders of the Universalist Church in America. He visited Price on his trip to England in 1787 bringing with him a letter of introduction from Benjamin Rush. See Benjamin Rush to R.P., 29 July 1787.

To John Adams

Oct. 16th 1785

Dr Price presents his respects to Mr Adams. The inclosed Receipt secures the assurance of M. Houdon's life from the day on which it is dated.[1] The

---

ORIGINAL: The Adams Papers, Massachusetts Historical Society.   TEXT: Original, with the kind permission of the Trustees of the Adams Papers.

1. Jean Antoine Houdon (1741–1828), the sculptor, had agreed to go to America to "take the figure" of General Washington. On 7 July 1785, Thomas Jefferson wrote to Adams from Paris asking him to find out what it would cost to insure Houdon's life in London for the journey to America and his return to France. On 4 Aug. Adams replied:

"Houdons Life may be insured for five Per cent. two for the Life and three for the Voyage. I mentioned it at Table with several Merchants: they all agreed that it would not be done for less. But Dr Price, who was present undertook to enquire and inform me. His answer is, that it may be done at an office in Hackney, for five Per Cent. He cannot say yet for less, but will endeavour to reduce it a little."

Jefferson wrote to Adams on 10 Aug. asking him to arrange for Houdon's life to be insured for 15,000 livres turnois. He also asked that the policy should run from 27 July until Houdon's return to Paris. Eventually, after some delay—due apparently to Price's having forgotten to make the necessary arrangements—Adams was able to inform Jefferson that Price had completed the transaction. On 19 Oct. 1785, he wrote:

"I am to acquaint you Sir that Dr Price has transacted the business respecting Mr Houdon. The Money is paid, but the policy is not quite ready but the Doctor has promised that it shall be sent in a few days, when it will be forwarded to you."

On 24 Oct. he wrote:

"The Insurance is made upon Houdons Life for Six months from the 12 of October. I have paid Thirty two pounds Eleven Shillings Praemium and Charges, which you will please give me Credit for. I could not persuade them to look back, as they say, they never ensure but for the future and from the date of the Policy."

(See *The Adams-Jefferson Letters*, ed. Lester J. Cappon, 2 vols. (University of N. Carolina Press, 1959), I, 39, 42, 48, 53, 57–58, 84–86).

The Assurance on Houdon's life was arranged with the Equitable Assurance Society (now the Equitable Life Assurance Society). The following is an extract from the minutes of the Weekly Court for 12 Oct. 1785:

"Thomas Jeffreyson Esq. Envoy from the United States to the Court of France, by his agent William Morgan was assured ×56 in the sum of six hundred and seventy pounds for the term of six calendar months on the life of—Houdon, Sculptor at Paris, now on his passage to Virginia in North America, age forty years, and the said Mr Jeffreyson having paid the premium of seven pounds sixteen shillings and sixpence and four pounds four shillings for entrance, and having executed the Covenant etc. it is ordered that a policy be issued accordingly.

Ordered that the Policy this day granted to Thomas Jeffreyson for assuring £670 for 6 months on the life of—Houdon be not vacated by the said Mr Houdon's dying upon the Seas in his passage from France to Virginia, or during his Residence there or in his return from thence to France Mr Jeffreyson having paid an extra premium of twenty pounds two shillings for such Risques.

N.B. It is understood and agreed that in case of the decease of—Houdon and of a Claim being made in virtue of the Policy of assurance this day granted to Mr Jeffreyson, Proof is to be made by the assured of the said Mr Houdon's having been in perfect health on this day of the date of the Policy, and a Minute to this effect is to be indorsed on the Policy."

Policy itself will be ready in a few days. The whole expence being 31 guineas. Dr Price is in debt to Mr Adams two guineas. Mr Higginson's letter contains much information; and Dr Price is much obliged to Mr Adams for the perusal of it.

"x 56" in the above refers to a proposal book no longer extant. The charge of thirty one guineas was made up as follows:

Premium	7 16 6	
Entrance	4 4 –	
Policy Money	8 6	
	12 9	
Risque of voyage and residence overseas	20 2	
(3% of sum assured)		
	£32 11	

I am indebted to Mr M.E. Ogborn for his kindness in sending me the details of this document, and to the Equitable Life Assurance Society for their kindness in allowing me to reproduce it.

From Joseph Clarke

Dublin, Oct. 22, 1785.

Sir,

Encouraged by your approbation of my former letter, I will take the liberty of stating to you a few more facts and observations, which I hope you will judge an Appendix to it of some importance.

With the view of ascertaining how far some of the foregoing conjectures are well founded, and of determining with greater precision the more obvious differences between the male and female sex in infancy, I began in the month of July last by weighing forty children, twenty of each sex, and by taking the dimensions of their heads. In the months of August and September I repeated the same experiment twice, taking such children as appeared to have arrived at the full period of gestation promiscuously as they happened to be born.

I weighed them all a few hours after birth, before they had taken food, and before purgative medicines had time to operate. For this purpose, I made use of a small spring or pocket steelyard, which weighs any thing (not heavier than a few pounds) appended to it with sufficient accuracy. To this was attached a flannel bag, into which the children were put, at first, naked; but this I soon found very troublesome. The nurses often wanted time sufficient to assist me,

---

PRINTED: *Phil. Trans.*, LXXVI (1786), part 2, 356–62. TEXT: *Phil. Trans.* Note in *Phil. Trans.* preceded by note (a) in text. An abstract and extracts from the Registry kept at the Lying Hospital Dublin, published as an appendix to Clarke's letter in *Phil. Trans.* are not reproduced here.

and timid mothers were afraid of their infants catching cold; I was therefore obliged to weigh them with their cloaths on, and to subtract a certain quantity from the gross weight of each child, according as it was full, middling, or light cloathed. Whatever inaccuracy this may have introduced, as to the real weight of the children, it can but little influence their comparative weights, or the differences between the two sexes, which it was my object to ascertain.

For measuring their heads, I made use of a piece of painted or varnished linen tape, divided into inches, halves, and quarters. The varnish has the good effect of preventing the length of such a measure being readily affected by variations in the humidity of the atmosphere, &c.; and it has little or no elasticity. In this part of the experiment then I can pretend to considerable accuracy. I took first the greatest circumference of the head from the most prominent part of the occiput around over the frontal sinuses; and, secondly, the tranverse dimension from the superior and anterior part of one ear, across the fontanelle, to a similar part of the opposite ear. These dimensions appeared to me the most likely to afford data for determining the respective sizes of the brain in the different sexes. The result was as follows:

Twenty males			Twenty females		
Weight. lbs. &c.	Circumf. of heads. Inches.	Dimensions from ear to ear Inches.	Weight. lbs. &c.	Circumf. of heads. Inches.	Dimen. from ear to ear. Inches.
		Experiment 1.			
$149\frac{1}{2}$	282	152	$137\frac{1}{4}$	272	143
		Experiment 2.			
$144\frac{1}{2}$	277	$146\frac{1}{4}$	135	272	147
		Experiment 3.			
148	280	$147\frac{1}{2}$	132	273	$143\frac{1}{4}$
		Totals.			
442	839	$445\frac{3}{4}$	$404\frac{1}{4}$	817	$433\frac{1}{4}$
		Average weight, &c.			
7 lbs. 5 oz.7dr.	14	$7\frac{1}{4}$	6lbs. 11oz.6dr.	$13\frac{5}{8}$	$7\frac{2}{9}$

Having found the relative proportions between the sexes to turn out thrice with so much uniformity, and observing them to correspond pretty nearly with some experiments, made for very different purposes by the late Professor ROEDERER,[1] of Gottingen, I did not think it necessary to prosecute the subject farther.

Upon the whole, it may be observed, that the difference of weight between the male and female at birth may be rated at about nine ounces, or nearly a twelfth part of the original weight. In the circumference of their heads there is a difference of near half an inch, or about a 28th or 30th part; and the same proportion of a 28th is pretty nearly preserved in the transverse dimension. It is evident, as the bony passage through which infants pass is of a certain determined capacity, that, were their heads equally incompressible with those of adults, the difference of half an inch in their size would often prove fatal to them. By the compressibility of their heads, however, in *well formed* women, this difficulty is by time surmounted. The effects which such a compression on the *brain* may produce, have not hitherto been well attended to.

In reckoning children, weighing from $5\frac{1}{2}$ to $6\frac{1}{2}$, 6 pounds weight, and from $6\frac{1}{2}$ to $7\frac{1}{2}$, 7, and so forth, in order to avoid fractions, I find the numbers of males and females, arranged according to their weight, to stand as follow.

	Males.								**Females.**						
lbs.	4	5	6	7	8	9	10	lbs.	4	5	6	7	8	9	10
No	0	3	6	32	16	2	1	No	2	9	14	25	8	2	0

Hence it appears, that the majority of males runs thus: seven, eight, six, five; whilst that of the females is seven, six, five, eight. Hence also appears the merciful dispensations of Providence towards the female sex; for when deviations from the medium standard occur, it is remarkable, that they are much more frequently below than above this standard. In 120 instances there are only five children exceeding eight pounds and a half in weight. The same may be observed with regard to the size of their heads. Only six measured above $14\frac{1}{2}$ inches in circumference, and these all of the male sex; five measured $14\frac{3}{4}$, and one 15. In transverse dimensions only four exceeded $7\frac{3}{4}$, the largest of which was $8\frac{1}{2}$; whereas deviations under the standard in these particulars were very numerous, never however under 12 around and $6\frac{1}{4}$ across.

In the year 1753, Dr ROEDERER published a Paper, *De pondere et longitudine Infantum recens natorum*, in the Commentaries of the Royal Society of Gottingen, of which the celebrated HALLER[2] was the principal institutor, and long the president. In this Paper he proves, in the clearest manner, by incontestible experiments, the absurdity of the ideas of obstetric writers with regard to the progress of the ovum during gestation, and the weight of the foetus after birth. He shews, although they state the weight of the foetus, come to the full time, to be from 12 to 14 or 16 pounds, that it is more generally 6 or 7, and very rarely exceeds eight. This deserves particular notice for two reasons; first, because it serves to shew how little dependence is to be placed on the assertions of authors who copy each other servilely, without having recourse to experiment even in the most obvious cases; and, secondly, because this paper

---

1. Jean-Georges Roederer (1726–63), obstetrician. He lectured at Gottingen from 1751. His works were published under the title *Opuscula Medica* at Gottingen in 1763. *Nat. Biog. Gén.*
2. Albrecht von Haller (1708–77), Swiss physiologist.

has been overlooked by some of the most celebrated writers and teachers of midwifery now living. What idea are we to form of the accuracy of one of our latest systematic writers, who (telling us that he has been a practitioner of midwifery, in a capital city, for twenty years, and a teacher for more than twelve) states, in one page of his work, that the weight of a foetus at eight months is about seven pounds; and on the opposite page, that at full time it weighs from twelve to fourteen pounds?[a]

Of 27 Children, carried to the full period of gestation, weighed and measured in length by ROEDERER, without any attention to the difference of sex, I find, that 18 were of the male and 9 of the female sex; and that the average weight of the former was about 6 lbs. 9 oz., that of the latter about 6 lbs. 2 oz. 2 dr. Whether he and I used the same weights, I cannot exactly say. He observes, that he used the civil pound of Gottingen, which I can easily perceive consisted of 16 ounces, as mine did; but whether a German ounce be the same with ours, I have not *data* to determine. The average length of the males measured by him is about $20\frac{1}{3}$ inches, and of the females about $19\frac{17}{18}$. He weighed also the placentae of 21 lying-in women, 16 of whom had borne male children, and five female. The average weight of the former was 1lb. $2\frac{1}{2}$oz.; that of the latter 1lb. 2oz. hence it appears, that in other circumstances, besides those I have taken notice of, the male and female sex differ. So far I thought it necessary to take extracts from Dr ROEDERER's paper, as his observations and mine throw light on each other, and add confirmation to both.

The limits of this letter will not permit me, Sir, to trespass much farther on your patience. There is one circumstance or two so intimately connected with my former letter, that I cannot pass them over in silence. Having found that males suffer more in the birth than females. I was desirous of knowing whether the chance of the mother's recovery was thereby in any degree affected; and to determine this I was once more at the pains of turning over our registry with care. I found, that of 214 women, dead of single children, 50 were delivered of still-born males, and 15 of stillborn females; 76 of living males, and 73 of living females, Of the 15 dead of twins, 6 had twins one of each sex; 6 others had twins both of the male sex; and three had twins both of the female sex. All of which twins (two or three excepted), it is very remarkable, survived the death of their mothers. It would appear then, that the life of the mother is principally endangered in those cases where the bulk of the male's head precludes the possibility of his being brought into the world alive, either by the efforts of nature or art. The conception of twins we have observed to be more fatal to the mother than that of single children. The average weight of 12 twins, which have occurred to me of late, I find to be 11 lbs. a pair. The largest pair weighed

---

(a.) See a Treatise of Midwifery (p. 88 and 89) Divested of *Technical* Terms and *Abstruse Theories*, by A. Hamilton, M.D. 8° edit. London, 1781. [Alexander Hamilton (1739–1802) was a professor of midwifery in the University of Edinburgh.]

13 lbs. and the least $8\frac{1}{2}$. From some rude attempts made to ascertain the weight of the contents of the gravid uterus in cases of twin and single children, I am inclined to think, that they are to each other as about 15 to 10, or perhaps $14\frac{1}{2}$ to $9\frac{1}{4}$.

Believe me, Sir, with great respect, &c.

J. Clarke.

To Thomas Jefferson

Newington Green Oct. 24th 1785

Dear Sir,

Dr Rogers,[1] the bearer of this, is the son of Dr Rogers of New=York.[2] He has been for some time in this country studying Physick; and he intends, I find, to spend this winter at Paris with a view to farther improvement. I cannot help taking this opportunity which he offers me to convey to you a few lines to acknowledge the receipt of the letter with which I was favoured in August last,[3] and to return you my thanks for it. The account you give of the prevailing sentiments in the united states with respect to the Negro=slavery, and of the probability of its abolition in all the states except the *Carolinas* and *Georgia*, has comforted me much. It agreed with an account which I have had from Mr Laurens, who at the same time tells me that in his own state he has the whole country against him. You do me much honour by the wish you express that I would address an exhortation on this subject to the young persons under preparation for public life in the College of William and Mary at Williamsburgh. But I cannot think of writing again on any political subject. What I have done in this way has been a deviation from the line of my profession to which I was drawn by the American war. Divinity and Morals will probably occupy me entirely during the remainder of a life now pretty far spent. My heart is impressed with a conviction of the importance of the sentiments I have address'd to the united states; but I must now leave these sentiments to make their way for themselves, and to be approved or rejected just as events and the judgements of those who may consider them shall determine. It is a very

---

ORIGINAL: Library of Congress. PRINTED: *Jefferson*: Boyd, VIII, 667–69. TEXT: Original.

1. See R.P. to Benjamin Rush, 14 Oct. 1784.

2. John Rodgers (1727–1811), Presbyterian divine. Born at Boston, Mass. Entered the Presbyterian Ministry in 1747, being ordained and instituted at St George's New Castle County, Delaware in 1749. Minister at New York from 1765 until 1818. Elected DD at Edinburgh in 1768 on Franklin's recommendation. Became Vice-Chancellor of the University of the State of New York in 1784.

3. Thomas Jefferson to R.P., 7 Aug. 1785.

happy circumstance for *Virginia* that its young men are under the tuition of so wise and virtuous a man as you say Mr Wythe is. Young men are the hope of every state; and nothing can be of so much consequence to a state as the principles they imbibe and the direction they are under. Able and liberal and virtuous tutors in all the colleges of America would infallibly make it in time such a seat of liberty, peace and science as I wish to see it.

I find myself very happy in the conversation and friendship of Mr Adams. I have lately managed for him the Assurance of Mr Houdon's life, but of this he will himself give you an account.

I see with pain the disagreeable turn which affairs are likely to take between this country and yours. I am grieved for the prejudices by which we are governed. From an opinion of the necessity of maintaining our Navigation laws against America, and that its interest together with the weakness of the federal government will always secure the admission of our exports, we are taking the way to lose the friendship and the trade of a world rapidly increasing and to throw its whole weight into the scale of France. Such is our policy. I have given my opinion of it; but without the hope of being regarded. The united states, however, may be gainers by this policy if it puts them upon strengthening their federal government; and if also it should check their rage for trade, detach them from their slavery to foreign tinsel, and render them more independent by causing them to seek all they want within themselves.

We are, at present, much encouraged here by the rapid rise of our stocks; and the influx of money occasioned by a turn of exchange in our favour which has hardly been ever known in an equal degree.

Accept, Sir, of the repetition of my assurances that I am, with all the best wishes and particular respect, your obliged and very obedient and humble servant

Richd Price

Dr Rogers will be made happy by any notice you may take of him.

To James Bowdoin

Newington=Green Oct 25th 1785

Sir,

I return you many thanks for your letter of the 12th of August last and for the memoirs with which it was accompany'd. It gives me much pleasure to find

---

ORIGINAL: Massachusetts Historical Society.   TEXT: Original, with the kind permission of the Massachusetts Historical Society.

that the American Academy of arts and sciences is honoured by a President so attentive to the interest of science and so capable of promoting it.[1] I shall be glad to see the volume of Memoirs which, I suppose, has before this time been printed and publish'd at Boston. May the American Academy flourish, and my hopes be verify'd of seeing the united states distinguish'd as seats of science, liberty, and virtue.

My sentiments of light are the same with those you defend in your first[2] and second memoir;[3] and your observations in answer to Dr Franklin's objections are, I think, decisive. Your Ideas also of an Orb surrounding visible nature and of concentric Orbs beyond it containing myriads of systems of worlds all so disposed as to cause the power of Gravity itself to preserve them in their original order. These Ideas open the imagination and lead to enlarged views of the grandeur of the Universe.[4] You propose them also with a diffidence and caution which are the general characteristics of wisdom, and which on such a subject are particularly proper. You will, therefore, I dare say, not be displeased with me for observing that Mr Herschel's late discoveries in the heavens have overthrown some of your arguments for the existence of such orbs.[5] An account of these discoveries has been given in two of the last Numbers of the Philosophical Transactions; and you may probably before this time have found in them that the appearance of the *Milky Way* is occasioned certainly by the blended light of a vast multitude of stars; that the heavens are full of *Nebulae*; that many of the *Nebulae* are resolvable into clusters of stars and others so distant as not to be so resolvable by Mr Herschel's largest magnifiers; that very probably our sun with the planets that move round it is one system in the milky way; and that the milky way itself with all the starry heavens discoverable by the naked eye form a cluster which appears a Nebula to distant Nebulae. Mr Herschel has also, in some former volumes of the Philosophical Transactions, shewn, contrary to an intimation of yours, that the solar system moves, and he has gone so far as even to point out the

---

1. James Bowdoin was the first President of the American Academy of Arts and Sciences. See Vol. I, 232.

2. "Observations upon an Hypothesis for Solving the Phenomena of Light: with Incidental Observations, tending to show the Heterogeniousness of Light, and of the Electric Fluid, by their Intermixture, or Union, with each other", *Memoirs of the American Academy of Arts and Sciences* (Boston, 1785), I, 187–94.

3. "Observations on Light, and the Waste of Matter in the Sun and Fixt Stars, occasioned by the Constant Efflux of Light from them", ibid., 195–207.

4. "Observations Tending to Prove, by Phenomena and Scripture, the Existence of an Orb, which Surrounds the Whole Visible Material System; and which may be necessary to Preserve it from Ruin, to which, without such a Counter-Balance, it seems liable by that Universal Principle in Matter, Gravitation," ibid., I, 208–46.

5. "Account of some Observations tending to Investigate the Construction of the Heavens,' *Phil. Trans.*, LXXIV (1784), 437–51; "On the Construction of the Heavens", *Phil. Trans.*, LXXV (1785), 213–66.

direction of its motion; and if our system moves it is most likely that other systems move.[6]

I must add, that it appears to me that since the light of the sun extinguishes the light of the moon and stars, it must have a much greater effect in extinguishing the light of an Orb so distant as that which you suppose, and that for this reason it seems impossible that the azure colour of the sky in a bright day should not be the light of the sun reflected by the air. Were this the light of an Orb beyond the fixed stars its white as well as its azure parts would appear in the day time; and they would appear fainter or brighter just as their light was more or less obliterated by the light of the sun and also the moon.

I beg leave further to observe, that the mean distance of Mr Herschel's planet being about 18 times the distance of the earth, the number of miles contained in this distance cannot exceed about 2000 millions. In p. 38 you have intimated that it is 5000 millions. I think I sent some time ago to Mr Willard an account of the Elements of the orbit of this planet as they have been determined by some of the best European Astronomers.[7]

I return you my best thanks for your readiness to assist Mr Lewis and tho' the offer you made of your kindness to him did not answer the end intended by it, he is equally obliged to you. I am truly sorry for the disagreeable situation of affairs between this country and yours. I lament the policy we are likely to pursue, and dread its consequences. It may prove fatal to us should we lose by it the trade and friendship of your increasing world and throw them entirely into the scale of France. The united states, however, will in my opinion profit by it should it check among them the luxury, the inequality, selfishness and avarice foster'd by trade, and teach them frugality, simplicity of manners, and the necessity of strengthening their federal union.

Permit me to congratulate you on your elevation to the station of Governor of your state.[8] Nothing, next to the testimony of a good conscience, can be more agreeable than such a proof of the approbation of free and enlighten'd citizens. It is an honour much greater than being by descent King of Great Britain or France. I doubt not but the state of Massachusetts will profit much by your integrity and abilities.

Dr Franklin had left Europe at the time I received your letter to him; and, therefore, I have burnt it without opening it.

Under a very grateful sense of your Excellency's kind attention and with all the best wishes and great respect I am

Your very obedient and humble servant

Rich*d* Price

---

6. "On the Proper Motion of the Sun and Solar System; with an Account of Several Changes that have happened among the Fixed Stars since the Time of Mr Flamsteed", *Phil. Trans.*, LXXIII (1783), 247–83.

7. Price sent an account of Herschel's discovery of Uranus to Willard in his letter of 6 Oct. 1783.

8. See R.P. to James Bowdoin, 31 May 1785, n.2.

P.S. I am very happy in the acquaintance of Mr Adams, and wish he was more encouraged in his Negotiations. This letter was written in October and kept in hopes of a direct conveyance to Boston, but not being able to find this I have sent it by way of New=York. I hope Mr Temple is safely arrived.

To the Marquis of Lansdowne

Newington Green Oct: 29*th* 1785

My Lord,

I have been for some time wishing and intending to address a few lines to your Lordship to thank you for the presents of Pine=apples and Game which have been sent me; but having nothing else of any consequence to write about I have omitted it. I was glad to learn from Count Sarsfield that he had left your Lordship and Lady Lansdown well. I returned from my visit to Yarmouth in the beginning of September after spending a month there agreeably with my Nephew,[1] the Brother of Mr Morgan in Chatham place, who last spring removed from Norwich to Yarmouth in order to be near the sea and also to live among his wife's relations who are some of the principal dissenters there. I found him full or ardor in Philosophical pursuits but too destitute of the means of gratifying his wishes. Like many other dissenting ministers his income, since he has had a family is become too narrow for him, and he is obliged to apply himself to the education of pupils; an employment for which I believe, he is extremely well qualify'd. He has two pupils, but wishes for three or four more.

I am sorry I could not have the pleasure of seeing Lord Wycombe before he went abroad. He honoured me with an obliging Note before he set out; and I should have called upon him had I known sooner of his being in town.

Mr Pitt, I fancy, must feel that he has lost ground lately. I wish, indeed, that instead of wasting a whole year on his *Irish* propositions he had endeavoured to bring about an amicable commercial settlement with America and to establish a plan of redemption. These appear to me objects of the first importance. The first has been neglected so long that there is reason to fear it will never be accomplish'd. A letter which I lately received from Mr Jefferson at Paris tells me "that his country and mine are getting into a ferment against one another; that certainly the issue will be one or other of two extremes, there being no medium between countries that once loved so much; that the decision is at present in the power of this country, but that it will not be so long."[2] Our

---

ORIGINAL: Bowood.   TEXT: Original, with the kind permission of the Marquis of Lansdowne.

1. George Cadogan Morgan, who married Anne "Nancy" Hurry.
2. A free rendering of a passage in Thomas Jefferson's letter to R.P., 7 Aug. 1785.

retention of the Posts between Canada and New=England; the language of some of our great men in Parliament, and our restraints on the trade of America are likely to produce the worst effects. Perhaps I may be wrong; but I find it impossible not to lament the prejudices by which we are governed. From an apprehension of the necessity of maintaining the Navigation laws, and that our exports will always force their way, we are pursuing measures which will deprive us of the trade and friendship of a world rapidly increasing and throw it entirely into the scale of *France*. During the war the cry was that our essential interests depended on keeping the colonies. Now it seems to be discover'd that they are of no use to us. The policy of The King of France's ministers is different. They are now offering to take from them duty free that oil which we have prohibited and with which we will not allow them to pay their debts.

They are forming a contract with them for that supply of masts which used to be sent to this country. They are also, I am informed, proposing a contract to them for tobacco. The returns to be made in French exports.

Mrs Price send her best respects. She continues much the same; but I am sometimes alarmed by the apprehension that the difficulty with which she speaks will end in the total loss of the powers of speaking.

Dr Priestley has lately received a request, attended with an offer of any compensation, from Lord Bristol[3] to remove to Ireland to educate his son; But he is so well satisfy'd with his situation at Birmingham that nothing can induce him to quit it.

I hope your Lordship will excuse this scribble, and always believe me to be with sincere wishes of your and Lady Lansdown's happiness and invariable regard

Your Lordship's most obedient
and humble servant
Rich*d* Price

---

3. Frederick Augustus Hervey (1730–1803), fourth Earl of Bristol. Bishop of Derry from 1768 and Chaplain General to the Irish Volunteers from 1782.

To Benjamin Franklin

Newington=Green Nov 5*th* 1785

Dear Friend,

I send you with this a pamphlet at the end of which you will find an account of a remedy which has been lately try'd with success in the sad malady with which you are troubled. I have been led to this by the remarkable relief which

---

ORIGINAL: American Philosophical Society.   PRINTED: *Franklin*: Bigelow, XII, 375 (incomplete). TEXT: Original, with the kind permission of the American Philosophical Society.

it has lately given in this malady to a gentleman among my acquaintance. This gentleman is Mr Barrett, Brother in law to Mr Hollis[1] in Great Ormond= Street. After going thro' more misery than can be express'd and being long confined, he now enjoys a considerable degree of ease and is able to go about in a carriage. Knowing this fact I could not make myself easy without communicating it to you together with an account of the remedy.

I heard a few days ago with particular pleasure of your safe arrival at Philadelphia, and of the joy with which you were received there. We had been alarmed here by accounts in the public papers of your being taken by an *Algerine* private and carried into slavery. I was so foolish as to believe this account when I first read it, but a little inquiry and consideration soon convinced me that the distress it gave me was groundless. May you still live to be happy in the respect and gratitude of your country, and to bless it by your counsel. It was a mortification to me that I could not make one of the friends who had the pleasure of being with you at Southhampton. I return you many thanks for the kind lines you sent me from thence. They gave me great pleasure.

I received some time ago from Mr Vaughn[2] a Diploma constituting me a member of the Philosophical Society at Philadelphia.[3] Will you be so good as to convey to the President and other members of the Society, in whatever manner you may think proper, my very grateful acknowledgements. I cannot but be impress'd by the honour they have done me; and I hope they will accept my wishes of their increasing credit and prosperity, to which, were it in my power, I should be glad to contribute.

I am sorry for the hostile aspect of affairs between this country and yours. The general cry during the war was, that the colonies were too important to be given up and that our essential interests depended on keeping them. It seems now to be discover'd among us that they are of no use to us; and the issue may be, that we shall lose the trade and friendship of an increasing world, and throw it into the scale of *France*. Our restraints, however, will do good to the united states should their effect be to oblige them to strengthen their federal government, to check their rage for trade, and to render them more independent by causing them to find all they want within themselves.

Should you happen to see Mr Vaughn, or any of his family deliver my kind compliments to them. With every respectful sentiment and the most affectionate regard I am ever yours

Rich*d* Price

Mrs Price sends her respects. She continues sadly depress'd and crippled by the Palsy.

---

1. Timothy Hollis (see Vol. I, 177).
2. John Vaughan (see *re* John Vaughan, 10 Jan. 1782).
3. Price was elected a member of the American Philosophical Society on 28 Jan. 1785.

From William Foster

Reverend and Respected Sir,

    I have not till now acknowledg'd the receipt of your esteemed letter with one of your excellent address to the Inhabitants of the United States. You will please to accept my sincere thanks therefor. I most sincerely hope you will not finally be dissatisfy'd at the conduct of these States. This present embarrass'd situation makes them appear in a more disadvantageous light than they deserve. I doubt not but in the course of two or three years they will wear a very different aspect.

    I have taken the freedom of putting a cask of Cranberries on board our Ship call'd the Hero, John Young Commander. marked R.P. which Captain Young will deliver to your order. They are esteemed the most acceptable sauce in use and hope will meet your acceptance. Shall esteem it a particular favour if you'll command me in any thing of the growth or produce of this Country either for your self or any of your very Honourable friends, and am

Your oblig'd and very humble servant
Wm Foster

P.S. Have received a packet from Cambridge and now forward it by Captain Young

---

ORIGINAL: American Philosophical Society. TEXT: Original, with the kind permission of the American Philosophical Society.

From William Hazlitt

Dear Sir,

    I wrote a short letter[1] to you above a year ago, which, I believe, you have received, as the answers I have had to those which accompanied it were an evidence that the whole packet arrived safe. Notwithstanding some untoward circumstances; I still hope that the American Revolution will be finally beneficial to the whole human race. I, therefore, wish you to continue your benevolent exertions to meliorate and enlighten this people, and to arouse

---

ORIGINAL: American Philosophical Society. PRINTED *M.H.S.P.* (1903), p. 334. TEXT: Original, with the kind permission of the American Philosophical Society.
    1. See William Hazlitt to R.P., 19 Oct. 1784.

them to improve and perfect their several forms of government. No man living can influence them so much as you. You are furnished, I know, almost every day with an ample detail of the state of things here. But you have one correspondent, I mean Dr Rush of Philadelphia, whose information I cannot help cautioning you to receive with diffidence. He is the tool of a party, whilst his vanity leads him to imagine himself the principal, who are labouring to destroy the present constitution of Pennsylvania, and to introduce in its room one which is in a great measure aristocratical, and, in my opinion, very inimical to liberty. He hates Dr Ewing, on account of his superior abilities, and particularly because he is a friend to the present constitution, and has fifty times his influence. He made a very scurrilous and base attack upon the Doctor, when he was at a great distance from Philadelphia, and, what particularly characterises him with me, is, that he represented the Doctor as an iniquitous man, on account of his catholicism, thinking that this measure would effectually ruin him with the public. After pretending that he himself was my very good friend he, upon mere suspicion, proclaimed me a Socinian in the News papers and reproached Dr Ewing as an unprincipled hypocrite, because that he, being a Presbyterian, was affectionately attached to me, and had warmly recommended me to be the pastor of a church at Carlisle, and the principal of that University. This conduct, so ungentlemanlike with respect to me, and so inconsistent with his own past professions of esteem and friendship, and that great assiduity with which he affected to serve me, disgusted me exceedingly, and made me think meanly of him ever since. I was first introduced to Dr Rush by Mr John Vaughan. He, then, paid me many fulsome compliments, congratulated the country upon the acquisition of such a man as he said I was, told me that he had heard me preach, and that my sentiments were too enlarged, and my compositions too elegant for the undiscerning multitude, but lamented that there were not many such, in the country, to cultivate a rational mode of thinking, and to disperse that darkness which overspread it. He afterwards talked to me, in the same strain, and promised me great things. But, when he found, that there was a popular clamour against me, as the Editor of Dr Priestley's Appeal etc. printed at Philadelphia,[2] he coldly told me, that he was contented with the religion of his ancestors. This declaration then lowered him much in my estimation. But, still, I did not think him capable of that subsequent conduct which I mentioned above. Dr Latrop[3] of Boston is as worthy a man as in America. He is friendly, generous, and without guile. On whatever accounts he sends you from his own knowledge you may absolutely depend. Dr Chauncy, you know, is thoroughly honest. But he takes it for granted, that the world will continually be growing worse until

2. An edition of Joseph Priestley's *An Appeal to the Serious and Candid Professors of Christianity* was published in Philadelphia in 1784. (*Nat. Union Cat.*)

3. John Lathrop, Minister of the Second Church in Boston. See William Hazlitt to R.P., 19 Oct. 1784.

the consummation of all things. Besides, his warm temper frequently leads him into mistakes. Mr Clarke is very sensible and ingenious, whilst he possesses a great share of vanity. There are some other intelligent and very worthy ministers in Boston, particularly Howard,[4] Everitt,[5] and Elliot[6]. The late Dr Mather,[7] though a treasury of valuable historical anecdotes, was as weak a man as I ever knew. He took it for granted, that his last letter to you would make you a trinitarian, just as he supposed that his last letter to Dr Lardner[8] made him die of a broken heart. I am sorry that the people of England are squandering away great sums of money, in endeavouring to raise Nova Scotia into consequence. The Old Settlers and the Refugees hate one another. The former are removing here, as fast as they can sell their farms. The others are a horribly abandoned set, who damn the king and the country, and who are, some few excepted, determined to stay no longer there than they are supported in idleness by Great Britain, or a permission be granted them to return to the United States. I am now by the desire of Mr Vaughan, at Kennebec River, where, according to present appearances, I shall probably settle.[9] I wish that you were young enough to think of a Tour through this continent. Your presence would do much good. I am, dear Sir, your very affectionate and humble servant.

W. Hazlitt

If you should have the leisure to write to me, be pleased to direct to me at Boston N. England.

---

4. Simeon Howard, DD (1733–1804), graduated at Harvard in 1758 and succeeded Jonathan Mayhew at the West Church, Boston in May 1767. See J.W. Thornton, *The Pulpit of the American Revolution* (Boston, 1860), pp. 358ff.

5. Oliver Everett (1732–1802), Minister of the New South Church in Boston, and father of Alexander Hill Everett (1790–1847) and Edward Everett (1794–1865), the celebrated Unitarian preacher. Oliver Everett, a graduate of Harvard, became pastor of New South Church in 1781, and was a close friend of Dr James Freeman of King's Chapel who carried his congregation over to Unitarianism in 1787. See P.R. Frothingham *Edward Everett* (Boston and New York, 1925).

6. Andrew Eliot, see Vol. I, 53.

7. Samuel Mather, see Samuel Mather to R.P., 22 July 1784.

8. Nathaniel Lardner (1684–1768), Independent minister. His main work, *The Credibility of the Gospel History* was published in fourteen volumes in the period 1727 to 1757 and is devoted to reconciling discrepancies in the Biblical narratives. It proved to be an invaluable source of information for scholars working on the authorship of the New Testament. His *A Letter writ in the year 1730, concerning the question, whether the Logos supplied the place of a Human Soul in the Person of Jesus Christ* (London, 1759) was an influential document in the development of Socinian thought in Britain. See *Autobiography*, pp. 92–93.

9. On the invitation of Samuel Vaughan, Hazlitt went to a new settlement at Hallowell on the Kennebec River. He spent the winter there and then moved to Dorchester, near Boston. See W. Carew Hazlitt, *Four Generations of a Literary Family*, 2 vols. (London, 1897), I, 44.

From Benjamin Rush

Phil*a* Nov*r* 26. 1785

Dear Sir,

The bearer Richard Peters Esqr.[1] bore an active and distinguished part in the cabinet in bringing about the late american revolution. His principles—his conduct and his fortune have procured him the first rank in our Country. He wishes to pay his respects to the friends of liberty and mankind in great Britain. I have therefore for this purpose taken the liberty of introducing him to you, and have no doubt but he will give you such accurate and authentic information of our affairs as will be highly satisfactory to you.

With great respect I am D[ea]r Sir your sincere friend and humble servant

Benj*n* Rush

ORIGINAL: The Historical Society of Pennsylvania. TEXT: Original, with the kind permission of The Historical Society of Pennsylvania.

1. Richard Peters (1744–1828), lawyer. He graduated from the College of Philadelphia in 1761, and was admitted to the bar in 1763. He was appointed a captain of the militia in May 1775, and a member of the Board of War in 1777. In 1782 he was elected to Congress for a year. In 1787 he became a member, and later Speaker, of the Pennsylvania Assembly.

To the Marquis of Lansdowne

Newington=Green Nov 29th 1785

My Lord

I know not how to avoid sending your Lordship a few lines to thank you for the obliging letter with which I was favoured a few days ago. The account I gave of our situation with respect to America is, I believe, true. The Defensive alliance lately concluded between France and Holland is another event which seems to have a threatening aspect.[1] Our ministers became alarmed about it when too late; and in order to prevent it made the most extraordinary proposals to the Dutch. They went so far, if I am rightly informed, as even to offer to pay the ten millions of florins to the Emperor for them, to guarantee the treaty with him, and to relax our Acts of Navigation in their favour. I am much mistaken if there will not be the same kind of After=wisdom and repentance

ORIGINAL: Bowood. TEXT: Original, with the kind permission of the Marquis of Lansdowne.

1. The Treaty of Fontainebleau, at which the French mediated between Holland and Austria, was signed on 8 Nov. 1785. It was followed on 10 Nov. by the conclusion of a Franco-Dutch Alliance. Each state guaranteed the other the possession of all its territories, engaged to assist the other when attacked, and agreed to enter no treatise detrimental to the interest of the other. See Lecky, V, 78.

when a similar union takes place between *France* and the united states, and the trade and friendship of that increasing world, which we might have secured and from which we might have derived greater advantages than ever, are lost and become the means of adding to the power and increasing the naval force of France. I am apt to think that one circumstance which contributes to produce the tardiness of our ministers with respect to America is the apprehension, that which ever side they take the party called the coalition is determined to take the opposite side and to raise a clamour. His party has already too much to go upon in the Irish Propositions and the alliance between France and Holland. I am told by some of Mr Pitt's friends that he is much encouraged by the productiveness of the Revenue, and determined to establish a sinking Fund this winter. I should have more hope were your Lordship concerned in the direction of our affairs; and I am very sorry to learn from your Lordship's letter that there is no probability of this. Mr Arthur Lee concludes a letter which I have received lately from him with these words—"I lament Col Barre's loss of sight as one who has a particular esteem for him. It seems to me that there never was a measure more strongly stamped with folly and effrontery than the coalition. My situation gave me a particular opportunity of knowing the great merit of Lord Shelburne in making the peace and acceding to the Independence of the United States. My esteem for him remains unalter'd; and you will oblige me by remembering me to him and to Col: Barre".

Mrs Price thanks your Lordship for your kind notice of her. She continues in her usual state. Our best respects wait on Lady Lansdown. Col. Barre, I hear, is at Bath. Should you see him, I wish to be kindly remember'd to him. In hopes of the pleasure of seeing you in town in January and with all the best wishes and great regard

I am your Lordship's
Most obedient and humble servant
Rich*d* Price

From George Washington

Nov., 1785

G. Washington presents his most respectful compliments to Dr Price. With much thankfulness he has received, and with the highest gratification he has read, the doctor's excellent observations on the importance of the American revolution,[1] and the means of making it a benefit to the world. Most devoutly is

---

PRINTED: G. Bancroft, *History of the Formation of the Constitution of the United States of America* (New York), I, 466. TEXT: Bancroft.

1. *Observations on the Importance of the American Revolution.*

it to be wished that reasoning so sound should take deep root in the minds of the revolutionists. But there is cause to apprehend that the inconveniences resulting from ill-founded jealousies and local politics must be felt ere a more liberal system of federal government is adopted. The latter I am persuaded will happen, but its progress may be slow—unless, as the revolution itself was, it should be precipitated by the all-grasping hand of..., or the illiberal and mistaken policy of other nations.

For the honourable notice of me in your address, I pray you to receive my warmest acknowledgements, and the assurance of the sincere esteem and respect which I entertain for you.

To William Adams

Newington=Green Dec 3d 1785

Dear Sir,

I have received with great pleasure your obliging letter, and the night before it arrived I had likewise received very safely your present of Brawn. I had so little reason to expect such a present, and it is so acceptable to me and a testimony of your kind remembrance of me that I know not how to thank you sufficiently for it. I can truly say that there are few in the world of whom I think with equal respect or whom I honour so much. Mrs Price desires I would add her particular acknowledgements to my own. She feels very sensibly the notice you take of her in your letter; and as she is fond of Brawn she will be often oblig'd to renew her respectful remembrance of you. She is sadly crippled in her limbs and often much depress'd in her spirits; but, I thank God, the humiliating disease which has attacked her, has never affected her understanding. By the last of her Paralytic strokes she was for some days almost deprived of her power of swallowing and speaking. She still speaks imperfectly, and is in a great degree incapable of reading, writing, dressing and feeding herself. My life upon the whole has been a happy life and I have great reason for gratitude to the giver of it. This illness of Mrs Price's has been my greatest affliction. I am now in my grand Clima[c]teric and find myself advanced into the evening of life. May God make it a serene evening; and, after that night of death which is coming upon us all, raise us up to a better life.

My book on morals having been for some time out of print, I am busily employ'd in revising it with a view to a 3d edition which I hope will be

ORIGINAL: Gloucestershire County Records Office. TEXT: Original with the kind permission of the Gloucestershire County Records Office.

publish'd some time or other in the spring.[1] All the alterations and additions I shall throw together in Notes at the end; and among these Notes I shall probably introduce one in which I shall express the disappointment I have met with in reading Mr Paley's Lectures on the principles of moral and political Philosophy.[2] Indeed I have never read a book which has disappointed me more.

I deliver'd in the summer to my congregation at Hackney a set of sermons on the different schemes of Christianity in which after stating the chief of these schemes, I gave my reasons for rejecting Socinianism and prefering the middle scheme between it and the Trinitarian and Calvinistic schemes. In consequence of a petition from the congregation, I have promised to publish them and I am now transcribing them; and this is another business that employs me.[3]

I have heard that the Bishop of Exeter[4] has lately informed his Clergy that alterations must be made in the Church=service and constitution, and assured them that they *will* be made. I know that he, and the Bishops of Landaff[5] and St Asaph[6] are very liberal, and will, I doubt not, do all they can to promote the reformation so much wanted. I have received this week a printed copy of the Book of Common prayer as alter'd and reformed by the Episcopalians at Boston in New=England. They have excluded from it every thing that is to me exceptionable; and were the church=service such as they have made it, I could heartily joyn in it and use it. This is the consequence of being at liberty.

Deliver my kind respects to Miss Adams. Wishing you, my dear friend, every valuable enjoyment and all that can make the remainder of an useful and important life happy, I am, with the truest affection and esteem,

Your obliged and very humble servant

Rich*d* Price

---

1. The third edition of *Review* was not published until 1787. In an appendix (pp. 485–87; Raphael's ed., pp. 282–84) Price strongly criticized Paley's *The Principles of Moral and Political Philosophy* which had been published in 1785. Price's criticisms centred on Paley's definitions of obligation and right, on his psychological egoism, on his account of the significance of subscription to religious tests; and, in political philosophy, on his definition of civil liberty, his rejection of the doctrine of the social contract, his defence of standing armies, and his interpretation of the constitution.

2. William Paley (1743–1805), Archdeacon of Carlisle.

3. These sermons were published under the title *Sermons on the Christian Doctrine* in 1787. See R.P. to Mr Cotton, 26 Aug. 1785.

4. John Ross was Bishop of Exeter from Jan. 1778 until his death in 1792. Not long after his consecration he preached a sermon to the House of Lords "in which he urged that toleration should be extended and that the fullest legal security should be given to the Dissenters for the free exercise of their worship." See Arthur Warne, *Church and Society in Eighteenth Century Devon* (Newton Abbott, 1969), p. 28.

5. Richard Watson (1737–1816) became Bishop of Llandaff in 1782. Previous appointments included Professor of Chemistry at Cambridge (1764), Regius Professor of Divinity at Cambridge (1772), and Archdeacon of Ely (1771). Elected FRS in 1769. For a discussion of Watson's liberal views in theology and other matters see Timothy Brain, "Richard Watson and the Debate on Toleration in the late Eighteenth Century", *The Price–Priestley Newsletter*, No. 2 (1976), 4–26.

6. Jonathan Shipley.

My friend Dr Priestley is about printing four volumes in Octavo in defence of Socinianism.[7] The first volume he has just sent me and I am going to read it. We differ much in Metaphysics and Divinity, but with perfect respect for one another.

---

7. Joseph Priestley, *An History of Early Opinions concerning Jesus Christ, compiled from Original Writers proving that the Christian Church was at first Unitarian*, 4 vols. (Birmingham, 1786).

To Ezra Stiles

Newington=Green Dec 5th 1785

Rev:d and Dear Sir,

I received about three weeks ago your letter inclosing one to Mr Lovell's wife and another to his son. I have since convey'd these letters to Frome, the town in Somersetshire and within 20 miles of Bristol mention'd in them, and got some gentlemen there to enquire after the family they describe. The answer I have received is that, after a particular search it cannot be found that any such person as Mr Lovell describes has after [?] lived there or that any one of the family he describes is now or ever has been living there. Some of the oldest men in the town say that no such person in trade has lived there in their time, nor can they remember they have ever heard of a man who was missing there and had left a wife and seven children. If Parishioners and in low circumstances, it is thought the wife would have made an application to the Parish for relief; but no trace of any such application can be discover'd.

There are, it seems, two other places that go by the name of Frome, one in Gloucestershire and the other in Dorsetshire, but they are obscure villages, and Frome in Somersetshire being the only place of this name much known and answering to Mr Lovell's account, I have not thought it worth while to make an enquiry in either of these places; nor do I know how easily to make it. I shall desire the enquiry at Frome in Somersetshire to be continued, and will inform you should I succeed, of which, however, I have no hope. In the meantime it will be right to examine Mr Lovell again. The story he tells is so circumstantial, as you have given it from him, that I know not how to suspect any imposition; and yet it seems strange that he should have lived in America fifteen years without having, long before this time, made an enquiry after such a family as, he says, he left behind him. I shall be glad, therefore, to hear from you again on this subject.

ORIGINAL: Yale University Library. TEXT: Original, with the kind permission of Yale University Library.

I writ to you I think about two or three months ago by Mr Hubbard, and sent you a copy of an Edition of my Observations on the American Revolution publish'd in London which, I hope, you have received.[1]

There are, I find, in your state several episcopal churches; and some time ago a Bishop[2] was consecrated for them by some Nonjuring Bishops in Scotland. I admire the liberality of the state in admitting him, And I am told also, that the people of the state have made collections toward helping these churches to repair their places of worship. Such harmony between different religious sects is what I wish much to spread; but I am afraid you will find in Dr Seabury the foolish pride and haughtiness of a man who thinks he belongs to a higher order and considers himself as elevated above the other ministers in the state. I hope you will be able to teach him more humility and wisdom.

Being in haste I can only add that I am, Dear Sir,

truly and respectfully yours
Rich*d* Price

---

1. See R.P. to Ezra Stiles, 2 Aug. 1785.
2. Samuel Seabury, see Jonathan Trumbull, the Elder, to R.P., 29 Apr. 1785.

From Nathaniel Gorham

Boston Dec*r* 26 1785

Dear Sir,

Your esteemed favours accompanied with your very valuable Books I received and took care to disperse them in a manner likely to answer the best purpose. They have been reprinted here and have been universally read and much approved. I was soon after my return chosen Speaker of our Assembly[1] which with my other avocations has so much engrossed my time as to prevent my paying my respects to you sooner, but though late I am sure nobody does it more respectfully or sincerely. I shall never forget your marks of attention and kindness to me. I wish our confederated Government was stronger and our finances better arranged, but I hope for the best. I shall set of tomorrow with Mr Hancock[2] the President to take my seat in Congress, when if I find any thing worth your notice I will do myself the honor of writing you from N. York.

ORIGINAL: The New York Historical Society.   TEXT: Original with the kind permission of the New York Historical Society.

1. See R.P. to Joseph Willard, 6 Oct. 1783.
2. John Hancock (1737–93). President of the Continental Congress from May 1775 to Oct. 1777. The first to sign the Declaration of Independence. Governor of Massachusetts from 1780 to 1785 and from 1787 to 1793 On 23 Nov. Hancock was elected President of Congress. (Boatner, p. 483.)

I want, Sir, to ask your advice on a matter of very considerable importance to an individual here which may be thus stated. Some years ago, Sir Arthur Haselrig[3] had an only son[4] who came to this Country and after living a dissolute life for some time married a very worthy and amiable Young Lady,[5] *Daughter* to a Mr Walter[6] the Congregational Minister of Roxbury, by whom he had three children, one son[7] and two daughters[8] and then returned to England and still lived in such a manner as to displease his Father. Old Sir Arthur, being deceived as to the character of his Son's wife and her connections, previous to his Death settled £200 a year on his son who died in the Fleet prison, and by his Will gave all his very great landed Estate to Lord Maynard[9] with limitations if Lord Maynard died without issue to his Lord Maynard several Brothers, and if they all died without issue then to revert to his own family, viz the three children above mentioned, the son first and if he failed of issue to the daughters. The case now is that the several Maynards are all dead without issue except the present Lord,[10] who is somewhat advanced as I am informed, as well as his Wife.[11] He has no children. His heir apparent as to the estate in question is the young Sir Arthur Haselrig, about 30 years old, the son of the above marriage, who has been married several years and has no children and who is very infirm Man now in the East Indies. The two daughters reside in this Country, the eldest of which is marri[e]d to a worthy Man, a Congregational Clergyman who has been dismissed from his Parish and is rather in low circumstances. And it would conduce much to his and his wife's comfort if they could raise a sum of money from their prospect[12] to this estate, which I was informed by a relation of theirs now in England amounts to th[letter torn] thousand sterling per annum laying in all most all the Midland Counties in England. They think as Lord Maynard is near sixty years old, his Wife about 50, and no person between Lord Maynard and them except the Brother in

---

3. Sir Arthur Hesilrige, the seventh baronet (d. 1763). In 1725 he married Hannah Sturges who was reputed to be the model for Richardson's Pamela. (*Burke's Peerage*, 1104.)

4. Sir Robert Hesilrige, the eighth baronet. (Ibid.)

5. Sarah Waller, daughter of Nathaniel Waller of Roxburgh, New England. (Ibid.)

6. i.e. Nathaniel Waller. (Ibid.)

7. Sir Arthur Hesilrige, the ninth baronet, who died in 1805. (Ibid.)

8. Sarah, who married David Henley, and Hannah who married Revd Thomas Abbott. (Ibid.)

9. Charles, Baron Maynard of Estaines ad Turrim (c. 1690–1775). Sometime Fellow of Christ's College, Cambridge, he was appointed Recorder of Saffron Walden in 1749 and from 1763 to 1769 was Lord Lieutenant of Suffolk. He was created Viscount Maynard in 1766. (*Complete Peerage*, VIII, 602–604.)

10. Charles, Viscount Maynard of Easton Lodge (1752–1824). He married Anne Parsons (or Horton, see n. 11) in June or July 1776. (Ibid.)

11. Anne Parsons was the daughter of a Bond Street tailor who lived with Hoghton or Horton, a slave trader, with whom she went to Jamaica. Returning to England she achieved notoriety by becoming the mistress of the third Duke of Grafton. (Ibid.)

12. The expectations of the two daughters of the Revd Waller must have been disappointed because Lord Maynard (who lived until 1824) and Sir Arthur Hesilrige (who lived until 1805), were not as infirm in 1785 as Nathaniel Gorham had been led to suppose.

India, that money might be had, provided they engaged to pay a much larger sum if they ever possessed the estate. I shall be exceedingly obliged if you will think on this subject and write me your opinion, directed for me at N. York; if your avocations will admit of your doing it soon, you will exceedingly oblige me, and in the meantime I remain with every sentiment of esteem and regard, Sir, Your most Humble Servant

Nathaniel Gorham

From William Pitt

8th January, 1786.

Dear Sir,

The subject of the papers which I enclose will I am sure be an apology for the liberty I take in troubling you, and in requesting your opinion upon them. When you have had sufficient leisure to consider them, I should be greatly obliged to you, if you will allow me to hope for the pleasure of seeing you at any time that is convenient to you. The situation of the revenue certainly makes this the time to establish an effectual Sinking Fund. The general idea of converting the *three per cents* into a fund bearing a higher rate of interest, with a view to facilitate redemption, you have on many occasions suggested, and particularly in the papers you were so good to send me last year.[1] The rise of the Stocks has made a material change since that period, and I am inclined to think something like the plan[2] I now send you may be more adapted to the present circumstances. There may be, I believe, some inaccuracies in the calculations, but not such as to be very material. Before I form any decisive opinion, I wish to learn your sentiments upon it; and shall think myself obliged to you for any improvement you can suggest, if you think the principle a right one; or for any other proposal which from your knowledge of the subject you may think preferable.

[No signature]

PRINTED: Richard Price, *Observations on Reversionary Payments*, 6th ed., 2 vols. (London, 1803), I, 318–19. TEXT: *Observations on Reversionary Payments*.

1. See R.P. to John Wilkes, 28 Apr. 1785.

2. Pitt's scheme provided for the conversion of £107 millions of the 3 per cents into a 5 per cent stock, an operation that would require an increase in interest charges of £510,000 per annum. The remainder of the annual surplus would be used to reduce the principal of the 5 per cent stock.

To William Pitt

Newington=Green Jany 9th 1786

Sir,

I think myself much honoured by your letter[1] and the communication of the papers which accompany'd it. I shall be glad to peruse them and to send you as soon as I can what may occur to me in considering them. I rejoyce to find that you intend this sessions to establish a plan of redemption. It is impossible that any greater service should be done to the public, or that a minister should engage in any undertaking that will do him greater honour should it succeed. It is of particular importance that the plan should be the most efficient that can be contrived; and it must require a good deal of deliberation to find out such a plan. I need not say that any assistance I can give is always ready as far as it can be of any use. The late rise of the stocks has made some alterations necessary in those tables which I sent you some time ago; and I have lately composed a supplement to them which I will send you as soon as I can get it properly copy'd. With the greatest respect I am, Sir,

Your very obedient and humble servant
Rich*d* Price

ORIGINAL: PRO 30/8/169. TEXT: Original, with the kind permission of the Public Record Office.
1. William Pitt to R.P., 8 Jan. 1786.

To William Pitt

Newington-Green Jany 12th 1786

Dear Sir,

I take the liberty to request your inspection of the inclosed tables. The first of them will shew that an annual surplus without any aid whatever may be employ'd much more efficiently in sinking the public debts, than by the measure of conversion proposed in the papers which you have done me the honour to send me. This measure redeems, as is shewn in these papers, a capital of 107 millions in the 3 per cents in 44 years, and creates a free Revenue after this term of £4.210,000. The first of the inclosed tables will prove that the same surplus employ'd as there stated will be equally efficient in a much less period, that in the *same* period it will redeem a capital of 123 millions, and

---

ORIGINAL: PRO 30/8/169. TEXT: Original, with the kind permission of the Public Record Office.

create a free Revenue of £5.418.227 paying always at *par* after the three first payments; but that paying the 3 per cents at 90 from the 30th year it will redeem 132 millions, and create a free revenue of £5.687,364.

This seems to me to give a decisive preference to this method of applying such a surplus; and it is an additional very strong recommendation of it that it produces its effects without any other management than is necessary to prevent interruption, and also without the necessity of procuring the consent of the public creditors, and consequently without the possibility of miscarrying. On the contrary; the success of the measure of conversion as explained in these papers, depending on the consent of the public creditors, must be very doubtful. Indeed, I cannot help thinking that it would not succeed; and I need not say what harm would be done to a minister by attempting in this case an unsuccessful measure. The chief argument in favour of it is that it would render more than half the million surplus incapable of being diverted, and therefore an interruption less hurtful. But the truth seems to be that it will render an interruption more hurtful by taking from the public for ever that part of the surplus; whereas, on the other plan the whole of it will remain for ever free, and, in case of an interruption, return to the public with the addition of that part of the revenue which it had made free *before* the interruption.

The reason of the great difference in respect of efficiency between this measure and the plan in the first table is that the former, in consequence of applying more than half the surplus to the purpose of conversion, effects no more than would be effected by the whole surplus were it apply'd to the redemption of the 3 *per cents* at so high a price as 90 or to debts bearing little more than 3 per cent interest; whereas the latter begins with the 3 per cents so low as 75, and after redeeming these low for three years proceeds to debts bearing 4 and 5 per cent interest for 26 years afterwards.

The conversion proposed in the 3d table is very different in its nature. It is a conversion by which the operations of a Fund consisting of a million *per Ann* surplus is so much aided as to give a free revenue in 34 years of $4\frac{1}{2}$ millions after giving back to the public this surplus itself, the temporary annuities which lapsed to it, and also the whole annual expence occasioned by the conversion.

I imagine, likewise, that this is a conversion which could not but be accepted by the public creditors. In this case there is a settled market price to guide us; and there can be no doubt but that the stockholders would eagerly advance any payment less than the market price. Whereas, in the other case, we have no such guide; and, in my opinion, the prospect of a reduction of 30 *per cent* in the capital of a favourite stock which owes its disproportionate value chiefly to its high capital would operate so strongly on the imaginations of the stockholders as to cause it to be scouted tho' demonstrably advantageous. I may, however, be mistaken in this expectation; and I refer these observations entirely to the decision of your judgment.

The calculations in the papers you have sent to me seem to be made skillfully and justly; but it will be very difficult to make the people in the Alley understand them; nor is there, as I think, any occasion for putting this upon them, a plan easy, simple and not possible to be defeated being much more efficient:

May I request leave to keep your papers a few days longer? Some farther observations have occurr'd to me in examining them; but being afraid of saying any thing too hastily, I wish to re=consider them, after which I will take the liberty to write again to you.

I have the honour to be, with great respect,

Your most obedient and humble servant

Rich*d* Price

From Mathon de la Cour

Lyon 14 Janvier 1786

Monsieur,

Daignez recevoir l'hommage de la vive et eternelle reconnoissance d'un homme qui n'a pas l'honneur d'etre connu de vous, mais qui vous a cependant l'une des plus grandes obligations qu'un homme de lettres puisse avoir a une autre. L'illustre M. franklin m'a envoyé un ouvrage pretieux a la suite duquel vous avez joint la traduction du Testament de Fortuné Ricard, bagatelle qui a eu quelque succès en France parce que l'idée en a paru neuve.[1] J'avois cherché a y laisser entrevoir quelque vues d'utilité publique et j'en suis bien recompensé puisque vous avez daigné vous occuper quelque momens de mon ouvrage et la faire connoitre a une nation aussi estimable que la vôtre. Etre traduit n'est rien en comparaison de l'honneur de l'être par vous. Je ne saurois assez vous exprimer à quel point j'y suis sensible et le serai toute ma vie. Je profite du départ d'un de mes compatriots pour l'angleterre pour vous faire parvenir mes très sincères remercimens. Je vous prie d'accepter un discours sur la décadence des lois de Lycurgue.[2] Je souhaiterois bien que cet ouvrage méritât l'approbation d'un juge aussi eclairé de la constitution des états, mais mon but en vous l'offrant est surtout de vous faire parvenir l'hommage de ma

ORIGINAL: Cyfarthfa Castle Museum. TEXT: Original, with the kind permission of the Cyfarthfa Castle Museum. Price notes on the reverse: A letter from Mr de la Core at Lyon, author of the Testament of Fortune Ricard dated Jan 14th 1786. Answered.

1. See Benjamin Franklin to R.P., 1 Feb. 1785. Price had included a translation of Mathon de la Cour's *Testament de Fortuné Ricard* in the 1785 edition of *Observations on the Importance of the American Revolution.*

2. *Par Quelles Causes et par Quels Degrès les Loix de Lycurgue se sont alterées chez les Lacédémoniens jusqu'a ce qu'elles ayent été aneantiés.* (Lyon and Paris, 1767).

reconnoissance en vous présentant comme dans les anciens sacrifices les premiers de mes travaux en litterature.

J'ai l'honneur d'être avec la considération le plus respectueux

Monsieur
Votre très humble et tres obeissant serviteur
Mathon de la Cour
des academies de Lyon, Villefranche

From William Pitt

Holwood Hill, 15th January, 1786

Dear Sir,

I am much obliged to you for the observations you have been so good to send me on the papers I troubled you with. They appear to me on the whole very convincing. I shall think myself much obliged to you, if you would do me the honor to call any morning after Tuesday next in Downing Street, when you have done with the papers. And if it should be in your power to let me know the day before, and to fix an early hour, I can be certain of being at leisure. The reason of my making this request is, that I think some points may occur which may be better explained in conversation than by writing, and I am anxious to avail myself to the utmost of your assistance, where it may be so material,[1]

I am, dear Sir, with great truth and esteem,
Your most obedient and faithful servant,
W. Pitt

PRINTED: Richard Price, *Observations on Reversionary Payments*, 6th ed., 2 vols. (London, 1803), I, 320–21. TEXT: *Observations on Reversionary Payments*.

1. The interview was arranged for 19 January.

To William Pitt

Newington=Green Jan*y* 18*th* 1786

Dear Sir

I now return you the papers which I received last week, and hope I have not put you to any inconvenience by keeping them so long. The principal observations, additional to those in my letter of thursday last, which have occurred to me in perusing them are the following.

The calculation in P. 15 on which most that follow are grounded goes on the

---

ORIGINAL: PRO 30/8/169. TEXT: Original, with the kind permission of the Public Record Office.

principle that a *perpetual* annuity consisting of a rate of interest on a capital is of the same value with an annuity *for a term* which is equal to the *perpetual* annuity with the addition of the annual sum which in that term will, in consequence of being improved at that rate of interest, accumulate to the capital. Thus, in the calculation to which I refer, the annuity (£3.710,000) being the amount of 5 per cent on a principal or capital of £74.200,000 is of the same value with an annuity for 44 years of £4.210,000 because the excess (£500,000) of this last annuity above the former is the annual sum which at 5 *per cent* compound interest will accumulate to £74.200,000. This is the exact value of the former annuity (£3,710,000) when the rate of interest in the stocks is 5 per cent. But when the rate of interest in the stocks is lower (suppose 4 per cent) the fair value of the same perpetual annuity (that is, the annuity for 44 years equivalent to it) is this perpetual annuity with the annual sum added (£800,000 nearly) which will at 4 *per cent* compound interest accumulate to a 4 per cent capital producing £3.710,000; that is, a capital of £92.750,000. The equivalent annuity, therefore, is on these suppositions £4.510,000. And the stockholders ought either to be paid this equivalent annuity, or be discharged at £125 for every £5[?]. Determining the equivalent temporary annuity from a *higher* rate of interest, and then the value of it from a *lower*, can never bring out a legitimate conclusion. The truth is, that the perpetual annuity under consideration is an annuity which is to be always redeemed more or less below its proper capital as the interest of money shall happen to be more or less below 5 *per cent*; and this diminishes its value, and makes the method of calculation just described improper when apply'd to it. It is an annuity the price of which will be always kept down by its having a fix'd capital at which it will be redeemed however low the current interest may be. On the contrary; the *temporary* Annuity suppos'd to be substituted for it is an annuity which, having no fixed capital, will be always rising in its price in proportion nearly to the fall of interest.

It is difficult to discover how the stock=holders would calculate were such a proposal as that in these papers made to them. Perhaps, a proper way of guessing at this may be the following.

The 5 per cents at the time of writing this are at 104½; and the *consols* at 70½. An addition, therefore, of £2 to the interest of a £100 3 per cent capital (making it a 5 *per cent* capital) is valued at £34, and consequently an addition of 9s. 6d. would be valued at £8. 1s. 6d. for as 2 is to 9s. 6d. so is £34 to ¢8. 1s. 6d. In the same circumstances £3 interest on a 5 *per cent* capital appears to be valued at £62. 14s. for as 5 is to 3 so is 104½ to 62 $\frac{7}{10}$ which is less by £7. 16s. than 70½, the price of £3 interest on a 3 per cent capital. The propos'd addition of interest (that is, 9s. 6d.) would, therefore, give a profit of 5s. 6d. on every £100 three per cent capital thus converted. But this is a profit much too small to induce the stock-holders to consent to such a conversion, should they happen to reckon the new 5 per cents of no more value or of but little more value than the present 5 per cents. All depends, therefore, on the question whether they would estimate them at a value considerably greater than the present 5 per cents. I imagine the contrary for the following reasons.

First, there is at present little expectation of a scheme of redemption which will not be interrupted before it has discharged 25 millions; and, therefore, the certainty that no part of the present 5 per cents shall be redeemed 'till this has been done has a very great effect. On the contrary; the stock=holders will reckon upon the redemption of a part of the new 5 per cents immediately, and, consequently on the immediate commencement of a loss, which loss will increase every year with every successive redemption till at last, should the plan meet with no interruption, the market=price of these 5 per cents will necessarily be brought to par let the other stocks be ever so high. This will be true supposing all the Consolidated 3 per cents subscribed; but should only a part of them be subscribed, this effect will be greater because the period of redemption will be shorter; and the stockholders seeing this, and fearing perhaps that but a small part will be subscribed, will be deterred from subscribing at all. For these reasons, I incline to think that the comparison which the stock=holders will make between the old and new 5 per cents will not be so much in favour of the latter as to furnish them with a sufficient inducement to accept of them in exchange for the 3 per cents with the addition of 9s:6d *per Ann* to the interest of every £100 three per cent stock reduced into $69\frac{1}{2}$ five per cent stock. I am indeed, apprehensive of very bad consequences from the proposals of such a reduction of the capital of the 3 per cents.

Such are my sentiments on this subject. I send them to you in compliance with the request with which you have honoured me, and should you think them in any instance wrong I shall hope for your candour.

I had writ the greatest part of this letter before I received yours yesterday; and I think it best to convey it to you with the enclosed papers before I give myself the pleasure of waiting upon you tomorrow morning. I have kept these papers entirely to myself nor have I taken any notice of the contents of them to any one. The papers likewise which I took the liberty to convey to you last week[1] containing three Tables with some general remarks have not yet been seen by any person except the Copyist.

I am, Sir, with the greatest respect,
Your very obedient and humble servant
Rich*d* Price

---

1. See R.P. to W. Pitt, 12 Jan. 1786.

To William Pitt[1]

Newington Green Feby 1st 1786

Dear Sir,

Thinking that possibly it may be agreeable to you to see the inclosed Table, I take the liberty to convey a copy of it to you. I shall make no other communication of these tables being satisfied that the business which is the object of them is in the best hands, and only wishing that a measure so efficacious in assisting a plan of redemption as that in the 3d of the Tables I lately sent you, may be consider'd and left open to adoption.[1]

With the greatest respect I am, Sir,
Your most obedient and humble servant
Richd Price

ORIGINAL: PRO 30/8/169. TEXT: Original, with the kind permission of the Public Record Office.

1. On 19 January Price met Pitt at Downing Street. In their discussion of the measures required to initiate a programme of debt redemption, Pitt seems to have accepted the validity of Price's criticism of his proposals and to have invited him to submit further alternative plans. In the King's Speech on 24 January the intention of introducing a plan for the redemption of the National Debt was declared. In reply to Pitt's invitation, Price submitted "Three Plans for Shewing the Progress and Effect during 40 years of a Fund consisting of a Million *per ann.* as is therein express'd and apply'd to the Redemption of the Public Debts." (For the text of these plans see *Observations on Reversionary Payments*, 6th ed., I, 322–35.)

Index